Wellington's History of the Peninsular War

Wellington's History of the Peninsular War

Battling Napoleon in Iberia 1808–1814

FRONTLINE
BOOKS

Published in 2019 by Frontline Books,
an imprint of Pen & Sword Books Ltd,
47 Church Street, Barnsley, S. Yorkshire, S70 2AS

www.frontline-books.com

ISBN: 978 1 52673 763 2

For more information on our books, please visit
www.frontline-books.com, email info@frontline-books.com
or write to us at the above address.

Printed and bound by TJ International

Pen & Sword Books Ltd incorporates the imprints of Pen & Sword
Archaeology, Atlas, Aviation, Battleground, Discovery,
Family History, History, Maritime, Military, Naval, Politics,
Social History, Transport, True Crime, Claymore Press,
Frontline Books, Praetorian Press,
Seaforth Publishing and White Owl

For a complete list of Pen and Sword titles please contact
PEN & SWORD LTD
47 Church Street, Barnsley, South Yorkshire, S70 2AS, England
E-mail: enquiries@pen-and-sword.co.uk

Or

PEN AND SWORD BOOKS
1950 Lawrence Rd, Havertown, PA 19083, USA
E-mail: Uspen-and-sword@casematepublishers.com

Contents

List of Maps   vii

Bibliography   xvii

Introduction   xix

Chapter 1   1808   1

Chapter 2   Memorandum of Operations In 18091   21

Chapter 3   Memorandum of Operations in 18101   43

Chapter 4   Memorandum of Operations In 18111   67

Chapter 5   1812 to 1814   99

Appendix I   British Officers mentioned in
                       Wellington's Dispatches   133

Appendix II   Wellington's Armies 1808–1814   223

Endnotes   279

Index   289

Contents

Chapter 1

Chapter 2

Chapter 3

Chapter 4

Chapter 5

Chapter 6

Chapter 7

List of Maps

1. The Battle of Vimiero
2. The Battle of Oporto
3. The Talavera Campaign
4. Battle of Fuentes d'Onoro, 3 May
5. Battle of Fuentes d'Onoro 5 May
6. Cuidad Rodrigo
7. Badajoz
8. The Vittoria Campaign

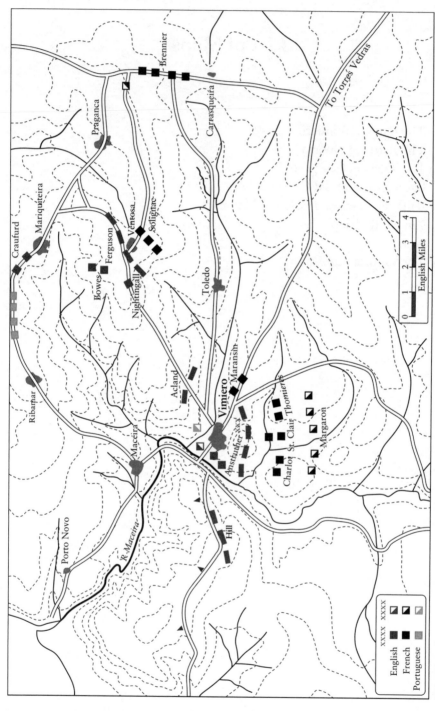

The Battle of Vimiero

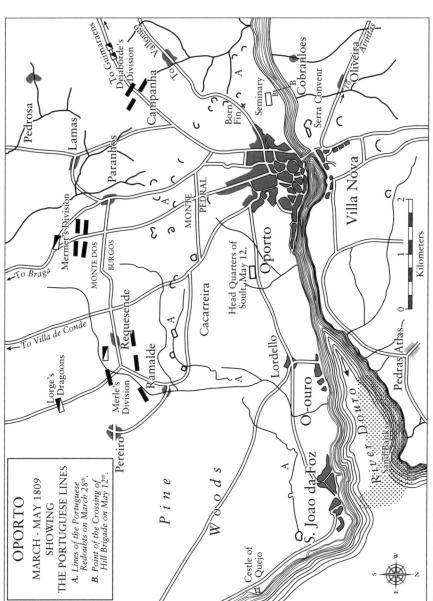

The Battle of Oporto

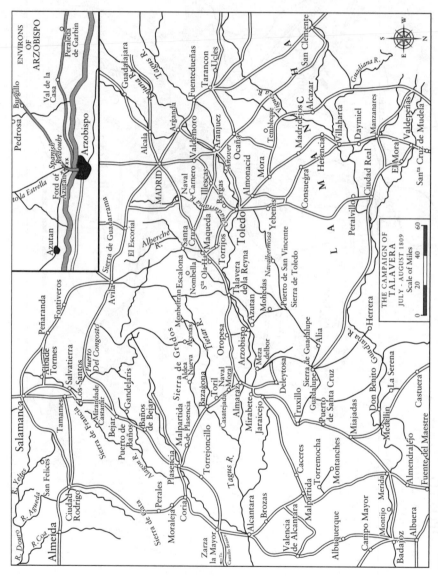

The Talavera Campaign

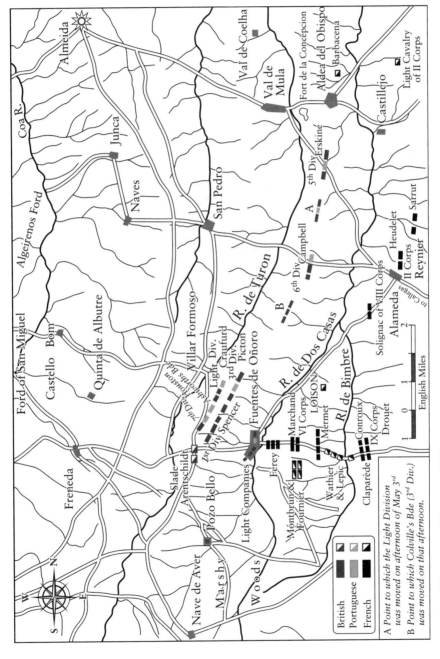

Battle of Fuentes d'Onoro, 3 May

Almeida

Coa R.

Val de Coelha

Fort de la Concepcion
Aldea del Obispo

Barbacena

Light Cavalry
of II Corps

Val de Mula

Castillejo

Algeirenos Ford

Junca

5th Div Erskine

Naves

San Pedro

Ford of San-Miguel

A

6th Div Campbell

Heudelet

Sarrut

Quinta de Albutre

R. de Turon

II Corps
Reynier

Castello Bom

B

Solignac of VIII Corps

Alameda

to Callegas

Villar Formoso

Light. Div.
Craufurd
3rd Div.
Picton

Fuentes de Oñoro

R. de Dos Casas

2nd Div
Houston's Bde

Freneda

Spencer

1st Div

R. de Bimbre

Marchand
VI Corps
LOISON
Mermet

Conroux
IX Corps
Droüet

Slade
Arentschildt
Pozo Bello

Ferey

Wathier
& Lepic

Claparède

Móntbrun &
Fournier

Light Companies

English Miles

Nave de Aver

Marshy

Woods

N
S
W
E

British

Portuguese

French

A Point to which the Light Division
was moved on afternoon of May 3rd

B Point to which Colville's Bde (3rd Div.)
was moved on that afternoon.

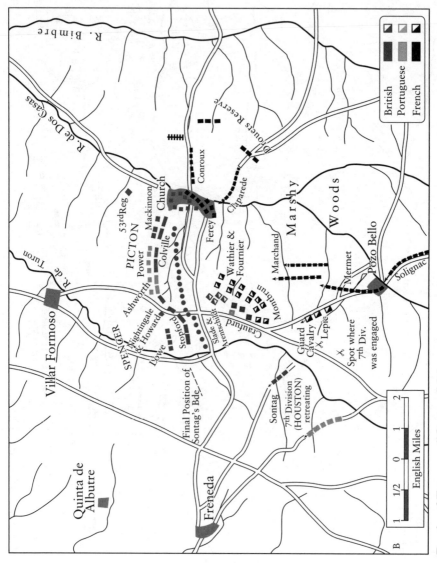

Battle of Fuentes d'Onoro 5 May

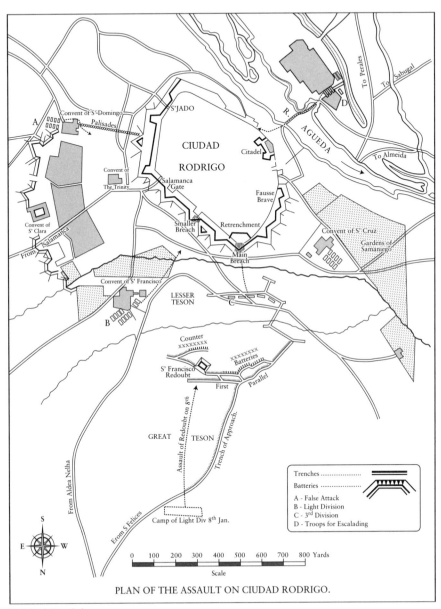

PLAN OF THE ASSAULT ON CIUDAD RODRIGO.

Cuidad Rodrigo

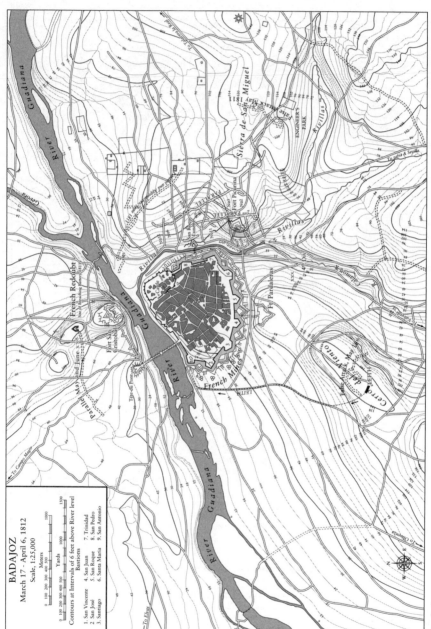

BADAJOZ
March 17 - April 6, 1812
Scale, 1:25,000

Meters
0 100 200 300 400 500   1000

Yards
0 100 200 300 400 500   1000   1500

Contours at Intervals of 6 feet above River level

Bastions

1. San Vincente   4. San Juan   7. Trinidad
2. San José   5. San Roque   8. San Pedro
3. Santiago   6. Santa Maria 9. San Antonio

Badajoz

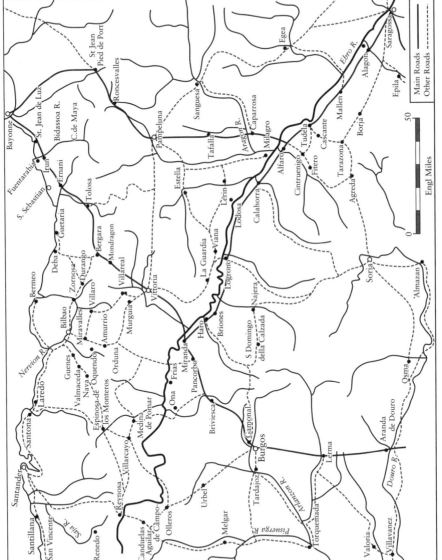

The Vittoria Campaign

Bibliography

Colonel John Gurwood,	*The Dispatches of Field Marshal the Duke of Wellington during his Various Campaigns in India, Denmark, Portugal, Spain, the Low Countries and France from 1789 to 1815* (new and enlarged edition; 12 volumes, London 1852)
WO25/3998	Field Officers Commissions
WO25/744-823	Statement of Services similar to above dating to 1809-10
1818 Pension Return:	*A return of the names of the officers in the Army who receive pensions for the loss of limbs, or for wounds; specifying, the rank they held at the time they were wounded, their present rank, the nature of the cases, the places where and the year when wounded, the amount of their pensions, and the dates from which they commence.* War Office 30th April 1819.
Army List	
Bulloch, J.M.	*Territorial Soldiering in the North East of Scotland* Aberdeen 1914
Challis, Lionel	*The Peninsula Roll Call* https://www.napoleon-series.org/research/biographies/GreatBritain/Challis/c_ChallisIntro.html
Dalton, Charles	*The Waterloo Roll Call* 2nd Edn, London 1904
Esdaile, Charles	*The Peninsular War: A new history* London 2002

Esdaile, Charles (ed.)	*The Duke of Wellington: Military Dispatches* London 2014
Gentleman's Magazine	
Glover, Richard	*Peninsular Preparation: The Reform of the British Army 1795-1809* Cambridge 1963
Hall, Dr John A.	*Biographical Dictionary of Officers Killed and Wounded 1808-1814* London 1998
Hart, H.G.	*The New Annual Army List* (1840)
McGuigan, R. and Burnham R.	*Wellington's Brigade Commanders* Barnsley 2017
Oman, Sir Charles	*A History of the Peninsular War* (7 Vols.) Oxford 1902-1930
Oman, Sir Charles	*Wellington's Army* London 1913
Oxford Dictionary of National Biography (ODNB)	
Philippart, John	*The Royal military calendar, or Army service and commission book. Containing the services and progress of promotion of the generals, lieutenant-generals, major-generals, colonels, lieutenant-colonels, and majors of the army, according to seniority: with details of the principal military events of the last century* (5 vols. London 1820)
Reid, Stuart	*Wellington's Army in the Peninsula 1809-14* Oxford 2004
Reid, Stuart	*Wellington's Highland Warriors* Barnsley 2010
Reid, Stuart	*Wellington's Officers* (3 vols) Leigh on Sea 2008
Ward, S.G.P.	*Wellington's Headquarters* Oxford 1957

Introduction

The Duke of Wellington once remarked that:

> The history of a battle, is not unlike the history of a ball. Some individuals may recollect all the little events of which the great result is the battle won or lost, but no individual can recollect the order in which, or the exact moment at which, they occurred, which makes all the difference as to their value or importance.

Yet surprisingly enough he himself did in fact write a history of the early part of the Peninsular War. It took the form of a series of memoranda, the first being a narrative of the operations culminating in the battles of Rolica and Vimeiro, which was prepared by way of evidence to the inquiry into the Convention of Cintra in 1808. Additionally, at the end of each of the three following years he took the time to pen lengthy and insightful narratives of the military and political operations in the Peninsula over the preceding 12 months.

Generally speaking these memoranda have been neglected by editors and historians, no doubt because they disturb the ordinary chronological sequence of the correspondence. Consequently, although included within Lieutenant Colonel Gurwood's monumental collection of the Duke's dispatches, they have never before been published consecutively in the form of a continuous narrative.

Sadly, Wellington does not appear to have written similar memoranda covering two remaining years of the war, but for the sake of completeness a selection of his dispatches for 1812, 1813 and those first few months of 1814 are included to draw the story to its end in southern France.

It will be noticed that there are some irregularities in the spelling of certain words and of many place names. These have been retained in the manner they were presented in Wellington's communications to maintain their authenticity.

Stuart Reid

Chapter 1

1808

*I*n 1807 with the active and indeed enthusiastic co-operation of its then Spanish allies a French army, under Marshal Junot, invaded Portugal. However, in the following year Spain was abruptly turned from an ally of France into a deadly enemy by a maladroit French coup, which toppled the decadent Bourbon monarchy and purposed to place Napoleon's brother Joseph on the Spanish throne instead. Viewed dispassionately this act in itself, and the promised liberal reforms, might both be accounted a good thing, but it provoked a national uprising and as a matter of course completely cut off the French army of Portugal. For a variety of reasons this was already isolated and effectively confined to the immediate environs of Lisbon. Only the fact that one of the first acts of the occupiers had been to dismantle the Portuguese Army[1] preserved the French from immediate annihilation, but Junot's situation was precarious and became even more so when Great Britain decided to intervene. Over the past 100 years successive British governments had a history of launching inadequate expeditionary forces at the continent of Europe with no clear notion of what they were to do once they arrived. Consequently, even when the expeditions did not end in disaster, they tended to be expensive failures. This time, the Government originally intended launching an expedition against what is now Venezuela, but when Spain abruptly switched from being an enemy to an ally in the struggle against Napoleonic France, the government nimbly redeployed the expeditionary force, and its commander, Sir Arthur Wellesley to the Iberian Peninsula instead.

The precise objective of the expedition was still more than a little hazy and having sailed from Cork, Wellesley was placed in the slightly ridiculous position of negotiating first with the Spanish and then the Portuguese authorities as to where his troops might land. Northern Spain was the first choice, largely through convenience, but the Spaniards themselves declined the assistance of British troops, while intimating that money and arms would be very welcome. The Portuguese were more accommodating but it rapidly became clear that the French were present in far greater numbers than expected. Wellesley already had the authority to call upon a small division under Major General Sir Brent Spencer, based on Gibraltar[2], but as time went by additional contingents from further afield were gradually drawn in to the scheme, and in the end as the numbers swelled, the Duke *of York and the rest of the military high command at the Horse Guards contrived to place no fewer than three officers over Wellesley's head; Sir Hew Dalrymple, Sir Harry Burrard and Sir John Moore. The first two were Guards officers who owed their appointments to personal influence rather than any discernible military talents, while the third, Sir John Moore, was already in command of an expeditionary force sent to the Baltic. Once arrived all three officers would outrank Wellesley simply by seniority.[3]*

As it happens, Wellesley succeeded in landing and winning two splendid victories outside Lisbon just as the first of his nemeses arrived, and the French, finding their position untenable entered negotiations for a capitulation, which resulted in the Convention of Cintra. By this treaty the French were not only allowed to return safely home but were carried there in British ships. While there was some justification for conceding these generous terms, it caused what might be called "a fearful row at home" and soon all three of the generals concerned; Dalrymple, Burrard and Wellesley, faced a court of inquiry.[4]

The first of Wellington's memoranda of operations presented here was written up as a statement of evidence for that inquiry.[5] As was always to be the case, although otherwise lucid and comprehensive, it records the fact of battles taking place but provides no detail as to how they were fought and won, and so his original despatches describing the battles of Rolica and Vimeiro have been interpolated into at the appropriate point in the text.

Memoranda of Operations 1808

I received the orders of His Royal Highness the Commander in Chief on the 15th of June. I received the instructions of the Secretary of State, of the 30th of June, in Dublin, on the 3d of July, and I set out from thence on the 5th, and arrived at Cork on the 6th of July.

I sailed from Cork on the 12th of July, with about 9064 men, including the 4th Royal Veteran Battalion, 275 artillery and drivers, and about 300 cavalry, of which 180 were mounted.[6]

I sailed from Cork in the *Donegal*[7] on the 12th of July; I went on board the *Crocodile*[8] on the 13th, and sailed to Corunna, where I arrived on the 20th of July. I there found that the French had, on the 14th, defeated the armies of Castille and Galicia under Generals Cuesta and Blake[9]; but, having sounded the Junta respecting their wish to have the assistance of the army under my command, in the existing crisis of their affairs, they declared explicitly that they did not want the assistance of troops; but eventually arms and ammunition, and money immediately. A sum of 200,000. for their use had arrived on the 20th, and their requisition for arms and ammunition was sent home immediately. The Junta of Galicia at the same time expressed the greatest anxiety that the troops under my command should be employed in driving the French out of Portugal, as they were persuaded that the Spaniards of the north and south of the Peninsula could never have any decided success independently of each other, and could never make any great simultaneous effort to remove the French from Spain, till they should be driven from Portugal, and the British troops in that kingdom should connect the operations of the northern and the southern Spanish armies. The Junta of Galicia, at the same time, strongly recommended to me to land in the north of Portugal, in order that I might bring forward and avail myself of the Portuguese troops, which the government of Oporto were collecting in the neighbourhood of that city.

I sailed from Corunna on the 22d, and joined the fleet off Cape Finisterre next day, and quitted it again at night, and went to Oporto, in order to hold a conference with the Bishop, and the General Officers in the command of the Portuguese troops. On my arrival at Oporto on the 24th, I received a letter from the Admiral, Sir Charles Cotton, in which he recommended to me to leave the troops either at Oporto, or at the mouth of the Mondego river; and to proceed to Lisbon in a frigate to communicate with him before I should determine upon the plan of operations, and the landing place.

The result of the conference which I had on the night of the 24th with the Bishop and the General Officers of the Portuguese army, was an agreement, that about 5000 Portuguese troops should be sent forward to co-operate with me against the enemy;[10] that the remainder of the Portuguese troops, amounting to about 1500, and a Spanish corps of about 1500 men, then on its march from Galicia, and another small Spanish corps of about 300 men, and all the Portuguese armed peasantry should remain in the neighbourhood of Oporto, and in the province of Tras os Montes; a part to be employed in the blockade of Almeida, and a part in the defence of the province of Tras os Montes, which province was supposed to be threatened by an attack from the French corps under Marshal Bessieres, since the defeat of the Spanish armies under Blake and Cuesta at Rio Seco, on the 14th of July.

The Bishop of Oporto likewise promised to supply the army under my command with mules and other means of carriage, and with slaughter cattle.

I sailed from Oporto on the morning of the 25th, and joined the fleet, and settled with Captain Malcolm that it should go to Mondego Bay; and I left it again that night, and went to the mouth of the Tagus to confer with the Admiral. I joined him on the evening of the 26th; and I there received letters from General [Sir Brent] Spencer[11], at Puerto Santa Maria, in which he informed me that he had landed his corps in Andalusia, at the request of the Junta of Seville, and he did not think it proper to embark it again till he should receive further orders from me; and he appeared to think that my presence in Andalusia, and the assistance of the troops under my command, were necessary to enable General Castanos to defeat General Dupont.

As I was of opinion that the most essential object for the Spaniards, as well as for us, was to drive the French from Portugal, and that neither his corps nor mine were sufficiently strong when separate to be of much service anywhere, and that when joined they might effect the object which had been deemed of most importance in England, and in Galicia, I immediately dispatched orders to General Spencer to embark his troops, unless he should be actually engaged in an operation which he could not relinquish without loss to the Spaniards, and to join me off the coast of Portugal.

The result of the information which I received from General Spencer, of the strength of the French army in Portugal, was, that they consisted of more than 20,000 men. The accounts of their numbers which I received from the Admiral, and had received from the Portuguese, did not make their force so large; but, upon the whole, I was induced to believe that they had not less than from 16,000 to 18,000 men. Of this number they had from 600 to 800 in the Fort of Almeida, 600 or 800 in Elvas, 800 in Peniche, 1600 or 1800 in Setuval, and the remainder were considered about 14,000 disposable for the defence of Lisbon, and the forts on the Tagus. The whole of this disposable force was at this time in the neighbourhood of Lisbon, excepting about 2400 men at Alcobaca, under General Thomiere.

I considered with the Admiral the propriety of carrying into execution any of the proposed plans of attack upon the Tagus, or upon the coast in the neighbourhood of the Rock at Lisbon; and it appeared to us both that all the attacks upon the river, which had been proposed to Government, were impracticable; that the attack upon Cascaes Bay was likewise so; that a landing in any of the small bays in the neighbourhood of the Rock was a matter of considerable difficulty at any time, and that there was a risk that if a part of the army, or even the whole army were landed, the state of the surf which prevails upon the whole coast of Portugal might prevent the disembarkation of the rear in the one case, and of the stores and provisions which were necessary in the other. At all events, the disembarkation would be made in the neighbourhood of the whole disposable force of the French army; and the British troops would be exposed to their attack on their landing, probably in a crippled state, and certainly not in a very efficient state.

By making our disembarkation in one of the bays near the Rock of Lisbon, it was certain that we should not have the advantage which, at that time, we expected to derive from the co-operation of the Portuguese troops.

It appeared to us that the fort of Peniche, which was garrisoned by the enemy, would prevent the disembarkation under the shelter of that peninsula; and therefore it appeared to the Admiral and to me, that it would be most advisable to disembark the troops in the Mondego river.

I quitted the Admiral off' the Tagus on the 27th, and joined the fleet of transports off the Mondego on the 30th.

I there received information from Government, dated the 15th of July, that they intended to reinforce the army under my command with 5000 men, under the command of Brigadier General [Wroth Palmer] Acland, in the first instance, and eventually with the corps consisting of 10,000 men, which had been under the command of Sir John Moore in Sweden; and that Sir Hew Dalrymple was appointed to command the army. I was likewise directed to carry into execution the instructions which I had received, if I conceived that my force was sufficiently strong.

Besides these dispatches from Government, I received information on my arrival at the Mondego of the defeat of the French corps under Dupont by the Spanish General under Castanos, on the 20th of July,[12] and I was convinced that General Spencer, if he did not embark immediately upon receiving intelligence of that event, would do so as soon as he should receive my orders of the 26th of July; I therefore considered his arrival as certain, and I had reason to expect the arrival of General Acland's corps every moment, as I had been informed that it was to sail from Harwich and the Downs on the 19th of July.

I also received accounts at the same time that General Loison had been detached from Lisbon across the Tagus into Alemtejo on the 27th of July, in order to subdue the insurrection in that province, and open the communication with Elvas. The insurgents had lately been joined by about 1000 men from the Spanish army of Estremadura, and the insurrection had made considerable progress, and was become formidable in Alentejo.

I therefore considered that I might commence the disembarkation of the troops, without risk of their being attacked by superior numbers before one or both the reinforcements should arrive ; and I was induced to disembark immediately, not only because the troops were likely to be better equipped, and more able to march in proportion as they should have been longer on shore ; but because I had reason to believe that the Portuguese had been much discouraged by seeing the troops so long in the ships after the fleet had arrived in Mondego Bay; and I was certain they would suspect our inclination or our ability to contend with the French, if they had not been disembarked as soon as I returned from the Tagus. I therefore determined to disembark as soon as the weather and the state of the surf would permit us, and we commenced the disembarkation on the 1st of August.

The difficulties of landing, occasioned by the surf, were so great, that the whole of the corps were not disembarked till the 5th, on which day General Spencer arrived, and his corps on the 6th. He had embarked at Puerto Santa Maria on the 21st of July, when he had heard of the defeat of Dupont by Castanos, and had not received the dispatches addressed to him by me on the 26th of July. General Spencer disembarked on the 7th and 8th, on which night the whole army was in readiness to march forward.

From the 1st of August to that day the time had been usefully spent in procuring the means for moving with the army the necessary stores, provisions, and baggage, and in arranging those means in the most advantageous manner to the different departments: the cavalry and the artillery received a large remount of horses, means were procured of moving with the army a sufficient supply of ammunition and military stores, and a seasonable supply of hospital stores; but I determined to march towards Lisbon by that road which passes nearest to the sea coast, in order that I might communicate with Captain Bligh of the *Alfred*, who attended the movements of the army with a fleet of victuallers and store ships. The communication with this fleet, however, it was obvious, would be very precarious, as well on account of the state of the surf on the coast, in the different points of rendezvous which had been settled, as because it might happen that it would be more advantageous to the army to take another line of march, passing farther inland.

I therefore made arrangements for carrying with the army such a supply of the articles of first necessity as should render it independent of the fleet till it should reach the Tagus, if circumstances should prevent the communication with the fleet, or should render it advantageous to relinquish it.

In the same period of time I also armed the Portuguese troops, and ascertained, as far as lay in my power, the degree of their discipline and efficiency, and recommended and superintended their organization. I offered such a sum of money, as the funds of the army could afford, to defray any expense which if. might be deemed necessary to incur in their equipment for the field, which was declined by the Portuguese General officers; and I met these gentlemen at Monte Mor Velho on the 7th, and arranged with them the plan of our operations and march, which was delayed for the main body of the army till the 10th, at their desire, for the convenience of the Portuguese troops.

On the 8th I wrote a letter to Sir Harry Burrard[13], which I left with Captain Malcolm of the *Donegal*, to be delivered to him upon his arrival at the Mondego, detailing all the circumstances of our situation, and recommending for his consideration a plan of operations for the corps under the command of Sir John Moore.

The advanced guard marched on the 9th, supported by the brigades under General [Rowland] Hill and General [Ronald Craufurd] Ferguson, as I had heard that General Laborde had collected his own corps and General Thomiere's, consisting of from 5 to 6000 men, in the neighbourhood of Leyria, which place he threatened, as it contained a magazine formed for the use of the Portuguese army. On the 10th the main body followed, and the advanced guard arrived at Leyria on the 10th, and the main body on the 11th.

I received a letter from Mr. Stuart[14] and Colonel [William] Doyle at Coruna, on the 10th, detailing the inefficient state of the Galician army under General Blake, that that General had separated his troops, which consisted of infantry, from the cavalry under General Cuesta, and that neither were in a condition to act offensively against Bessieres, or even to follow that General if he should march into Portugal, or to attack him if he should make any considerable detachment to that quarter. At the same time I received the intelligence of the retreat of Joseph Bonaparte from Madrid on the 29th July; and I concluded that Bessieres, instead of moving out, or detaching towards Portugal, would cover the retreat of Joseph Bonaparte towards the French frontier. Whether he did so or not, it was obvious to me that I should have time for my operations against Junot before Bessieres could arrive in Portugal to interrupt them; and it was probable that General Acland's corps, or Sir John Moore's, would arrive and land in Portugal before Bessieres could come from the north of Spain.

Adverting therefore to the advanced state of the season, the necessity of communicating with the sea coast, and the certainty that that communication would be nearly impracticable after the month of August, and to the still dispersed state of the French forces in Portugal, I considered it to be important to endeavor to perform those operations to which the army was equal, and for which it was fully equipped and prepared, without loss of time.

The Portuguese army, consisting of about 6000 men, including 500 cavalry, arrived at Leyria on the 12th, where the whole force was then assembled.

The French General Loison, who had been detached across the Tagus into Alentejo, on the 26th or 27th of July, with between 5 and 6000 men, had withdrawn the greatest part of the garrison of Setuval, consisting of 1600 men, by which he had been joined, and he had immediately marched towards Evora, where he defeated and dispersed a Spanish detachment, consisting of 1000 men, and the force of the insurrection[15] of Alentejo collected in that town; he then marched to Elvas, re-victualled that place, suppressed the insurrection, and re-established the French authority in Alentejo, and made arrangements for the purchase and collection of the grain of that province. He crossed the Tagus again at Abrantes, and marching down that river, he arrived at Thomar, about sixteen miles to the south east from Leyria, on the evening of the 11th, on which day the British army arrived at Leyria.

The corps under Laborde was at the same time at Alcobaca, about sixteen miles from Leyria to the south west, and the object of the French officers had evidently been to join at Leyria before the British troops could arrive there.

This town is on the high road from Lisbon to the north of Portugal, to the eastward of which, and nearly parallel to the road, there is a chain of high mountains which runs from Leyria nearly to the Tagus, over which chain there is no good passage for carriages. In consequence of the early arrival, therefore, of the British troops at Leyria, General Loison was obliged to return to the southward before he could effect his junction with General Laborde, who was thus exposed to be attacked when alone, and was attacked on the 17th of August.

All the arrangements for the march having been made and communicated to the Portuguese officers, the army marched on the 13th in two columns to Calvario, and on the 14th in two columns to Alcobaca, from whence General Laborde had retreated in the course of the preceding night. The Portuguese troops had not marched from Leyria as had been arranged and as I had expected, under the pretence that they had no provisions; and I received on the 13th in the evening a letter from Colonel [Nicholas] Trant, who was employed by me to communicate with the Portuguese General, in which he informed me of the General's intention to halt at Leyria, unless I should consent to supply the Portuguese troops with provisions from the British commissariat on the march to Lisbon. He also explained a plan of operations which General Freire proposed to carry into execution, by which he would have been left without any communication with the British army, exposed to be attacked by the French army, if they should choose to abandon the defence of Lisbon and the Tagus, and proceed to the northward and eastward; or even if they should be compelled to retire after an action with the British troops.

In my reply to this communication I pointed out the impossibility of my complying with the demand for provisions, and the danger which would result from the adoption of the plan of operations proposed for the Portuguese corps.

I urged the Portuguese General, in the most earnest terms, to co-operate with me in the deliverance of his country from the French, if he had any regard to his own honor, to the honor of his country, or of his Prince; and I pointed out to him the resources of which he could avail himself to feed the army. I then proposed to him that, if he should not march with his whole corps, he should send to join me 1000 regular infantry, all his light troops and his cavalry, which troops I engaged to feed, as the utmost I could undertake to perform in that way.

These troops, in numbers 1000 regular infantry, 400 light troops, and 250 cavalry, joined me at Alcobaca, on the evening of the 14th, with Colonel Trant, and remained with me during the remainder of the operations.

The main body of the Portuguese corps, instead of carrying into execution the plan of operations which I had originally proposed, or that which General Freire had substituted, adopted the measure of safety which I had recommended in the event of his determination not to join me, and remained at Leyria, and afterwards at Caldas and Obidos till the 22nd of August.

On the arrival of the army at Alcobaca, I immediately opened a communication with Captain Bligh, of the *Alfred*, who had been for two days waiting with the fleet of victuallers and store ships off Nazareth. A supply of bread and oats was immediately landed; and I appointed Peniche, which place I intended to reconnoitre as our next point of communication.

The army marched on the 15th, in two columns to Caldas, where it halted the 16th to allow the commissariat to come up, and to receive the supplies which had been landed at Nazareth. On the 15th in the evening there was a skirmish between the troops of the advanced guard of Laborde's corps and our riflemen, in which the latter sustained some loss. But we kept possession of the post at Obidos, which commands the valley of Caldas.

Throughout that day we had reason to believe that General Loison, who had moved from Rio Mayor on the evening of the 16th, would be found on Laborde's right, and the disposition for the attack was made accordingly.

The battle of Rolica 17 August 1808[16]

The French General Laborde having continued in his position at Rolica, since my arrival at Caldas on the 15th instant, I determined to attack him in it this morning. Rolica is situated on an eminence, having a plain in its front, at the end of a valley, which commences at Caldas, and is closed to the southward by mountains, which join the hills forming the valley on the left. Looking from Caldas, in the centre of the valley and about eight miles from Rolica, is the town and old Moorish fort of Obidos, from whence the enemy's picquets had been driven on the 15th; and from that time he had posts in the hills on both sides of the valley, as well as in the plain in front of his army, which was posted on the heights in front of Rolica, its right resting upon the hills, its left upon an eminence on which was a windmill, and the whole covering four or five passes into the mountains on his rear.

I have reason to believe that his force consisted of at least 6000 men, of which about 500 were cavalry, with five pieces of cannon; and there was some reason to believe that General Loison, who was at Rio Mayor yesterday, would join General Laborde by his right in the course of the night.

The plan of attack was formed accordingly, and the army, having broken up from Caldas this morning, was formed into three columns. The right, consisting of 1200 Portuguese infantry, 50 Portuguese cavalry, destined to turn the enemy's left, and penetrate into the mountains in his rear. The left, consisting of Major General Ferguson's and Brig. General [Barnard Foord] Bowes's brigade of infantry, three companies of riflemen, a brigade of light artillery, and twenty British and twenty Portuguese cavalry, was destined, under the command of Major General Ferguson, to ascend the hills at Obidos, to turn all the enemy's posts on the left of the valley, as well as the right of his post at Rolica. This corps was also destined to watch the motions of General Loison on the enemy's right, who, I had heard, had moved from Rio Mayor towards Alcoentre last night. The centre column, consisting of Major General Hill's, Brig. General [Sir Miles] Nightingall's, Brig. General [James Catlin] C. Craufurd's and Brig. General Henry Fane's brigades (with the exception of the riflemen detached with Major General Ferguson), and 400 Portuguese light infantry, the British and Portuguese cavalry, a brigade of 9 pounders, and a brigade of 6 pounders, was destined to attack General Laborde's position in the front.[17]

The columns being formed, the troops moved from Obidos about 7 o'clock in the morning. Brig. General Fane's riflemen were immediately detached into the hills on the left of the valley, to keep up the communication between the centre and left columns, and to protect the march of the former along the valley, and the enemy's posts were successively driven in. Major General Hill's brigade, formed in three columns of battalions, moved on the right of the valley, supported by the cavalry, in order to attack the enemy's left; and Brig. Generals Nightingall and Craufurd moved with the artillery along the high road, until at length the former formed in the plain immediately in the enemy's front, supported by the light infantry companies, and the 45th Regiment of Brig. General Craufurd's brigade; while the two other regiments of this brigade (the 50th and 91st), and half of the 9 pounder brigade, were kept up as a reserve in the rear.

Major General Hill and Brig. General Nightingall advanced upon the enemy's position, and at the same moment Brig. General Fane's riflemen were in the hills on his right, the Portuguese in a village upon his left, and Major General Ferguson's column was descending from the heights into the plain. From this situation the enemy retired by the passes into the mountains with the utmost regularity and the greatest celerity; and notwithstanding the rapid advance of the British infantry, the want of a sufficient body of cavalry was the cause of his suffering but little loss on the plain.

It was then necessary to make a disposition to attack the formidable position which he had taken up.

Brig. General Fane's riflemen were already in the mountains on his right; and no time was lost in attacking the different passes, as well to support the riflemen as to defeat the enemy completely.

The Portuguese infantry were ordered to move up a pass on the right of the whole. The light companies of Major General Hill's brigade, and the 5th Regiment, moved up a pass next on the right; and the 29th Regiment, supported by the 9th Regiment, under Brig. General Nightingall, a third pass; and the 45th and 82d regiments, passes on the left.

These passes were all difficult of access, and some of them were well defended by the enemy, particularly that which was attacked by the 29th and 9th regiments. These regiments attacked with the utmost impetuosity, and reached the enemy before those whose attacks were to be made on their flanks.

The defence of the enemy was desperate; and it was in this attack principally that we sustained the loss which we have to lament, particularly of that gallant officer, the Hon. Lieut. Colonel [George Augustus Frederick] Lake, who distinguished himself upon this occasion. The enemy was, however, driven from all the positions he had taken in the passes of the mountains, and our troops were advanced in the plains on their tops. For a considerable length of time the 29th and 9th regiments alone were advanced to this point, with Brig. General Fane's riflemen at a distance on the left, and they were afterwards supported by the 5th Regiment, and by the light companies of Major General Hill's brigade, which had come upon their right, and by the other troops ordered to ascend the mountains, who came up by degrees.

The enemy here made three most gallant attacks upon the 29th and 9th regiments, supported as I have above stated, with a view to cover the retreat of his defeated army, in all of which he was, however, repulsed; but he succeeded in effecting his retreat in good order, owing principally to my want of cavalry, and, secondly, to the difficulty of bringing up the passes of the mountains, with celerity, a sufficient number of troops and of cannon to support those which had first ascended. The loss of the enemy has, however, been very great, and he left three pieces of cannon in our hands.

I cannot sufficiently applaud the conduct of the troops throughout this action. The enemy's positions were formidable, and he took them up with his usual ability and celerity, and defended them most gallantly. But I must observe, that although we had such a superiority of numbers employed in the operations of this day, the troops actually engaged in the heat of the action were, from unavoidable circumstances, only the 5th, 9th, 29th, the riflemen of the 95th and 60th, and the flank companies of Major General Hill's brigade; being a number by no means equal to that of the enemy. Their conduct therefore deserves the highest commendation.

I cannot avoid taking this opportunity of expressing my acknowledgments for the aid and support I received from all the General and other Officers of this army: I am particularly indebted to Major General Spencer for the advice and assistance I received from him; to Major General Ferguson, for the manner in which he led the left column; and to Major General Hill, and Brig. Generals Nightingall and Fane, for the manner in which they conducted the different attacks which they led.

I derived most material assistance also from Lieut. Colonel [John Goulstone Price] Tucker and Lieut. Colonel [James] Bathurst, in the offices of Deputy Adjutant and Deputy Quarter Master General, and from the Officers of the Staff employed under them. I must also mention that I had every reason to be satisfied with the artillery under Lieut. Colonel [William] Robe. I have the honor to enclose herewith a return of killed, wounded, and missing.

	Officers	Non-commissioned officers and drummers	Rank and File	Horses	Total loss of Officers, Non-commissioned Officers, and Rank And File
Killed	4	3	63	1	70
Wounded	20	20	295	2	335
Missing	4	2	68	..	74

During the action a French officer, who was dying of his wounds, informed me that they had expected Loison to join them that day at one o'clock by their right, which was the reason for which they stood our attack, that their numbers were 6000, and that their loss had been severe. Intelligence to the same purport was received from other prisoners, and as a small patrole of French infantry appeared at no great distance from the left of our position on the 17th at dusk, and I heard that Loison's corps was at that moment arriving at Bombarral, which was about five miles from the field of battle, I conclude that the junction had been intended, and was prevented only by our early attack.

At all events great caution was necessary in all the movements of that day; and indeed the nature of the ground over which the troops were obliged to move rendered a very rapid attack impossible.

The two French corps joined on that night, and retired beyond Torres Vedras, which was ten miles from the field of battle towards Cabeca de Montachique. My intention was to march to Torres Vedras on the morning of the 18th; and the troops were under arms, and the orders for the march had been issued, when I received from General [Robert] Anstruther an account of his arrival on the coast, and of his junction with Captain Bligh. My original intention had been to employ the corps under General Acland and General Anstruther in the siege of Peniche, if I should find it necessary to undertake it; or if I should not, to send them down the coast to effect a landing in some of the bays in the neighbourhood of the Rock of Lisbon, in the rear of the enemy, while I should press upon their front. But the disappointment which I experienced in the hope of co-operation of the Portuguese troops, which were with me in the action of the 17th, and, above all, the determined and gallant resistance of the enemy in that action, induced me to be of opinion that I ought to land General Anstruther' s Brigade, and General Acland's when it should arrive, and to join those troops to the army.[18]

I therefore marched on the 18th to Lourinha, from whence I communicated again with General Anstruther, and on the 19th to Vimieiro, which appeared on the whole to be the position best calculated to secure the junction of General Anstruther, at the same time that it was a march in advance on our route. On account of the calms, the fleet which was anchored off the Berlings could not stand in till late on the 19th, and General Anstruther did not land till that evening, and he formed a junction with two brigades detached from our left on the morning of the 20th, and took his position in the advanced guard.

Between the 18th and 20th the French corps had assembled at and about Torres Vedras, the troops last arrived under Junot forming the advanced guard, in a strong position in front of the town; and the divisions of Laborde and Loison the main body, in another strong position behind it.

Their cavalry was very active throughout the days of the 19th and 20th, they covered the whole country, patrolled frequently up to our position, and on the 20th one patrole was pushed into the rear of our right, as far as the landing place at Maceira.

Under these circumstances we could gain no detailed information of the enemy's position, excepting that it was very strong and occupied by their whole force.

My intention was to march on the morning of the 21st, and orders were issued accordingly. I should have pushed the advanced guard as far as the heights of Mafra, and should have halted the main body about four or five miles from that place. By this movement the enemy's position at Torres Vedras would have been turned, and I should have brought the army into a country of which I had an excellent map, and topographical accounts, which had been drawn up for the use of the late Sir Charles Stuart[19]; and the battle, which it was evident would be fought in a few days, would have had for its field a country of which we had a knowledge, and not very distant from Lisbon, into which town, if we had been successful, we might have entered with the retreating enemy.

I was informed in the middle of the day of the 20th, that General Acland's brigade was in the offing, and I made arrangements for their disembarkation as soon as they should arrive; and in the evening of this day Sir Harry Burrard arrived in Maceira roads in the Brazen. He immediately assumed the command of the army.[20]

The battle of Vimeiro 21 August 1808[21]

The village of Vimeiro stands in a valley, through which runs the river Maceira; at the back, and to the westward and northward of this village, is a mountain, the western point of which touches the sea, and the eastern is separated by a deep ravine from the heights, over which passes the road which leads from Lourinha, and the northward to Vimeiro. The greater part of the infantry, the 1st, 2d, 3d, 4th, 5th, and 8th brigades, were posted on this mountain, with eight pieces of artillery, Major General Hill's brigade being on the right, and Major General Ferguson's on the left, having one battalion on the heights separated from the mountain. On the eastern and southern side of the town is a mill, which is entirely commanded, particularly on its right, by the mountain to the westward of the town, and commanding all the ground in the neighbourhood to the southward and eastward, on which Brig. General Fane was posted with his riflemen, and the 50th Regiment, and Brig. General Anstruther with his brigade, with half a brigade of 6 pounders, and half a brigade of 9 pounders, which had been ordered to the position in the course of last night. The ground over which passes the road from Lourinha commanded the left of this height, and it had not been occupied, excepting by a picquet, as the camp had been taken up only for one night, and there was no water in the neighbourhood of this height.

The cavalry and the reserve of artillery were in the valley, between the hills on which the infantry stood, both flanking and supporting Brig. General Fane's advanced guard.

The enemy first appeared about 8 o'clock in the morning, in large bodies of cavalry on our left, upon the heights on the road to Lourinha; and it was soon obvious that the attack would be made upon our advanced guard and the left of our position; and Major General Ferguson's brigade was immediately moved across the ravine to the heights on the road to Lourinha, with three pieces of cannon; he was followed successively by Brig. General Nightingall, with his brigade and three pieces of cannon, Brig. General Acland, and his brigade, and Brig. General Bowes, with his brigade. These troops were formed (Major General Ferguson's brigade in the first line, Brig. General Nightingall's in the second, and Brig. General Bowes's and Acland's in columns in the rear) on those heights, with their right upon the valley which leads into Vimeiro, and their left upon the other ravine, which separates these heights from the range which terminates at the landing place at Maceira. On the last mentioned heights the Portuguese troops, which had been in the bottom near Vimeiro, were posted in the first instance, and they were supported by Brig. General C. Craufurd's brigade.

The troops of the advanced guard, on the heights to the southward and eastward of the town, were deemed sufficient for its defence, and Major General Hill was moved to the centre of the mountain, on which the great body of the infantry had been posted, as a support to these troops, and as a reserve to the whole army; in addition to this support, these troops had that of the cavalry in the rear of their right.

The enemy's attack began in several columns upon the whole of the troops on this height; on the left they advanced, notwithstanding the fire of the riflemen, close to the 50th Regiment, and they were checked and driven back only by the bayonets of that corps. The 2d batt. 43d Regiment was likewise closely engaged with them in the road which leads into Vimeiro; a part of that corps having been ordered into the churchyard, to prevent them from penetrating into the town. On the right of the position they were repulsed by the bayonets of the 97th Regiment, which corps was successfully supported by the 2d batt. 52d, which, by an advance in column, took the enemy in flank.

Besides this opposition given to the attack of the enemy on the advanced guard by their own exertions, they were attacked in flank by Brig. General Acland's brigade, in its advance to its position on the heights on the left, and a cannonade was kept up on the flank of the enemy's columns by the artillery on those heights.

At length, after a most desperate contest, the enemy was driven back in confusion from this attack, with the loss of seven pieces of cannon, many prisoners, and a great number of Officers and soldiers killed and wounded. He was pursued by a detachment of the 20th light dragoons, but the enemy's cavalry were so much superior in numbers, that this detachment has suffered much, and Lieut. Colonel [Charles] Taylor was unfortunately killed.

Nearly at the same time the enemy's attack commenced upon the heights on the road to Lourinha: this attack was supported by a large body of cavalry, and was made with the usual impetuosity of French troops. It was received with steadiness by Major General Ferguson's brigade, consisting of the 36th, 40th, and 71st regiments, and these corps charged as soon as the enemy approached them, who gave way, and they continued to advance upon him, supported by the 82d, one of the corps of Brig. General Nightingall's brigade, which, as the ground extended, afterwards formed a part of the first line by the 29th Regiment, and by Brig. General Bowes' s and Acland's brigades; whilst Brig. General C. Craufurd's brigade and the Portuguese troops, in two lines, advanced along the height on the left. In the advance of Major General Ferguson's brigade, six pieces of cannon were taken from the enemy, with many prisoners, and vast numbers were killed and wounded.

The enemy afterwards made an attempt to recover part of his artillery, by attacking the 71st and 82d regiments, which were halted in a valley in which it had been taken. These regiments retired from the low grounds in the valley to the heights, where they halted, faced about, and fired, and advanced upon the enemy, who had by that time arrived in the low ground, and they thus obliged him again to retire with great loss.

In this action, in which the whole of the French force in Portugal was employed, under the command of the Due D'Abrantes[22] in person, in which the enemy was certainly superior in cavalry and artillery, and in which not more than half of the British army was actually engaged, he has sustained a signal defeat, and has lost thirteen pieces of cannon, twenty-three ammunition waggons, with powder, shells, stores of all descriptions, and 20,000 rounds of musket ammunition. One General Officer has been wounded (Brenier) and taken prisoner, and a great many Officers and soldiers have been killed, wounded, and taken.

The valor and discipline of His Majesty's troops have been conspicuous upon this occasion, as you, who witnessed the greatest part of the action, must have observed; but it is a justice to the following corps to draw your notice to them in a particular manner: viz., the Royal artillery, commanded by Lieut. Colonel Robe; the 20th light dragoons, which has been commanded by Lieut. Colonel Taylor; the 50th Regiment, commanded by Colonel [George Townshend] Walker; the 2d batt. 95th Foot, commanded by Major [Robert] Travers; the 5th batt. 60th Regiment, commanded by Major [William] Davy; the 2d batt. 43d, commanded by Major [Edward] Hull; the 2d batt. 52d, commanded by Lieut. Colonel [John] Ross; the 97th Regiment, commanded by Lieut. Colonel Lyon; the 36th Regiment, commanded by Colonel [Robert] Burne; the 40th, commanded by Lieut. Colonel [James] Kemmis; the 71st, commanded by Lieut. Colonel Pack; and the 82d Regiment, commanded by Major [Henry] Eyre.

In mentioning Colonel Burne and the 36th Regiment upon this occasion, I cannot avoid adding that the regular and orderly conduct of this corps throughout the service, and their gallantry and discipline in action, have been conspicuous.

I must take this opportunity of acknowledging my obligations to the General and Staff Officers of the army. I was much indebted to Major General Spencer's judgment and experience in the decision which I formed in respect to the number of troops allotted to each point of defence, and for his advice and assistance throughout the action. In the position taken up by Major General Ferguson's brigade, and in its advances upon the enemy, that Officer showed equal bravery and judgment; and much praise is due to Brig. General Fane and Brig. General Anstruther for their gallant defence of their position in front of Vimeiro, and to Brig. General Nightingall, for the manner in which he supported the attack upon the enemy made by Major General Ferguson.

Lieut. Colonel G. Tucker, and Lieut. Colonel Bathurst, and the Officers in the departments of the Adjutant and Quarter Master General, and Lieut. Colonel [Henry] Torrens and the Officers of my personal staff, rendered me the greatest assistance throughout the action.

I have the honor to enclose herewith a return of the killed, wounded and missing.[23]

	Officers	Non-commissioned officers and drummers	Rank and File	Horses	Total loss of Officers, Non-commissioned Officers, and Rank And File
Killed	4	3	128	30	135
Wounded	37	31	466	12	534
Missing	2	3	46	1	51

With that the campaign was over. Sir Hew Dalrymple had also arrived to take command and the French General Kellermann came in with a proposition to suspend hostilities, with a view to make a Convention for the evacuation of Portugal by the French, This was followed by the inevitable French surrender, a success which in the way of things might have redounded greatly to the credit of those who had done least to deserve it, were it not for the fact that under the terms of the resulting convention, the French were not merely allowed to march away, but were to be safely returned home in British ships. Objectively it was a cheap price to pay for such a complete victory, but such was the outrage in Britain at this latter stipulation, that the triumvirate of generals who had actually signed the instrument found themselves facing that court of inquiry. All three were exonerated, thanks to their various friends in high places, but only Wellesley was ever to be employed again.

In the meantime, Sir John Moore had assumed command of the army and marched it into Spain, only to be chased out again, and on 16 January 1809 was killed in the Battle of Corunna. Only the Lisbon garrison, under Sir John Cradock, remained. He too expected to be wafted away to safety in due course, but instead of writing off the Iberian adventure as yet one more expensive fiasco, the government took the courageous decision to renew the fight, to commit more men and treasure to the war in the Peninsula.

At the beginning of March, when tasked by Castlereagh with advising on the practicality of defending Portugal, Wellesley firmly responded that:

I have always been of opinion that Portugal might be defended, whatever might be the result of the contest in Spain; and that in the mean time the measures adopted for the defence of Portugal would be highly useful to the Spaniards in their contest with the French.

My notion was, that the Portuguese military establishments, upon the footing of 40,000 militia and 30,000 regular troops, ought to be revived; and that, in addition to these troops, His Majesty ought to employ an army in Portugal amounting to about 20,000 British troops, including about 4000 cavalry. My opinion was, that even if Spain should have been conquered, the French would not have been able to overrun Portugal with a smaller force than 100,000 men ; and that as long as the contest should continue in Spain this force, if it could be put in a state of activity, would be highly useful to the Spaniards, and might eventually have decided the contest ...

The whole of the army in Portugal, Portuguese as well as British, should be placed under the command of British Officers. The Staff of the army, the Commissariat in particular, must be British; and these departments must be extensive in proportion to the strength of the whole army which will act in Portugal, to the number of detached posts which it will be necessary to occupy, and in a view to the difficulties of providing and distributing supplies in that country. In regard to the detail of these measures, I recommend that the British army in Portugal should be reinforced as soon as possible with some companies of British riflemen, with 3000 British or German cavalry; that the complement of ordnance with that army should be made thirty pieces of cannon, of which two brigades of 9 pounders; that these pieces of ordnance should be completely horsed; that twenty pieces of brass (12 pounders) ordnance upon travelling carriages should be sent to Portugal, with a view to the occupation of certain positions in the country; that a corps of engineers for an army of 60,000 men should be sent there, and a corps of artillery for sixty pieces of cannon.

I understand that the British army now in Portugal consists of 20,000 men, including cavalry. It should be made up 20,000 infantry at least, as soon as possible, by additions of Riflemen and other good infantry, which by this time may have been refitted after the campaign in Spain.

The reinforcements may follow, as the troops shall recover from their fatigues.

The first measures to be adopted are to complete the army in Portugal with its cavalry and artillery, and to horse the ordnance as it ought to be. As soon as this shall be done the General and Staff Officers should go out; as it may be depended upon that as soon as the newspapers shall have announced the departure of Officers for Portugal, the French armies in Spain will receive orders to make their movements towards Portugal, so as to anticipate our measures for its defence. We ought therefore to have everything on the spot, or nearly so, before any alarm is created at home respecting our intentions.

Besides the articles above enumerated, 30,000 stands of arms, clothing and shoes, for the Portuguese army, should be sent to Lisbon as soon as possible.[24]

Thus it all began. Justified by this confident assessment Castlereagh confirmed on 2 April 1809 that the necessary troops would be found and that Wellesley would command.

Chapter 2

Memorandum of Operations In 1809[1]

The British army, intended for the service in Portugal and Spain, was complete in the end of April, with the exception of one brigade of infantry not arrived, and some troops expected from Gibraltar, when relieved by others to be sent from Portugal.[2] Sir Arthur Wellesley landed at Lisbon on the 23rd of April.

At that time the French had got possession of Zaragoza. Marshal Soult held Oporto and the northern provinces of Portugal. The battle of Medellin had been fought on the 29th of March; and General Cuesta was endeavoring to recover from its effects, and to collect an army again at Monasterio, in the mountains of the Sierra Morena. The French, under Marshal Victor, were in possession of the Guadiana, and had their advanced posts as forward as Los Santos. Sebastiani was at Ciudad Real, and held in check the army of La Carolina, at that time under the command of General Vanegas[3], consisting of about 12,000 men. Ney was in possession of Galicia; Salamanca was held by a small detachment of French troops; St. Cyr was in Catalonia with his corps of 25,000 men; and Kellerman, who had succeeded Bessieres in the command of the 6th Corps, was at Valladolid. Mortier, with his corps, and the Due D'Abrantes, with the 8th Corps, at Zaragoza.

The Portuguese army was totally disorganized, and nearly annihilated; and the Spanish troops were scarcely able to hold their positions in the Sierra Morena.

The Marquis de la Romana[4], who had been with his corps on the frontiers of Portugal, near Chaves, from the period of the embarkation of the British army at Coruna, in the month of January, till the month of March, had moved from thence when Soult invaded Portugal by Chaves, and afterwards moved towards the Asturias with his army, and went himself into that province.

Sir John Cradock gave the command to Sir Arthur Wellesley on the 27th of April; and on the same day the orders were given for the collection and march of the troops, preparatory to the attack of Soult at Oporto.

Oporto 12 May 1809[5]

The advanced guard and the cavalry had marched on the 7th [May], and the whole had halted on the 8th, to afford time for Marshal [William Carr] Beresford with his corps to arrive upon the Upper Douro.

The infantry of the army was formed into three divisions for this expedition, of which two, the advanced guard, consisting of the King's German Legion, and Brig. General R. [Richard] Stewart's brigade, with a brigade of 6 pounders, and a brigade of 3 pounders, under Lieut. General [Hon. Edward] Paget; and the cavalry under Lieut. General [Sir William] Payne; and the brigade of Guards, Brig. General [Sir Alexander] Campbell's and Brig. General [John] Sontag's brigades of infantry, with a brigade of 6 pounders, under Lieut. General [Sir John Coape] Sherbrooke, moved by the high road from Coimbra to Oporto: and one, composed of Major General Hill's and Brig. General [Allan] Cameron's brigades of infantry, and a brigade of 6 pounders, under the command of Major General Hill, by the road from Coimbra to Aveiro.

On the 10th in the morning, before daylight, the cavalry and advanced guard crossed the Vouga, with the intention to surprise and cut off four regiments of French cavalry, and a battalion of infantry and artillery, cantoned in Albergaria Nova and the neighbouring villages, about eight miles from that river, in the last of which we failed; but the superiority of the British cavalry was evident throughout the day. We took some prisoners and their cannon from them; and the advanced guard took up the position of Oliveira.

On the same day Major General Hill, who had embarked at Aveiro on the evening of the 9th, arrived at Ovar, in the rear of the enemy's right; and the head of Lieut. General Sherbrooke's division passed the Vouga on the same evening.

On the 11th, the advanced guard and cavalry continued to move on the high road towards Oporto, with Major General Hill's division in a parallel road which leads to Oporto from Ovar.

On the arrival of the advanced guard at Vendas Novas, between Souto Redondo and Grijo, they fell in with the outposts of the enemy's advanced guard, which were immediately driven in; and shortly afterwards we discovered the enemy's advanced guard, consisting of about 4,000 infantry and some squadrons of cavalry, strongly posted on the heights above Grijo, their front being covered by woods and broken ground. The enemy's left flank was turned by a movement well executed by Major General [Sir John] Murray, with Brig. General Langwerth's brigade of the King's German Legion[6]; while the 16th Portuguese Regiment of Brig. General Richard

Stewart's brigade attacked their right, and the riflemen of the 95th, and the flank companies of the 29th, 43rd, and 52nd of the same brigade, under Major [Gregory Holman Bromley] Way, attacked the infantry in the woods and village in their centre.

These attacks soon obliged the enemy to give way; and Brig. General the Hon. Charles Stewart led two squadrons of the 16th and 20th dragoons, under the command of Major [William Williams] Blake, in pursuit of the enemy, and destroyed many and took several prisoners.

On the night of the 11th the enemy crossed the Douro, and destroyed the bridge over that river.

It was important, with a view to the operations of Marshal Beresford, that I should cross the Douro immediately; and I had sent Major General Murray in the morning with a battalion of the King's German Legion, a squadron of cavalry, and two 6 pounders, to endeavor to collect boats, and, if possible, to cross the river at Avintas, about four miles above Oporto; and I had as many boats as could be collected brought to the ferry, immediately above the towns of Oporto and Villa Nova.

The ground on the right bank of the river at this ferry is protected and commanded by the fire of cannon, placed on the height of the Serra Convent at Villa Nova; and there appeared to be a good position for our troops on the opposite side of the river, till they should be collected in sufficient numbers.

The enemy took no notice of our collection of boats, or of the embarkation of the troops, till after the first battalion (the Buffs) were landed, and had taken up their position, under the command of Lieut. General Paget, on the opposite side of the river.

They then commenced an attack upon them, with a large body of cavalry, infantry, and artillery, under the command of Marshal Soult, which that corps most gallantly sustained, till supported successively by the 48th and 66th regiments, belonging to Major General Hill's brigade, and a Portuguese battalion, and afterwards by the first battalion of detachments[7] belonging to Brig. General Richard Stewart's brigade.

Lieut. General Paget was unfortunately wounded soon after the attack commenced, when the command of these gallant troops devolved upon Major General Hill.

Although the French made repeated attacks upon them, they made no impression; and at last, Major General Murray having appeared on the enemy's left flank on his march from Avintas, where he had crossed; and Lieut. General Sherbrooke, who by this time had availed himself of the enemy's weakness in the town of Oporto, and had crossed the Douro at the ferry between the towns of Villa Nova and Oporto, having appeared upon their right with the brigade of Guards, and the 29th Regiment; the whole retired in the utmost confusion towards Amarante, leaving behind them five pieces of cannon, eight ammunition tumbrils, and many prisoners.

The enemy's loss in killed and wounded in this action has been very large, and they have left behind them in Oporto 700 sick and wounded.

Brig. General the Hon. Charles Stewart then directed a charge by a squadron of the 14th dragoons, under the command of Major Hervey, who made a successful attack on the enemy's rear guard.

In the different actions with the enemy, of which I have above given your Lordship an account, we have lost some, and the immediate services of other valuable Officers and soldiers.

In Lieut. General Paget, among the latter, I have lost the assistance of a friend, who had been most useful to me in the few days which had elapsed since he had joined the army.

He had rendered a most important service at the moment he received his wound, in taking up the position which the troops afterwards maintained, and in bearing the first brunt of the enemy's attack.

[Felton Elwell] Hervey also distinguished himself at the moment he received his wound in the charge of the cavalry on this day.

I cannot say too much in favor of the Officers and troops. They have marched in four days over eighty miles of most difficult country, have gained many important positions, and have engaged and defeated three different bodies of the enemy's troops.

I beg particularly to draw your Lordship's attention to the conduct of Lieut. General Paget, Major General Murray, Major General Hill, Lieut. General Sherbrooke, Brig. General the Hon. Charles Stewart; Lieut. Colonel [William Howe] Delancey, Deputy Quarter Master General, and Captain [Henry Francis] Mellish, Assistant Adjutant General, for the assistance they respectively rendered General the Hon. Charles Stewart in the charge of the cavalry this day and on the 11th ; Major Colin Campbell, Assistant Adjutant General, for the assistance he rendered Major General Hill in the defence of his post ; and Brig. General the Hon. Charles Stewart in the charge of the cavalry this day; and Brigade Major Fordyce, Captain [Edward] Currie, and Captain [Clement]Hill, for the assistance they rendered General Hill.

I have also to request your Lordship's attention to the conduct of the riflemen and of the flank companies of the 29th, 43d, and 52d regiments, under the command of Major Way of the 29th; that of the 16th Portuguese Regiment, commanded by Colonel Machado, of which Lieut. Colonel

[Sir John Milley] Doyle is Lieut. Colonel; that of the brigade of the King's German Legion, under the command of Brig. General Langwerth; and that of the two squadrons of the 16th and 20th light dragoons, under the command of Major Blake of the 20th in the action of the 11th : and the conduct of the Buffs, commanded by Lieut. Colonel [Archibald] Drummond; the 48th, commanded by Colonel [George Henry]Duckworth; and 66th, commanded by Major [James Patrick] Murray, who was wounded; and of the squadron of the 14th dragoons, under the command of Major Hervey in the action of this day.

I have received the greatest assistance from the Adjutant General and Quarter Master General Colonel [George] Murray, and from all the Officers belonging to those departments respectively throughout the service, as well as from Lieut. Colonel Bathurst and the Officers of my personal staff; and I have every reason to be satisfied with the artillery and Officers of engineers.

I send this dispatch by Captain [Hon. Leicester Fitzgerald Charles] Stanhope, whom I beg to recommend to your Lordship's protection: his brother, the Hon. Major [Lincoln Edwin Robert] Stanhope, was unfortunately wounded by a sabre whilst leading a charge of the 16th light dragoons on the 10th instant.

Return of Ordnance captured on the 12th May, 1809.

Ten 12 pounders; twelve 8 pounders; eighteen 4 pounders; sixteen 3 pounders; two howitzers.

Abstract of the Killed, Wounded, and Missing in the Army under the command of Lieut. General the Right Hon. Sir A. Wellesley, K.B., in action with the French Army under the command of Marshal Soult, on the 10th, 11th, and 12th of March, 1809.[8]

	Officers	Serjeants	Rank and File	Horses	Total loss of Officers, Non-commissioned Officers, and Rank and File
Killed	1	–	42	–	43
Wounded	17	1	150	–	168
Missing	–	–	17	..	17

Soult was driven from Oporto on the 12th of May, and on the 18th he entered Galicia, closely pursued by the British and Portuguese troops, having lost all his cannon, his military chest, many stands of arms, baggage, &c. &c., and bringing with him not more than 8000 men of his corps.

In the mean time the following events had occurred in other parts. Ney, in conjunction with Kellerman, had invaded the Asturias, which province they entered on the beginning of May; the Marquis de la Romana having escaped from Gijon in a sloop of war.

The inhabitants of Vigo, aided by Captain Mackinlay of the *Lively*, had taken possession of that town; and, in the absence of Ney and Soult from Galicia, had pushed their parties as far as Lugo, which town they had attacked.

Marshal Victor repassed the Guadiana about the 12th or 13th of May, and detached a division across the Tagus at Alcantara on the 14th. This division retired again in a few days, probably as soon as it had heard of the success of the 12th against Soult; but Sir Arthur Welleslev having discontinued the further pursuit of Soult on the 18th of May, and having on the 19th received the accounts of the passage of the Tagus of this division, immediately gave orders for the return of the troops to the southward, and set out himself.

The leading troops arrived at Coimbra, on the Mondego, on the 26th of May; but Sir Arthur Wellesley having in the meantime heard that the French division which had passed the Tagus at Alcantara had recrossed that river, discontinued the rapidity of the march which he had at first ordered, and the British troops did not arrive on the Tagus till between the 7th and 12th of June.

They halted here till the 27th of June, partly to receive supplies of money, and of shoes, and of other articles of equipment wanting, and to give rest to the men and horses after the rapid marches they had made to the frontier of Galicia and back again.

It was also desirable to receive the reinforcements of the 48th and 61st regiments expected from Gibraltar, and the 23rd Dragoons arrived from England, before any further operations were entered upon.

During this time the French brought Ney's corps out of Asturias back into Galicia; and on the 6th of June they made an attempt, in conjunction with a detachment from Soult's corps, to obtain possession of Vigo, In their attempt upon the bridge of San Payo they failed entirely; and Soult failed equally in all his endeavors to bring to action on the River Sill the corps of the Marquis de la Romana, which had again in the beginning of the month of June assembled near Orense, upon the frontiers of Portugal.

The Marquis de la Romana having retired from Orense towards Vigo, Soult determined to withdraw from Galicia altogether, leaving Ney's corps alone in that province; and he marched in the end of June to Zamora, on the Duero, in order to re-equip and refit his army. Ney, finding himself too weak to maintain Galicia when alone, also evacuated that province in the middle of July, and posted himself at Astorga.

As soon as Victor found that the British army had arrived upon the Tagus, he began to retire from Estremadura on the 14th and 15th of June; and he finally crossed the Tagus at Almaraz on the 24th of June, two days before the British army broke up from Abrantes, &c. to march to Plasencia.

Kellerman's corps evacuated Asturias and Biscay, and returned to Valladolid; and Mortier's corps was at Leon. Suchet having defeated Blake at Belchite on the 18th June, had returned to Zaragoza; and the corps of St, Cyr was employed in the blockade of Gerona.

The Spanish army under General Cuesta, which had been reinforced with cavalry and infantry, and had been refitted with extraordinary celerity since the action of Medellin, had advanced from Monasterio in the middle of May, when Victor had crossed the Guadiana to support the division which he had detached over the bridge of Alcantara; and General

Cuesta made an attack upon a fortified post which the enemy had left at Merida. In this attack he did not succeed; the enemy maintained their post at Merida, and General Cuesta had his head quarters at Fuentes del Maestre till the end of June, when the enemy evacuated Estremadura, and passed the Tagus at Almaraz, upon hearing of the arrival of the British army upon that river at Abrantes.

In the end of June General Cuesta fixed his head quarters at the Puerto de Mirabete, opposite Almaraz, having a division of his army at Arzobispo.

Thus, then, in the end of June, the Spanish army under Cuesta was upon the Tagus; the French, under Victor, at Talavera de la Reyna; Sebastiani had retired from Ciudad Real, and had arrived near Toledo; and Vanegas's corps, which had likewise been reinforced, had advanced into La Mancha. The French had evacuated Galicia, with the exception of Ney's corps, which left that province at a later period, and arrived at Astorga in the middle of July. Mortier was at Leon, Soult at Zamora, Kellerman at Valladolid, Suchet at Zaragoza, and St. Cyr engaged in the blockade of Gerona. The British army broke up from Abrantes, &c., on the 27th of June to march to Plasencia, in order to co-operate with the Spanish troops in an endeavor to drive the French from the south of Spain.

The Commanding Officer of the King's troops in Portugal is alone responsible for this operation, for which the motives were various. First, adverting to the general state of the war in Spain, as well as in Germany, it appeared to be desirable to make an effort at that time in Spain. Secondly, the means appeared to be adequate to the object in view. General Cuesta had under his immediate command 38,000 men, and General Vanegas 18,000; and the British army was not less than 20,000 men, besides General Robert Craufurd's brigade, which had landed at Lisbon on the 28th of June, and was to commence its march to join the army immediately. Against these troops were to be opposed 28,000 men under Victor, and 12,000 under Sebastiani; and whatever the King could bring from the garrison of Madrid, and his guards.

It was not known till the beginning of July that even Soult had evacuated Galicia, in a state, as appears by the intercepted letters taken on General Francheschi, very unfit for service; nor that Ney had quitted that province and gone to Astorga, till late in July; and Mortier and Kellerman were supposed still to be in the Asturias and Biscay.

The difficulties of the operation were calculated; but it was supposed that the orders of the Spanish Government would furnish the means of transport and provisions that were or might be required, as they had expressed the greatest anxiety for the co-operation of the British troops. The means of transport were known to exist in the country, and the harvest about to be reaped, it was imagined, would have afforded an abundance of provisions.

The troops which broke up from Abrantes and the neighbourhood on the 27th of June reached Plasencia between the 7th and 10th of July, on which day Sir A. Wellesley went over to the Puerto de Mirabete, to confer and concert a plan of operations with General Cuesta. The objects of the plan were to bring into operation upon the enemy, at the same time, the British army and the two Spanish corps, under Cuesta and Vanegas, in such a manner as to prevent the enemy from bringing his concentrated force to bear upon either.

It was impossible for the corps of Cuesta and Vanegas, issuing from the defensive positions which they had occupied in Estremadura and La Mancha respectively, to join, or to have any military communication in this operation, excepting by Talavera and the bridge of Toledo; and it was obvious that unless the enemy should be alarmed for the safety of Madrid by one of the corps, he would fall with his whole collected strength upon the other. It was necessary to divide the attention of the enemy as much as possible, and to choose such a line of march for each corps as to prevent the enemy from opposing the march of either by natural obstacles, or by any thing excepting detachments from his own concentrated force.

General Vanegas was therefore ordered by Cuesta to direct his march by Tembleque, Tarancon, and Fuentiduena to Arganda, where he was to be on the 22nd of July, the day appointed for the arrival of the combined British and Spanish armies at Talavera. By passing by Fuentiduena, General Vanegas could have crossed the Tagus at a ford, and nothing could have prevented his arrival at his station but the opposition of the enemy. This was all that was wished for; - at the same time that, if he had been opposed by a corps too strong for him, his retreat was always open to the mountains of Cuenca; and the enemy could not have followed him in strength, and could not have undertaken any operation against La Carolina, pressed as they would have been on the other flank by the combined armies.

The only corps with which it was supposed that the combined armies would have had to engage, were the corps of Victor, Sebastiani, and the King. The other French corps in Spain were understood to be otherwise occupied; and at all events it was conceived that the occupation of the Puerto de Banos by General Cuesta's detachment, and of the Puerto de Perales by the garrison of Ciudad Rodrigo, and by the position of Marshal Beresford's corps on the frontiers of Portugal, would have prevented the enemy from penetrating into Estremadura by the passes in the rear of the army.

Sir Arthur Wellesley returned to Plasencia on the 12th, and found that the hopes were disappointed which he had formed of drawing from Ciudad Rodrigo, and other places in Castille, the means of transport which he had required, and which had been supplied by those places in the preceding year to the army under Sir John Moore. He still considered it necessary, however, to carry into execution the plan of operations agreed upon with General Cuesta, as he was unwilling to disappoint that General; and as General Vanegas' corps, which it was supposed would have commenced its operations, would have been exposed to risk; and, moreover. Sir A. W. expected that the army would have been supplied with provisions from the Vera de Plasencia till it should be supplied with means of transport from Seville, for which General Cuesta had written, or from La Mancha. Sir A. W., however, gave notice that he should co-operate only in the first operation, which should put General Cuesta in possession of the passage of the Alberche, and of the course of the Tagus, and should enable him to communicate with General Vanegas, until the wants of the British army should be supplied.

A part of the British army, consisting of about 1000 Portuguese troops under Sir Robert Wilson, (and which corps had been reinforced by two Spanish battalions,) was to march according to the plan through the Vera de Plasencia, on the left of the combined armies, to Escalona, on the Alberche. This corps marched on the 15th of July, and the British army, according to the plan agreed upon, commenced its march on the 17th and 18th of July; the 23rd Dragoons and 48th Regiment having joined the army while it was at Plasencia, and the 61st being expected to join on the 18th.

Sir Robert Wilson arrived at Escalona on the 22nd, and the combined armies at Talavera on the same day; and they drove in the enemy's outposts. On the 23rd arrangements were made, and the British army had marched and was in column near the Alberche to attack the French corps of Victor, posted on the heights beyond the river; but General Cuesta preferred to delay the attack till the following morning; and when the troops were formed on that morning at daylight, it was found that the enemy had withdrawn during the night.

General Cuesta then continued his march in pursuit of them to Santa Olalla; but they had gone to Torrijos, and thence even farther, to Bargas, The main body of the British remained at Talavera; with a division of infantry at Cazalegas to keep up the communication with General Cuesta; and another at Cardiel, on the Alberche, to keep up the communication with Sir Robert Wilson at Escalona.

The scarcity of provisions had been so great since the 20th, owing to the failure of the magistrates and inhabitants of the Vera de Plasencia to perform the contracts into which they had entered with a British Commissary, to supply at Talavera 240,000 rations before the 24th, that the British army was totally unable to move. The armies remained on the 25th in the positions taken up on the 24th, and the enemy collected all his force at Bargas.

It appears that General Vanegas had not obeyed the orders he had received, to direct his march upon Fuentiduena and Arganda. The enemy therefore had no apprehension from his operations, and they collected their whole force to oppose the combined armies. They attacked Cuesta's outposts at Torrijos on the morning of the 26th, and drove them in ; and General Cuesta retired with his army on that day to the left bank of the Alberche, the British division still remaining at Cazalegas, the division at Cardiel having joined; and on the 27th General Cuesta crossed the Alberche, and took up his position near Talavera; and the British troops retired from Cazalegas, one division remaining as an outpost in the woods opposite the enemy's position on the Alberche, the other going to its position near Talavera.

A general action being obviously to be expected on the 26th, Sir Robert Wilson was ordered from Escalona to join the army with his corps, through the mountains by Marrupe. The enemy attacked the outposts in the woods on the 27th, which retired to the position occupied by the army; and on that night, and on the 28th, followed the battle of Talavera.

Talavera 27-28 July 1809 [9]

General Cuesta followed the enemy's march with his army from the Alberche, on the morning of the 24th, as far as Santa Olalla, and pushed forward his advanced guard as far as Torrijos. For the reasons stated to your Lordship in my dispatch of the 24th[10] I moved only two divisions of infantry and a brigade of cavalry across the Alberche to Cazalegas, under the command of Lieut. General Sherbrooke, with a view to keep up the communication between General Cuesta and me, and with Sir Robert Wilson's corps at Escalona.

It appears that General Venegas had not carried into execution that part of the plan of operations which related to his corps, and that he was still at Daymiel, in La Mancha; and the enemy, in the course of the 24th, 25th, and 26th, collected all his forces in this part of Spain, between Torrijos and Toledo, leaving but a small corps of 2000 men in that place.

This united army thus consisted of the corps of Marshal Victor, of that of General Sebastiani, and of 7000 or 8000 men, the guards of Joseph Buonaparte, and the garrison of Madrid; and it was commanded by Joseph Buonaparte, aided by Marshals Jourdan and Victor, and by General Sebastiani.

On the 26th, General Cuesta's advanced guard was attacked near Torrijos and obliged to fall back; and the General retired with his army on that day to the left bank of the Alberche, General Sherbrooke continuing at Cazalegas, and the enemy at Santa Olalla.

It was then obvious that the enemy intended to try the result of a general action, for which the best position appeared to be in the neighbourhood of Talavera; and General Cuesta having consented to take up this position on the morning of the 27th, I ordered General Sherbrooke to retire with his corps to its station in the line, leaving General [Randoll] Mackenzie with a division of infantry and a brigade of cavalry as an advanced post in the wood, on the right of the Alberche, which covered our left flank.

The position taken up by the troops at Talavera extended rather more than two miles: the ground was open upon the left, where the British army was stationed, and it was commanded by a height, on which was placed en echelon, as the second line, a division of infantry under the orders of Major General Hill.

There was a valley between the height and a range of mountains still farther upon the left, which valley was not at first occupied, as it was commanded by the height before mentioned; and the range of mountains appeared too distant to have any influence on the expected action.

The right, consisting of Spanish troops, extended immediately in front of the town of Talavera, down to the Tagus. This part of the ground was covered by olive trees, and much intersected by banks and ditches. The high road leading from the bridge over the Alberche was defended by a heavy battery in front of a church, which was occupied by Spanish infantry.

All the avenues of the town were defended in a similar manner. The town was occupied, and the remainder of the Spanish infantry was formed in two lines behind the banks on the road which led from the town and the right to the left of our position.

In the centre, between the two armies, there was a commanding spot of ground, on which we had commenced to construct a redoubt, with some open ground in its rear. Brig. General Alexander Campbell was posted at this spot with a division of infantry, supported in his rear by General Cotton's brigade of dragoons and some Spanish cavalry.

At about 2 o'clock on the 27th, the enemy appeared in strength on the left bank of the Alberche, and manifested an intention to attack General Mackenzie's division[11]. The attack was made before they could be withdrawn; but the troops, consisting of General Mackenzie's and Colonel [Rufane Shaw] Donkin's brigades, and General [George] Anson's brigade of cavalry, and supported by General Payne with the other four regiments of cavalry in the plain between Talavera and the wood, withdrew in good order, but with some loss, particularly by the 2d batt. 87th Regiment, and the 2d batt. 31st regiment, in the wood.

Upon this occasion, the steadiness and discipline of the 45th Regiment, and the 5th batt. 60th Regiment, were conspicuous, and I had particular reason for being satisfied with the manner in which Major General Mackenzie withdrew this advanced guard.

As the day advanced, the enemy appeared in larger numbers on the right of the Alberche, and it was obvious that he was advancing to a general attack upon the combined armies. General Mackenzie continued to fall back gradually upon the left of the position of the combined armies, where he was placed in the second line in the rear of the Guards, Colonel Donkin being placed in the same situation farther upon the left, in the rear of the King's German Legion.

The enemy immediately commenced his attack, in the dusk of the evening, by a cannonade upon the left of our position, and by an attempt with his cavalry to overthrow the Spanish infantry, posted, as I have before stated, on the right. This attempt entirely failed.

Early in the night, he pushed a division along the valley on the left of the height occupied by General Hill, of which he gained a momentary possession; but Major General Hill attacked it instantly with the bayonet, and regained it. This attack was repeated in the night, but failed; and again, at daylight on the morning of the 28th, by two divisions of infantry, and was repulsed by Major General Hill.

Major General Hill has reported to me, in a particular manner, the conduct of the 29th Regiment, and of the 1st batt 48th Regiment, in these different affairs, as well as that of Major General [Christopher] Tilson and Brig. General R. Stewart.

We lost many brave Officers and soldiers in the defence of this important point in our position; among others, I cannot avoid mentioning Brigade Major [Alexander] Fordyce and Brigade Major [Daniel] Gardner; and Major General Hill was himself wounded, but I am happy to say but slightly.

The defeat of this attempt was followed about noon by a general attack with the enemy's whole force upon the whole of that part of the position occupied by the British army.

In consequence of the repeated attempts upon the height upon our left, by the valley, I had placed two brigades of British cavalry in that valley, supported in the rear by the Duque de Alburquerque's division of Spanish cavalry.[12]

The enemy then placed light infantry in the range of mountains on the left of the valley, which were opposed by a division of Spanish infantry, under Lieut. General Bassecourt.

The general attack began by the march of several columns of infantry into the valley, with a view to attack the height occupied by Major General Hill. These columns were immediately charged by the 1st German hussars and 23d light dragoons, under Brig. General Anson, directed by Lieut. General Payne, and supported by Brig. General Fane's brigade of heavy cavalry; and although the 23d dragoons suffered considerable loss, the charge had the effect of preventing the execution of that part of the enemy's plan.[13]

At the same time, he directed an attack upon Brig. General Alexander Campbell's position in the centre of the combined armies, and on the right of the British. This attack was most successfully repulsed by Brig. General Campbell, supported by the King's Regiment of Spanish cavalry and two battalions of Spanish infantry, and Brig. General Campbell took the enemy's cannon.

The Brig. General mentions particularly the conduct of the 97th, the 2d batt. 7th, and of the 2d batt. of the 53d Regiment; and I was highly satisfied with the manner in which this part of the position was defended.

An attack was also made at the same time upon Lieut. General Sherbrooke's division, which was in the left and centre of the first line of the British army. This attack was most gallantly repulsed by a charge with bayonets by the whole division; but the brigade of Guards, which were on the right, having advanced too far, they were exposed on their left flank to the fire of the enemy's batteries, and of their retiring columns, and the division was obliged to retire towards the original position, under cover of the second line of General Cotton's brigade of cavalry, which I moved from the centre, and of the 1st batt. 48th Regiment. I had moved this last regiment from its position on the height as soon as I observed the advance of the Guards, and it was formed in the plain, and advanced upon the enemy, and covered the formation of Lieut. General Sherbrooke's division.

Shortly after the repulse of this general attack, in which apparently all the enemy's troops were employed, he commenced his retreat across the Alberche, which was conducted in the most regular order, and was effected during the night, leaving in our hands twenty pieces of cannon, ammunition, tumbrils, and some prisoners.

Your Lordship will observe, by the enclosed return, the great loss which we have sustained of valuable Officers and soldiers in this long and hard fought action with more than double our numbers. That of the enemy has been much greater. I have been informed that entire brigades of infantry have been destroyed; and indeed the battalions which retreated were much reduced in numbers.

I have particularly to lament the loss of Major General Mackenzie, who had distinguished himself on the 27th, and of Brig. General Langwerth, of the King's German Legion, and of Brigade Major [Richard] Beckett, of the Guards.

Your Lordship will observe that the attacks of the enemy were principally, if not entirely, directed against the British troops. The Spanish Commander in Chief, his Officers and troops, manifested every disposition to render us assistance, and those of them who were engaged did their duty; but the ground which they occupied was so important, and its front at the same time so difficult, that I did not think it proper to urge them to make any movement on the left of the enemy while he was engaged with us.

I have reason to be satisfied with the conduct of all the Officers and troops. I am much indebted to Lieut. General Sherbrooke for the assistance I received from him, and for the manner in which he led on his division to the charge with bayonets; to Lieut. General Payne and the cavalry, particularly Brig. General Anson's brigade, to Major Generals Hill and Tilson, Brig. Generals Alexander Campbell, Richard Stewart, and Cameron, and to the divisions and brigades of infantry under their command respectively; particularly to the 29th Regiment, commanded by Colonel [Daniel] White; to the 1st batt. 48th, commanded by Colonel [Charles] Donellan; afterwards when that Officer was wounded, by Major [George] Middlemore; to the 2d batt. 7th, commanded by Lieut. Colonel Sir W. Myers; to the 2d batt. 53d, commanded by Lieut. Colonel [George Ridout] Bingham; to the 97th, commanded by Colonel [Sir James Frederick] Lyon; to the 1st batt. of detachments, commanded by Lieut. Colonel [William] Bunbury; to the 2d batt. 30th, commanded by Major Watson; the 45th, commanded by Lieut. Colonel [William] Guard; and to the 5th batt. 60th, commanded by Major Davy.

The advance of the brigade of Guards was most gallantly conducted by Brig. General H. Campbell; and, when necessary, that brigade retired and formed again in the best order.

The artillery, under Brig. General [Sir Edward] Howorth, was also throughout these days of the greatest service; and I had every reason to be satisfied with the assistance I received from the Chief Engineer, Lieut. Colonel [Richard] Fletcher; the Adjutant General, Brig. General the Hon. C. Stewart; the Quarter Master General, Colonel Murray; and the Officers of those departments respectively; and from Lieut. Colonel Bathurst, and the Officers of my personal Staff.

I also received much assistance from Colonel O'Lalor, of the Spanish service, and from Brig. General [Samuel Ford] Whittingham, who was wounded in bringing up the two Spanish battalions to the assistance of Brig. General Alexander Campbell.

Return of the numbers of killed, wounded and missing of the army under the command of Lieut. General the Hon. Sir Arthur Wellesley, K.B. in action with the French army commanded by King Joseph Buonaparte in person, at Talavera de la Reyna, on the 27th and 28th July, 1809.[14]

	Officers	Serjeants	Rank and File	Horses	Total loss of Officers, Non-commissioned Officers, and Rank and File
Killed	40	28	789	211	857
Wounded	195	165	3553	71	3913
Missing	9	15	629	159	653

The enemy retired in the evening and during the night of the 28th, and took up a position, with a rear guard of 10,000 men, on the heights of Cazalegas, beyond the Alberche. The British army and Spanish armies, which had been joined on the evening of the 29th by General Robert Craufurd's brigade of infantry, remained on the field of battle of Talavera, with their advanced posts, consisting of General Craufurd's brigade, in the woods, nearly in the place in which they had been on the 27th.

On the 29th, General Venegas went to Aranjuez, and made an attack upon a post of about 2000 men, which the enemy had left at Toledo. The King with the reserve, therefore, and Sebastiani's corps, went to oppose his advance, while Victor was left to watch the combined armies.

On the 31st, Sir Robert Wilson's corps, which had been called to the army when the general action was expected, and had arrived at Marrupe, returned towards Escalona; and the enemy's rear guard at Cazalegas retired on the same night, and went to Maqueda.

On the 30th, accounts had been received by General Cuesta that rations for a corps of 12,000 men had been ordered at Fuente Roble, north of the Puerto de Banos; and for 24,000 men at Los Santos, near the same place; supposed to be for the corps of Soult, which was known to have been at Zamora in the end of June, and for which equipments had been called for by Soult. It was expected, however, that the troops in the Puerto would make some resistance, and would stop their march; or that Soult might have been induced to desist from it by the position of Marshal Beresford's corps, or by the accounts he would have received of the victory at Talavera on the 28th of July.

It has already been stated that the Portuguese army in April was totally disorganized, and nearly annihilated; at the same time it had been necessary to employ the few men who were in the service in the expedition against

Soult, and in the defensive measures adopted for the security of the western frontier, when the army marched on that expedition.

When the British army was about to enter Spain in the end of June, there was no longer any danger for the north of Portugal; and it was desirable that advantage should be taken of the leisure which this security afforded, to collect in one camp the disposable part of the Portuguese army, in which Marshal Beresford should have an opportunity of forming and organizing the troops,

A camp on the frontiers of Beira, between Ciudad Rodrigo and Almeida, was considered the best situation for this purpose; and it had this additional recommendation, that the Portuguese corps, to which a British brigade was to be added, principally for the purpose of example, would protect the only vulnerable part of the Portuguese frontier which was exposed to attack; added to the security of the left of the British army; and, above all, protected the passage into Estremadura by the Puerto de Perales. From this situation, also, this Portuguese corps could have been brought with advantage in a subsequent part of the campaign, when it was hoped that the troops would be formed; but it was neither intended nor expected that Marshal Beresford's corps should co-operate, except as above stated, in the first operations of the months of July and August.

Notwithstanding the hopes entertained that Soult's march might have been stopped, or that he might have been induced to desist from it, it was desirable, as General Cuesta had not confidence in the exertions of the troops in the Puerto, that they should be reinforced; but he declined to reinforce them, and persisted in his refusal to do so till the morning of the 2nd of August, when he detached General Bassecourt with his division for that purpose. In the mean time the troops in the Puerto had retired without firing a shot, and had gone to the bridge over the Tagus at Almaraz, which they took up; and Soult entered Plasencia unresisted on the 1st of August.

It was then necessary to take decisive measures to re-establish the communication with Portugal, and for this purpose the British army marched on the morning of the 3rd to Oropesa, leaving General Cuesta's division in charge of the post at Talavera, and of the hospital. On that day, for the first time, General Cuesta received accounts, apprizing him of the real strength of the army which Soult had brought with him into Estremadura, which consisted of 34,000 men, and he imagined that the British corps was not equal to a contest with such numbers. He therefore immediately determined to withdraw from Talavera, and to join the British army at Oropesa; and thus he lost the hospital, and exposed the combined armies to be attacked in front and rear at the same time.

Soult's army arrived at Navalmoral on the evening of the 3rd; and in this position stood between the combined armies and the bridge of Almaraz, which it was supposed was removed, but most probably was, or it might have been, easily destroyed. The only retreat which remained was by the bridge of Arzobispo. There was a direct road to this bridge from Talavera de la Reyna, by Calera, and another direct from Navalmoral, each of them passing at not less than ten or twelve miles' distance from Oropesa, the station at which the combined armies were assembled on the morning of the 4th instant.

Besides these circumstances attending the only retreat the armies had it was to be observed that the enemy had now collected in Estremadura all the disposable force which he had in Galicia and Castille, with the exception of the corps of Kellerman, which still remained at Valladolid: 34,000 men were known to be added to the force already opposed to the combined armies; and it was obvious that they must retire across the Tagus, and take up a defensive position on that river.

Accordingly, the British army having halted at Oropesa on the night of the 3rd, marched early on the 4th to Arzobispo, and immediately crossed the Tagus; and the Spanish army, which had marched from Talavera, on the night of the 3rd, halted during the early part of the day of the 4th at Oropesa, and marched, and arrived at Arzobispo on the evening of the 4th.

On the 5th, the British army continued its march, and the advanced guard was placed upon the Mesa de Ibor, to secure that passage; and on the 6th the army arrived at the Mesa de Ibor, and the advanced guard at the Casas del Puerto, on the Tagus, opposite Almaraz; and on the 7th, the head of the column of the army arrived at Deleytosa, which place was reached on the 8th and 9th by the rear divisions.

The Spanish army in the mean time crossed the Tagus on the 5th, and the head quarters were removed to Peraleda de Garbin on the 7th, leaving an advanced guard at the bridge of Arzobispo; which was surprised on the 8th, and lost many men, and 30 pieces of cannon.

On the 11th of August the head quarters of the British army were transferred to Jaraicejo, leaving Deleytosa open for the Spanish army, to which place their head quarters were removed on the 13th; General Cuesta having resigned the command of the army on the 12th.

While this was going on on the left, General Vanegas was attacked at Aranjuez by Sebastiani and the King on the 5th; in which action he had some success. But he then resolved to retire to the Sierra Morena, and actually marched as far as Temblecque, He then altered this resolution, and he returned to Almonacid on the 11th, where he was attacked and defeated, with the loss of 4000 men. He then retired into the mountains of the Sierra Morena.

When the French evacuated Old Castille in the end of the month of July, to collect their armies in Estremadura, the Duque del Parque, the Commandant of Ciudad Rodrigo, sent a detachment from his garrison to take possession of Salamanca. This circumstance, and the probable early arrival of Romana's corps in Old Castille from Galicia, and the certainty that the position taken up by the allied armies was of such a nature, that no effort which they could make would dislodge them from it, induced the enemy to march the corps of Soult and Ney to Plasencia on the 9th, 10th, and 11th; and to send the latter into Castille through the Puerto de Banos, on the 12th of August. Ney there fell in with, and defeated Sir Robert Wilson's detachment; which, after the combined armies had retired from Talavera and Oropesa to Arzobispo, had been unable to reach the latter place; and had marched through the Vera de Plasencia, and the Puerto de Tornavacas; and was on its march when Ney passed through the Puerto de Banos.

Thus, in the middle of August, Ney was at Salamanca; Kellerman at Valladolid; Soult at Plasencia; Mortier at Oropesa and Arzobispo; Victor at Talavera and Toledo; and Sebastiani in La Mancha: while the British army was at Jaraicejo; General Eguia[15] at Deleytosa (General Cuesta having resigned); and General Vanegas at La Carolina, in the Sierra Morena.

On the 20th of August, the British army having suffered from extreme distress of provisions, broke up from its positions at Jaraicejo and the Casas del Puerto, the latter of which was occupied by the Spanish troops; and it moved with its head quarters to Badajoz, on the 3rd of September, and occupied a position on the frontiers of Spain and Portugal, in which, while it would give protection to both countries, it would be enabled to subsist with ease; and it would be possible to give the troops the refreshments they required, as well as the clothing and equipments which they wanted; and it has remained in that position.

The Portuguese army, under Marshal Beresford, also withdrew nearly about the same time within the Portuguese frontier, and went into cantonments.

In the mean time, the Spanish army of Estremadura was reduced to the number of 6000 men at Deleytosa; and General Eguia commenced his march with the remainder towards La Mancha in the middle of September. Nearly about the same period, 13,000 men of the corps of the

Marquis de la Romana arrived in the neighbourhood of Ciudad Rodrigo, from Galicia; and the command was taken from the Marquis, and given to the Duque del Parque[16]. The Duque immediately put himself at their head, and marched to Villa Vieja, and threatened the French posts towards Salamanca; but the enemy having reconnoitred him, and having drawn in all their detachments with a view to attack him, the Duque del Parque retired from Villa Vieja on the 23rd, to the neighbourhood of Ciudad Rodrigo.

The forward movement by the Duque del Parque, which the French conceived to be connected with a movement to be made by the British army, and with the march of General Eguia into La Mancha, induced Soult to abandon Plasencia on the 1st of October; and he moved to Oropesa. The Duque del Parque then occupied the strong position of Tamames, on the Castille side of the Puerto de Banos; in which he was attacked on the 19th October by General Marchand, in the command of Ney's corps, Ney having gone to France; and the French were defeated, with the loss of one piece of cannon. The Duque del Parque was joined on the following day by Ballasteros' division of the Marquis de la Romana's corps; and he then marched forward, and took possession of Salamanca on the 25th, the enemy having retired towards the Duero.

These events in Old Castille induced the enemy to withdraw some of the troops from Estremadura; and an army was collected there, consisting of Ney's, Kellerman's, and a part of Mortier's corps, amounting to 36,000 men, under the command of Marshal Mortier. The arrival of these troops in Old Castille obliged the Duque del Parque again to retire; and he arrived at Bejar, where he placed his head quarters on the 8th of November. The movements of General Eguia into La Mancha from Estremadura, in the middle of September, induced the French to move a large corps of 30,000 men under Victor, into that province; when the Spaniards retired to the Sierra Morena; and the French again withdrew their troops to the Tagus.

But the events which had occurred in Castille in October, particularly the battle at Tamames, induced the Spanish Government to believe that a favorable opportunity offered for obtaining possession of Madrid; and they directed General Areyzaga[17], who had, in October, taken the command of the army of La Mancha, to move forward and push for the possession of Madrid. He marched on the 3rd November, and reached Los Barrios, near Ocana on the 10th. He made an attack upon a French corps of 5000 men, which occupied that town on the night of the 10th, in which he lost some men and horses; and the French made good their retreat. He then moved to Santa Cruz de la Zarza on the 13th, where he remained till the 18th; and having heard of an enemy's corps in his front, at Arganda, which was about to pass the Tagus on his right at Fuentiduena, while there was another corps of 25,000 men at Aranjuez and Ocana, he returned to Los Barrios, and prepared to attack the French corps in his front. He found, however, on the morning of the 19th, that the French were likely to anticipate his attack; and he formed his army, consisting of 50,000 men, in the rear of Ocana. The French attacked him with 25,000 men, and completely defeated and dispersed the Spanish army, taking 55 pieces of cannon. The head quarters arrived at La Carolina on the 22nd; and very few men had been collected on the 28th. The French did not pursue farther than Villarta.

In the mean time, the Duque de Alburquerque, who had assumed the command of the army of Estremadura, in the beginning of November, marched to Arzobispo, when the French collected their troops on the Upper Tagus to oppose Areyzaga.

The French also, with the same view, drew out of Old Castille, on the 13th and 14th of November, a part of the troops which they had sent into that province to oppose the Duque del Parque. The Duque, upon finding Old Castille weakened, moved forward from Bejar on the 17th of November, and arrived at Alba de Tormes on the 28th, with his advanced guard at Carpio. It was there attacked by a French corps assembled from Valladolid, &c., but the French were repulsed with some loss. The Duque then moved forward to Fresno; but retired again on the 26th, in consequence of orders from the Junta.

By this time also, the French had reinforced again their corps in Old Castille; and the Duque was attacked on the 27th and 28th on his retreat, and at Alba de Tormes, and suffered considerably. He continued his retreat, however, towards Ciudad Rodrigo and the mountains; and on the 29th, when within two leagues of Tamames, the troops were alarmed by the appearance of 30 dragoons in their rear, and dispersed.

There was no enemy, however, at hand to take advantage of this panic; and it was expected that they would be collected again. While this was going on in Old Castille, the Junta ordered the Duque de Alburquerque to fall back with his corps on the Guadiana; and thus to give up the position of the Puerto de Mirabete, on the Tagus, and the Mesa de Ibor.

These circumstances, and the necessity that the British army should be north of the Tagus, when the enemy's reinforcements should arrive, induced Sir Arthur Wellesley to put the British army in motion to cross that river immediately. He had long had that movement in contemplation; and had given notice of it to the Junta.

The object in occupying this proposed position, is to be at the point of defence of Portugal; to divert the attention of the French from the south of Spain when they shall receive their reinforcements, and thus give time to the Spanish Government to repair their losses. The filling of the rivers, and the destruction of the roads, will, with a very few troops, be a sufficient defence in the winter for the south of Spain. The same events which might impede the march of the British army to the north of Portugal, if longer delayed, would be fatal to Portugal, and might be so to the British army, if the enemy were to be able to invade that kingdom during the winter. It is absolutely necessary, therefore, to cross the Tagus immediately; and it may be depended upon, that the enemy's first effort upon receiving his reinforcements will be upon the troops north of the Tagus. The contents of this Memorandum must show the great use the British army has been to Spain and Portugal. Since they arrived in April, the French have destroyed three Spanish armies, Blake's, Areyzaga's, and Del Parque's; and yet they can do nothing. They have been obliged to evacuate the north of Portugal, Galicia, South Estremadura, and they hold but part of La Mancha; and also to keep their force concentrated in Old Castille, and about Madrid.

If' the Spaniards had not lost two armies lately, we should keep up the ball for another year. But as it is! – but I won't despair!

Chapter 3

Memorandum of Operations in 1810[1]

Te last memorandum, on the operations of the British army in the Peninsula, ended with the breaking up of the British army from its position on the frontiers of Estremadura and Aleritejo, and its march to a position in Upper Beira, between the Mondego and the Tagus, in the middle of December, 1809.

The reasons for this movement were the following:

First, it was believed that the French were aware that, till they could dislodge the British army from Lisbon and the Tagus, they could not hope to make any successful invasion of Andalusia, or any progress in obtaining possession of that country. This belief was confirmed by their conduct after the battle of Ocana, in the month of November. The events of that battle, and the state to which it reduced the Spanish army, afforded them the best opportunity of entering Andalusia unopposed, and of taking possession even of Cadiz itself; but instead of pursuing their advantages, they turned their troops back immediately into Old Castille, and gave ground for belief that their line of operations would be in that quarter.

Secondly, there was every reason to believe that large reinforcements would enter Spain during the winter, which might be thrown immediately upon the frontier of Portugal.

Thirdly, the swelling of the rivers Tagus and Guadiana, which had occurred in some degree, had opposed a material obstacle to the advance of the French through Estremadura, and the expected rains were likely to render the roads quite impracticable; which, added to the means of defence remaining in the province, under the Duque de Alburquerque, left it in a state of apparent safety from invasion.

The British army had completed its march by the 15th January, and had taken up its cantonments with their right at Guarda, their left extending towards the Douro, and the advanced posts on the Coa. The head quarters were placed at Viseu.

At this time, the strength of the British army was 19,500 rank and file: 2800 of that number were cavalry, leaving 16,700 infantry, of which 800 were at Lisbon. A division of infantry of 4400 men had been left on the Tagus at

Abrantes, under the command of Lieut. General Hill, as the foundation of the corps to be formed under his command, to carry on operations on the frontiers of Alentejo and Estremadura, if, contrary to all appearances and expectation, the enemy should invade that part of the country. With the exception of the hussars, the cavalry also were left upon the Tagus for the convenience of receiving forage, which we were informed that the province of Upper Beira could not supply.

The Portuguese army was at this time in a state not fit for service, owing principally to the want of clothing, and those equipments which are necessary to all soldiers in a winter campaign. Their discipline, organization, and equipment had been in some degree thrown back by their operations in the preceding summer; and it was determined, if possible, not to move them from the cantonments which they occupied in the interior of the country till the last moment, in order to give them as much time to be formed and equipped as might be possible, while the British troops should occupy the frontiers.

The force and position of the allies at that time were as follows: About 24,000 men, which had been collected of the fugitives from the battle of Ocana, were at La Carolina, occupying the principal passes of the Sierra Morena; about 12,000 men, under the Duque de Albuquerque, were at Medellin, upon the Guadiana; and about 20,000 men[2], which had been collected together after the Duque del Parque's action at Alba, were at St. Martin de Trebejo, in the Sierra de Gata. There were 6000 or 8000 men, under General Mahy, at Astorga and Villa Franca, in Galicia; and there was a garrison in Ciudad Rodrigo. It had been repeatedly recommended to the Spanish Government to reinforce the corps under the Duque de Alburquerque. If this corps had been stronger, and the operations of the Spanish troops could have been reckoned upon, it could have defended the passage of the Tagus at Almaraz; and if the enemy, instead of attempting that operation, had pushed their whole force through La Mancha, as they afterwards did, this corps might have been thrown upon their right flank by the valley of the Guadiana. The enemy's force consisted of, and was disposed as follows: The corps of Sebastiani (the 4th), Victor (the 1st), and Mortier (the 5th), were disposed of about the Tagus and Madrid; and Soult, the King's guards, and Dessolle's reserve, composed an army of about 65,000 men. Soult's corps was at Talavera de la Reyna, and in that neighbourhood, and consisted of about 12,000 men. Ney's corps (the 6th) was in Old Castille; and, by the time the British army arrived in Beira, it had been joined by the reinforcements, and consisted of 32,000 men; and towards the middle of the month of January, the Duc d'Abrantes, or the 8th corps, consisting of 27,000 men, also entered Spain.

Besides these corps, which are immediately the subject of this memorandum, there was the 3rd corps, under Suchet, in Aragon, and the army of Catalonia, put under Augereau, and then under Macdonald, in Catalonia, which have been engaged in the operations of the campaign against the Spanish armies of Valencia and Catalonia; but the operations are quite distinct from those which have been carried on on the western and southern side of the Peninsula, and they will not be noticed any further.

The first operation which the enemy undertook, as soon as their reinforcements entered Spain was to force the passes of the Sierra Morena. After manoeuvring for some days at the foot of the mountains, they carried the passes almost without opposition on the part of the Spanish army, which retired in several directions. The greater part, under General Areyzaga himself, retired to Jaen, and thence to Grenada, which towns they successively abandoned, and thence into Murcia; and this body has since formed the army of Murcia. A part retired into the Sierra de la Honda, and thence to Gibraltar, from whence it was removed to Cadiz; and a part, under the Visconde de Gand, retired to Seville, and thence into the Condado de Niebla, where it has since remained, under the command of General Copons; and one division, and the artillery, crossed the Guadalquivir at Seville, and went to Monasterio, in Estremadura; from whence the artillery was sent to Badajoz, and the troops went and embarked at Ayamonte.

After passing the Sierra Morena, the French pushed their left, the corps of Sebastiani, towards Jaen; and the 1st corps, with the King's guards and reserve, went, under the King, to Seville and Cadiz. The Duque de Alburquerque, however, passed the Sierra Morena from his position on the Guadiana, by Guadalcanal, nearly at the same time with the French, and arrived at Xerez, and occupied the Isla de Leon, before the French approached the place.

While these movements were making, the Central Junta was dissolved. Previous to the dissolution of that body, they had ordered the march of the corps under the command of the Duque del Parque from Castille into Estremadura; and, with the exception of 3000 men under General Carrera, it marched on the [   ]³. Nearly at the same time the Marquis de la Romana was appointed to resume the command of this corps.

The wants and the situation of the Portuguese army at that period of time have been already pointed out. It would have been impossible to move them, without incurring the risk of rendering them useless during the campaign. Including the cavalry (with the exception of General Slade's brigade, attached to General Hill's corps), the whole British army that could be brought into operation on the frontiers of Castille, between the middle and end of January, was less than 15,000 men, to which the Portuguese army might have added 10,000 or 12,000 men, if it had been deemed expedient to draw these troops into the field at that time, notwithstanding the considerations above referred to.

Against this force was Ney's corps at Salamanca; and Junot's, or the 8th, was on its march within the Spanish frontier; and at all events it was known in the end of January that the effect had been produced in Andalusia, which it would have been the object of any diversion to prevent. The passes of the Sierra had been carried without opposition; the Spanish army had been dispersed; Seville, the seat of government, with its arsenals and establishments, was in the possession of the French; and Cadiz itself was threatened. No operation, which should not have been performed by a most powerful and superior body of troops well supported, could have produced any diversion to avert the consequences of this state of things.

It was obvious that the French were in an error when they entered Andalusia. They should have begun by turning their great force against the English in Portugal, holding in check the Spanish force in Andalusia, as they had done in the preceding spring. Andalusia would then have fallen an easy conquest to them; but in the manner in which they have proceeded, they have been obliged to bring corps after corps out of Andalusia against Portugal; Cadiz, &c., have in the mean time become strengthened, as has Portugal; and it is doubtful whether they will ever obtain possession of either.

This view of the subject, and the knowledge that the cause would eventually be fought for in Portugal, and the certainty that the enemy had the means of collecting a superior force to ours, even if he had not already been reinforced, prevented us from incurring any risk to create a diversion in January. Besides, the weather was such as to prevent all operations; and the suspicion which was always entertained that the reinforcements were within reach when the enemy made their movements to the southward, were the principal reasons.

As soon as it was known in Portugal that the French had entered Andalusia, and that the Spanish Government desired to have assistance to defend Cadiz, the 79th, 87th, and 94th regiments, and two companies of artillery, were detached there in the beginning of February, under Major General [Hon. William] Stewart, and the 20th Portuguese Regiment. Nearly at the same time, accounts were received that the 2nd corps of the French army were entering Estremadura, in concert with, and supported by, the 5th corps (Mortier's) from Andalusia. The 5th corps had left Seville on the 2nd and 3rd February, apparently to disperse a fugitive division of Areyzaga's army, which had crossed the Guadalquivir, but these retired towards Ayamonte, sending their artillery to Badajoz.

It appears that the French Government had imagined that the invasion of Andalusia, the possession of Seville and its arsenals, &c., and the dissolution of the Central Junta, would be deemed misfortunes of such magnitude, as that all resistance would cease; and on the same day, the 12th of February, they summoned the places of Cadiz, Badajoz, Ciudad Rodrigo, and Astorga.

Immediately upon receiving information of the entry of the French into Estremadura, General Hill was put in motion on the 12th February, with his own British division; two brigades of Portuguese infantry, about 4000 strong, under Major General [Sir John] Hamilton; one brigade of British cavalry, about 1000, under Major General Slade; and [the] 4th Regiment of Portuguese cavalry; and one brigade of German, and two of Portuguese, artillery. This corps was ordered, in the first instance, to Portalegre; and General Hill was directed to co-operate with the Spanish troops lately under the command of the Duque del Parque, then supposed to have crossed the Tagus; and to prevent the enemy, if possible, from carrying on any serious operation against Badajoz.

The enemy retired from Badajoz when they heard of General Hill's arrival at Portalegre. Ciudad Rodrigo was summoned by Marshal Ney with two divisions of his corps, and he retired again upon the Tormes, upon finding the advanced guard of the British army crossing the Coa; and Astorga was summoned by General Loison, with the third division of Ney's corps, who remained in that neighbourhood for some time. Loison was afterwards relieved by the 8th corps, under Junot; and he approached nearer to Salamanca.

From this time no movement of importance was made by either party, till towards the middle of March, when the French corps in Estremadura broke up, and Mortier marched to the southward; and Regnier, with Soult's corps, remained in the neighbourhood of Merida.

The allied British and Spanish troops on the frontiers of Portugal and Estremadura were then in some degree superior in numbers to the French corps remaining in Estremadura, and the question whether the latter should be attacked or not was then well considered. In the consideration of every question of this description, there are certain topics which must be reviewed, and the following are of the number:

First, the object in this case would have been, if possible, to cripple, or entirely destroy, the 2nd corps of the army which remained in Estremadura; but it is apprehended that this object would have been impracticable. Even supposing that General Hill's and the Marquis de la Romana's corps joined had been deemed sufficiently strong to attempt to remove the 2nd corps from its position on the Guadiana, they could not have prevented its retreat either to the Sierra Morena, or along the valley of the Guadiana to Ciudad Real, or between the Tagus and the Guadiana towards Arzobispo. The attack must have been made in one concentrated body, on one side or the other of the Guadiana; and the allies would have been able only to choose which way the enemy should retreat, supposing them to have been able to force his retreat.

'Secondly, the means to effect this object consisted in about 12,000 men, cavalry and infantry, half British and half Portuguese, under General Hill, and about 10,000 Spanish troops, under the Marquis de la Romana, whose corps had been much reduced by sickness and want; and General Carrera, with 3000 men, had remained in Old Castille. Against these the enemy had not less than 16,000 men; for the 2nd corps, as well as the others, had received reinforcements.

Thirdly, the risks to be incurred in this expedition consisted in the probability that the 2nd corps would be joined by the 5th corps again, before any serious impression could have been made upon the 2nd corps. The Marquis de la Romana had at this time but little of any cavalry, and the Spanish cavalry is notoriously bad. The Portuguese cavalry was but newly formed; and the reliance in respect to that arm, in that open country, would have been upon the 1100 British cavalry. The 2nd corps was always stronger in cavalry than the allies in Estremadura; but if the 2nd corps had been rejoined by the 5th, not only would the enemy's superiority in cavalry have been increased, but in infantry also; and the retreat of the allies to the strong places would have been hurried at least, if not difficult.

Fourthly, the difficulties in the undertaking, besides those of the season, are of the same description with those which have attended, and invariably must attend, every operation which has been attempted in the Peninsula.

There is an old military proverb respecting these operations which is strictly and invariably true, and that is, that "if they are attempted with small numbers they must fail; if with large, the army must starve". The inhabitants of Spain and Portugal will not part with their provisions, even for money. There are no great markets for corn in any part of the Peninsula, excepting the seaports, and some of the very large and populous cities, and the inhabitants subsist generally upon stores formed in their own houses, or buried under ground; and if they are deprived of any considerable portion of their supply for the year, they must either starve, or must go to seek for a fresh supply at a great distance, as no neighbour has any to sell. These circumstances account at the same time for the difficulties which the allied armies experienced, while the enemy can subsist with facility. The force used by the allies to obtain subsistence from the country consists in the influence of the civil magistrates: that used by the French is terror. They force from the inhabitants, under pain of death, all that they have in their houses for the consumption of the year, without payment, and are indifferent respecting the consequences to the unfortunate people. The British armies cannot, and the natives will not, follow this example, although the latter go nearest to it. Still, however, no Spanish officer could venture to carry his requisitions for provisions on any town much further than the influence of the civil magistrate would go to procure them; and the Spanish troops have always been in want, where the French armies have afterwards found subsistence. When the Marquis de la Romana and his officers were asked whether they would insure the subsistence of the troops upon this expedition, supposing it were undertaken, they answered that they could not; and indeed their own army was at this moment in the utmost distress in their cantonments, and literally perishing for want. Upon the whole, then, comparing the only object which could be acquired by this expedition with the risk to be incurred, and the difficulty of the undertaking, it was thought best not to attempt it.

The next event of any importance that occurred was, in the commencement of April, the formal attack of Astorga by the 8th corps, under the Due d'Abrantes. At this time the expediency of attempting a diversion in favor of the Spaniards, by making a forward movement into Castille, was again considered.

In the end of March, the British army in Portugal consisted of about 22,000 rank and file, of which 2733 were cavalry. Of the cavalry, 1072, and of the infantry, 5112, were with General Hill in Alentejo, and 400 men at Lisbon, leaving in Beira about 15,000 effective rank and file, cavalry and infantry.

About this time the Portuguese army were becoming in a better state of equipment, and we might have drawn twelve regiments of regular infantry, and four of chasseurs, making about 14,000 effective rank and file, to the army, exclusive of the Portuguese troops with General Hill. This would have made the allied army in Beira about 30,000 men.

With this force we should have had to attack Marshal Ney at the head of his own corps, which was more numerous than ours (infinitely superior in cavalry), in a strong position at Salamanca; having it in his power to draw towards him either the whole or any part of Junot's corps, or of the body of troops under Kellerman in Old Castille, between the time at which he would have heard of our passing the Agueda and that of our arrival at Salamanca, supposing that he had ever allowed us to reach that place. It may be supposed that we might have drawn a part, if not the whole, of Hill's corps into Beira for this operation; but even with the whole of that corps we were not equal to the operation, and should not have succeeded in obliging the French to raise the siege of Astorga. But if the whole of that corps had been brought from the frontiers of Alentejo to those of Beira, the enemy would have entered the former province, and there was nothing between them and Lisbon. To this add, that all the arguments respecting the difficulties for subsistence in the proposed expedition into Estremadura in March were stronger in respect to that in contemplation into Castille in the end of that month and beginning of April, and the weather rendered all operations at that time impracticable. Astorga fell on the 22nd of April, the magazine having been kept in a church, and it blew up. On the 24th, the 3rd division of Marshal Ney's corps was put in motion from its cantonments towards Ciudad Rodrigo; and it took up its ground on the 26th, and blockaded the place, on the right of the Agueda. On the same day the British advanced guard went to Gallegos, and the communication with the place was open from that time till the 10th of June.

The British army in Beira was put in motion on the 26th of April, and their cantonments were closed up to the front. The head quarters were moved on that day to Celorico from Viseu. There is no doubt but that if the British army had been moved forward to the Agueda in the end of April, Loison's division must have moved from its position in the neighbourhood of Ciudad Rodrigo, or the whole of the 6th corps must have been brought up to its support. But the temporary removal of Loison's division could not prevent the French from making the siege of Ciudad Rodrigo, when the state of the weather and rivers would permit them. They had then 57,000 effective men in the 6th and 8th corps in Castille, besides the troops under Kellerman, and some under Serras; and if Loison had been obliged to retire by our troops, it would have only been for a time. Ciudad Rodrigo would have gained nothing by this retreat, for the communication with the town by the left of the Agueda was open as long as it could be under any circumstances; while our troops would have suffered all the inconvenience and sickness which would have resulted from drawing them out of their cantonments before the rains were over. Ciudad Rodrigo could have been saved only by such a diversion on the part of General Mahy in Galicia[4], and of the inhabitants and guerrillas of Castille, when the French armies were drawn together for the siege, as should have obliged the French to detach troops to quell the insurrection, or to force Mahy to retreat again to his mountains, and thus render the besieging army of such a strength as that we might have ventured to attack it But General Mahy made no movement; the inhabitants looked on with apathy, only abusing us that we did not involve ourselves in the same peril with Ciudad Rodrigo.

The British army in Portugal, on the 1st of June, consisted of 25,000 rank and file, of which number 3261 were cavalry; 5381 infantry, and 449 cavalry, were with General Hill; and about 2000 infantry were at Lisbon; leaving in Beira about 17,000 men, of which number about 14,000 were infantry. Of the 2000 men at Lisbon, about 1500 belonged to the royals [3/1st or Royal Regiment], the 9th and 38th regiments, which regiments had been in Walcheren, and it was not deemed expedient to move them from Lisbon till the season should have entirely settled; and they were not moved till the end of June.[5]

The Portuguese army, on the 1st of June, consisted of 29,200 effective rank and file, cavalry, infantry, and artillery. Of this number about 1200 cavalry, and 5000 infantry, and 300 artillery, were with General Hill, leaving about 23,000 effective men. There were five regiments of infantry in garrisons, one at Cadiz, three regiments and two battalions of the Lusitanian legion unfit to be brought into the field; making, with the cavalry, also unfit, not less than 10,000 effective men, which would leave about 14,000 in Beira; making, in June, our army in Beira, including artillery, of about 32,000 effective men, which was the largest we were ever able to collect upon that frontier.

The three Walcheren regiments, the three inefficient regiments of Portuguese infantry, the two battalions of the Lusitanian legion, and three battalions of militia, and three brigades of Portuguese artillery, were collected as a reserve upon the Zezere in the beginning of July, under the command of General [James] Leith; but these corps were not fit to be joined to the army till the end of September. I had sent Colonel M'Mahon's brigade of infantry away from it in May, as being unfit.[6]

On the 25th June the head quarters were removed to Almeida, in order to be nearer the scene of action; and on the 1st July they were moved to Alverca, as being more centrally situated in respect to our own troops.

Every thing was done which could enable the British army to endeavor to save Ciudad Rodrigo, if it had been practicable; but it was impracticable to attempt it, unless it could be supposed that we should beat an army nearly double the strength of the allied army, having nearly four times the number of cavalry, in a country admirably adapted to the use of that arm. The place surrendered on the 11th July.

After the surrender of Ciudad Rodrigo, the enemy's movements were for some time uncertain, and we could not learn from them his intentions. We knew that Regnier had been ordered to cross the Tagus, and to manoeuvre upon Alcantara, with a view to support the attack upon Ciudad Rodrigo. But he did not carry that measure into execution till about the 18th of July; and his movement was followed immediately by that of General Hill, who crossed the Tagus likewise at Villa Velha, and took up a position in Regnier's front, in Lower Beira.

At length, on the 24th of July, the enemy attacked General Craufurd's division, near Almeida, with the whole of Ney's corps, and obliged it to cross the Coa with some loss.[7]

It had been desirable to maintain our posts beyond the Coa as long as possible, as well to observe the movements of the enemy as to keep up the communication with Almeida; but it was not intended to fight an action beyond the Coa. It was necessary to withdraw the troops from the bridge of Almeida that night; and the enemy's advanced guard passed it in the morning, and Almeida was invested.

The enemy having passed the Coa in force, it was necessary to withdraw the division of infantry which was at Pinhel, which was liable to be attacked in front by the 8th corps, and on its flank by the 6th; and on the 26th the advanced guard was drawn back to Fraxedas, and the army was concentrated between Guarda and Trancoso.

The enemy's designs were still uncertain. From the movements of the 2nd and 8th corps, and from the delay to make any preparations for the siege of Almeida, and from the advanced state of the season, it was thought most probable that he could not attempt that operation, but would advance into Portugal by the roads which lead through Lower Beira, forcing back General Hill's corps, and turning the right of that under my command; or that he would fall with his concentrated force upon both the flanks and the centre of the corps under my command, and hurry them in their retreat, which must have been made by one road only. The infantry of the army was therefore thrown back one march into the valley of the Mondego, still keeping a division upon Guarda; and General Hill was ordered to Sarzedas, in Lower

Beira; Colonel Le Cor's division of militia keeping the communication between General Hill and the army.

At length, on the 15th of August, the enemy's design to attack Almeida became manifest; and the army was concentrated again between Trancoso and Guarda; and the advanced guard was moved to Fraxedas, as well to oblige the enemy to concentrate his army for the siege, and thus give scope and opportunity to the guerrillas and other troops in Spain to carry on their operations, as to be in a situation to take advantage of any opportunity which offered to strike a blow against the enemy.

The place surrendered on the 27th of August, owing to the magazine having been blown up; and on the 28th the infantry of the army was again thrown into the valley of the Mondego.

In order to render more clear the nature of these and the subsequent operations, it is necessary to point out that the two great entrances into Portugal, between the Tagus and the Douro, are on different sides of the great range of mountains called the Estrella. The rivers Zezere and Mondego rise in the Estrella, and take their course on different sides of that mountain. The former runs a considerable distance to the southward and westward, and then to the southward, and falls into the Tagus at Punhete; the latter runs first to the northward as far as Celorico, where it turns to the westward, and falls into the sea at Figueira. Guarda stands upon the eastern extremity of the Estrella, and there the mountain can be passed; and there is no road by which troops can pass the mountains from the valley of the Zezere and the valley of the Mondego, excepting nearly as far to the westward as the Ponte da Murcella, over the Alva. This river likewise rises in the Estrella, and runs in a north westerly direction into the Mondego, into which it falls about five leagues above Coimbra.

From this general description, it will be obvious that the British army could not be concentrated for any operation to the eastward of the Alva, without laying open to the enemy one of the great entrances into the country. General Hill's corps could not have joined that under my command, without passing by or to the eastward of Guarda. Regnier was always in his front, and he might immediately have occupied the passes of Lower Beira; and then the safety of the army, and of the capital, would have depended upon the operations of the reserve on the Zezere.

If the reserve had been joined to the army, it would not have been sufficiently strong to undertake any operation of importance; and any accident to General Hill, who was not so strong as Regnier, would have exposed all our interests to ruin. If we could have collected the reserve, which consisted of about 1500 British infantry and 4000 Portuguese troops, and General Hill's corps of about 12,000 men, and the corps in Beira of about 32,000, making a total of less than 50,000 men, we should have had less by 7000 men than the 6th and 8th corps, without including Serras, Bonnet, or Kellerman; and the 2nd corps, consisting of 16,000 or 17,000, might either have been thrown upon us, or might have been moved through Lower Beira at once upon Lisbon, as there would have been nothing between them and Lisbon in the supposed case. It was therefore determined to observe the movements of the enemy, and to concentrate the army in the first favorable situation that should be found, after they should manifest their line of attack. If they had made their attack by two lines, most probably the army could not have been concentrated till it reached the neighbourhood of Lisbon; but it was thought probable, from their movements, that they were to make it in one concentrated body by the valley of the Mondego, and measures were taken to concentrate the army on the Serra da Murcella, on the Alva.

It was never imagined that they could make the march they did across the Mondego, through Upper Beira. The ground, however, on the north of the Mondego, was not unknown; and the measures which had been taken, with a view to the concentration of the British army on the Alva, facilitated the movement of the troops across the Mondego, and their concentration on Busaco.

On the 4th of September, the head quarters, which had been moved to Celorico on the 28th of August, were moved to Gouveia, in consequence of the collection of the enemy's force upon the Upper Coa, and his movements towards Alverca. They remained there till the 16th, on which day the heads of two corps (the 2nd and 6th) of the enemy entered Celorico, and the third (the 8th) Trancoso; the former crossed the Mondego again to Fornos. The army was then put in motion, and took up a position, and was concentrated upon the position of Busaco.

The British army in Portugal, at the time of the battle of Busaco, consisted of 27,188 rank and file, of which number 2839 were cavalry: 2200 infantry were at Lisbon, 1900 of which just arrived: 1350 infantry were on their march to join, leaving in the battle not quite 24,000 men. The Portuguese army at the same time consisted of 26,800 effective rank and file of infantry, and 3375 cavalry. Of the infantry, 1350 were at Elvas, 1142 at Cadiz, and 563 at Abrantes; leaving 23,800 infantry in the battle. Of the cavalry, 500 were at Elvas, 600 at Badajoz, 500 north of the Douro, and 200 at Lisbon, leaving 1375 with the army; making a total of 25,175.

The two armies amounting to about 49,000 men, besides artillery, of which there were four brigades and two troops of British, and six brigades of Portuguese.

The French army consisted of eighty-nine battalions of infantry, which, according to the latest returns, consisted of 56,000 men; fifty four squadrons of cavalry, of 8000 men; and about 6000 artillery. The whole army, including sappers, &c., was not less than 72,000 men.

Busaco 27 September 1810[8]

While the enemy was advancing from Celorico and Trancoso upon Viseu, the different divisions of militia and ordenanza were employed upon their flanks and rear; and Colonel Trant with his division attacked the escort of the military chest and reserve artillery near Tojal, on the 20th instant. He took 2 officers and 80 prisoners, but the enemy collected a force from the front and rear, which obliged him to retire again towards the Douro. I understand that the enemy's communication is completely cut off, and he possesses only the ground upon which his army stands.

On the 21st the enemy's advanced guard pushed on to Sta Combadao, at the junction of the rivers Criz and Dab; and Brig. General [Denis] Pack retired across the former and joined Brig. General Craufurd at Mortagoa, having destroyed the bridges over those two rivers.

The enemy's advanced guard crossed the Criz, having repaired the bridge, on the 23rd, and the whole of the 6th corps was collected on the other side of the river. I therefore withdrew the cavalry through the Serra de Busaco, with the exception of three squadrons, as the ground was favourable for the operation of that arm.

On the 25th, the whole of the 6th and of the 2nd corps crossed the Criz in the neighbourhood of Sta Combadao; and Brig. General Pack's brigade and Brig. General Craufurd's division retired to the position which I had fixed upon for the army on the top of the Serra de Busaco. These troops were followed in this movement by the whole of the corps of Ney and Regnier (the 6th and the 2nd); but it was conducted by Brig. General Craufurd with great regularity, and the troops took their position without sustaining any loss of importance.

The 4th Portuguese caqadores, which had retired on the right of the other troops, and the piquets of the 3rd Division of infantry, which were posted at St Antonio de Cantaro, under Major Smyth of the 45th Regiment, were engaged with the advance of Regnier's corps in the afternoon, and the former showed that steadiness and gallantry which others of the Portuguese troops have since manifested.

The Serra de Busaco is a high ridge which extends from the Mondego in a northerly direction about eight miles. At the highest point of the ridge, about two miles from its termination, is the convent and garden of Busaco. The Serra de Busaco is connected by a mountainous tract of country with the Serra de Caramula, which extends in a north easterly direction beyond Viseu, and separates the valley of the Mondego from the valley of the Douro. On the left of the Mondego, nearly in a line with the Serra de Busaco, is another ridge of the same description, called the Serra da Murcella, covered by the river Alva, and connected by other mountainous parts with the Serra d'Estrella.

All the roads to Coimbra from the eastward lead over the one or the other of these Serras. They are very difficult for the passage of an army, the approach to the top of the ridge on both sides being mountainous.

As the enemy's whole army was on the right of the Mondego, and it was evident that he intended to force our position, Lieut. General Hill crossed that river by a short movement to his left, on the morning of the 26th, leaving Colonel Le Cor with his [Portuguese] brigade on the Serra da Murcella, to cover the right of the army, and Brig. General Fane, with his division of Portuguese cavalry and the 13th light dragoons, in front of the Alva, to observe and check the movements of the enemy's cavalry on the Mondego.

With this exception, the whole army was collected upon the Serra de Busaco, with the British cavalry observing the plain in the rear of its left, and the road leading from Mortagoa to Oporto, through the mountainous tract which connects the Serra de Busaco with the Serra de Caramula.

The 8th corps joined the enemy in our front on the 26th, but he did not make any serious attack on that day. The light troops on both sides were engaged throughout the line.

At six in the morning of the 27th the enemy made two desperate attacks upon our position, the one on the right, the other on the left of the highest part of the Serra. The attack upon the right was made by two divisions of the 2nd corps, on that part of the Serra occupied by the 3rd Division of infantry. One division of French infantry arrived at the top of the ridge, where it was attacked in the most gallant manner by the 88th Regiment, under the command of Lieut. Colonel [John Alexander Dunlop Agnew] Wallace, the 45th, under the command of Lieut. Colonel the Hon. R. Meade,[9] and by the 8th Portuguese Regiment, under the command of Lieut. Colonel [James Dawes] Douglas, directed by Major General [Thomas] Picton. These three corps advanced with the bayonet, and drove the enemy's division from the advantageous ground which they had obtained. The other division of the 2nd corps attacked farther on the right, by the road leading by St Antonio de Cantaro, also in front of Major General Picton's division. These were repulsed, before they could reach the top of the ridge, by the 74th, under the command of Lieut. Colonel the Hon. R.[Richard Le Poer] Trench, and the brigade of Portuguese infantry of the 9th and 21st regiments, under the command of Colonel Champelmond, directed by Colonel Mackinnon. Major General Leith also moved to his left to the support of Major General Picton, and aided in the defeat of the enemy by the 3rd battalion of Royals, the 1st battalion of the 9th, and the 2nd battalion of the 38th regiments. In these attacks Major Generals Leith and Picton, Colonels [Henry] Mackinnon and Champelmond, of the Portuguese service, who was wounded, Lieut. Colonel Wallace, Lieut. Colonel the Hon. R. Meade, Lieut. Colonel [Charles] Sutton, of the 9th Portuguese, Major Smyth of the 45th, who was afterwards killed, Lieut. Colonel Douglas, and Major Birmingham[10], of the 8th Portuguese Regiment, distinguished themselves.

Major General Picton reports the good conduct of the 9th and 21st Portuguese regiments, commanded by Lieut. Colonel Sutton and Lieut. Colonel A. Bacellar, and of the Portuguese artillery, under the command of Major Arentschildt. I have also to mention, in a particular manner, the conduct of Captain Dansey of the 88th.

Major General Leith reports the good conduct of the Royals, 1st battalion[11], and 9th, and 2nd battalion of the 38th regiments; and I beg to assure your Lordship that I have never witnessed a more gallant attack than that made by the 88th, 45th, and 8th Portuguese regiments, on the enemy's division which had reached the ridge of the Serra.

On the left the enemy attacked with three divisions of infantry of the 6th corps, on the part of the Serra occupied by the light division of infantry commanded by Brig. General Craufurd, and by the brigade of Portuguese infantry commanded by Brig. General Pack.

One division of infantry only made any progress to the top of the hill, and they were immediately charged with the bayonet by Brig. General Craufurd, with the 43rd, 52nd, and 95th, and the 3rd Portuguese cacadores, and driven down with immense loss.

Brig. General Coleman's brigade[12] of Portuguese infantry, which was in reserve, was moved up to the right of Brig. General Craufurd's division, and a battalion of the 19th Portuguese Regiment, under the command of Lieut. Colonel MacBean, made a gallant and successful charge upon a body of another division of the enemy, which was favourable to penetrate in that quarter.

In this attack, Brig. General Craufurd, Lieut. Colonels [Sir Thomas Sidney] Beckwith, of the 95th, and [Robert] Barclay, of the 52nd, and the Commanding Officers of the regiments, distinguished themselves.

Besides these attacks, the light troops of the two armies were engaged throughout the 27th; and the 4th Portuguese Cacadores, and the 1st and 16th regiments, directed by Brig. General Pack, and commanded by Lieut. Colonel [Dudley St. Leger] Hill, Lieut. Colonel Luis de Regoa, and Major [Richard] Armstrong, showed great steadiness and gallantry.

The loss sustained by the enemy in his attack of the 27th has been enormous. I understand that the Generals of division, Merle, Loison, and Maucune are wounded, and General Simon was taken prisoner by the 52nd Regiment; and 3 Colonels, officers, and 250 men.

The enemy left 2000 killed upon the field of battle, and I understand from the prisoners and deserters that the loss in wounded is immense.

The enemy did not renew his attack, excepting by the fire of his light troops on the 28th; but he moved a large body of infantry and cavalry from the left of his centre, to the rear, from whence I saw his cavalry in march on the road from Mortagoa over the mountains towards Oporto.

Having thought it probable that he would attempt to turn our left by that road, I had directed Colonel Trant, with his division of militia, to march to Sardao, with the intention that he should occupy the mountains, but unfortunately he was sent round by Oporto, by the General Officer commanding in the north, in consequence of a small detachment of the enemy being in possession of S. Pedro do Sul; and, notwithstanding the efforts which he made to arrive in time, he did not reach Sardao till the 28th at night, after the enemy were in possession of the ground.

As it was probable that, in the course of the night of the 28th, the enemy would throw the whole of his army upon the road, by which he could avoid the Serra de Busaco and reach Coimbra by the high road of Oporto, and thus the army would have been exposed to be cut off from that town or to a general action in less favourable ground, and as I had reinforcements in my rear, I was induced to withdraw from the Serra de Busaco.

The enemy did break up in the mountains at eleven at night of the 28th, and he made the march I expected. His advanced guard was at Avelans, on the road from Oporto to Coimbra, yesterday, and the whole army was seen in march through the mountains. That under my command, however, was already in the low country, between the Serra de Busaco and the sea; and the whole of it, with the exception of the advanced guard, is this day on the left of the Mondego.

Although, from the unfortunate circumstance of the delay of Colonel Trant's arrival at Sardao, I am apprehensive that I shall not succeed in effecting the object which I had in view in passing the Mondego and in occupying the Serra de Busaco, I do not repent my having done so. This movement has afforded me a favourable opportunity of showing the enemy the description of troops of which this army is composed; it has brought the Portuguese levies into action with the enemy for the first time in an advantageous situation; and they have proved that the trouble which has been taken with them has not been thrown away, and that they are worthy of contending in the same ranks with British troops in this interesting cause, which they afford the best hopes of saving.

Throughout the contest on the Serra, and in all the previous marches, and those which we have since made, the whole army have conducted themselves in the most regular manner. Accordingly all the operations have been carried on with ease; the soldiers have suffered no privations, have undergone no unnecessary fatigue, there has been no loss of stores, and the army is in the highest spirits.

I have received throughout the service the greatest assistance from the General and Staff Officers. Lieut. General Sir Brent Spencer has given the assistance his experience enables him to afford me; and I am particularly indebted to the Adjutant and the Quarter Master Generals, and the officers of their departments and to Lieut. Colonel Bathurst, and the officers of my personal staff; to Major General Howorth and the Artillery, and particularly to Lieut. Colonel Fletcher, Captain Chapman, and the officers of the Royal Engineers. I must likewise mention Mr. Kennedy, and the officers of the Commissariat, which department has been carried on most successfully.

I should not do justice to the service, or to my own feelings, if I did not take this opportunity of drawing your Lordship's attention to the merits of Marshal Beresford. To him exclusively, under the Portuguese Government, is due the merit of having raised, formed, disciplined, and equipped the Portuguese army, which has now shown itself capable of engaging and defeating the enemy.

I have besides received from him all the assistance which his experience and abilities, and his knowledge of this country, have qualified him to afford me.

I enclose a return of the killed and wounded of the allied armies in the course of the 25th, 26th, and 27th.

Return of the Killed, Wounded, and Missing of the Army under the Command of Lieut. General Viscount Wellington, K.B., on the 25th and 26th of September, and in the action with the French Army, commanded by Marshal Massena, at Busaco, on the 27th of September, 1810.[13]

	Officers	Serjeants	Rank and File	Horses	Total loss of Officers, Non-commissioned Officers, and Rank and File
Killed	11	6	180	5	197
Wounded	62	32	920	12	1014
Missing	1	3	54	10	58

It would have been impossible to detach a corps from the army to occupy the Serra de Caramula after the action of the 27th September, when it was found that Colonel Trant had not arrived at Sardao. But that corps might have been hard pressed, and obliged to retreat, in which case it must have made its retreat upon Sardao and the north of Portugal. It could not have rejoined the army; and its services would have been wanting in the fortified position near Lisbon. It was therefore determined to rely upon Colonel Trant to occupy the Serra de Caramula, whose line of operations and of retreat was to the northward. Nothing that could have been done (excepting to detach a large corps) could have prevented the French from throwing a large force into the Serra de Caramula. Even after their loss on the 27th, they had at least 12,000 or 14,000 men more than we had, and good as our position was, theirs was equally good. When they took the road of the Serra de Caramula, therefore, there was nothing for it but to withdraw from Busaco.

After quitting Busaco, there was no position which we could take up with advantage, in which we could be certain that we could prevent the enemy from getting to Lisbon before us, till we reached the fortified positions in front of that place, in which we arrived on the 8th of October; and we finally took up our ground on the 15th. Shortly after we arrived, the Marquis de la Romana joined us with about 5000 effective rank and file.

In the beginning of the month of November, the British army in Portugal consisted of 29,497 rank and file, of which 2479 were cavalry; and 465 infantry were at Lisbon.

The effectives of the Portuguese army consisted as follows: Infantry, 26,500, of which were at Elvas 1500, at Cadiz 1173, and at Abrantes 1500, leaving 22,400 with the army. The effective cavalry consisted of 2637, of which were at Elvas 163, Abrantes 76, in the north 130, and Estremadura 600; leaving about 1500 cavalry with the army and at Lisbon; making the Portuguese army about 24,000 men. The British army was 29,000, and the Spanish army 5000, and the artillery made altogether about 60,000 men of the allies.

The French army, at this time, could not have consisted of more than from 50,000 to 55,000 effective men. Their losses by death, desertion, and sickness, must have been considerable; but still they could not, in the beginning of November, be reduced lower than the numbers above stated.

The question of attacking them was then well considered, and it was determined not to carry the measure into execution. In fact, the chances of success were much against us. The enemy's force, but little inferior in numbers, was much superior in quality to a large part of ours. Their position, as is the case in all strong countries, was nearly as good as our own. We could not have used our artillery against it. We could not have attempted to turn it without laying open some of the roads to Lisbon, of which the enemy would infallibly have taken advantage. The French have shown, throughout the war in the Peninsula, but particularly in the last campaign in Portugal, that they invariably operate upon the flanks and rear, and communications of their enemy, never having any anxiety about their own; and, in fact, till they have beaten their enemy in the field, they never possess more than the ground they stand upon. This fact is proved in Portugal by their having lost their hospital and every thing belonging to it at Coimbra, only on the day their head quarters left that place; by the difficulty they have, and the constant losses they incur, in sending officers and messengers en courier, and by their total want of intelligence.

This system is the consequence of the mode in which they subsist their armies. They plunder every thing they find in the country. Every article, whether of food or raiment, and every animal, and vehicle of every description, is considered to belong of right, and without payment, to the French army; and they require a communication with their rear only for the purpose of conveying intelligence and receiving orders from the Emperor.

Other armies cannot exist without a communication with their rear. The British army, in particular, must not lose its communication with its port of embarkation; and this is the principal cause of the great difficulties experienced in a contest with the French.

On the 14th of November, the French broke up from their position in front of the allies, with their right upon Sobral, and their left upon the Tagus, and retired by different routes to Santarem. They here took a strong position, occupying the hill of Santarem with the 2nd corps as the head of their cantonments, having the 8th corps to support it on its right; and the 6th corps, in a second line, at Torres Novas, Golegao, or towards the Zezere, over which river they had bridges; and they occupied Punhete as a tete de pont. They were followed closely by the allied army; and from the intelligence received on the 17th from the left of the Tagus of the movements of the enemy from Santarem, it was believed that the army was in full retreat; and that nothing remained at Santarem excepting, at the utmost, the 2nd corps as a rear guard.

The intelligence (which was received from Major General Fane) was confirmed by the probability that a retreat was the enemy's intention. It was obvious that, as a military body, it was the measure which it was most expedient for them to adopt.

By a retreat into Spain, they would, first, have been able to provide their army with plenty of food during the winter.

Secondly, they would have been able to put them into good and quiet cantonments.

Thirdly, they would have been able to provide their numerous sick with surgeons, medicines, &c., the whole of which they had lost.

Fourthly, they would have been able to clothe and re-equip their troops with shoes, &c., which they required.

Fifthly, they must have been perfectly aware that even should they be of insufficient strength to hope to make any impression upon the position of the allies in Portugal, they would experience no difficulty in regaining the position of Santarem from the frontier.

And sixthly, they must have been aware that as long as they remained in the country, its cultivation would be impeded; and that by remaining they cut up by the roots the resources which were to enable them to attack the allies upon a future occasion.

These reflections confirmed the intelligence which had been received, that the enemy were in full retreat; and it was believed that the only troops on Santarem were of the 2nd corps.

General Hill was therefore detached across the Tagus with the corps which had been under his command on the 18th, and head quarters were moved to Cartaxo; and, on the 19th, when a sufficient body of troops to support the advanced guard had arrived, the orders were given, not, as is supposed, to attack the position of Santarem, but to cross the Rio Mayor river at different points, and attack the enemy's outposts upon it, to enable us to reconnoitre more closely the position of Santarem, and see whether it was practicable to attack the post, and what the enemy's real object was in maintaining himself there.

Owing to a mistake of the road by a brigade of guns, the attack could not be made as was intended, and in fact ordered; and in the course of that night and the following morning so much rain had fallen as to render it impracticable to cross the Rio Mayor, or indeed scarcely to move the troops at all. We still, however, continued to work on with our troops on the right of the position of Santarem, on which side it appeared most practicable to approach it, till the 22nd, when the enemy brought up troops of the 8th corps from their rear, and drove in our piquets beyond the bridge of Calhariz.

From this circumstance, and others of which we obtained a knowledge at about the same time, it was then obvious that they had their whole army between Santarem and the Zezere.

The question of attacking the enemy on Santarem was then well considered; and the notion was relinquished, as the plan was impracticable at that moment, on account of the state of the roads and rivulets, as well as because it was obvious that the enemy had their whole army collected in certainly the strongest position in Portugal. We could not succeed without immense loss; and we could not make the attempt at that time without incurring the risk of having some of our detachments insulated and cut off from all communication with the others.

About this time we heard of the movements of the enemy's reinforcements on the frontier; and General Silveira had, in November, been successful in an affair with an advanced guard which had been pushed across the Coa. This was the advanced guard of a division formed under General Gardanne, consisting of convalescents belonging to the three corps in Portugal, of 1500 men, which had been sent into Spain in October as an escort to General Foy; and of two or three battalions belonging to the 8th corps, which had been detached to General Serras by order of the Emperor, and were exclusive of the eighty-nine battalions which entered Portugal. The whole were supposed to amount to 8000 men.

After the affair with Silveira, the enemy retired across the Coa again, and went by the Upper Coa by Sabugal, and entered Portugal through Lower Beira, leaving the Estrella to the north on their right hand. They advanced till they reached the Tagus, when they suddenly turned about, on the 25th November, and retired into Spain, more in the manner of the flight of a mob than of the march of troops. The ordenanza of Lower Beira followed them and did them much mischief; and they suffered much from the badness of the weather.

On the 13th of December, a division of the 9th corps (which consisted of about twenty-six battalions of infantry, and had entered Spain in September) broke up from Ciudad Rodrigo with this same division of Gardanne, in consequence of an order received from Paris, to make another attempt to enter Portugal. This division consisted of eleven battalions, and, with Gardanne's, was supposed to be from 13,000 to 16,000 men: they must have been at least 10,000 men. They reached the army about the 27th or 29th December, having been attacked by Colonel Wilson's division of militia on their passage of the Alva, and suffered some loss. They brought no provisions or stores with them.

Since that period, and indeed ever since they took up the position of Santarem, the attention of the enemy has been principally devoted to discover the means of passing the Tagus; and they view our corps on the left of the Tagus, which has continued there, with the utmost jealousy. The general report in their army, when they retired from Sobral, was, and my opinion is, that they intended immediately to cross the Tagus, and establish themselves in Alentejo, from which they were prevented by the passage of General Hill over that river on the 18th of November; and they are still prevented by the position of his corps, now under the command of Sir William Beresford, on the left of the Tagus.

From this memorandum, which applies to events up to the close of the year 1810, it will appear that we had done every thing in our power for the allies. Till lately, we have always been inferior in number, and infinitely inferior in description of troops to the enemy; and, adverting to the instructions which I received, and their spirit and meaning as explained by other letters, I do not think that I should have been justified in attempting more than I have done. Indeed, since the enemy have occupied the position of Santarem, it would have been impossible to attempt any thing, owing to the bad state of the roads, and the swelling of the rivulets, by the rain.

NOTE. When Regnier passed the Tagus in July, we were aware that Mortier would replace him in Estremadura; but the Marquis de la Romana considered his corps to be sufficient not only to keep him in check, but to beat him out of the province. In this last expectation he was disappointed very much by the misconduct of his officers, and a large part of his army was defeated by Mortier on the 11th of August.[14] The Marquis, however, still continued to hold his ground; and a brigade of Portuguese dragoons soon joined him, which had been detached to reinforce him in cavalry from the reserve which I had formed on the Tagus.

After Mortier had defeated this corps, he withdrew again into Andalusia, and the Marquis de la Romana followed him, and had some successes against his small posts. Mortier then advanced again into Estremadura, and the Marquis de la Romana retired; and on the 14th of September the Portuguese cavalry defeated that of the enemy near Fuente de Cantos.[15]

The state of affairs in Portugal had induced the Marquis de la Romana to turn his attention to this side, at about this time; and he had determined to join the allied army with a part of his corps, leaving the divisions of Mendizabel and Ballesteros, and the cavalry, and all the garrisons, in Estremadura.

Mortier, upon hearing of the battle of Busaco, retired again into Andalusia on the 8th of October; and the Marquis de la Romana was entirely at liberty to break up in Estremadura, and to join the allies without risk to the interests of that province.

Chapter 4

Memorandum of Operations In 1811[1]

The last memorandum on the operations in the Peninsula, brought them down to the end of the year 1810, when a division of the 9th corps, with other troops, which had before endeavored to join Massena from the frontiers of Castille, through Lower Beira, arrived, and took their station on the right of the enemy's army at Leyria. These troops, supposed to be from 8000 to 10,000 men, had been annoyed on their march by Colonel Wilsons detachment on the Alva.

The other division of the 9th corps under Claparede, amounting also to about 10,000 men, remained on the frontier, and by their manoeuvres kept General Silveira in check during the march of the division under Drouet, by the valley of the Mondego. Silveira attacked their advanced guard at Pontedo Abade, on the 30th December, 1810, and was defeated; and he was himself attacked and defeated at Villa da Ponte on the 11th of January; and he retired, first to Lamego, and thence across the Douro. Claparede advanced upon Lamego; but General Bacellar having placed the divisions of militia, under the command of General [James] Miller and of Colonel Wilson, on his flanks and his communications, he was obliged to retire, and went to Guarda, to which place he had been ordered by Massena.

But the principal occurrence in the commencement of this year was the movement, from Andalusia, of a large force into Estremadura, in order to create a division in favor of Massena.

The army of the south, under the command of Soult, consisted of the 1st corps, which was engaged in the operations of the siege of Cadiz; of the 4th corps, which was at Grenada; and of the 5th corps, one division of which, under Gazan, could with difficulty maintain its ground in Estremadura against the Spanish division of Mendizabal and Ballesteros, whilst the other division, under Girard, was employed in the Condado de Niebla, and in keeping open the communication between Seville and the besieging army of Cadiz. The whole amount of the army of the south could not be less in the beginning of the year than 50,000 men.

Soult broke up from Cadiz with about 5000 men on the 21st December, and collected at Seville the troops destined for the invasion of Estremadura.

He had with him about 20,000 men, including a very large body of cavalry; to oppose which there were the Spanish divisions of Mendizabal and Ballesteros which amounted to about 10,000 men, a brigade of Portuguese cavalry, and about 1500 Spanish cavalry, making altogether about 2300 cavalry. There were, besides, garrisons in Badajoz and Campo Mayor, Alburquerque, and Valencia de Alcantara; and Don Carlos de Espana's[2] brigade, about 2000 men, which was on the right of the British army near Abrantes, was considered disposable for service in Estremadura.

If this corps had been left entire, and had been prudently managed, it would have been fully sufficient, even though not joined by the other troops belonging to the army of the Marquis de la Romana, incorporated with the British army, to prevent the enemy from passing the Guadiana, which was full at that season of the year.

But the first measure adopted by the Spanish Government, on the same day, the 21st December, that Soult broke up from Cadiz, was to order Ballesteros, with a part of his division, into the Condado de Niebla. Notwithstanding that we received at Cartaxo, on the 29th December, the accounts of Soult having broken up from before Cadiz, the Spanish General Mendizabal did not hear of this circumstance for some days afterwards; and the first he heard of it was from us. He was quite unprepared for his retreat, which was hurried; and he retired in a manner different, and making a different disposition from that which was recommended and ordered.

He had been ordered to break the bridges of Merida and Medellin, and to defend the passages of the Guadiana. He retired upon Badajoz and Olivenca; and the engineer officer who was sent to destroy the bridge of Merida, instead of obeying the orders he received, made a report which was sent to Cartaxo to the Marquis de la Romana, and asked for orders. The town of Merida itself was not defended; and the consequence was, that an advanced guard of French cavalry took Merida, which post 400 French troops had held in June in the year 1809, against the whole Spanish army, with this additional disadvantage, that the river Guadiana was then fordable, and that the Spanish troops were in possession of all the avenues to the town.

General Mendizabal, in making his retreat upon Badajoz and Olivenca, threw 3000 men of General Ballesteros' division into the latter, the others having marched under General Ballesteros by order of the Government, into the Condado de Niebla. The division of General Mendizabal retired upon Badajoz, with all the cavalry, excepting a small body which marched upon Merida.

There were various reports of the movements of the French; and in fact it was but little known in what direction, and with what object, they were moving. It was at one time positively stated, that they had passed the bridge of Merida on the 15th of January, and that they were moving towards the bridge of Almaraz, on the Tagus; at another time it was reported that they were encamped at Caceres; but at last it was found that they did not cross the Guadiana in any force, but blockaded the troops of General Ballesteros' division in Olivenca.

This blockade was made on the 15th and continued till the 23rd of January, when the garrison surrendered. Two or three attempts were made by General Mendizabal to raise the blockade, but without success; and as the garrison at last surrendered, before the enemy had attacked the place, and without being distressed for provisions, it is believed that the place was sold.

During the month of January, the Marquis de la Romana was taken very ill at Cartaxo, of which illness he died on the 23rd of that month. He had ordered Don Carlos de Espana's brigade to march as soon as he heard of the danger of Ballesteros' detachment from the advance of the French troops, and he afterwards ordered that the remainder of the troops which had been incorporated with the British army should move from Villa Franca, where they had been cantoned. They moved on the 30th of January.

From the period at which we had heard of the movement of the French from Cadiz, and particularly, latterly, I had frequent conversation with him regarding the situation of affairs in Estremadura; and as he was unwell, I wrote, in the shape of a memorandum, my opinions on the plan of operations to be pursued, as well for the objects of the war in general, as for the particular purpose of saving Olivenca, or rather for relieving the troops in that place, respecting whom the Marquis was particularly anxious.

The Marquis died three days after he had received this memorandum; but not till after he had circulated it among the officers under his command, and had desired them to attend to it. A reference to the memorandum, and to the letters and dispatches of that day, will show how far they attended either to the first or to the last.

After two attempts were made to raise the blockade of Olivenca, the place surrendered on the 23rd January; and the enemy invested Badajoz, on both sides of the Guadiana, on the 27th of January, and broke ground on the left of the river on the 29th.

The Spanish generals were not decided respecting the measures which they should adopt in the circumstances in which they stood. But at length the troops, which had quitted the allied army on the 20th of January, were ordered to advance to Badajoz. They immediately re-established the communication between Elvas and Badajoz, obliging the French cavalry to retire beyond the Evora; and then having entered the town, they attempted to raise the siege by making a sortie upon the enemy's works. They were driven back with loss; and having remained in the town, the communication between Elvas and Badajoz was again cut off by the enemy's cavalry,

The Spanish troops however came out of the town again on the 9th of February, and at last took the position on the heights of San Christoval, which was recommended to them. They did not however adopt any measure to fortify this position, nor did they adopt any of the other measures recommended to them, particularly that of sending away from Badajoz the bridge of boats, the want of which was afterwards found to be so fatal to the cause.

The Spanish army, about 10,000 strong, and having besides about 2000 cavalry, including General Madden's Portuguese brigade, remained in the position at San Christoval, till the 19th February, having the Evora in their front, and that river and the Guadiana between them and the enemy, on which day they were surprised by between 5000 and 6000 French troops, and totally destroyed as a military body; their camp and artillery being taken, and the whole body not killed or taken dispersed, except the Portuguese brigade of cavalry, and a few hundred Spaniards. About 2000 of the troops escaped into Badajoz.

An examination of the letters written at this period to Mr. Wellesley and the Secretary of State, will show my anxiety for the relief of Badajoz, and the measures which I recommended for that object. The most effectual measure of any would undoubtedly have been to detach a body of British troops to that part of the country; but a moment's reflection on the relative numbers of the two armies at that time on the Tagus, and on the extent and nature of the positions which we had to occupy, will shew that it was impossible to venture to detach, from our army at least, till the reinforcements then expected should have arrived in the Tagus.

Massena had come into Portugal with 72,000 men, of which he had lost 10,000 at the battle of Busaco, and its consequences; and it is a large allowance to suppose that he had in January lost 10,000 more by deaths, prisoners, deserters, and killed in various little affairs which had occurred. This would reduce his original number to 52,000 men; and an aide de camp of his, who was taken in December, reported that the army had that number before Drouet joined.

To this number Drouet, in December, and Foy in January, added about 12,000 men, making 64,000; and Claparede was at Guarda with between 8000 and 10,000 men; of the 64,000, about 14,000 may have been sick, as the army were very sickly; and there would have remained on the Tagus fit for service about 50,000 men.

The British army on the 20th January, consisted of 41,040 men; of which number there were sick, 6715; on command, 1974; prisoners of war, 1586; and there remained present fit for duty, 30,765. Of this number, the 2nd battalion 88th (485), were at Lisbon, and the 2nd battalion 58th, at Torres Vedras; leaving about 30,000 for service; of which number 1655 were cavalry.

The Portuguese army, joined with the British for service in the field, at the same time amounted to about 32,000 effective men, exclusive of the garrisons of Abrantes and Elvas, in each of which there were two regiments of infantry, one regiment of infantry at Cadiz, and one regiment of infantry (the 24th) with General Silveira. The object of the French General at this time was undoubtedly to pass the Tagus; and he had his choice of making the attempt in a course of about thirty miles from Santarem to the Zezere, and even higher than the junction of that river. It was necessary to guard that whole course of the river; for which it is conceived that 14,000 men could not be deemed more than sufficient.

The remainder of the army, about 40,000 men, was on the right of the Tagus, opposed to the whole French army; and it must be observed, that if the enemy had been able to advance, either with their 50,000 men, or after being joined by Claparede, they would have been opposed by very unequal numbers, as some days must have elapsed before the troops on the left of the Tagus could have been brought across the river.

The detachment which it would have been necessary to make, in order to effect any good at Badajoz, or even to have been in safety, adverting to the mode in which the Spanish troops have usually conducted themselves, ought to have been about 13,000 men; which numbers, it is obvious, could not be spared from the army from the end of January to the 19th of February.

Reinforcements to the amount of 6000 or 7000 men were daily expected; which afterwards arrived in the beginning of March. It was hoped that the Spaniards would risk nothing, and would be able to hold out till these reinforcements should arrive, when it was intended to detach a sufficient force to effect the object at Badajoz, before anything else should be attempted against Massena.

The delay of all measures against Massena's position continued to be absolutely necessary on account of the state of the roads and rivers in the country; even if our force had been deemed sufficient to attack him.

The result of the battle of the 19th February, however, destroyed all hopes of being able, even when the reinforcement should arrive, to make such a detachment from the army as should be able to relieve Badajoz; more particularly as the Spaniards, having neglected to remove the bridge from Badajoz to Elvas, the troops which should attempt to relieve Badajoz had no choice left, in respect to the mode of crossing the Guadiana. They must have passed by the bridge of Badajoz.

It was then determined to attack Massena, as soon as the reinforcements should arrive, by which time it was hoped that the roads and rivulets would become practicable. In the meantime the Governor of Badajoz was requested to hold out to the last moment.

Massena however retired from his position on the night of the 5th of March, before our troops, which had arrived at Lisbon in the 1st day of March, could join the army. The British troops were immediately put in motion in pursuit of the French army; those on the left of the Tagus, by Abrantes and the Zezere; and those on the Rio Mayor river, by the different routes leading in the direction which the enemy had taken.

A letter was written to General Leite, the governor of Elvas, from Santarem on the 6th, to request him to apprise the governor of Badajoz of Massena's retreat, and to assure him that support and relief would be sent to him without loss of time.

This support was accordingly ordered to march on the 8th, as soon as the enemy's retreat was found to be decided.

When the enemy retired, it appeared at first that their intention was to go by the road of Thomar and Espinhal, leaving Coimbra on their left; and it was not certain that they had taken the high road by Pombal, till the 9th: on that morning a most favorable report was received of the state of affairs at Badajoz. It appeared that the garrison had not suffered; that the fire of the place was superior to that of the enemy; and that one of the enemy's six battering guns had been dismounted by the fire of the place. Under these circumstances, when it was found on the afternoon of the 9th, that the enemy had collected their army in a strong position at Pombal, it was deemed expedient to order the 4th Division, and General [Hon. George] De Grey's brigade of cavalry (which had been ordered to march on the 10th to join the 2nd, and General Hamilton's division[3], on the left of the Tagus, as soon as the bridge should be laid for them), to march upon Pombal, to co-operate in the attack which it was intended to make upon the enemy on the 11th.

These troops accordingly joined, and the enemy retired; but the garrison of Badajoz surrendered on the 10th of March.

The mode of the enemy's retreat on the 11th, and the fact that they were still stronger than we were, and might have taken up the position of Coimbra and the Mondego, unless hurried beyond that town, caused the continued detention of the 4th Division, and General De Grey's brigade of cavalry, till the operations of the 13th forced the enemy past Coimbra and enabled us to communicate with that town.

The troops for Badajoz were immediately put in motion to return to the south, but unfortunately we that night heard of the fall of that fortress on the 10th. These accounts were accompanied by reports of the enemy immediately threatening Campo Mayor; and if it had not been desirable to prevent them from extending their conquests on that side, the fall of Badajoz facilitated to such a degree their entry into Portugal, and Badajoz was so much nearer to Lisbon than the point at which we then found ourselves, that it would have been impossible to continue the pursuit of Massena even for one march, without providing for the security of our right flank, by placing a large corps on the Tagus,

Thus, then, it was still necessary to make this detachment, notwithstanding that the original object for which it was destined was lost.

The pursuit of Massena was continued with uniform success from that period till he finally crossed the Agueda on the 9th of April. Our reinforcements, however, were not all arrived in Portugal, and those which had arrived, did not join the army till the end of March. Even then we were infinitely inferior to the enemy in numbers, particularly when he approached the frontier, and was joined by Claparede's division of the 9th corps from Guarda. Our movements were, therefore, necessarily cramped, and we were obliged to proceed with caution, when the utmost activity would have been desirable.

Let any body now advert to the difference of the result of Massena's invasion of Portugal, if the operations on the Guadiana in the month of January had been carried on as they ought; if the Spanish Regency had not drawn Ballesteros from Estremadura at the moment that province was attacked; if his troops had not been shamefully sold in Olivenca; if the battle of the 19th of February had not been lost, and the Spanish army annihilated; and, finally, if Badajoz itself had not been shamefully sold to the enemy on the day after the Governor was informed that relief would be sent to him.

As soon as the French were driven across the Agueda, Almeida was invested; and it will be seen in a subsequent part of this memorandum, the enemy made an attempt in May to relieve the place. What would have been the result of that attempt, nay, more, would it ever have been made, if we had had 22,000 men in the ranks, which were at that time in Estremadura?

If our attention had not been preferably, and with part of our army necessarily, carried into Estremadura, in consequence of the events in that province, in the months of January, February, and March, what would have been the result of an attempt to obtain possession of Ciudad Rodrigo in May, after the fall of Almeida, by the concentrated force and resources of the allied army?

But other circumstances occurred, not yet adverted to in this memorandum, which show still more clearly the fatal effects of the Spanish system of military operations. Notwithstanding that General Ballesteros was weak, and that he ought never to have been removed from Estremadura, he held his ground against a French corps which attacked him on the 25th of January.[4] A part of the French force in Estremadura was consequently withdrawn from that province, and the force engaged in the siege of Badajoz was reduced.

Another event occurred highly advantageous in all its circumstances to the state of affairs in Estremadura. In consequence of the diminution of the force before Cadiz in December, 1810, the British and Spanish authorities conceived that a fair opportunity offered of making an attack upon the blockading army by the besieged. This attack was fixed for the 28th of February, but owing to contrary winds, and a variety of circumstances, could not take place till the 6th of March. On that day the battle of Barrosa was fought, four days before the surrender of Badajoz; and in all probability, if Badajoz had held out one day longer, the enemy would not have remained to take possession of the place.

The troops which were detached from the army at Condeixa on the 14th of March, did not arrive at Portalegre till the 22nd of that month. Campo Mayor, which had been regularly attacked by the enemy on the 14th, surrendered on the 22nd. Marshal Sir William Beresford, having collected his corps, advanced against the enemy; surprised them at Campo Mayor on the 25th, which place they abandoned. Their cavalry fled into Badajoz, leaving behind them a regiment of infantry, and all their cannon. Unfortunately the excessive impetuosity of the troops (the 13th light dragoons in particular) prevented Sir W. Beresford from taking the advantage which he intended to take of these events. Some of the 13th dragoons were taken on the bridge, between the tete du pont and the gate of Badajoz.

The instructions to Sir William Beresford were to pass the Guadiana as soon as he should have possession of Campo Mayor, and to blockade Badajoz, till the means for attacking the place regularly could arrive. Unfortunately here again our operations were frustrated by the conduct of the Spaniards.

One of the objects particularly recommended to their attention was to send to Elvas the bridge of boats that was in Badajoz. This had been repeatedly desired before, and the reasons for urging the measure again were particularly stated in that memorandum. This was the only bridge in the possession of the allies; and if it had been at Elvas, Marshal Beresford could have passed the Guadiana, and have blockaded Badajoz on the 26th March, and in all probability the place would have fallen into our hands as Campo Mayor had, or as Almeida subsequently did, as it was at that time unprovided with stores or with provisions.

As it was, he could not pass the Guadiana till the 4th April, and could not advance till the 6th or 7th; and in the intermediate time the enemy threw into the place all the provisions and stores which it required to last till the enemy were enabled finally to relieve it in the middle of June.

When the French crossed the Agueda on the 9th of April, they left Almeida to its fate, and it was immediately invested and blockaded by our troops. The enemy retired beyond the Tormes, some of them even beyond the Douro, and abandoned Ciudad Rodrigo as well as Almeida. Our army, however, was scarcely strong enough to maintain the blockade of Almeida, and certainly could not have maintained that of Ciudad Rodrigo – Indeed the state of the Agueda rendered it impossible for us to draw supplies across that river.

The enemy having passed the Douro, Almeida being invested, and matters appearing tolerably quiet on the frontiers of Castille, the head quarters were moved on the 15th of April into Alentejo, and arrived at Elvas on the 20th. Sir William Beresford had crossed the Guadiana on the 4th of April, and had blockaded both Badajoz and Olivenca. The garrison of the latter place having refused to surrender, guns were brought from Elvas, and Lieut. General [Galbraith Lowry] Cole forced the place to surrender on the 15th of April.

In the mean time Sir William Beresford advanced with the 2nd Division of infantry, and General Hamilton's division, and the cavalry, as well to force the enemy to retire from Estremadura entirely, as to give support to General Ballesteros, who had been obliged to retire into that province from the Condado de Niebla.

Marshal Beresford surprised the enemy's cavalry on the 16th of April, at Los Santos, and defeated them with considerable loss.

Badajoz was reconnoitred on the 22nd, and the general plan for the attack was fixed. But unfortunately the rain which had fallen in the third week in April, swelled the Guadiana considerably; and the bridge which Marshal Sir William Beresford had constructed under Jurumenha, with great trouble and difficulty, and after much delay, was swept away in the night of the 23rd of April.

Marshal Sir William Beresford was consequently instructed to delay the operations of the siege till he should have re-established the bridge, or till the river should become fordable.

The Marshal was likewise instructed and authorized to fight a battle, in case he should think it expedient, in order to save the siege of Badajoz; and these instructions applied as well to the corps under General Blake, which landed about this time at Ayamonte.

All these arrangements being made, the head quarters were again transferred to the frontiers of Castille. They quitted Elvas on the 25th of April, and arrived at Alameda on the 28th. Intelligence had been received that orders had arrived from Paris, for Massena to make an attempt to raise the blockade of Almeida; in which attempt Marshal Bessieres was to co-operate with part of the army of the north.

The enemy's army was collected at Ciudad Rodrigo in the end of April, but the same fall of rain which had swelled the rivers in Estremadura, likewise swelled those in Castille, and they did not advance till the 2nd of May.

Fuentes d'Onoro 3–5 May 1811[5]

The enemy's whole army, consisting of the 2d, 6th, and 8th corps, and all the cavalry which could be collected in Castille and Leon, including about 900 of the Imperial Guard, crossed the Agueda at Ciudad Rodrigo on the 2d instant.

The battalions of the 9th corps had been joined to the regiments to which they belonged in the other three corps; excepting a division consisting of battalions belonging to regiments in the corps doing duty in Andalusia; which division likewise formed part of the army.[6]

As my object in maintaining a position between the Coa and the Agueda, after the enemy had retired from the former, was to blockade Almeida, which place I had learned from intercepted letters, and other information, was ill supplied with provisions for its garrison, and as the enemy were infinitely superior to us in cavalry, I did not give any opposition to their march, and they passed the Azava on that evening, in the neighborhood of Espeja, Carpio, and Gallegos.

They continued their march on the 3d, in the morning, towards the Dos Casas, in three columns; two of them, consisting of the 2d and 8th corps, to the neighborhood of Almeida and Fort Concepcion, and the third column, consisting of the whole of the cavalry, and the 6th and that part of the 9th corps which had not already been drafted into the other three.

The allied army had been cantoned along the river Dos Casas, and on the sources of the Azava, the Light division at Gallegos and Espeja. This last fell back upon Fuentes de Onoro, on the Dos Casas, with the British cavalry, in proportion as the enemy advanced, and the 1st, 3d, and 7th divisions were collected at that place; the 6th Division, under Major General [Sir Alexander] Campbell, observed the bridge at Alameda; and Major General Sir William Erskine, with the 5th division, the passages of the Dos Casas at Fort Concepcion and Aldea del Obispo. Brig. General Pack's brigade, with the Queen's Regiment from the 6th division, kept the blockade of Almeida; and I had prevailed upon Don Julian Sanchez to occupy Nave d'Aver with his corps of Spanish cavalry and infantry.

The Light Division were moved in the evening to join Major General Campbell, upon finding that the enemy were in strength in that quarter; and they were brought back again to Fuentes de Onoro on the morning of the 5th, when it was found that the 8th corps had joined the 6th on the enemy's left.

Shortly after the enemy had formed on the ground on the right of the Dos Casas, on the afternoon of the 3d, they attacked with a large force the village of Fuentes de Onoro, which was defended in a most gallant manner by Lieut. Colonel [William] Williams, of the 5th batt. 60th Regiment, in command of the light infantry battalion belonging to Major General Picton's division[7], supported by the light infantry battalion in Major General Nightingall's brigade, commanded by Major [Robert Henry] Dick of the 42d Regiment, and the light infantry battalion in Major General Howard's brigade, commanded by Major [Archibald] McDonnell of the 92d, and the light infantry battalion of the King's German Legion, commanded by Major [Karl August] Aly, of the 5th battalion of the line, and by the 2d batt. 83d Regiment, under Major [Henry William] Carr.

The troops maintained their position: but having observed the repeated efforts which the enemy were making to obtain possession of the village, and being aware of the advantage which they would derive from the possession in their subsequent operations, I reinforced the village successively with the 71st Regiment under Lieut. Colonel the Hon. H. [Henry] Cadogan, and the 79th under Lieut. Colonel [Phillips] Cameron, and the 24th under Major [Thomas] Chamberlain. The former, at the head of the 71st Regiment, charged the enemy, and drove them from a part of the village of which they had obtained a momentary possession.

Nearly at this time Lieut. Colonel Williams was unfortunately wounded, but I hope not dangerously; and the command devolved upon Lieut. Colonel Cameron of the 79th.

The contest continued till night, when our troops remained in possession of the whole.

I then withdrew the light infantry battalions, and the 83d Regiment, leaving the 71st and 79th regiments only in the village, and the 2d batt. 24th Regiment to support them.

On the 4th the enemy reconnoitred the position which we had occupied on the Dos Casas river; and during that night they moved the Due d'Abrantes' corps from Alamcda to the left of the position occupied by the 6th corps, opposite to Fuentes de Onoro.

From the course of the reconnaissance on the 4th I had imagined that the enemy would endeavour to obtain possession of Fuentes de Onoro, and of the ground occupied by the troops behind that village, by crossing the Dos Casas at Pozo Velho; and in the evening I moved the 7th Division, under Major General [Sir William] Houstoun, to the right, in order, if possible, to protect that passage.

On the morning of the 5th the 8th corps appeared in two columns, with all the cavalry, on the opposite side of the valley of the Dos Casas and Pozo Velho; and as the 6th and 9th corps also made a movement to their left, the Light Division, which had been brought back from the neighborbood of Alameda, were sent with the cavalry, under Sir Stapleton Cotton, to support Major General Houstoun; while the 1st and 3d divisions made a movement to their right, along the ridge between the Turon and Dos Casas rivers, corresponding to that of the 6th and 9th corps, on the right of the Dos Casas.

The 8th corps attacked Major General Houstoun's advanced guard, consisting of the 85th Regiment, under Major [Aeneas] Macintosh, and the 2d Portuguese cacadores, under Lieut. Colonel [Robert] Nixon, and obliged them to retire; and they retired in good order, although with some loss. The 8th corps being thus established in Pozo Velho, the enemy's cavalry turned the right of the 7th Division, between Pozo Velho and Nave d'Aver, from which last place Don Julian Sanchez[8] had been obliged to retire; and the cavalry charged.

The charge of the advanced guard of the enemy's cavalry was met by two or three squadrons of the different regiments of British dragoons, and the enemy were driven back; and Colonel La Motte, of the 13th chasseurs, and some prisoners, taken.

The main body were checked and obliged to retire by the fire of Major General Houstoun's division; and I particularly observed the Chasseurs Britanniques, under Lieut. Colonel [William Cornwallis] Eustace, as behaving in the most steady manner; and Major General Houstoun mentions in high terms the conduct of a detachment of the Duke of Brunswick's light infantry.[9]

Notwithstanding that this charge was repulsed, I determined to concentrate our force towards the left, and to move the 7th and Light divisions and the cavalry from Pozo Velho towards Fuentes de Onoro, and the other two divisions.

I had occupied Pozo Velho and that neighborhood, in hopes that I should be able to maintain the communication across the Coa by Sabugal, as well as provide for the blockade, which objects it was now obvious were incompatible with each other; and I therefore abandoned that which was the least important, and placed the Light Division in reserve in the rear of the left of the 1st Division, and the 7th Division on some commanding ground beyond the Turon, which protected the right flank and rear of the 1st Division, and covered the communication with the Coa, and prevented that of the enemy with Almeida by the roads between the Turon and that river.

The movement of the troops upon this occasion was well conducted, although under very critical circumstances, by Major General Houstoun, Brig. General Craufurd, and Lieut. General Sir Stapleton Cotton. The 7th Division was covered in its passage of the Turon by the Light Division, under Brig. General Craufurd; and this last, in its march to join the 1st Division, by the British cavalry.

Our position thus extended on the high ground from the Turon to the Dos Casas. The 7th Division, on the left of the Turon. Covered the rear of the right; the 1st Division, in two lines, were on the right; Colonel [Charles] Ashworth's brigade, in two lines, in the centre; and the 3d Division, in two lines, on the left; the Light Division and British artillery in reserve; and the village of Fuentes in front of the left. Don Julian's infantry joined the 7th Division in Frcneda; and I sent him with his cavalry to endeavour to intercept the enemy's communication with Ciudad Rodrigo.

The enemy's efforts on the right part of our position, after it was occupied as I have above described, were confined to a cannonade, and to some charges with his cavalry, upon the advanced posts. The regiments of the 1st Division, under Lieut. Colonel [George] Hill of the 3d Regiment of Guards, repulsed one of these; but as they were falling back they did not see the direction of another in sufficient time to form to oppose it, and Lieut. Colonel Hill was taken prisoner, and many men were wounded, and some taken, before a detachment of the British cavalry could move up to their support.

The 2d batt. 42d Regiment, under [Robert Alexander Stewart] Lord Blantyre, also repulsed a charge of the cavalry directed against them.

They likewise attempted to push a body of light infantry upon the ravine of the Turon, to the right of the 1st Division, which were repulsed by the light infantry of the Guards under Lieut. Colonel [John Wright] Guise, aided by five companies of the 95th under Captain [Peter] O'Hare. Major General Nightingall was wounded in the course of the cannonade, but I hope not severely.

The enemy's principal effort was throughout this day again directed against Fuentes de Onoro; and, notwithstanding that the whole of the 6th corps were at different periods of the day employed to attack this village, they could never gain more than a temporary possession of it. It was defended by the 24th, 71st, and 79th regiments, under the command of Lieut. Colonel Cameron; and these troops were supported by the light infantry battalions of the 3d Division, commanded by Major [William] Woodgate; the light infantry battalions of the 1st Division, commanded by Major Dick, Major McDonald, and Major Aly; the 6th Portuguese caqadores, commanded by Major Pinto; by the light companies in Colonel Champelmond's Portuguese brigade, under Colonel Sutton; and those in Colonel Ashworth's Portuguese brigade, under Lieut. Colonel [Henry] Pynn, and by the piquets of the 3d Division, under the command of Colonel the Hon. R. Trench. Lieut. Colonel Cameron was severely wounded in the afternoon, and the command in the village devolved upon Lieut. Colonel the Hon. H. Cadogan.

The troops in Fuentes were besides supported, when pressed by the enemy, by the 74th Regiment, under Major Russell Manners, and the 1st batt. 88th Regiment, under Lieut. Colonel Wallace, belonging to Colonel Mackinnon's brigade; and on one of these occasions, the 88th, with the 71st and 79th, under the command of Colonel Mackinnon, charged the enemy, and drove them through the village; and Colonel Mackinnon has reported particularly the conduct of Lieut. Colonel Wallace, Brigade Major Wilde[10], and Lieut and Adjutant Stewart.

The contest again lasted in this quarter till night, when our troops still held their post; and from that time the enemy have made no fresh attempt on any part of our position.

The enemy manifested an intention to attack Major General Sir William Erskine's post at Aldea del Obispo on the same morning, with a part of the 2d corps; but the Major General sent the 2d batt. Lusitanian Legion across the ford of the Dos Casas, which obliged them to retire.

In the course of last night the enemy commenced retiring from their position on the Dos Casas; and this morning, at daylight, the whole was in motion. I cannot yet decide whether this movement is preparatory to some fresh attempt to raise the blockade of Almeida, or is one of decided retreat; but I have every reason to hope that they will not succeed in the first, and that they will be obliged to have recourse to the last. Their superiority in cavalry is very great, owing to the weak state of our horses, from recent fatigue and scarcity of forage, and the reduction of numbers in the Portuguese brigade of cavalry with this part of the army, in exchange for a British brigade sent into Estremadura with Marshal Sir William Beresford, owing to the failure of the measures reported to have been adopted to supply horses and men with food on the service.

The result of a general action, brought on by an attack upon the enemy by us, might, under those circumstances, have been doubtful; and if the enemy had chosen to avoid it, or if they had met it, they would have taken advantage of the collection of our troops to fight this action, and throw relief into Almeida.

From the great superiority of force to which we have been opposed upon this occasion, your Lordship will judge of the conduct of the Officers and troops. The actions were partial, but very severe, and our loss has been great. The enemy's loss has also been very great, and they left 400 killed in the village of Fuentes, and we have many prisoners. I particularly request your attention to the conduct of Lieut. Colonel Williams, and Lieut. Colonel Cameron, and Lieut. Colonel the Hon. H. Cadogan; and to that of Colonel Mackinnon and Lieut. Colonel [William] Kelly, 24th Regiment; of the several Officers commanding battalions of the line and of light infantry, which supported the troops in Fuentes de Onoro; likewise to that of Major Macintosh of the 85th, and of Lieut. Colonel Nixon, of the 2d cacadores, and of Lieut. Colonel Eustace, of the Chasseurs Britanniques, and of Lord Blantyre.

Throughout these operations I have received the greatest assistance from Lieut. General Sir Brent Spencer, and all the General Officers of the army; and from the Adjutant and Quarter Master General, and the Officers of their several departments, and those of my personal Staff.

Return of the Killed, Wounded, and Missing, of the Army under the Command of Lieut. General Viscount Wellington, K.B., in the affairs at Fuentes de Onoro, on the 3d and 5th May, 1811.

	Officers	Serjeants.	Rank and File	Horses	Total loss of Officers, Non-commissioned Officers, and Rank and File
Killed	11	16	208	49	235
Wounded	81	72	1081	101	1234
Missing	7	0	300	5	317

They attacked us at Fuentes de Onoro on the 3rd and 5th, but could make no impression upon us, and at length retired on the 10th, and the whole were across the Agueda on that night.

In the middle of the night of the 10th, after the blockade was completely resumed in force. General Brenier, the Governor of Almeida, blew up the place, and made his escape with his garrison across the bridge of Barba de Puerco. This event was to be attributed to a variety of unfortunate circumstances.

First, the Officer commanding the Queen's Regiment, who was close to the place, was not aware of the nature of the explosion which he heard, or that the garrison escaped, and made no movement.[11]

Secondly, the Officer commanding the 4th Regiment, who had been ordered to Barba de Puerco, at one o'clock on the 10th, when the French retired, missed his road; and although the distance he had to march was only three miles, he did not reach Barba de Puerco till the morning of the 11th, after the French had arrived there.[12]

Thirdly, the 8th Portuguese Regiment had been ordered to march from its cantonments at Junga to Barba de Puerco, in case an explosion should be heard. These orders were obeyed; the regiment marched to Barba de Puerco, and arrived before the French, and before Major General Campbell, with the 4th and 36th regiments; but finding nothing there but a piquet of cavalry, and the commanding officer believing that he had mistaken the nature of the explosion, returned again to his cantonments.

The 3rd and 7th divisions were ordered off to Estremadura on the 13th and 14th; and accounts having been received on the 15th that Soult was about to advance from Seville, the head quarters were again removed on the following day to Elvas, where they arrived on the 19th. Sir William Beresford had invested Badajoz on both sides of the Guadiana on the 4th, and he broke ground on the 8th. He lost some men on the right of the river, in front of the tete du pont, on the first day, and a considerable number in a sortie made by the enemy on the 10th. On the 12th, the Marshal heard of the collection of a large body of troops by Marshal Soult, in the neighbourhood of Seville, and of their march towards Estremadura, and he immediately raised the siege; and, according to the instructions and recommendation left with them, he and the Spanish Generals collected their troops on the Albuera rivulet.

The battle of Albuera was fought on the 16th May, on the ground pointed out in those instructions. That which was most conspicuous in the battle of Albuera was the want of discipline of the Spaniards. These troops behaved with the utmost gallantry, but it was hopeless to think of moving them. In the morning the enemy gained an eminence which commanded the whole extent of the line of the allies, which either was occupied, or was intended to be occupied, by the Spanish troops. The natural operation would have been to re-occupy this ground by means of the Spanish troops; but that was impossible. The British troops were consequently moved there; and all the loss sustained by those troops was incurred in regaining a height which ought never for a moment to have been in possession of the enemy.

After the battle of Albuera, the enemy retired leisurely to Llerena and Guadalcanal.

It was obvious, from the immense superiority of cavalry which they showed in that battle, and that, as the allies were but little superior in total strength, and had beaten them with difficulty, and could derive no great advantage from their success, it was hopeless to attack Soult in the position which he had taken at Llerena. There was nothing to prevent him from retiring upon Seville, or even upon the troops engaged in the blockade of Cadiz, if he should have found himself so pressed as to render that measure necessary; and the arrival of reinforcements, which it will appear he had reason to expect, would have placed in a state of risk the troops which would have obliged him to take this step. But this reasoning supposes that Soult would have considered himself under the necessity of retiring from the strong position of Llerena and Guadalcanal, in consequence of the measures which we might have adopted in Estremadura in the end of May. I believe there is no foundation for this hypothesis.

The allies' troops, which were sent from the frontiers of Castille, and arrived at Campo Mayor on the 23rd and 24th of May, were rather more than equal to the loss sustained in the battle of Albuera, and in the first siege of Badajoz. It had been obvious in the battle of Albuera, that we could not reckon upon the Spaniards in any affair of manoeuvre, and therefore that we could not rely upon them in such an operation as the attack of Soult's army in the positions of Guadalcanal and Llerena.

But the effect of these operations, even if well executed, could only be to force Soult to fall back for a time; and here the question arose whether it was worth while to attempt it. It was known that Drouet had marched with 17 or 19 battalions of the 9th corps, belonging to the army of Portugal, from Salamanca, on the 16th or 17th of May, destined for a reinforcement to Soult; and it was calculated that these battalions would join Soult on or about the 8th of June.

Under these circumstances, it was deemed better not to lose the time between the 25th of May and the 8th of June by an attempt to attack Soult, which appeared hopeless; and to take advantage of our superiority in the battle of Albuera, and in the early arrival of our reinforcements, to make a vigorous attack upon Badajoz.

Accordingly, the place was reinvested on the 25th of May, and the fire was opened on the 2nd of June.

There appeared every ground for belief that we should have been able to obtain possession of the place before the day on which it was possible that Soult could advance for its relief. It is certain that its possession depended upon the possession of the outwork of San Christoval, which commanded the point of attack in the castle. This outwork was deemed to be in a state to be taken by storm on the 6th, and again on the 9th. Both attempts failed; and the question whether Badajoz could be taken or not in the time which remained, during which the allied army could be applied to that operation, came to be one of means, upon which we were decidedly of opinion that we had it not in our power to take the place; and therefore we raised the siege on the 10th, although we continued the blockade till the 17th.

While the operations of the second siege of Badajoz were going on, accounts were received that Marshal Marmont was about to move from Salamanca into Estremadura, in order to aid Soult in his operations for the relief of Badajoz.

The first movements of the army were upon Ciudad Rodrigo, into which place Marmont introduced a convoy on the 6th of June. Lieut. General Sir Brent Spencer retired across the Coa; and Marmont then turned about, and marched through the Puerto de Banos, to Plasencia. Lieut. General Sir Brent Spencer made a corresponding movement on Castello Branco, at which place he received intelligence of the enemy having had posts on the Alagon, and the cavalry in Coria, and some doubts were entertained of their intention to cross the Tagus. The head of their army, however, crossed that river on the 12th, and arrived at Truxillo on the 13th; and the advanced guard was at Merida, and in communication with Soult, on the 15th.

Soult had broken up from Llerena and Guadalcanal on the 12th, as soon as he was joined by Drouet; and he moved upon Zafra, and his advanced guard to Los Santos, on the 13th. The allied army were immediately concentrated upon Albuera, with the exception of the 3rd and 7th divisions, which kept the blockade of Badajoz. But the accounts of the arrival at Truxillo of the advanced guard of the army of Portugal having arrived at Albuera, and Soult having made a movement from Zafra on Almendralejo, having thus shown that he knew of the arrival of that army, it was deemed expedient to retire across the Guadiana.

As far as we could form a judgment, the French had at that time assembled in Estremadura 60,000 men, of which 7000 were cavalry.

The British army consisted of
        Cavalry, 1,671
        Infantry, 11,812

The Portuguese,
        Cavalry, 900
        Infantry, 12,885

and General Blake had about 8000 men.

The head of Sir Brent Spencer's column did not join till the 20th, the 5th Division not till the 24th. The strength of the whole army when collected together was,
        British Infantry, 25,123
        Portuguese Infantry, 18,926
        British Cavalry, 3,197
        Portuguese Cavalry, 1,200

It would have been, impossible for the allies to maintain the blockade of Badajoz with the strength which they could produce against that of the enemy, in the days which intervened between the 17th and 24th of June; nor could the allies pretend to attack the enemy in Estremadura, composed as they were, being, after all, even including the Spaniards and Sir Brent Spencer, inferior in numbers, particularly of cavalry, and very inferior in composition.

These circumstances were stated in a conference with General Blake on the 14th June, at Albuera, and in a previous letter to him; and he was urged either to co-operate with the allied British and Portuguese army; or, having crossed the Guadiana at Jurumenha, to move down the right bank, and to cross that river at Mertola, and to endeavor to obtain possession of Seville, while the enemy's attention should be drawn to us on the frontier of Alentejo. General Blake preferred the last operation, and he recrossed the Guadiana on the 22nd of June.

But, instead of moving at once upon Seville, he attempted to obtain possession of Niebla on the 30th of June, where the enemy had only 300 men, in which attempt he failed; and Soult having, towards the end of the month of June, discovered General Blake's movement, and detached a body of troops into Andalusia, General Blake embarked at Ayamonte on the 6th of July.

While this was going on, the allied British and Portuguese army took a position on the 19th of June between Elvas and Campo Mayor. The particular object in taking this position was to protect those places, and to insure the arrival into them of the convoys of provisions and stores destined for their supply. The enemy reconnoitred the position of the army on the 22nd June, but they never showed any inclination to attack it.

The armies remained opposite to each other till the 14th July, when Marmont retired across the Tagus, and cantoned his army about Plasencia, &c. and along the Tagus to Talavera; and Drouet removed the 5th corps to Zafra. Before these troops separated, the allies were certainly stronger than the enemy in infantry: the enemy were strongest in cavalry; but the attack of the enemy would have answered no purpose, excepting to oblige them to retire from Estremadura. That object was likely to be accomplished without incurring the risk of an attack with inferior numbers of cavalry, and without exposing the troops to the inconvenience of making long marches in Estremadura in that season.

The enemy having retired from Estremadura, the question regarding the future operations of the army was maturely considered, and it was determined to remove the seat of the war to the frontiers of Castille, The grounds of that decision were,

First; that in that season we could not venture to under-take any thing against Badajoz.

Secondly; that we were not strong enough to venture into Andalusia.

Thirdly; that from all the information I had received, the strength of the northern army was less than that of the south, and that the army of Portugal, which was destined to oppose us in whatever point we should direct our operations, was not likely to be so strongly supported in the north as in the south.

In this supposition I was mistaken. The army of the north, even before the reinforcements arrived, was stronger than that in the south; but it must be observed that there is nothing so difficult as to obtain information of the enemy's numbers in Spain. There is but little communication between one town and another; and although the most minute account of numbers which have passed through one town can always be obtained, no information can be obtained of what is passing in the next. To this add, that the disposition of the Spaniards naturally leads them to exaggerate the strength and success of themselves and their friends, and to despise that of the enemy, and it will not be matter of surprise that we should so often have been misinformed regarding the enemy's numbers.

The first intention was to remain in the cantonments of the Alentejo, which had been taken up as soon as Marmont had retired, till the train and stores should have been brought up from Oporto, to make the attack upon Ciudad Rodrigo. The march of the troops would consequently not have taken place till the beginning of September. The movement was made in the end of July and beginning of August, for the following reasons.

In the end of July it was discovered, that notwithstanding Marshal Bessieres had evacuated the Asturias and Astorga when Marmont moved into Estremadura in the beginning of July, and had thereby increased the disposable force under his command, Don Julian [Sanchez] had been so successful in the blockade of Ciudad Rodrigo, that up to that moment the enemy had not been able to keep open any communication with the place, or to supply it at all with provisions.

A return of the supplies in the place, when it was left by Marmont in the beginning of June, had likewise been intercepted, from which it appeared that the provisions would be exhausted by the 20th of August. It was therefore determined to send the army across the Tagus immediately, and to blockade Ciudad Rodrigo, if it should not have been supplied; and if it should, to canton the army in Lower Beira, till the train and stores should have arrived.

We did not receive intelligence that the place had been supplied till we went so forward as to disclose our design against the place. But there were two other reasons for taking up cantonments for the summer in Castille rather than in Lower Beira: one was, that in Castille we could procure supplies of provisions, which we much wanted, and we could procure none in Beira; the other was, that by threatening Ciudad Rodrigo, we were likely to relieve Galicia, and General Abadia's army from the attack with which both were threatened by the army of the north.

We accordingly made the blockade of Ciudad Rodrigo in the first week in August, and continued it from that time forward. The train for the siege would have arrived at Almeida in the first week of September. But before that period, accounts were received of the arrival in Spain of the enemy's reinforcements. It was also discovered by an intercepted return of the army of the north, that they were much stronger than they had been supposed in July, when the plan was determined upon to make the siege of Ciudad Rodrigo. Under these circumstances, and as Almeida was not in a state to give security to the heavy train and its stores, it was determined not to bring the equipment forward, and to confine our efforts to the blockade of Ciudad Rodrigo.

In the third week of September, the enemy collected the whole army of the north, (with the exception of Bonnet's division, which observed Abadia's movements on the side of Galicia,) and two divisions from Navarre, which had recently come from Calabria, and five divisions, and all the cavalry of the army of Portugal, to escort a convoy to Ciudad Rodrigo. They had not less than 60,000 men, of which, more than 6000 were cavalry, to which we could oppose about 40,000. If we had fought a battle to maintain the blockade of Ciudad Rodrigo, we must have had the river Agueda, and the place in our rear; and if defeated, a retreat was impossible.

Although we did not fight a battle to protect the blockade of Ciudad Rodrigo, the army was assembled on the left of the Agueda, and a partial engagement, highly honorable to the troops, was fought at El Bodon on the 25th of September.

El Bodon 25 September 1811[13]

The enemy commenced their movements towards Ciudad Rodrigo with the convoys of provisions from the Sierra de Bejar, and from Salamanca, on the 21st instant, and on the following day I collected the British army in positions, from which I could either advance or retire without difficulty, and which would enable me to see all that was going on, and the strength of the enemy's army.

The 3d Division, and that part of Major General Alten's brigade of cavalry which was not detached, occupied the range of heights which are on the left of the Agueda: having their advanced guard, under Lieut. Colonel Williams, of the 60th, on the heights of Pastores, within three miles of Ciudad Rodrigo; the 4th Division was at Fuente Guinaldo, where I had strengthened a position with some works; the Light Division on the right of the Agueda, having their right resting upon the mountains which separate Castille and Estremadura. Lieut. General Graham commanded the troops on the left of the army, which were posted on the Lower Azava; the 6th Division, and Major General Anson's brigade of cavalry, being at Espeja, and occupying Carpio, Marialva, &c.

Don Carlos de Espana observed the Lower Agueda with Don Julian Sanchez's cavalry and infantry.

Lieut. General Sir Stapleton Cotton, with Major General Slade's, and Major General De Grey's brigades of cavalry, were on the Upper Azava, in the centre, between the right and left of the army, with General Pack's brigade at Campillo; and the 5th Division was in observation of the Pass of Perales, in the rear of the right, the French General Foy having remained and collected a body of troops in Upper Estremadura, consisting of part of his own division of the army of Portugal, and a division of the army of the centre; and the 7th Division was in reserve at Alamedilla.

The enemy first appeared in the plain near Ciudad Rodrigo, on the 23d; and retired again in a short time; but on the 24th, in the morning, they advanced again in considerable force, and entered the plain by the roads of Santi-espiritus and Tenebron; and before evening they had collected there all their cavalry, to the amount of about 6000 men, and four divisions of infantry, of which one division was of the Imperial Guard; and the remainder of the armies were encamped on the Guadapero, immediately beyond the hills which surround the plain of Ciudad Rodrigo.

On the morning of the 25th the enemy sent a reconaissance of cavalry towards the Lower Azava, consisting of about fourteen squadrons of the cavalry of the Imperial Guard. They drove in our posts on the right of the Azava, but having passed that river, the Lanciers de Berg were charged by two squadrons of the 16th, and one of the 14th light dragoons, and driven back; they attempted to rally and to return, but were fired upon by the light infantry of the 61st Regiment, which had been posted in the wood on their flank, by Lieut. General [Sir Thomas] Graham; and Major General Anson pursued them across the Azava; and afterwards resumed his posts on the right of that river. Lieut. General Graham was highly pleased with the conduct of Major General Anson's brigade; and Major General Anson particular mentions Lieut. Colonel Hervey, and Captain [Thomas William] Brotherton, of the 14th, and Captain [James] Hay and Major [Edward Charles] Cocks, of the 16th.

But the enemy's attention was principally directed during this day to the position of the 3d Division, in the hills between Fuente Guinaldo and Pastores. About 8 in the morning, they moved a column, consisting of between thirty and forty squadrons of cavalry, and fourteen battalions of infantry, and twelve pieces of cannon, from Ciudad Rodrigo, in such a direction, that it was doubtful whether they would attempt to ascend the hills by La Encina, or by the direct road of El Bodon, towards Fuente Guinaldo; and I was not certain by which road they would make their attack, till they actually commenced it upon the last.

As soon as I saw the direction of their march, I had reinforced the 2d batt. 5th Regiment, which occupied the post on the hill over which the road passes to Guinaldo, by the 77th Regiment, and the 21st Portuguese Regiment, under the command of Major General the Hon. C. [Charles] Colville, and Major General Alten's brigade, of which only three squadrons remained which had not been detached, drawn from El Bodon; and I ordered there a brigade of the 4th Division from Fuente Guinaldo, and afterwards from El Bodon, the remainder of the troops of the 3d Division, with the exception of those at Pastores, which were too distant.

In the meantime, however, the small body of troops in this post sustained the attack of the enemy's cavalry and artillery. One regiment of French dragoons succeeded in taking two pieces of cannon which had been posted on a rising ground on the right of our troops; but they were charged by the 2d batt. 5th Regiment, under the command of Major [Henry] Ridge, and the guns were immediately retaken.

While this operation was going on the flank, an attack was made on the front by another regiment, which was repulsed in a similar manner by the 77th Regiment; and the three squadrons of Major General Alten's brigade charged repeatedly different bodies of the enemy which ascended the hill on the left of the two regiments of British infantry, the Portuguese regiment being posted in the rear of their right.

At length, the division of the enemy's infantry which had marched with the cavalry from Ciudad Rodrigo, were brought up to the attack on the road of Fuente Guinaldo, and seeing that they would arrive and be engaged before the troops could arrive either from Guinaldo or El Bodon, I determined to withdraw our post, and to retire with the whole on Fuente Guinaldo. The 2d batt. 5th Regiment, and the 77th Regiment, were formed into one square, and the 21st Portuguese Regiment into another, supported by Major General Alten's small body of cavalry and the Portuguese artillery.

The enemy's cavalry immediately rushed forward, and obliged our cavalry to retire to the support of the Portuguese regiment; and the 5th and 77th regiments were charged on three faces of the square by the French cavalry, but they halted and repulsed the attack with the utmost steadiness and gallantry. We then continued the retreat, and joined the remainder of the 3d division, also formed in squares, on their march to Fuente Guinaldo, and the whole retired together in the utmost order, and the enemy never made another attempt to charge any of them; but were satisfied with firing upon them with their artillery, and with following them.

Lieut. Colonel Williams with his light infantry, and Lieut. Colonel the Hon. R. Trench with the 74th Regiment, retired from Pastores across the Agueda; and thence marched by Robleda, where they took some prisoners, and recrossed the Agueda, and joined at Guinaldo in the evening.

I placed the 3d and 4th divisions, and General Pack's brigade of infantry, and Major General Alten's, Major General De Grey's, and Major General Slade's brigades of cavalry in the position at Fuente Guinaldo on the evening of the 25th, and ordered Major General R. Craufurd to retire with the Light Division across the Agueda, the 7th Division to form at Albergueria, and Lieut. General Graham to collect the troops under his command at Nave d'Aver, keeping only posts of observation on the Azava; and the troops were thus formed in an echellon, of which the centre was in the position at Guinaldo; and the right upon the pass of Perales; and the left at Nave d'Aver; Don Carlos de Espana was placed on the left of the Coa; and Don Julian Sanchez was detached with the cavalry to the enemy's rear.

The enemy brought up a second division of infantry from Ciudad Rodrigo in the afternoon of the 25th; and in the course of that night, and of the 26th, they collected their whole army in front of our position at Guinaldo; and not deeming it expedient to stand their attack in that position, I retired about three leagues, and on the 27th formed the army as follows: viz., the 5th Division on the right, at Aldea Velha; the 4th, and light dragoons, and Major General Alten's cavalry, at the Convent of Sacaparte, in front of Alfayates;

the 3d and 7th divisions in second line, behind Alfayates; and Lieut. General Graham's corps on the left at Bismula, having their advanced guard beyond the Villar Mayor river; and Lieut. General Sir Stapleton Cotton's cavalry near Alfayates, on the left of the 4th division, and having General Pack's and General M'Mahon's brigades at Rebolosa, on their left. The piquets of the cavalry were in front of Aldea da Ponte, beyond the Villar Mayor river; and those of General Alten's brigade beyond the same river, towards Forcalhos.

It had been the enemy's intention to turn the left of the position of Guinaldo by moving a column into the valley of the Upper Azava, and thence ascending the heights in the rear of the position by Castillejos; and from this column they detached a division of infantry and fourteen squadrons of cavalry to follow our retreat by Albergueria, and another body of the same strength followed us by Forcalhos. The former attacked the piquets of the cavalry at Aldea da Ponte, and drove them in; and they pushed on nearly as far as Alfayates. I then made General [Hon. Edward] Pakenham attack them with his brigade of the 4th division, supported by Lieut. General the Hon. L. [Lowry] Cole, and the 4th division, and by Sir Stapleton Cotton's cavalry; and the enemy were driven through Aldea da Ponte, back upon Albergueria, and the piquets of the cavalry resumed their station.

But the enemy having been reinforced by the troops which marched from Forcalhos, again advanced about sunset and drove in the piquets of the cavalry from Aldea da Ponte, and took possession of the village.

Lieut. General Cole again attacked them with a part of General Pakenham's brigade, and drove them through the village; but night having come on, and as General Pakenham was not certain what was passing on his flanks, or of the numbers of the enemy, and he knew that the army were to fall back still further, he evacuated the village, which the enemy occupied, and held during the night.

On the 28th, I formed the army on the heights behind Soito; having the Serra de Meras on their right, and the left at Rendo, on the Coa; about a league in rear of the position which they had occupied on the 27th. The enemy also retired from Aldea da Ponte, and had their advanced posts at Albergueria; and as it appears that they are about to retire from this part of the country, and as we have already had some bad weather, and may expect more at the period of the equinoctial gales, I propose to canton the troops in the nearest villages to the position which they occupied yesterday.

I cannot conclude this report of the occurrences of the last week, without expressing to your Lordship my admiration of the conduct of the troops engaged in the affairs of the 25th instant. The conduct of the 2d batt. 5th Regiment, commanded by Major Ridge, in particular, affords a memorable example of what the steadiness and discipline of the troops, and their confidence in their Officers, can effect in the most difficult and trying situations. The conduct of the 77th Regiment, under the command of Lieut. Colonel [John] Bromhead, was equally good, and I have never seen a more determined attack than was made by the whole of the enemy's cavalry, with every advantage of the assistance of a superior artillery, and repulsed by these two weak battalions. I must not omit also to report the good conduct on the same occasion, of the 21st Portuguese Regiment, under the command of Colonel Bacellar, and of Major Arentschildt's artillery. The Portuguese infantry were not actually charged, but were repeatedly threatened, and they showed the utmost steadiness and discipline, both in the mode in which they prepared to receive the enemy, and in all the movements of a retreat made over six miles of plain in front of a superior cavalry and artillery.

The Portuguese artillerymen attached to the guns, which were for a moment in the enemy's possession, were cut down at their guns.

The infantry upon this occasion were under the command of Major General the Hon. C. Colville; Lieut. General Picton having remained with the troops at El Bodon; and the conduct of Major General Colville was beyond all praise.

Your Lordship will have observed by the details of the action which I have given you, how much reason I had to be satisfied with the conduct of the 1st hussars and 11th light dragoons of Major General Alten's brigade. There were not more than three squadrons of the two regiments on the ground, this brigade having for some time furnished the cavalry for the outposts of the army, and they charged the enemy's cavalry repeatedly; and notwithstanding the superiority of the latter, the post would have been maintained if I had not preferred to abandon it to risking the loss of these brave men by continuing the unequal contest under additional disadvantages, in consequence of the immediate entry of fourteen battalions of infantry into the action, before the support which I had ordered up could arrive. Major General Alten, and Lieut. Colonels [Henry John] Cumming and Arentschildt, and the Officers of these regiments, particularly distinguished themselves upon this occasion.

I have also to mention that the Adjutant General, Major General the Hon. C. Stewart, being upon the field, gave his assistance as an Officer of cavalry with his usual gallantry.

In the affair of the 27th, at Aldea da Ponte, Brig. General Pakenham and the troops of the 4th Division, under the orders of Lieut. General the Hon. G. L. Cole, likewise conducted themselves remarkably well.

His Serene Highness, the Hereditary Prince of Orange, accompanied me during the operations which I have detailed to your Lordship, and was for the first time in fire; and he conducted himself with a spirit and intelligence which afford a hope that he will become an ornament to his profession.

The enemy having collected for the object of relieving Ciudad Rodrigo the army of the north, which were withdrawn from the attack they had commenced on General Abadia in Galicia, in which are included twenty two battalions of the Imperial Guards, and General Souham's division of infantry, composed of troops recently arrived in Spain from the army of Naples, and now drawn from the frontier of Navarre, where they had been employed in operations against Mina, together with five divisions and all the cavalry of the army called off Portugal, composing altogether an army of not less than 60,000 men, of which 6000 cavalry and 125 pieces of artillery, I could not pretend to maintain the blockade of Ciudad Rodrigo, nor could any effort which I could make prevent or materially impede the collection of the supplies or the march of the convoy for the relief of that place. I did all that I could expect to effect without incurring the risk of great loss for no object; and as the reports as usual were so various in regard to the enemy's real strength, it was necessary that I should see their army in order that the people of this country might be convinced that to raise the blockade was a measure of necessity, and that the momentary relief of Galicia, and of Mina, were the only objects which it was in my power immediately to effect.

Return of the Killed, Wounded, and Missing, of the Army under the Command of General Viscount Wellington, K.B., in an affair with the Enemy on the Heights of El Bodon, on the 25th, and near Aldea da Ponte, on the 27th September, 1811.

	Officers	NCOs and drummers	Rank and File	Total loss of Officers, Non-commissioned Officers, and Rank and File
Killed	1	1	40	42
Wounded	16	13	156	185
Missing	–	1	33	34

The object of taking a position so near to the enemy was to force them to show their army. This was an object, because the people of the country, as usual, believed and reported that the enemy were not so strong as we knew them to be; and if they had not seen the enemy's strength, they would have entertained a very unfavorable opinion of the British army, which it was desirable to avoid. This object was accomplished by the operations at the close of September.

Although the removal of the army from the Alentejo did not accomplish all the objects which were in view when the movement was made, it had the effect of obliging the enemy to collect their whole force for the relief of Ciudad Rodrigo, and to abandon all their other operations and objects. The army of the north were obliged to discontinue their operations against Abadia, and still further, to call to their assistance two divisions which had recently arrived from Calabria and were employed in Navarre against the guerrilla Mina. Mina's success in Navarre has consequently been extraordinary, and his numbers have rapidly increased.

After the operations for the relief of Ciudad Rodrigo, it was determined to persevere in the same system till the enemy should make some alteration in the disposition of their force, and to continue to threaten Ciudad Rodrigo with an attack, in order to keep a large force of the enemy employed to observe our operations, and to prevent them from undertaking any operation elsewhere.

To this system we were forced, not less by the relative force of the two armies, than by the extraordinary sickness of our own troops. All the soldiers who had recently arrived from England, and all those who had been in Walcheren, and vast numbers of officers, were attacked by fever, not of a very violent description, but they were rendered unable to perform any duty, and those who recovered, relapsed upon making any exertions. Even if an opportunity had offered, therefore, for undertaking anything on this side, the unfortunate state of the army would have prevented it.

It would not have answered to remove the army to the frontiers of Estremadura, where a chance of effecting some important object might have offered; as in that case General Abadia would have been left to himself, and would have fallen an easy sacrifice to the army of the north. We availed ourselves of the opportunity which offered of striking a blow against Girard in Estremadura; by which the country between the Tagus and the Guadiana, was relieved from the enemy.

But little notice has been taken in this memorandum of the operations of the Spaniards, which having been confined principally to the eastern coast of the Peninsula, have been but little influenced by those on the western side. Tortosa was surrendered by treachery on the 2nd of January, as Lerida had been but a short time before. The troops under Suchet then prepared to attack Tarragona, which place was taken by storm on the 28th June.

In the course of the winter, it had appeared by an intercepted letter to be Soult's intention to attack Carthagena, in order to be prepared to attack Valencia on both sides in concert with Suchet. He attempted to carry this intention into execution in the month of July, after he had obliged General Blake to embark at Ayamonte. General Blake, however, went with his army by sea to the coast of Murcia, and landed it there in August, while Soult moved in that direction by Granada. It appears that General Blake quitted the army as soon as it had formed a junction with the army of Murcia, called the third army, and he proceeded to Valencia, leaving General Freire in the command of the troops in Murcia. The French advanced from Granada, but the Spaniards did not retreat in time, and their loss was very great. They had time, however, to reassemble their dispersed divisions, and the people in Murcia took arms, and partly on this account, partly on account of the prevalence of the yellow fever at Carthagena, and throughout Murcia, and partly because the movement of the allied British and Portuguese army upon Ciudad Rodrigo, rendered necessary a concentration of the French forces in the Peninsula, Soult returned to the westward, and arrived at Seville on the 17th September.

In the mean time, Suchet, having been joined by reinforcements from France, and having dispersed the troops which General Lacy had attempted to collect in Catalonia, penetrated into the kingdom of Valencia. General Blake had been since August preparing for the defence of that city, and he collected there the army of Valencia, and others from Aragon and Catalonia; and latterly, General Mahy marched from Murcia to join him with the troops which General Blake had brought from Cadiz, and a part of the third army, i.e., that of Murcia.

Suchet having gained possession of Oropesa, commenced an attack on the castle of Saguntum on the 29th September. He made several attempts to obtain possession of this castle by storm, in all of which he failed, and at last, having brought up a few heavy guns, he broke ground regularly before the place, and made a breach in its wall. He made several attempts to carry the breach by storm, in all of which he failed.

As soon as General Blake was joined at Valencia by the troops from Murcia, under General Mahy, he moved out from Valencia on the 24th October, and on the 25th attacked Suchet, and was defeated, with the loss of some prisoners and eight pieces of cannon. The French immediately summoned the garrison of Saguntum to surrender, which they did upon capitulation. Suchet advanced upon Valencia, and it is understood that he opened his fire upon a part of the intrenched position occupied by Blake in front of the town on the 25th of November. It is likewise stated, that on the 2nd of December, there was a severe action at Valencia, in which the French suffered considerably.

These circumstances, and the movement of Marmont's army towards Toledo, as is supposed, to aid Suchet, have induced us to make preparations for the siege of Ciudad Rodrigo. By these measures we shall bring Marmont back, and probably oblige the army of the north to reassemble.

Since Suchet has been in Valencia, the guerrillas have been very active and enterprising in Aragon and Navarre. Mina defeated a detachment of 1100 men, sent against him, only three of whom escaped; and besides other advantages of small amount, he and the Empecinado, and Duran, having joined, it is reported that they had taken the garrison of Daroca, consisting of 2400 men.

When General Blake embarked on the 6th July from the mouth of the Guadiana, he left there General Ballesteros with a division of troops, which likewise embarked, and went to the Sierra de Ronda on the 24th of August. He has been very successful against the French by his light operations in rear of the army, blockading Cadiz; and he has always a secure retreat open upon Gibraltar. In order to aid General Ballesteros, and to give additional security to Tarifa, Colonel [John Byne] Skerrett, with about 1200 men, was detached thither from Cadiz on the 10th of October. By this measure the French were obliged to retire from San Roque on the night of the 21st of October, in which position they had kept Ballesteros blockaded under the guns of Gibraltar; and Ballesteros did them much mischief in their retreat, and in a subsequent attack which he made upon one of their detachments at Bornos. He was afterwards again obliged to retire in the end of November under protection of the guns of Gibraltar; and Colonel Skerrett, and the Spanish General Copons, to Tarifa. The object of the French on this occasion was to attack Tarifa, while they should keep Ballesteros blockaded. But they had commenced to retire on the 12th December.

From this memorandum it will be seen, that if the Spaniards had behaved with common prudence, or if their conduct had been even tolerably good, the result of Massena's campaign in Portugal must have been the relief of the south of the Peninsula.

We had to contend with the consequences of the faults of some, the treachery of others, and the folly and vanity of all. But although our success has not been what it might and ought, we have at least lost no ground, and with a handful of British troops fit for service, we have kept the enemy in check in all quarters since the month of March.

Till now they have gained nothing, and have made no progress on any side. It is to be apprehended that they will succeed in Valencia; but I believe there is no man who knows the state of affairs in that province, and has read Suchet's account of his action with Blake on the 25th of October, who does not believe that, if Blake had not fought that action, Valencia would have been safe. Are the English Ministers and Generals responsible for the blunders of Blake.

Chapter 5

1812 to 1814

*S**adly, Wellington wrote no memoranda of operations for the years 1812 and 1813, no doubt because the effective stalemate of the preceding years was broken in a most dramatic fashion. The Emperor Napoleon had resolved on going to war with Russia and despite mobilising the rest of Europe to aid him in this grand design, his need for troops was such that not only were reinforcements curtailed, but large numbers of troops already serving in Spain were recalled. Yet at the same time, far from going on to the defensive until the Russian war was decided, the French armies were firmly instructed to act offensively. Inevitably, not only were they overstretched in carrying out their own operations, but containing Wellington's army was no longer possible – a fact cruelly underscored at the very start of the year by the Duke's seizure of the twin gateways between Spain and Portugal; Cuidad Rodrigo in the north, and Badajoz in the south.*

The Storm of Cuidad Rodrigo 19 January 1812[1]

I informed your Lordship, in my dispatch of the 9th, that I had attacked Ciudad Rodrigo, and in that of the 15th, of the progress of the operations to that period, and I have now the pleasure to acquaint your Lordship that we took the place by storm yesterday evening after dark.

We continued, from the 15th to the 19th, to complete the second parallel, and the communications with that work, and we had made some progress by sap towards the crest of the glacis. On the night of the 15th we likewise advanced from the left of the first parallel down the slope of the hill towards the convent of San Francisco to a situation from which the walls of the fausse braie[2] and of the town were seen, on which a battery for seven guns was constructed, and these commenced their fire on the morning of the 18th.

In the mean time, the batteries in the first parallel continued their fire; and, yesterday evening, their fire had not only considerably injured the defences of the place, but had made breaches in the fausse braie wall, and in the body of the place, which were considered practicable; while the battery on the slope of the hill, which had been commenced on the night of the 15th, and had opened on the 18th, had been equally efficient still farther to the left, and opposite to the suburb of San Francisco.

I therefore determined to storm the place, notwithstanding that the approaches had not been brought to the crest of the glacis, and the counterscarp of the ditch was still entire. The attack was accordingly made yesterday evening, in five separate columns, consisting of the troops of the 3rd and Light divisions, and of Brigadier General Pack's brigade[3]. The two right columns, conducted by Lieut. Colonel [Bryan] O'Toole of the 2nd cacadores, and Major Ridge of the 5th Regiment, were destined to protect the advance of Major General Mackinnon's brigade, forming the 3rd, to the top of the breach in the fausse braie wall; and all these, being composed of troops of the 3rd division, were under the direction of Lieut. General Picton.

The fourth column, consisting of the 43rd and 52nd regiments, and part of the 95th Regiment, being of the Light division, under the direction of Major General Craufurd, attacked the breaches on the left in front of the suburb of San Francisco, and covered the left of the attack of the principal breach by the troops of the 3rd Division; and Brig. General Pack was destined, with his brigade, forming the fifth column, to make a false attack upon the southern face of the fort.

Besides these five columns, the 94th Regiment, belonging to the 3rd Division, descended into the ditch in two columns, on the right of Major General Mackinnon's brigade, with a view to protect the descent of that body into the ditch and its attack of the breach in the fausse braie, against the obstacles which it was supposed the enemy would construct to oppose their progress.

All these attacks succeeded; and Brig. General Pack even surpassed my expectations, having converted his false attack into a real one; and his advanced guard, under the command of Major [Henry Blois] Lynch, having followed the enemy's troops from the advanced works into the fausse braie, where they made prisoners all opposed to them.

Major Ridge, of the 2nd batt. 5th Regiment, having escaladed the fausse braie wall, stormed the principal breach in the body of the place, together with the 94th Regiment, commanded by Lieut. Colonel [James] Campbell, which had moved along the ditch at the same time, and had stormed the breach in the fausse braie, both in front of Major General Mackinnon's brigade. Thus, these regiments not only effectually covered the advance from the trenches of Major General Mackinnon's brigade by their first movements and operations, but they preceded them in the attack.

Major General Craufurd, and Major General [John Ormsby] Vandeleur, and the troops of the Light Division, on the left, were likewise very forward on that side; and, in less than half an hour from the time the attack commenced, our troops were in possession of, and formed on the ramparts of the place, each body contiguous to the other. The enemy then submitted, having sustained a considerable loss in the contest.

Our loss was also, I am concerned to add, severe, particularly in officers of high rank and estimation in this army. Major General Mackinnon was unfortunately blown up by the accidental explosion of one of the enemy's expense magazines, close to the breach, after he had gallantly and successfully led the troops under his command to the attack. Major General Craufurd likewise received a severe wound while he was leading on the Light Division to the storm, and I am apprehensive that I shall be deprived for some time of his assistance.

Major General Vandeleur was likewise wounded in the same manner, but not so severely, and he was able to continue in the field.

I have to add to this list Lieut. Colonel [John] Colborne of the 52nd Regiment, and Major George Napier, who led the storming party of the Light Division, and was wounded on the top of the breach.

I have great pleasure in reporting to your Lordship the uniform good conduct, and spirit of enterprise, and patience, and perseverance in the performance of great labor, by which the General officers, officers, and troops of the 1st, 3rd, 4th, and Light divisions, and Brig. General Pack's brigade, by whom the siege was carried on, have been distinguished during the late operations.

Lieut. General Graham assisted me in superintending the conduct of the details of the siege, besides performing the duties of the General Officer commanding the 1st Division; and I am much indebted to the suggestions and assistance I received from him for the success of this enterprise.

The conduct of all parts of the 3rd Division, in the operations which they performed with so much gallantry and exactness on the evening of the 19th in the dark, afford the strongest proof of the abilities of Lieut. General Picton and Major General Mackinnon, by whom they were directed and led; but I beg particularly to draw your Lordship's attention to the conduct of Lieut. Colonel O'Toole, of the 2nd Cacadores, of Major Ridge of the 2nd Batt. 5th Foot, of Lieut. Colonel Campbell of the 94th Regiment, of Major [Russell] Manners of the 74th, and of Major [John] Grey of the 2nd Batt. 5th Foot who has been twice wounded during this siege.

It is but justice also to the 3rd Division to report that the men who performed the sap belonged to the 45th, 74th, and 88th regiments, under the command of Captain [George] Macleod of the Royal Engineers, and Captain [Alexander] Thompson of the 74th, Lieut. Beresford of the 88th, and Lieut. Metcalfe of the 45th, and they distinguished themselves not less in the storm of the place than they had in the performance of their laborious duty during the siege.

I have already reported, in my letter of the 9th instant, my sense of the conduct of Major General Craufurd, and of Lieut. Colonel Colborne, and of the troops of the Light Division, in the storm of the redoubt of San Francisco, on the evening of the 8th instant. The conduct of these troops was equally distinguished throughout the siege; and in the storm, nothing could exceed the gallantry with which these brave officers and troops advanced and accomplished the difficult operation allotted to them, notwithstanding that all their leaders had fallen.

I particularly request your Lordship's attention to the conduct of Major General Craufurd, Major General Vandeleur, Lieut. Colonel [Andrew Francis] Barnard of the 95th, Lieut. Colonel Colborne, Major [Edward] Gibbs, and Major Napier of the 52nd, and Lieut. Colonel [Charles] Macleod of the 43rd. The conduct of Captain [John] Duffy of the 43rd, and that of Lieut. [John] Gurwood of the 52nd Regiment, who was wounded, have likewise been particularly reported to me. Lieut. Colonel [George] Elder and the 3rd Cacadores were likewise distinguished upon this occasion.

The 1st Portuguese Regiment, under Lieut. Colonel Hill, and the 16th, under Colonel Campbell, being Brig. General Pack's brigade, were likewise distinguished in the storm, under the command of the Brigadier General, who particularly mentions Major Lynch.

In my dispatch of the 15th, I reported to your Lordship the attack of the convent of Sta Cruz by the troops of the 1st Division, under the direction of Lieut. General Graham, and that of the convent of San Francisco on the 14th instant, under the direction of Major General the Hon. C. Colville. The first mentioned enterprise was performed by Captain Laroche de Starkenfels, of the 1st Line Batt. King's German Legion, the last by Lieut. Colonel [Charles Amédée] Harcourt, with the 40th Regiment. This regiment remained from that time in the suburb of San Francisco, and materially assisted our attack on that side of the place.

Although it did not fall to the lot of the troops of the 1st and 4th divisions to bring these operations to a successful close, they distinguished themselves throughout their progress by the patience and perseverance with which they performed the labor of the siege. The brigade of Guards, under Major General H. [Henry Frederick] Campbell, were particularly distinguished in this respect.

I likewise request your Lordship's attention to the conduct of Lieut. Colonel [Richard] Fletcher, the chief engineer, and of Brigade Major [John Thomas] Jones, and the officers and men of the Royal Engineers. The ability with which these operations were carried on exceeds all praise; and I beg leave to recommend these officers to your Lordship most particularly.

Major [Alexander] Dickson of the Royal Artillery, attached to the Portuguese artillery, has for some time had the direction of the heavy train attached to this army, and has conducted the intricate details of the late operation, as he did that of the two sieges of Badajoz in the last summer, much to my satisfaction. The rapid execution produced by the well directed fire kept up from our batteries affords the best proof of the merits of the officers and men of the Royal Artillery, and of the Portuguese artillery, employed on this occasion; but I must particularly mention Brigade Major [John] May, and Captains [Harcourt Fort] Holcombe.

[William Greenshields] Power, [Thomas] Dynely, and [William Bolden] Dundas, of the Royal Artillery, and Captains Da Cunha and Da Costa, and Lieut. Silva, of the 1st Regiment of Portuguese artillery.

I have likewise particularly to report to your Lordship the conduct of Major [Henry] Sturgeon of the Royal Staff corps. He constructed and placed for us the bridge over the Agueda, without which the enterprise could not have been attempted; and he afterwards materially assisted Lieut. General Graham and myself in our reconnaissance of the place on which the plan of the attack was founded; and he finally conducted the 2nd Batt. 5th Regiment, as well as the 2nd Cacadores, to their points of attack.

The Adjutant General, and the Deputy Quarter Master General, and the officers of their several departments, gave me every assistance throughout this service, as well as those of my personal Staff; and I have great pleasure in adding that, notwithstanding the season of the year, and the increased difficulties of procuring supplies for the troops, the whole army have been well supplied, and every branch of the service provided for during the late operations, by the indefatigable exertions of Mr. Commissary General Bissett, and the officers belonging to his department.

The Mariscal de Campo, Don Carlos de Espana, and Don Julian Sanchez, observed the enemy's movements beyond the Tormes during the operations of the siege; and I am much obliged to them, and to the people of Castille in general, for the assistance I received from them. The latter have invariably shown their detestation of the French tyranny, and their desire to contribute, by every means in their power, to remove it.

I shall hereafter transmit to your Lordship a detailed account of what we have found in the place; but I believe that there are 153 pieces of ordnance, including the heavy train belonging to the French army, and great quantities of ammunition and stores. We have the Governor, General Barrie, about 78 officers, and 1700 men, prisoners.

I transmit this dispatch by my aide de camp. Major the Hon. A. [Alexander William] Gordon, who will give your Lordship any further details you may require; and I beg leave to recommend him to your protection.

Return of the Killed, Wounded, and Missing, of the Army under the command of General Viscount Wellington, K.B., during the siege and in the assault of Cuidad Rodrigo from the 8th to the 19th of January 1812.

	Officers	Serjeants.	Rank and File	Horses	Total loss of Officers, Non-commissioned Officers, and Rank and File
Killed	9	11	158	–	178
Wounded	70	35	713	–	818
Missing	–	–	7	–	7

The Storm of Badajoz 6-7 April 1812[4]

My dispatch of the 3rd instant will have apprized your Lordship of the state of the operations against Badajoz to that date; which were brought to a close on the night of the 6th, by the capture of the place by storm.

The fire continued during the 4th and 5th against the face of the bastion of La Trinidad; and the flank of the bastion of Sta Maria; and on the 4th, in the morning, we opened another battery of six guns in the second parallel against the shoulder of the ravelin of San Roque; and the wall in its gorge.

Practicable breaches were effected in the bastions above mentioned on the evening of the 5th; but as I had observed that the enemy had entrenched the bastion of La Trinidad, and the most formidable preparations were making for the defence, as well of the breach in that bastion, as of that in the bastion of Sta Maria, I determined to delay the attack for another day, and to turn all the guns in the batteries in the second parallel on the curtain of La Trinidad; in hopes, that by effecting a third breach, the troops would be enabled to turn the enemy's works for the defence of the other two; the attack of which would besides be connected by the troops destined to attack the breach in the curtain.

This breach was effected in the evening of the 6th, and the fire of the face of the bastion of Sta Maria, and of the flank of the bastion of La Trinidad being overcome, I determined to attack the place that night.

I had kept in reserve in the neighborhood of this camp, the 5th Division under Lieut. General [Sir James] Leith, which had left Castille only in the middle of March and had but lately arrived in this part of the country; and I brought them up on that evening. The plan for the attack was, that Lieut. General Picton should attack the castle of Badajoz by escalade with the 3rd Division; and a detachment from the guard in the trenches furnished that evening by the 4th Division, under Major [James] Wilson of the 48th Regiment, should attack the ravelin of San Roque upon his left, while the 4th Division under Major General the Hon. C. Colville, and the Light Division under Lieut. Colonel Barnard, should attack the breaches in the bastions of La Trinidad and Sta Maria, and in the curtain by which they are connected. The 5th Division were to occupy the ground which the 4th and Light divisions had occupied during the siege; and Lieut. General Leith was to make a false attack upon the outwork called the Pardaleras; and another on the works of the fort, towards the Guadiana, with the left brigade of the division under Major General Walker, which he was to turn into a real attack, if circumstances should prove favorable; and Brigadier General [Manley] Power, who invested the place with his Portuguese brigade on the right of the Guadiana, was directed to make false attacks on the tete de pont [bridgehead]., the Fort San Christoval, and the new redoubt called Mon Coeur.

The attack was accordingly made at ten at night; Lieut. General Picton preceding by a few minutes the attacks by the remainder of the troops. Major General Kempt led this attack, which went out from the right of the first parallel. He was unfortunately wounded in crossing the river Rivillas below the inundation; but notwithstanding this circumstance, and the obstinate resistance of the enemy, the castle was carried by escalade; and the 3rd Division established in it at about half-past eleven.

While this was going on, Major Wilson of the 48th carried the ravelin of San Roque by the gorge, with a detachment of 200 men of the guard in the trenches; and with the assistance of Major [John] Squire, of the Engineers, established himself within that work.

The 4th and Light divisions moved to the attack from the camp along the left of the river Rivillas, and of the inundation. They were not perceived by the enemy, till they reached the covered-way; and the advanced guards of the two divisions descended without difficulty into the ditch protected by the fire of the parties stationed on the glacis for that purpose; and they advanced to the assault of the breaches led by their gallant officers, with the utmost intrepidity. But such was the nature of the obstacles prepared by the enemy at the top and behind the breaches, and so determined their resistance, that our troops could not establish themselves within the place. Many brave officers and soldiers were killed or wounded by explosions at the top of the breaches; others who succeeded to them were obliged to give way, having found it impossible to penetrate the obstacles which the enemy had prepared to impede their progress. These attempts were repeated till after twelve at night; when, finding that success was not to be attained, and that Lieut. General Picton was established in the castle, I ordered that the 4th and Light divisions might retire to the ground, on which they had been first assembled for the attack.

In the mean time, Lieut. General Leith had pushed forward Major General [George Townshend] Walker's brigade on the left, supported by the 38th Regiment under Lieut. Colonel [John] Nugent, and the 15th Portuguese Regiment under Colonel Do Rego, and he had made a false attack upon the Pardaleras with the 8th Cacadores under Major [Dudley St. Leger] Hill. Major General Walker forced the barrier on the road of Olivenca, and entered the covered-way on the left of the bastion of San Vicente, close to the Guadiana. He there descended into the ditch, and escaladed the face of the bastion of San Vicente. Lieut. General Leith supported this attack by the 38th Regiment, and 15th Portuguese Regiment; and our troops being thus established in the castle, which commands all the works of the town, and in the town; and the 4th and Light divisions being formed again for the attack of the breaches, all resistance ceased; and at daylight in the morning, the Governor, General Philippon, who had retired to Fort St. Christoval, surrendered, together with General Vielande, and all the Staff, and the whole garrison. I have not got accurate returns of the strength of the garrison, or of the number of prisoners. But General Philippon has informed me that it consisted of 5000 men at the commencement of the siege, of which 1200 were killed or wounded during the operations; besides those lost in the assault of the place. There were five French battalions, besides two of the regiment of Hesse Darmstadt, and the artillery, engineers, &c.; and I understand there are 4000 prisoners.

It is impossible that any expressions of mine can convey to your Lordship the sense which I entertain of the gallantry of the officers and troops upon this occasion. The list of killed and wounded will show that the General Officers, the Staff attached to them, the Commanding, and other Officers of the regiments, put themselves at the head of the attacks which they severally directed, and set the example of gallantry which was so well followed by their men.

Marshal Sir William Beresford assisted me in conducting the details of this siege; and I am much indebted to him for the cordial assistance which I received from him, as well during its progress, as in the last operation which brought it to a termination.

The duties in the trenches were conducted successively by Major General the Hon. C. Colville, Major General Bowes, and Major General Kempt, under the superintendence of Lieut. General Picton. I have had occasion to mention all these officers during the course of the operations; and they all distinguished themselves, and were all wounded in the assault. I am particularly obliged to Lieut. General Picton for the manner in which he arranged the attack of the castle; for that in which he supported the attack, and established his troops in that important post.

Lieut. General Leith's arrangements for the false attack upon the Pardaleras, and that under Major General Walker, were likewise most judicious; and he availed himself of the circumstances of the moment, to push forward and support the attack under Major General Walker, in a manner highly creditable to him. The gallantry and conduct of Major General Walker, who was also wounded, and that of the officers and troops under his command, were conspicuous.

The arrangements made by Major General the Hon. C. Colville for the attack by the 4th Division, were very judicious; and he led them to the attack in the most gallant manner.

In consequence of the absence, on account of sickness, of Major General Vandeleur, and of Colonel Beckwith, Lieut. Colonel Barnard commanded the Light division in the assault, and distinguished himself not less by the manner in which he made the arrangements for that operation, than by his personal gallantry in its execution.

I have also to mention Brig. General [William Maundy] Harvey of the Portuguese service, commanding a brigade in the 4th Division, and Brig. General Champelmond, commanding the Portuguese brigade in the 3rd Division, as highly distinguished. Brig. General Harvey was wounded in the storm.

Your Lordship will see in the list of killed and wounded, a list of the Commanding Officers of regiments. In Lieut. Colonel [Charles] Macleod, of the 43rd Regiment who was killed in the breach. His Majesty has sustained the loss of an officer who was an ornament to his profession, and was capable of rendering the most important services to the country. I must likewise mention Lieut. Colonel [Edward] Gibbs of the 52nd, who was wounded, and Major [Peter] O'Hare of the 95th, unfortunately killed in the breach; Lieut. Colonel [George] Elder of the 3rd, and Major [John Henry] Algeo of the 1st Cacadores. Lieut. Colonel [Charles Amédée] Harcourt of the 40th, likewise wounded, was highly distinguished; and Lieut. Colonels [Sir Edward] Blakeney of the Royal Fusiliers, [William Howe] Knight of the 27th, [James] Erskine of the 48th, and Captain [John Thomas] Leaky, who commanded the 23rd Fusiliers, Lieut. Colonel Ellis having been wounded during the previous operation of the siege.

In the 5th Division I must mention Major [Dudly St.Leger] Hill of the 8th Cacadores, who directed the false attack upon the fort Pardaleras. It was impossible for any men to behave better than these did.

I must likewise mention Lieut. Colonel [Francis] Brooke of the 4th regiment, and Lieut. Colonel the Hon. G.[George] Carleton of the 44th, and Lieut. Colonel [George]Gray of the 30th, who was unfortunately killed. The 2nd Batt. 38th Regiment under Lieut. Colonel [John] Nugent, and the 15th Portuguese Regiment under Colonel Luiz do Rego, likewise performed their part in a very exemplary manner.

The officers and troops in the 3rd Division have distinguished themselves as usual in these operations. Lieut. General Picton has reported to me particularly the conduct of Lieut, Colonel Williams of the 60th, Lieut. Colonel [Henry] Ridge of the 5th, who was unfortunately killed in the assault of the castle; Lieut. Colonel [Thomas] Forbes of the 45th, Lieut. Colonel [John Forster] Fitzgerald of the 60th, Lieut. Colonel the Hon. R. Le P. Trench, and Lieut. Colonel [Russell] Manners of the 74th; Major William Henry Carr of the 83rd, and Major the Hon. H.[Hercules Robert] Pakenham, Assistant Adjutant General to the 3rd Division. He has likewise particularly reported the good conduct of Colonel [James] Campbell of the 94th, commanding Major General the Hon. Charles Colville's brigade, during his absence in command of the 4th Division, whose conduct I have so repeatedly had occasion to report to your Lordship.

The officers and men of the corps of engineers and artillery were equally distinguished during the operations of the siege and in its close.

Lieut. Colonel [Richard] Fletcher continued to direct the works, (notwithstanding that he was wounded in the sortie made by the enemy on the 19th of March,) which were carried on by Major [John] Squire and Major Burgoyne, under his directions. The former established the detachments under Major [James] Wilson, in the ravelin of San Roque, on the night of the storm; the latter attended the attack of the 3rd Division on the castle. I have likewise to report the good conduct of Major [John Thomas] Jones, Captain [William] Nicholas, and Captain [John Archer] Williams, of the Royal Engineers.

Major [Alexander] Dickson conducted the details of the artillery service during the siege, as well as upon former occasions, under the general superintendence of Colonel [Sir Haylett] Framingham, who, since the absence of Major General Borthwick, has commanded the artillery with the army.

I cannot sufficiently applaud the officers and soldiers of the Royal and Portuguese Artillery during the siege, particularly that of Lieut. Colonel [William] Robe, who opened the breaching batteries; Major [John] May, Captain [Robert] Gardiner, Major [Harcourt] Holcombe, and Lieut. [Daniel Macnamara] Bourchier of the Royal Artillery; Captain de Retberg of the German, and Major [Alexander] Tulloh of the Portuguese Artillery.

Adverting to the extent of the details of the ordnance department during this siege, to the difficulties of the weather, &c., with which Major Dickson had to contend, I must mention him most particularly to your Lordship.

The officers of the Adjutant and Quarter Master General's department rendered me every assistance on this occasion, as well as those of my personal Staff; and I have to add that I have received reports from the General Officers commanding divisions, of the assistance they received from the officers of those departments attached to them, the greatest number of whom, and of their personal Staff, are wounded.

In a former dispatch I reported to your Lordship the difficulties with which I had to contend, in consequence of the failure of the civil authorities of the province of Alentejo to perform their duty and supply the army with means of transport. These difficulties have continued to exist; but I must do Major General Victoria, the Governor of Elvas, the justice to report that he, and the troops under his command, have made every exertion, and have done every thing in their power to contribute to our success.

Marshal Soult left Seville on the 1st instant, with all the troops which he could collect in Andalusia; and he was in communication with the troops which had retired from Estremadura, under General Drouet, on the 3rd, and he arrived at Llcrena on the 4th. I had intended to collect the army on the Albuera rivulet, in proportion as Marshal Soult should advance; and I had requested Lieut. General Sir Thomas Graham to retire gradually upon Albuera, while Lieut. General Sir R. Hill should do the same on Talavera, from Don Benito,and the upper parts of the Guadiana.

I do not think it certain that Marshal Soult has made any decided movement from Llerena since the 4th, alhough he has patrolled forward with small detachments of cavalry, and the advanced guard of his infantry have been at Usagre.

None of the army of Portugal have moved to join him.

According to the last reports which I have received of the 4th instant, from the frontier of Castille, it appears that Marshal Marmont had established a body of troops between the Affueda and the Coa, and he had reconnoitred Almeida on the 3rd. Brig. General Trant's division of militia had arrived upon the Coa, and Brig. General Wilson's division was following with the cavalry, and Lieut. General the Conde d'Amarante was on his march, with a part of the corps under his command, towards the Douro.

It would be very desirable that I should have it in my power to strike a blow against Marshal Soult before he could be reinforced: but the Spanish authorities having omitted to take the necessary steps to provision Ciudad Rodrigo, it is absolutely necessary that I should return to the frontiers of Castille within a short period of time. It is not very probable that Marshal Soult will risk an action in the province of Estremadura, which it would not be difficult for him to avoid, and it is very necessary that he should return to Andalusia, as General Ballesteros was in movement upon Seville on the 29th of last month, and the Conde de Penne Villemur moving on the same place from the Lower Guadiana.

It will be quite impossible for me to go into Andalusia till I shall have secured Ciudad Rodrigo. I therefore propose to remain in the positions now occupied by the troops for some days; indeed a little time is required to take care of our wounded; and if Marshal Soult should remain in Estremadura I shall attack him; if he should retire into Andalusia, I must return to Castille.

I have the honor to enclose returns of the killed and wounded from the 31st March, and in the assault of Badajoz, and a return of the ordnance, small arms, and ammunition found in the place. I shall send the returns of provisions in the place by the next dispatch. This dispatch will be delivered to your Lordship by my aide de camp Captain [Charles Fox] Canning, whom I beg leave to recommend to your protection.

He has likewise the colors of the garrison, and the colors of the Hesse Darmstadt's regiment, to be laid at the feet of His Royal Highness the Prince Regent. The French battalions in the garrison had no eagles.

Return of the Killed, Wounded, and Missing, of the Army under the Command of General the Earl of Wellington, K.B., at the Siege and Capture of Badajoz, from the 18th March to 7th April, 1812, inclusive.

	Officers	Serjeants.	Rank and File	Horses	Total loss of Officers, Non-commissioned Officers, and Rank and File
Killed	72	51	912	–	1035
Wounded	306	216	3265	–	3787
Missing	–	1	62	–	63

The Portuguese loss is included in the above numbers

In the event Soult prudently looked to Andalucia, so Wellington marched north again and having satisfied himself as to the security of Cuidad Rodrigo, struck out for Salamanca and the army of Marshal Marmont. The city was soon liberated but the French at first proved more elusive before riposting with a counter-offensive, forcing the Allies to retreat once more towards Portugal. Marmont, however, overreached himself in his haste to bring Wellington to battle…

The Battle of Salamanca 22 July 1812[5]

My aide de camp, Captain [Robert Cotton St. John Trefusis] Lord Clinton, will present to your Lordship this account of a victory which the allied troops under my command gained in a general action, fought near Salamanca on the evening of the 22nd instant, which I have been under the necessity of delaying to send till now, having been engaged ever since the action in the pursuit of the enemy's flying troops.

In my letter of the 21st, I informed your Lordship that both armies were near the Tormes; and the enemy crossed that river, with the greatest part of his troops, in the afternoon, by the fords between Alba de Tormes and Huerta, and moved by their left towards the roads leading to Ciudad Rodrigo.

The allied army, with the exception of the 3rd Division, and General [Benjamin] D'Urban's cavalry, likewise crossed the Tormes in the evening by the bridge of Salamanca and the fords in the neighbourhood; and I placed the troops in a position, of which the right was upon one of the two heights called Dos Arapiles, and the left on the Tormes, below the ford of Sta Marta.

The 3rd Division, and Brig. General D'Urban's cavalry, were left at Cabrerizos, on the right of the Tormes, as the enemy had still a large corps on the heights above Babila-fuente, on the same side of the river; and I considered it not improbable that, finding our army prepared for them in the morning on the left of the Tormes, they would alter their plan, and manoeuvre by the other bank.

In the course of the night of the 21st, I received intelligence, of the truth of which 1 could not doubt, that General Clausel had arrived at Polios on the 20th, with the cavalry and horse artillery of the Army of the North, to join Marshal Marmont; and I was quite certain that these troops would join him on the 22nd or 23rd at latest.

There was no time to be lost therefore; and I determined that, if circumstances should not permit me to attack him on the 22nd, I would move towards Ciudad Rodrigo without further loss of time, as the difference of the numbers of cavalry might have made a march of manoeuvre, such as we have had for the last four or five days, very difficult, and its result doubtful.

During the night of the 21st, the enemy had taken possession of the village of Calvarassa de Arriba, and of the heights near it called Nuestra Senora de la Pefia, our cavalry being in possession of Calvarassa de Abaxo; and, shortly after daylight, detachments from both armies attempted to obtain possession of the more distant from our right of the two hills called Dos Arapiles.

The enemy, however, succeeded; their detachments being the strongest, and having been concealed in the woods nearer the hill than we were; by which success they strengthened materially their own position, and had in their power increased means of annoying ours.

In the morning, the light troops of the 7th Division, and the 4th Cacadores belonging to General Pack's brigade, were engaged with the enemy on the height called Nuestra Senora de la Pena, on which height they maintained themselves with the enemy throughout the day. The possession by the enemy, however, of the more distant of the Arapiles rendered it necessary for me to extend the right of the army en potence to the height behind the village of Arapiles, and to occupy that village with light infantry; and here I placed the 4th Division, under the command of Lieut. General the Hon. L. [Lowry] Cole: and although, from the variety of the enemy's movements, it was difficult to form a satisfactory judgment of his intentions, I considered that upon the whole his objects were upon the left of the Tormes. I therefore ordered Major General the Hon. E. [Edward] Pakenham, who commanded the 3rd Division in the absence of Lieut. General Picton, on account of ill health, to move across the Tormes with the troops under his command, including Brig. General D Urban's cavalry, and to place himself behind Aldea Tejada; Brig. General [Thomas] Bradford's brigade of Portuguese infantry, and Don Carlos de Espana's infantry, having been moved up likewise to the neighbourhood of Las Torres, between the 3rd and 4th divisions.

After a variety of evolutions and movements, the enemy appears to have determined upon his plan about two in the afternoon; and, under cover of a very heavy cannonade, which, however, did us but very little damage, he extended his left, and moved forward his troops, apparently with an intention to embrace, by the position of his troops, and by his fire, our post on that of the two Arapiles which we possessed, and from thence to attack and break our line, or, at all events, to render difficult any movement of ours to our right.

The extension of his line to his left, however, and its advance upon our right, notwithstanding that his troops still occupied very strong ground, and his position was well defended by cannon, gave me an opportunity of attacking him, for which I had long been anxious. I reinforced our right with the 5th Division, under Lieut. General Leith, which I placed behind the village of Arapiles, on the right of the 4th Division, and with the 6th and 7th divisions in reserve; and as soon as these troops had taken their station, I ordered Major General the Hon. E. Pakenham to move forward with the 3rd Division and General D'Urban's cavalry, and two squadrons of the 14th Light Dragoons, under Lieut. Colonel [Felton Elwell] Hervey, in four columns, to turn the enemy's left on the heights; while Brig. General Bradford's brigade, the 5th Division, under Lieut. General Leith, the 4th Division, under Lieut. General the Hon. L. Cole, and the cavalry under Lieut. General Sir Stapleton Cotton, should attack them in front, supported in reserve by the 6th Division, under Major General [Sir William Henry]

Clinton, the 7th, under Major General [John]Hope, and Don Carlos de Espana's Spanish division; and Brig. General [Denis] Pack should support the left of the 4th Division, by attacking that of the Dos Arapiles which the enemy held. The 1st and Light divisions occupied the ground on the left, and were in reserve.

The attack upon the enemy's left was made in the manner above described, and completely succeeded. Major General the Hon. E. Pakenham formed the 3rd Division across the enemy's flank, and overthrew every thing opposed to him. These troops were supported in the most gallant style by the Portuguese cavalry, under Brig. General D Urban, and Lieut. Colonel Hervey 's squadrons of the 14th, who successfully defeated every attempt made by the enemy on the flank of the 3rd Division.

Brig. General Bradford's brigade, the 5th and 4th divisions, and the cavalry under Lieut. General Sir Stapleton Cotton, attacked the enemy in front, and drove his troops before them from one height to another, bringing forward their right, so as to acquire strength upon the enemy's flank in proportion to the advance. Brig. General Pack made a very gallant attack upon the Arapiles, in which, however, he did not succeed, excepting in diverting the attention of the enemy's corps placed upon it from the troops under the command of Lieut. General Cole in his advance.

The cavalry under Lieut. General Sir Stapleton Cotton made a most gallant and successful charge against a body of the enemy's infantry, which they overthrew and cut to pieces. In this charge Major General [John Gaspard] Le Marchant was killed at the head of his brigade; and I have to regret the loss of a most able officer.

After the crest of the height was carried, one division of the enemy's infantry made a stand against the 4th Division, which, after a severe contest, was obliged to give way, in consequence of the enemy having thrown some troops on the left of the 4th Division, after the failure of Brig. General Pack's attack upon the Arapiles, and Lieut. General the Hon, L. Cole having been wounded.

Marshal Sir William Beresford, who happened to be on the spot, directed Brig. General [William Frederick] Spry's brigade of the 5th Division, which was in the second line, to change its front, and to bring its fire on the flank of the enemy's division; and, I am sorry to add that, while engaged in this service, he received a wound which I am apprehensive will deprive me of the benefit of his counsel and assistance for some time. Nearly about the same time Lieut. General Leith received a wound which unfortunately obliged him to quit the field. I ordered up the 6th Division, under Major General Clinton, to relieve the 4th, and the battle was soon restored to its former success.

The enemy's right, however, reinforced by the troops which had fled from his left, and by those which had now retired from the Arapiles, still continued to resist; and I ordered the 1st and Light divisions, and Colonel [Thomas William] Stubbs's Portuguese brigade of the 4th Division, which was reformed, and Major General William Anson's brigade, likewise of the 4th Division, to turn the right, while the 6th Division, supported by the 3rd and 5th, attacked the front. It was dark before this point was carried by the 6th Division; and the enemy fled through the woods towards the Tormes. I pursued them with the 1st and Light divisions, and Major General William Anson's brigade of the 4th Division, and some squadrons of cavalry under Lieut. General Sir Stapleton Cotton, as long as we could find any of them together, directing our march upon Huerta and the fords of the Tormes, by which the enemy had passed on their advance; but the darkness of the night was highly advantageous to the enemy, many of whom escaped under its cover who must otherwise have been in our hands.

I am sorry to report that, owing to this same cause, Lieut, General Sir Stapleton Cotton was unfortunately wounded by one of our own sentries after we had halted.

We renewed the pursuit at break of day in the morning with the same troops, and Major General Bock's[6] and Major General Anson's brigades of cavalry, which joined during the night; and, having crossed the Tormes, we came up with the enemy's rear of cavalry and infantry near La Serna. They were immediately attacked by the two brigades of dragoons, and the cavalry fled, leaving the infantry to their fate. I have never witnessed a more gallant charge than was made on the enemy's infantry by the heavy brigade of the King's German Legion, under Major General Bock, which was completely successful; and the whole body of infantry, consisting of three battalions of the enemy's 1st Division, were made prisoners.

The pursuit was afterwards continued as far as Penaranda last night, and our troops were still following the flying enemy.

Their head quarters were in this town, not less than ten leagues from the field of battle, for a few hours last night: and they are now considerably advanced on the road towards Valladolid, by Arevalo. They were joined yesterday on their retreat by the cavalry and artillery of the Army of the North, which have arrived at too late a period, it is to be hoped, to be of much use to them.

It is impossible to form a conjecture of the amount of the enemy's loss in this action; but, from all reports, it is very considerable. We have taken from them 11 pieces of cannon,* several ammunition waggons, 2 eagles, and 6 colors; and 1 General, 3 Colonels, 3 Lieut. Colonels, 130 officers of inferior rank, and between 6000 and 7000 soldiers are prisoners;† and our detachments are sending in more at every moment. The number of dead on the field is very large.

I am informed that Marshal Marmont is badly wounded, and has lost one of his arms; and that four General Officers have been killed, and several wounded.

Such an advantage could not have been acquired without material loss on our side; but it certainly has not been of a magnitude to distress the army, or to cripple its operations.

I have great pleasure in reporting to your Lordship that, throughout this trying day, of which I have related the events, I had every reason to be satisfied with the conduct of the General Officers and troops.

The relation which I have written of its events will give a general idea of the share which each individual had in them; and I cannot say too much in praise of the conduct of every individual in his station.

I am much indebted to Marshal Sir William Beresford for his friendly counsel and assistance, both previous to, and during the action; to Lieut. Generals Sir Stapleton Cotton, Leith, and Cole, and Major Generals Clinton, and the Hon. E. Pakenham, for the manner in which they led the divisions of cavalry and infantry under their command respectively; to Major General [Richard] Hulse, commanding a brigade in the 6th Division; Major General G. Anson, commanding a brigade of cavalry; Colonel [Samuel Venables] Hinde; Colonel the Hon. William Ponsonby, commanding Major General Le Marchant's brigade after the fall of that officer; to Major General W. Anson, commanding a brigade in the 4th Division; Major General [William Henry] Pringle, commanding a brigade in the 5th Division, and the division after Lieut. General [Sir James] Leith was wounded ; Brig. General [Thomas] Bradford; Brig. General Spry; Colonel Stubbs; and Brig. General Power, of the Portuguese service; likewise to Lieut. Colonel [James] Campbell of the

---

* The official returns only account for 11 pieces of cannon, but it is believed that 20 have fallen into our hands.

† The prisoners are supposed to amount to 7000; but it has not been possible to ascertain their number exactly, from the advance of the army immediately after the action was over.

94th, commanding a brigade in the 3rd Division; Lieut. Colonel [William] Williams of the 60th Foot ; Lieut. Colonel [John] Wallace of the 88th, commanding a brigade in the 3rd Division; Lieut. Colonel [Henry Walton] Ellis of the 23rd, commanding Major General the Hon. E. Pakenham's brigade in the 4th Division, during his absence in the command of the 3rd Division; Lieut. Colonel the Hon. C. [Charles John] Greville of the 38th Regiment, commanding Major General Hay's brigade in the 5th Division, during his absence on leave; Brig. General Pack; Brig. General the Conde de Rezende of the Portuguese service; Colonel [James Dawes] Douglas of the 8th Portuguese Regiment; Lieut. Colonel the Conde de Ficalho of the same regiment; and Lieut. Colonel [George Ridout] Bingham of the 53rd Regiment; likewise to Brig. General D'Urban and Lieut. Colonel Hervey of the 14th Light Dragoons; Colonel Lord Edward Somerset, commanding the 4th Dragoons; and Lieut. Colonel the Hon. F. [Frederick Cavendish] Ponsonby, commanding the 12th Light Dragoons.

I must also mention Lieut. Colonel [Alexander George] Woodford, commanding the light battalion of the brigade of Guards, who, supported by two companies of the Fusiliers, under the command of Captain [John] Crowder, maintained the village of Arapiles against all the efforts of the enemy, previous to the attack upon their position by our troops.

In a case in which the conduct of all has been conspicuously good, I regret that the necessary limits of a dispatch prevent me from drawing your Lordship's notice to the conduct of a larger number of individuals; but I can assure your Lordship that there was no officer or corps engaged in this action who did not perform his duty by his Sovereign and his country.

The Royal and German Artillery, under Lieut. Colonel [Haylett] Framingham, distinguished themselves by the accuracy of their fire wherever it was possible to use them; and they advanced to the attack of the enemy's position with the same gallantry as the other troops.

I am particularly indebted to Lieut. Colonel De Lancy, the Deputy Quarter Master General, the head of the department present, in the absence of the Quarter Master General, and to the officers of that department and of the Staff corps, for the assistance I received from them, particularly Lieut. Colonel the Hon. L. [Robert Lawrence] Dundas and Lieut. Colonel [Henry] Sturgeon of the latter, and Major [George] Scovell of the former; and to Lieut. Colonel [John] Waters, at present at the head of the Adjutant General's department at head quarters; and to the officers of that department, as well at head quarters as with the several divisions of the army; and Lieut. Colonel Lord Fitzroy Somerset, and the officers of my personal Staff. Among the latter I particularly request your Lordship to draw the attention of His Royal Highness the Prince Regent to His Serene Highness the Hereditary Prince of Orange, whose conduct in the field, as well as upon every other occasion, entitles him to my highest commendation and has acquired for him the respect and regard of the whole army.

I have had every reason to be satisfied with the conduct of the Mariscal de Campo Don Carlos de Espana, and of Brigadier Don Julian Sanchez, and with that of the troops under their command respectively; and with that of the Mariscal de Campo Don Miguel Alava, and of Brigadier Don Jose O'Lalor, employed with this army by the Spanish Government, from whom, and from the Spanish authorities and people in general, I received every assistance I could expect.

It is but justice likewise to draw your Lordship's attention upon this occasion to the merits of the officers of the civil departments of the army. Notwithstanding the increased distance of our operations from our magazines, and that the country is completely exhausted, we have hitherto wanted nothing, owing to the diligence and attention of the Commissary General Mr. Bissett, and the officers of the department under his direction.

I have likewise to mention that, by the attention and ability of Dr. M'Grigor, and of the officers of the department under his charge, our wounded, as well as those of the enemy, left in our hands, have been well taken care of; and I hope that many of these valuable men will be saved to the service.

Captain Lord Clinton will have the honor of laying at the feet of His Royal Highness the Prince Regent the eagles and colors taken from the enemy in this action.

I enclose a return of the killed and wounded.

Return of killed, wounded, and missing, of the allied army, in the battle near Salamanca, on the 22nd July 1812.

	Officers	Sergeants	R&F	Horses	Total	British	Port.	Spanish
Killed	41	28	625	114	694	388	304	2
Wounded	252	178	3840	133	4270	2714	1552	4
Missing	1	1	254	44	256	74	182	–

Wellington's great victory at Salamanca marked a turning point in the war. In the immediate term it facilitated the liberation of Madrid and although the campaign terminated disappointingly in a doomed attempt to capture the strategically important fortress of Burgos, the balance had decisively shifted in favour of the Allies. Moreover, Wellington himself had convincingly demonstrated that he was not only a consummate defensive fighter, but that he could attack as well. This was even more strongly under-scored when he marched out of Portugal for the last time in the following year to first turn the French out of a succession of defensive positions along the river-lines of northern Spain before utterly crushing them in the battle of Vittoria by orchestrating the advance of converging columns of troops:

The Battle of Vittoria 21 June 1813[7]

The enemy, commanded by King Joseph, having Marshal Jourdan as the Major General of the army, took up a position, on the night of the 19th instant, in front of Vitoria; the left of which rested upon the heights which end at La Puebla de Arganzon, and extended from thence across the valley of the Zadorra, in front of the village of Arinez. They occupied with the right of the centre a height which commanded the valley to the Zadorra. The right of their army was stationed near Vitoria, and was destined to defend the passages of the river Zadorra, in the neighbourhood of that city. They had a reserve in rear of their left, at the village of Gomecha. The nature of the country through which the army had passed since it had reached the Ebro, had necessarily extended our columns; and we halted on the 20th, in order to close them up, and moved the left to Murguia, where it was most likely it would be required. I reconnoitred the enemy's position on that day, with a view to the attack to be made on the following morning, if they should still remain in it.

We accordingly attacked the enemy yesterday, and I am happy to inform your Lordship, that the Allied army under my command gained a complete victory, having driven them from all their positions; having taken from them 151 pieces of cannon, waggons of ammunition, all their baggage, provisions, cattle, treasure, &c., and a considerable number of prisoners.

The operations of the day commenced by Lieut. General Sir Rowland Hill obtaining possession of the heights of La Puebla, on which the enemy's left rested, which heights they had not occupied in great strength. He detached for this service one brigade of the Spanish division under General Morillo;[8] the other brigade being employed in keeping the communication between his main body on the high road from Miranda to Vitoria, and the troops detached to the heights. The enemy, however, soon discovered the importance of these heights, and reinforced their troops there to such an extent, that Lieut. General Sir Rowland Hill was obliged to detach, first, the 71st regiment and the light infantry battalion of General [George Townshend] Walker's brigade, under the command of Lieut. Colonel the Hon. H. [Henry] Cadogan, and successively other troops to the same point; and the Allies not only gained, but maintained possession of these important heights throughout their operations, notwithstanding all the efforts of the enemy to retake them.

The contest here was, however, very severe, and the loss sustained considerable. General Morillo was wounded, but remained in the field; and I am concerned to have to report, that Lieut. Colonel the Hon. H. Cadogan has died of a wound which he received. In him His Majesty has lost an officer of great merit and tried gallantry, who had already acquired the respect and regard of the whole profession, and of whom it might have been expected that, if he had lived, he would have rendered the most important services to his country.

Under cover of the possession of these heights, Sir Rowland Hill successively passed the Zadorra, at La Puebla, and the defile formed by the heights and the river Zadorra, and attacked and gained possession of the village of Subijana de Alava, in front of the enemy's line, which the enemy made repeated attempts to regain.

The difficult nature of the country prevented the communication between our different columns moving to the attack from their stations on the river Bayas at as early an hour as I had expected; and it was late before I knew that the column, composed of the 3rd and 7th divisions, under the command of the Earl of Dalhousie, had arrived at the station appointed for them. The 4th and Light divisions, however, passed the Zadorra immediately after Sir Rowland Hill had possession of Subijana de Alava; the former at the bridge of Nanclares, and the latter at the bridge of Tres-puentes; and almost as soon as these had crossed, the column under the Earl of Dalhousie arrived at Mendoza; and the 3rd Division, under Lieut. General Sir Thomas Picton, crossed at the bridge higher up, followed by the 7th Division, under the Earl of Dalhousie. These four divisions, forming the centre of the army, were destined to attack the height on which the right of the enemy's centre was placed, while Lieut. General Sir Rowland Hill should move forward from Subijana de Alava to attack the left. The enemy, however, having weakened his line to strengthen his detachment on the hills/abandoned his position in the valley as soon as he saw our disposition to attack it, and commenced his retreat in good order towards Vitoria.

Our troops continued to advance in admirable order, notwithstanding the difficulty of the ground. In the mean time, Lieut. General Sir Thomas Graham, who commanded the left of the army, consisting of the 1st and 5th divisions, and General Pack's and Bradford's brigades of infantry, and General Bock's and Anson's of cavalry, and who had been moved on the 20th to Murguia, moved forward from thence on Vitoria, by the high road from that town to Bilbao. He had, besides, with him the Spanish division under Colonel Longa[9]; and General Giron[10], who had been detached to the left, under a different view of the state of affairs, and had afterwards been recalled, and had arrived on the 20th at Orduna, marched that morning from thence, so as to be in the field in readiness to support Lieut. General Sir Thomas Graham, if his support had been required.

The enemy had a division of infantry with some cavalry advanced on the great road from Vitoria to Bilbao, resting their right on some strong heights covering the village of Gamarra Mayor. Both Gamarra and Abechuco were strongly occupied as tetes de pont and the bridges over the Zadorra at these places. Brigadier General Pack with his Portuguese brigade, and Colonel Longa with his Spanish division, were directed to turn and gain the heights, supported by Major General Anson's brigade of light dragoons, and the 5th Division of infantry under the command of Major General Oswald, who was desired to take the command of all these troops.

Lieut. General Sir Thomas Graham reports, that in the execution of this service the Portuguese and Spanish troops behaved admirably. The 4th battalion of Cacadores, and the 8th Cacadores, particularly distinguished themselves. Colonel Longa being on the left, took possession of Gamarra Menor.

As soon as the heights were in our possession, the village of Gamarra Mayor was most gallantly stormed and carried by Major General [Frederick Philipse] Robinson's brigade of the 5th Division, which advanced in columns of battalions, under a very heavy fire of artillery and musketry, without firing a shot, assisted by two guns of Major [Robert] Lawson's brigade of artillery. The enemy suffered severely, and lost three pieces of cannon.

The Lieut. General then proceeded to attack the village of Abechuco with the 1st Division, by forming a strong battery against it, consisting of Captain [Saumaurez] Dubourdieu's brigade, and Captain [William Norman] Ramsay's troop of horse artillery; and under cover of this fire, Colonel [Colin] Halkett's brigade advanced to the attack of the village, which was carried; the light battalions having charged and taken three guns and a howitzer on the bridge. This attack was supported by General [Thomas] Bradford's brigade of Portuguese infantry.

During the operation at Abechuco the enemy made the greatest efforts to repossess themselves of the village of Gamarra Mayor, which were gallantly repulsed by the 5th Division, under the command of Major General Oswald. The enemy had, however, on the heights on the left of the Zadorra, two divisions of infantry in reserve; and it was impossible to cross by the bridges till the troops which had moved upon the enemy's centre and left had driven them through Vitoria.

The whole then co-operated in the pursuit, which was continued by all till after it was dark.

The movement of the troops under Lieut. General Sir Thomas Graham, and their possession of Gamarra and Abechuco, intercepted the enemy's retreat by the high road to France. They were then obliged to turn to the road towards Pamplona; but they were unable to hold any position for a sufficient length of time to allow their baggage and artillery to be drawn off. The whole, therefore, of the latter which had not already been taken by the troops in their attack of the successive positions taken up by the enemy in their retreat from their first position at Arifiez and on the Zadorra, and all their ammunition and baggage, and every thing they had were taken close to Vitoria. I have reason to believe that the enemy carried off with them one gun and one howitzer only.

The army under King Joseph consisted of the whole of the armies of the South, and of the Centre, and of four divisions and all the cavalry of the Army of Portugal, and some troops of the Army of the North. General Foy's division of the Army of Portugal was in the neighbourhood of Bilbao; and General Clausel, who commanded the Army of the North, was near Logrofio with one division of the Army of Portugal commanded by General Taupin, and General Van-der-Maesen's division of the Army of the North. The 6th Division of the allied army under Major General the Hon. E. Pakenham was likewise absent, having been detained at Medina de Pomar for three days, to cover the march of our magazines and stores.

I cannot extol too highly the good conduct of all the General Officers, Officers, and soldiers of the army in this action. Lieut. General Sir R. Hill speaks highly of the conduct of General Morillo and the Spanish troops under his command, and of that of Lieut. General the Hon. W. Stewart, and the Conde de Amarante[11], who commanded divisions of infantry under his directions. He likewise mentions the conduct of Colonel the Hon. R.

W. [Robert William] O'Callaghan, who maintained the village of Subijana de Alava against all the efforts of the enemy to regain possession of it, and that of Lieut. Colonel [John Charles] Rooke of the Adjutant General's department, and Lieut. Colonel the Hon. A. [Alexander] Abercromby of the Quarter Master General's department. It was impossible for the movements of any troops to be conducted with more spirit and regularity than those of their respective divisions, by Lieut. Generals the Earl of Dalhousie, Sir Thomas Picton, Sir Lowry Cole, and Major General Baron Charles Alten. The troops advanced in echelons of regiments in two, and occasionally three lines; and the Portuguese troops in the 3rd and 4th divisions, under the command of Brigadier General [Manly] Power and Colonel [Thomas William] Stubbs, led the march with steadiness and gallantry never surpassed on any occasion.

Major General the Hon. C. Colville's brigade of the 3rd Division was seriously attacked in its advance by a very superior force well formed, which it drove in, supported by General [William] Inglis's brigade of the 7th Division, commanded by Colonel [William] Grant of the 82nd. These officers and the troops under their command distinguished themselves.

Major General [John Ormsby] Vandeleur's brigade of the Light Division was, during the advance upon Vitoria, detached to the support of the 7th Division; and Lieut. General the Earl of Dalhousie has reported most favorably of its conduct. Lieut. General Sir Thomas Graham particularly reports his sense of the assistance he received from Colonel [William Howe] De Lancey, the Deputy Quarter Master General, and from Lieut. Colonel [Henry Frederick] Bouverie, of the Adjutant General's department, and from the officers of his personal staff; and from Lieut. Colonel the Hon. A. [Arthur Percy] Upton, Assistant Quarter Master General, and Major [James Archibald] Hope, Assistant Adjutant General, with the 1st Division; and Major General Oswald reports the same of Lieut. Colonel [George Henry Frederick] Berkeley of the Adjutant General's department, and Lieut. Colonel [William Maynard] Gomm of the Quarter Master General's department.

I am particularly indebted to Lieut. General Sir Thomas Graham, and to Lieut. General Sir Rowland Hill, for the manner in which they have respectively conducted the service entrusted to them since the commencement of the operations which have ended in the battle of the 21st; and for their conduct in that battle; as likewise to Marshal Sir W. Beresford for the friendly advice and assistance which I have received from him upon all occasions during the late operations.

I must not omit to mention likewise the conduct of General Giron, who commands the Galician army, who made a forced march from Orduna, and was actually on the ground in readiness to support Lieut. General Sir Thomas Graham.

I have frequently been indebted, and have had occasion to call the attention of your Lordship to the conduct of the Quarter Master General Sir George Murray, who in the late operations, and in the battle of the 21st of June, has again given the greatest assistance. I am likewise much indebted to Lord Aylmer, the Deputy Adjutant General, and to the officers of the departments of the Adjutant and Quarter Master General respectively; and also to Lord FitzRoy Somerset, and Lieut. Colonel [Colin] Campbell and those of my personal staff: and to Lieut. Colonel Sir Richard Fletcher, and the officers of the Royal Engineers.

Colonel his Serene Highness the Hereditary Prince of Orange was in the field as my aide de camp, and conducted himself with his usual gallantry and intelligence.

Mariscal de Campo, Don Luis Wimpffen, and the Inspector General Don Thomas O'Donoju, and the officers of the staff of the Spanish army have invariably rendered me every assistance in their power in the course of these operations; and I avail myself of this opportunity of expressing my satisfaction with their conduct; as likewise with that of Mariscal de Campo Don Miguel Alava; and of the Brig. General Don Jose O'Lalor, who have been so long and usefully employed with me.

The artillery was most judiciously placed by Lieut. Colonel [Alexander] Dickson, and was well served; and the army is particularly indebted to that corps.

The nature of the ground did not allow of the cavalry being generally engaged; but the General Officers commanding the several brigades kept the troops under their command respectively close to the infantry to support them, and they were most active in the pursuit of the enemy after they had been driven through Vitoria.

I send this dispatch by my aide de camp Captain [John] Fremantle, whom I beg leave to recommend to your Lordship's protection. He will have the honor of laying at the feet of His Royal Highness the colors of the 4th Batt. 100th Regiment, and Marshal Jourdan's baton of a Marshal of France taken by the 87th Regiment.

I enclose a return of the killed and wounded in the late operations, and a return of the ordnance, carriages, and ammunition taken from the enemy in the action of the 21st inst.[12]

Return of the killed, wounded and missing, of the Allied army at Vitoria, on the 21st June, 1813.

	Officers	Sergeants	R&F	Total	British	Spanish	Port.	Horses
Killed	33	19	688	740	501	89	150	92
Wounded	230	158	3782	4174	2807	464	899	68
Missing	-	1	265	266	-	-	-	26

1 serjeant, 2 drummers and 263 R. and F. have been returned missing by the several corps of the army, British and Portuguese. It is supposed that the greater number of them lost their regiments in the course of the night, and that very few of them have fallen into the hands of the enemy.[13]

The immediate result of this stunning victory was that Wellington was able to close up to the Pyrenees, where he was faced with the choice of attacking either Pamplona or San Sebastian. Lacking the resources to tackle both he opted to take the latter while merely blockading Pamplona. At the end of July the revived French, now commanded by Marshal Soult, attempted to force the passes through the mountains and relieve Pamplona, only to be stopped and beaten back in a series of hard-fought actions collectively known as the Battle of the Pyrenees. On 7 October the Allies crossed into France and by December, after now forgotten battles on the Nivelle and the Nive, were at Bayonne. The war had barely months still to run and after a fierce fight at Orthes on 27 February, Wellington closed in on Toulouse and the last battle.

The Battle of Toulouse 10 April 1814[14]

I have the pleasure to inform your Lordship that I entered this town this morning, which the enemy evacuated during the night, retiring by the road of Carcassone.

The continued fall of rain and the state of the river prevented me from laying the bridge till the morning of the 8th, when the Spanish corps and the Portuguese artillery, under the immediate orders of Lieut. General Don Manuel Freyrc, and the head quarters, crossed the Garonne.

We immediately moved forward to the neighbourhood of the town ; and the 18th Hussars, under the immediate command of Colonel [Richard Hussey] Vivian, had an opportunity of making a most gallant attack upon a superior body of the enemy's cavalry, which they drove through the village of Croix d'Orade, and took about 100 prisoners, and gave us possession of an important bridge over the river Ers, by which it was necessary to pass, in order to attack the enemy's position. Colonel Vivian was unfortunately wounded upon this occasion; and I am afraid that I shall lose the benefit of his assistance for some time.

The town of Toulouse is surrounded on three sides by the canal of Languedoc and the Garonne. On the left of that river, the suburb, which the enemy had fortified with strong field works in front of the ancient wall, formed a good tete de pont. They had likewise formed a tete de pont at each bridge of the canal, which was besides defended by the fire in some places of musketry, and in all of artillery from the ancient wall of the town. Beyond the canal to the eastward, and between that and the river Ers, is a height which extends as far as Montaudran, and over which pass all the approaches to the canal and town from the eastward, which it defends; and the enemy, in addition to the tetes de pont on the bridges of the canal, had fortified this height with five redoubts, connected by lines of entrenchments, and had, with extraordinary diligence, made every preparation for defence. They had likewise broken all the bridges over the Ers within our reach, by which the right of their position could be approached. The roads, however, from the Arriege to Toulouse being impracticable for cavalry or artillery, and nearly so for infantry, as reported in my dispatch to your Lordship of the 1st instant, I had no alternative, excepting to attack the enemy in this formidable position.

It was necessary to move the pontoon bridge higher up the Garonne, in order to shorten the communication with Lieut. General Sir Rowland Hill's corps, as soon as the Spanish corps had passed; and this operation was not effected till so late an hour on the 9th as to induce me to defer the attack till the following morning.

The plan, according to which I determined to attack the enemy, was for Marshal Sir William Beresford, who was on the right of the Ers with the 4th and 6th divisions, to cross that river at the bridge of Croix d' Grade, to gain possession of Montblanc, and to march up the left of the Ers to turn the enemy's right, while Lieut. General Don Manuel Freyre, with the Spanish corps under his command, supported by the British cavalry, should attack the front. Lieut. General Sir Stapleton Cotton was to follow the Marshal's movement with Major General Lord Edward Somerset's brigade of hussars; and Colonel Vivian's brigade, under the command of Colonel Arentschildt, was to observe the movements of the enemy's cavalry on both banks of the Ers beyond our left.

The 3rd and Light divisions, under the command of Lieut. General Sir Thomas Picton and Major General Charles Baron Alten, and the brigade of German cavalry, were to observe the enemy on the lower part of the canal, and to draw their attention to that quarter by threatening the tetes de pont, while Lieut. General Sir Rowland Hill was to do the same on the suburb on the left of the Garonne.

Marshal Sir William Beresford crossed the Ers, and formed his corps in three columns of lines in the village of Croix d'Orade, the 4th Division leading, with which he immediately carried Montblanc. He then moved up the Ers in the same order, over most difficult ground, in a direction parallel to the enemy's fortified position; and as soon as he reached the point at which he turned it, he formed his lines and moved to the attack. During these operations, Lieut. General Don Manuel Freyre moved along the left of the Ers to the front of Croix d'Orade, where he formed his corps in two lines with a reserve on a height in front of the left of the enemy's position, on which height the Portuguese artillery was placed; and Major General Ponsonby's brigade of cavalry in reserve in the rear.

As soon as formed, and that it was seen that Marshal Sir William Beresford was ready, Lieut. General Don Manuel Freyre moved forward to the attack. The troops marched in good order, under a very heavy fire of musketry and artillery, and showed great spirit, the General and all his Staff being at their head; and the two lines were soon lodged under some banks immediately under the enemy's entrenchments; the reserve and Portuguese artillery, and British cavalry, continuing on the height on which the troops had first formed. The enemy, however, repulsed the movement of the right of General Freyre's line round their left flank; and having followed up their success, and turned our right by both sides of the high road leading from Toulouse to Croix d'Orade, they soon compelled the whole corps to retire. It gave me great satisfaction to see that, although they suffered considerably in retiring, the troops rallied again as soon as the Light Division, which was immediately on their right, moved up; and I cannot sufficiently applaud the exertions of Lieut. General Don Manuel Freyre, the officers of the Staff of the 4th Spanish Army, and of the officers of the General Staff, to rally and form them again.

Lieut. General Mendizabal, who was in the field as a volunteer, General Ezpeleta, and several officers of the Staff and chiefs of corps, were wounded upon this occasion; but General Mendizabal continued in the field. The Regiment de Tiradores de Cantabria, under the command of Colonel Leon de Sicilia, kept its position, under the enemy's entrenchments, until I ordered it to retire.

In the mean time, Marshal Sir William Beresford, with the 4th division, under the command of Lieut. General Sir Lowry Cole, and the 6th Division, under the command of Lieut. General Sir Henry Clinton, attacked and carried the heights on the enemy's right, and the redoubt which covered and protected that flank; and he lodged those troops on the same height with the enemy; who were, however, still in possession of four redoubts, and of the entrenchments and fortified houses.

The badness of the roads had induced the Marshal to leave his artillery in the village of Montblanc; and some time elapsed before it could be brought to him, and before Lieut. General Don Manuel Freyre's corps could be reformed and brought back to the attack. As soon as this was effected the Marshal continued his movement along the ridge, and carried, with General Pack's brigade of the 6th Division, the two principal redoubts and fortified houses in the enemy's centre. The enemy made a desperate effort from the canal to regain these redoubts, but they were repulsed with considerable loss; and the 6th Division continuing its movement along the ridge of the height, and the Spanish troops continuing a corresponding movement upon the front, the enemy were driven from the two redoubts and entrenchments on the left; and the whole range of heights were in our possession. We did not gain this advantage, however, without severe loss; particularly in the brave 6th Division. Lieut. Colonel [James] Coghlan of the 61st, an officer of great merit and promise, was unfortunately killed in the attack of the heights. Major General [Denis] Pack was wounded, but was enabled to remain in the field; and Colonel [James Dawes] Douglas, of the 8th Portuguese Regiment, lost his leg; and I am afraid that I shall be deprived for a considerable time of his assistance.

The 36th, 42nd, 79th, and 61st, lost considerable numbers, and were highly distinguished throughout the day.

I cannot sufficiently applaud the ability and conduct of Marshal Sir William Beresford throughout the operations of the day; nor that of Lieut. Generals Sir Lowry Cole, Sir Henry Clinton, Major Generals Pack and Lambert, and the troops under their command. Marshal Sir William Beresford particularly reports the good conduct of Brigadier General D'Urban, the Quarter Master General, and General Brito Mozinho, the Adjutant General to the Portuguese army.

The 4th Division, although exposed on their march along the enemy's front to a galling fire, were not so much engaged as the 6th, and did not suffer so much; but they conducted themselves with their usual gallantry.

I had also every reason to be satisfied with the conduct of Lieut. General Don Manuel Freyre, Lieut. General Don Gabriel Mendizabal, Mariscal de Campo Don Pedro Barcenas, Brigadier General Don J. de Ezpeleta, Mariscal de Campo Don A. Garccs de Marcilla, and the Chief of the Staff Don E. S. Salvador, and the Officers of the Staff of the 4th Army. The officers and troops conducted themselves well in all the attacks which they made subsequent to their being re-formed.

The ground not having admitted of the operations of the cavalry, they had no opportunity of charging.

While the operations above detailed were going on, on the left of the army, Lieut. General Sir Rowland Hill drove the enemy from their exterior works in the suburb, on the left of the Garonne, within the ancient wall. Lieut. General Sir Thomas Picton likewise, with the 3rd Division, drove the enemy within the tete de pont on the bridge of the canal nearest to the Garonne; but the troops having made an effort to carry it they were repulsed, and some loss was sustained. Major General [Thomas] Brisbane was wounded; but I hope not so as to deprive me for any length of time of his assistance; and Lieut. Colonel [Thomas] Forbes, of the 45th, an officer of great merit, was killed.

The army being thus established on three sides of Toulouse, I immediately detached our light cavalry to cut off the communication by the only road practicable for carriages which remained to the enemy, till I should be enabled to make arrangements to establish the troops between the canal and the Garonne.

The enemy, however, retired last night, leaving in our hands General Harispe, General Baurot, General St. Hilaire, and 1600 prisoners. One piece of cannon was taken on the field of battle; and others, and large quantities of stores of all descriptions, in the town.

Since I sent my last report, I have received an account from Rear Admiral Penrose of the successes in the Gironde of the boats of the squadron under his command.

Lieut. General the Earl of Dalhousie crossed the Garonne nearly about the time that Admiral Penrose entered the river, and pushed the enemy's parties under General Lhuillier beyond the Dordogne. He then crossed the Dordogne on the 4th, near St. Andre de Cubzac, with a detachment of the troops under his command, with a view to the attack of the fort of Blaye. His Lordship found General Lhuillier and General Desbareaux posted near Etauliers, and made his disposition to attack them, when they retired, leaving about 300 prisoners in his hands. I enclose the Earl of Dalhousie's report of this affair.

In the operations which I have now reported, 1 have had every reason to be satisfied with the assistance I received from the Quarter Master and

Adjutant General, and the officers of those departments respectively; from Mariscal de Campo Don Luis Wimpffen and the officers of the Spanish Staff, and from Mariscal de Campo Don Miguel Alava; from Colonel Dickson, commanding the allied artillery; and from Lieut. Colonel Lord FitzRoy Somerset and the officers of my personal staff.

I send this dispatch by my aide de camp, Major Lord William Russell, whom I beg leave to recommend to your Lordship's protection.

Return of the killed, wounded and missing, of the Allied army at the battle of Toulouse, 10th April, 1814.

	Officers	Sergeants	R&F	Total	British	Spanish	Port.	Horses
Killed	31	21	543	595	312	205	78	62
Wounded	248	123	3675	4046	1795	1722	529	59
Missing	3	-	15	18	17	1	-	2

The End

Wellington to Lieut. General Sir John Hope, K.B. Toulouse, 16 April, 1814.[15]
I have been so much, occupied since I entered this town on the 12th instant, that I have not had leisure to write to you; and I am apprehensive that you will not have heard of the great events that have occurred. I will therefore give you an account of them in the order of their occurrence.

We beat Marshal Soult on the 10th, in the strong position which he took to maintain his position in Toulouse. The 11th was spent in reconnaissances towards the road of Carcassone, and in the arrangements to be adopted for shutting him in Toulouse entirely. The 11th at night he evacuated the town and marched by the road of Carcassone.

We entered the town about noon, and found the white flag flying, every body wearing white cockades, Buonaparte's statue thrown out of the window of the Capitol, and the eagles pulled down, &c...

In the afternoon Colonel Cooke and Colonel St. Simon arrived from Paris; the former sent by His Majesty's Minister with the King of Prussia to apprise me, and the latter sent by the Provisional Government of France to apprise Marshal Soult of the events which had occurred in the capital to the night of the 7th, when they quitted it.

Shortly after the entry of the allies, the Emperor Alexander published a proclamation, in which he declared the determination of the allies not to make peace with Buonaparte. The Senate immediately assembled, and decreed la Decheance [*forfeiture*] de Buonaparte; a Provisional Government has been appointed; and a constitution has been framed, under which Louis XVIII. is called to the throne of his ancestors; and Buonaparte has abdicated, accepting an establishment in the island of Elba, and a pension of 6,000,000 of litres, of which half for himself and the remainder for his family...

In consequence of these events, and finding that the allies had agreed with the Provisional Government for a suspension of hostilities, I have had with Marshal Soult a correspondence, of which I enclose you the copies, intending, if he should declare his submission to the Provisional Government, and to the constitution of the 6th April, to agree to a suspension of hostilities with him. But you will see, from his last letter, that he does not submit to that Government; the reason for which he stated to Colonel Gordon to be, that he could not give entire credit to Colonel St. Simon; and that he wished to have time to receive from some of the ministers of Napoleon an account of the events which had occurred. He was informed, however, both by Colonel Cooke and Colonel St. Simon, that they had been stopped at Blois by the gendarmerie attending the court of the Empress; and that, having been brought before the Minister at War, the Due de Feltre, this person had backed their passports in order that their mission might not be interrupted; at the same time declaring that his functions had ceased with the government of his late Sovereign. The conduct of Marshal Soult, therefore, can be considered in no other light than as prolonging the miseries of war without an object, excepting that of promoting a civil war in the country.

The garrison and corps of troops posted at Montauban, under the command of General Loverdo, having submitted to the Provisional Government, I have concluded a treaty to suspend hostilities with them; and I march tomorrow to follow Marshal Soult, and to prevent his army from becoming the noyau of a civil war in France.

I recommend to you to send this letter and all its enclosures to the Governor of Bayonne, in order that he may be made acquainted with the state of affairs at Paris and elsewhere in France; and that he may choose the line he will adopt. If he will acknowledge the Provisional Government, I have no objection to allow of a suspension of hostilities at Bayonne.

Wellington to Earl Bathurst, Toulouse, 19 April, 1814.[16]
On the evening of the 12th instant Colonel Cooke arrived from Paris to inform me of the events which had occurred in that city to the night of the 7th instant. He was accompanied by Colonel St. Simon, who was directed

by the Provisional Government of France to apprise Marshal Soult and Marshal Suchet of the same events.

Marshal Soult did not at first consider the information to be so authentic as to induce him to send his submission to the Provisional Government, but he proposed that I should consent to a suspension of hostilities to give him time to ascertain what had occurred; but I did not think it proper to acquiesce in this desire. I enclose the correspondence which passed on this occasion.

In the mean time I concluded on the 15th a convention for the suspension of hostilities with the General Officer commanding at Montauban, of which I enclose a copy; and the troops being prepared for moving forward, they marched on the 16th and the 1 7th towards Castelnaudary.

I sent forward on the 16th another officer who had been sent from Paris to Marshal Soult, and I received from him the following day the letter of which I enclose the copy, brought by the General of Division Comte Gazan, who informed me, as indeed appears by the Marshal's letter, that he had acknowledged the Provisional Government of France.

I therefore authorised Major General Sir George Murray and Mariscal de Campo Don Luis Wimpffen to arrange with General Gazan a convention for the suspension of hostilities between the allied armies under my command and the French armies under the command of Marshals Soult and Suchet, of which I enclose a copy.

This convention has been confirmed by Marshal Soult, though I have not yet received the final ratifications, as he waits for that of Marshal Suchet.

This General, apprehending that there might be some delay in the arrangement of the convention with Marshal Soult, has in the mean time sent here Colonel Ricard, of the Staff of his army, to treat for a convention for the suspension of hostilities with the army under his immediate command; and I have directed Major General Sir George Murray and the Mariscal de Campo Don Luis Wimpffen to agree to the same articles with this officer to which I had before agreed, as relating to the army under Marshal Suchet, with Comte Gazan.

British Officers mentioned in Wellington's Dispatches

This appendix contains outline biographies for all, or very nearly all, of the British officers mentioned or otherwise referred to in Wellington's various memoranda of operations and the associated dispatches printed here. Occasionally information on some individuals is sparse, but at the very least a basic career history is given, and to better understand it a brief explanation of the Army's structure and mechanics will be helpful.

The basic regimental structure was straightforward enough but naturally contained more than a few quirks. At the outset of the wars in 1793 infantry regiments normally comprised a single battalion of 10 companies, each of them commanded by a captain, seconded by a lieutenant, and at the bottom of the pile an ensign, who might instead be termed a second lieutenant in Fusilier and Rifle regiments, although there was no real difference between the two. The Footguards, considering themselves superior to the rest of creation, not only had more companies, but promoted their officers above those of ordinary regiments. A captain in the Footguards ranked as a lieutenant colonel in the army, while a lieutenant was similarly styled a Lieutenant and Captain. They did however have the sense to recognise that a newly commissioned ensign in the Footguards was as useless as one in the Line and so refrained from promoting them as well. Regimentally these apparent conceits made no practical difference; a captain was still no more than a company commander but, allied with the fact that there were more than enough Footguards companies available for actual service this system of dual rank meant that in addition to the battalions formed for service in the field, there was also a sizeable pool of senior officers belonging to the Footguards available for extra-regimental duty either on the staff or for special duties.

Returning to regiments of the Line; at the outset of the wars three of the 10 company commanders were also field officers, that is the colonel, lieutenant colonel and major. The first of these was of course a great man, and unless designated a colonel or lieutenant colonel commandant did not actually lead it on service. As his lieutenant was consequently in permanent charge of the company his efforts were rewarded with the dual title of captain-lieutenant or more properly captain-lieutenant and captain.[1]

It was also common for either or even both of the other field officers to be on detached duty and consequently on 1 September 1795 an additional lieutenant colonel and major were added to each battalion. (In practice there were rarely if ever four field officers on parade and the additional posts were really convenient billets for officers employed elsewhere). Then, on 27 May 1803 another circular from Horse Guards relieved the field officers of all duties as company commanders and added three captains to the establishment to take their places, abolishing the rank of captain-lieutenant in the process.

At the same time an increasing number of regiments acquired additional battalions although the process was inconsistent. Some units such as the 1st (Royal) Regiment had two battalions in the eighteenth century, but to all intents and purposes they were independent of each other. Now, created from the short-lived Battalions of Reserve, the new Second Battalions were intended to have a dual role as home defence units and as a depot for the service battalion. In practice it never worked so neatly and the Second Battalions frequently found themselves ordered abroad. What is relevant in term of officers' career paths is that in theory the junior officers in each grade were invariably posted to the Second Battalion while the seniors served in the First Battalion. This in turn meant that should say a lieutenant serving in the First Battalion be promoted he would be posted home as a captain into the Second Battalion.[2]

Cavalry regiments (including the Household ones) had a very similar structure, though the number of troops (as companies were designated) varied and included at least one and often two designated as a depot, which of course remained at home. As for the officers; junior subalterns were termed cornets rather than ensigns.

---

1 As such although ranking as the senior lieutenant he was by courtesy addressed as captain and on promotion took precedence among his peers according to the date of his original appointment as captain-lieutenant rather than his full captaincy.

2 There was obviously a degree of flexibility in that it was usually desirable for him to continue serving with the First Battalion until the senior captain from the First Battalion came out to fill the original vacancy. There was often an unfortunate sequel in that when the second battalions were disbanded in 1814 all their officers were placed on half pay irrespective of their actual seniority.

The Royal Artillery on the other hand was organised into battalions only for accountancy purposes and on service the companies acted independently. There was at this time an entirely separate Corps of Drivers and when serving in the field an artillery company would be linked with a company of drivers, as a "brigade" under the overall command of the gunner officer. The requirement for a much higher proportion of trained officers to ordinary artillerymen also meant that there was a captain-lieutenant in each company until 19 July 1804 when they became second captains.

Whatever the branch of service, all steps in rank were incremental and an officer had to pass through each in turn.[3] Seniority played a greater role in promotion than is commonly recognised, but in theory at least, except in the Royal Artillery and Royal Engineers (where promotion was indeed ruled entirely by seniority), it revolved around the purchase system; that is an aspiring hero could purchase his first commission and any subsequent promotions up to and including the rank of lieutenant colonel.[4] In practice

---

3 This did not apply to the rank of captain-lieutenant, except in the Royal Artillery. As the senior lieutenant in an infantry regiment he was automatically entitled to succeed to any free vacancy for a captaincy, however an ordinary lieutenant did not need to pass through that rank before purchasing a captaincy.

4 The purchase system like so much else in the Georgian Army is more frequently condemned than understood. While it was obviously open to abuse there was nothing unique in expecting a man to purchase or rather invest into his profession, whether he was a soldier, doctor, lawyer or any other professional – or for that matter to entre into an apprenticeship or acquire a share in a business. The prices paid for commissions is also deceptive. In the 1790s the regulated price of an ensign's commission was £400 and leaving aside the various clerks' fees and agents' fees that was exactly what it cost him. The next step, a lieutenant's commission was valued at £500 but in this case all that was actually paid was the "difference" of £100 and then with a captaincy valued at £1,500 he actually needed to find only £1,000 to purchase his company. On retirement, the full value was then achieved by reversing the process and receiving £1,000 from his successor, and £500 from those moving up behind him. This would then be sufficient to invest in an annuity which would provide a suitable pension. If he was unable to do so, because he had not purchased his commissions, he might instead retire on the Half Pay. Although it might appear cumbersome all the necessary transactions and paperwork were handled for him by the regimental agent, who could also arrange exchanges between the various units in their portfolio of clients.

Hand in hand with purchase was the Half Pay establishment, which again is little understood. While officers ordinarily expected to fund their retirement by realising the money which they had invested in their commissions, it was obviously impossible to find buyers for those commissions if their regiment was disbanded on the happy outbreak of peace. Consequently, surplus regiments were instead "reduced" to a cadre

this was usually unnecessary, since free commissions were virtually to be had for the asking providing the aspirant wasn't choosy about his destination. In 1810 only 19.5 percent of first commissions had been purchased and these accounted for 44 per cent of ensigns in the Footguards and 47 per cent of cavalry cornets. Moreover, in the 1800s it has been estimated that some 10 per cent of newly commissioned subalterns had previously served in the ranks, exclusive of those posted to Royal Veteran battalions, who were invariably ex-NCOs. Nor were commissions heritable property and consequently the death of an officer invariably created a free vacancy, filled by the most senior man in the rank below.

Once they reached the rank of captain, whether by purchase or otherwise, officers could also be promoted by brevet, conferring rank "in the Army", independent of their regimental status. This could be conferred individually as a reward for particular merit, or in order to give an officer the necessary seniority to command a mixed detachment or outpost. Frequently however it was indiscriminate; most famously in the case of the Victory Brevet of 1814 which advanced all those officers who had been serving since 1803. All general officers were promoted by brevet since their rank was again "in the Army" and ordinarily regimental rank was relinquished, while colonelcies of regiments were sinecures in the gift of the Crown.[5]

Staff Officers

In outline, the broader command and control of the Army was equally straightforward. Armies were commonly commanded in the field by

---

of officers who were then granted a pension referred to as Half pay. At this point some officers accepted their pension and faded away, but every encouragement was given to a two-way traffic whereby officers wishing to continue in service could exchange with officers in other corps who did need to retire but who were unable to sell out because their own commissions had not been purchased. Ordinary wastage within these phantom regiments also resulted in vacancies allowing officers to be placed on half pay temporarily for various reasons, such as taking up a staff appointment, or indeed for personal reasons.

5 Promotion of general officers was supposedly governed entirely by seniority, so that in order to promote a particular officer from say the rank of major general to lieutenant general (usually in order to give him the necessary seniority to take up a particular appointment) it was also necessary to promote all those officers senior to him at the same time – although there was no obligation to find employment for any of them!

lieutenant generals, while brigades were led by major generals or brigadier generals – the latter being a temporary appointment, not a rank, usually held by a colonel. The creation of permanent divisions required lieutenant generals to lead them and increasingly brigades fell to major generals rather than to brigadiers, although there was obviously a considerable amount of acting up. In order to assist them in their duties, major generals were allowed one aide de camp (ADC) maintained at public expense, while lieutenant generals had two and full generals three. General officers commanding armies were also allowed a military secretary to handle their paperwork and accounts. These were permanent staff appointments and the holders were required to relinquish regimental rank for its duration, and in the meantime "retire" on to Half Pay, in order that their parent battalions should not suffer by their absence. This official allotment was wholly inadequate of course on active service and in practice generals were also assisted not only by "Extra ADCs" temporarily seconded from convenient regiments[6], but by a whole host of permanent or departmental staff officers as well.

Aside from a general's personal assistants, the Army's staff was in fact divided between two principal departments; those of the Adjutant General and the Quartermaster General. The precise parameters of their respective responsibilities and indeed their primacy depended to a very considerable extent upon the men responsible for running them. Broadly speaking however in Wellington's Peninsular army, the Adjutant General's department was responsible for routine matters such as discipline, the collection of returns and the issue and implementation of regulations and standing orders. The Quartermaster General's department on the other hand was largely presided over in the Peninsula by the very capable George Murray and under his direction it was given, or at least abrogated to itself responsibility for the actual conduct of operations and everything necessary to facilitate them; including but by no means limited to the quartering or accommodation of the army, its movements and its transportation. Accordingly, the department became concerned with the reconnoitring and where necessary the improvement of the roads and bridges which the army would pass over and by a further logical extension of this function, reconnoitring of the enemy as well, maintaining contact with allied forces, including the Spanish guerrillas, and then preparing intelligence summaries

---

6 A surprising number of whom nominally belonged to one or other of the West India regiments!

based on the knowledge thus gained – most of which had traditionally fallen within the purview of the Adjutant General.[7]

To help the Adjutant General and Quartermaster General in the execution of their multitudinous duties they normally had two assistants apiece – lieutenant colonels or majors - conventionally designated by their initials as AAG (Assistant Adjutant General) and AQMG (Assistant Quartermaster General) respectively. At the next level down came their deputies – usually captains, or even subalterns – again referred to by their initials as DAAGs and DAQMGs.

This matrix was duplicated within the divisions with a small administrative staff assigned to each, comprising an Assistant Adjutant General and an Assistant Quartermaster General with a deputy apiece. Individual brigades however had to make do with the commander's ADCs and a single permanent staff officer, (usually in the shape of a captain), serving as brigade major.

The Officers

Hon. Alexander Abercromby (1784-1853)
Fourth and youngest son of Sir Ralph Abercromby, born 4 March 1784. Entered army as volunteer 100th (Gordon) Highlanders 1799. Served Helder 1799, Ferrol 1800 then Gibraltar and Egypt. ADC to Sir John Moore in Sicily, lieutenant colonel on staff Canada 28 January 1808 as Inspecting Field Officer of Militia. Served in Peninsula; Talavera, Busaco, temporarily commanded brigade at Albuera, later at Arroyo de Molinos and Almaraz. AQMG 4 February 1813 and attached to 6th Division, then temporarily to 2nd Division April to October 1813. Afterwards on leave until 16 January

---

7 The Quartermaster General even had his very own troops in the shape of the Royal Staff Corps. This comprised two branches. The first carried out a variety of functions which would later fall to the Royal Engineers. However at this period the RE were wholly concerned with the construction, maintenance and occasional destruction of fortified places, while Royal Staff Corps officers on the other hand looked after the more mundane but no less necessary jobs of building, maintaining and improving roads, bridges and the like – and even running the post office. The rank and file of the Corps were employed as gangers to oversee navvying work carried out by ordinary infantrymen or more commonly locally hired labourers. There was also a mounted detachment, initially known as the Corps of Staff Guides, and later as the Royal Staff Corps Cavalry, who were largely comprised of foreign mercenaries, and as their early title suggests primarily served as scouts and guides.

1814 when attached to 7th Division. Served at Vittoria, Pyrenees and Orthez. AQMG at Quatre Bras and wounded at Waterloo. Died 27 August 1853.

Commissions: cornet 2nd Dragoons 16 August 1799; lieutenant 52nd Foot 19 March 1800; captain 23rd Fusiliers 21 May 1801; major 100th Foot 17 July 1806 but exch. 81st Foot 7 January 1807; lieutenant colonel 28th Foot 10 December 1808; colonel (brevet) 4 June 1814; captain and lieutenant colonel Coldstream 25 July 1814.

> WO25/744 f17; WO25/3998; Dalton S. *Waterloo Roll Call,* (2nd Edn. London 1904); Hart, *New Annual Army List (1840); Oxford Dictionary of National Biography* (ODNB); Ward S.P.G. *Wellington's Headquarters* (Oxford UP 1957)

Sir Wroth Palmer Acland (1770-1816)
Son of Arthur Palmer Acland of Fairfield, Somerset born 16 March 1770. Embarked for Sir Charles Grey's expedition to the West Indies 1794 as a captain in the 3rd Foot but transferred instead to Lord Moira's French expedition and served on Jersey and in Flanders. Embarked once again for West Indies in 1796 but went to Madras instead before returning to England 1799 on grounds of ill-health which plagued him for the rest of his life. Brigadier Eastern District Staff 1804 but joined Sir James Craig's staff in Mediterranean in March 1805, fought at Maida then to South America with Whitelocke, before returning the Eastern District staff December 1807. Commanded Harwich contingent at Vimeiro, before returning home due to ill-health and taking part in Walcheren expedition 1809. Thereafter held a variety of home appointments, possibly because unfit for further service abroad. Died at Bath 8 March 1816.

Commissions: ensign 17th Foot 25 April 1787; lieutenant 4 June 1790; captain Independent Company 24 January 1792, half pay June 1791; exchanged to 3rd Foot 2 March 1793; major 19th Foot 19 March 1795, exchanged to the Coldstream Guards 10 May 1800; colonel (brevet) 25 September 1803; major general 1810; lieutenant general 4 June 1814.

> WO25/744; WO25/3998; McGuigan & Burnham *Wellington's Brigade Commanders* (Barnsley 2017)

John Henry Algeo (k.1813)
Served in Peninsula with Portuguese Army 1810-1813. Wounded at Badajoz and killed in action at the crossing of the Bidasoa October 1813.

Commissions: ensign 34th Foot 6 April 1797; lieutenant 54th Foot 3 July 1800, half pay 25 June 1802; lieutenant 14th Foot 25 December 1802; captain 34th

Foot 23 May 1805; major (staff Portugal) 26 September 1811.
> WO25/3998; Hall, John A. *The Biographical Dictionary of British Officers killed and wounded 1808-1814*

George Anson (1769-1849)

Second son of George Anson and Mary Vernon, born 12 August 1769. Served Jamaica 1792-1797 and Den Helder 1799. Went to Portugal 1809 as colonel 16th Light Dragoons, but on promotion to brigadier general was given first an infantry brigade and then a cavalry one which he commanded until 1813, when he obtained an appointment on the home staff. Died as Governor of Chelsea Hospital 4 November 1849.

Commissions: cornet 16th Light Dragoons 3 May 1786; lieutenant 16 March 1891; lieutenant 20th Light Dragoons 20 January 1792; captain 9 September 1792; major 25 December 1794; major 16th Light Dragoons 15 June 1797; lieutenant colonel 20th Light Dragoons 21 December 1797; lieutenant colonel 15th Light Dragoons 6 September 1798; colonel (brevet) 1 January 1805; lieutenant colonel 16th Light Dragoons 12 December 1805; major general 25 July 1810; lieutenant general 12 August 1819; general 10 January 1837.
> WO25/3998; Hart (1840); McGuigan & Burnham

Robert Anstruther (1768-1809)

Eldest son of Sir Robert Anstruther and Lady Janet Erskine, daughter of Earl of Kellie, born 3 March 1768. DQMG Egypt, took a brigade to Peninsula 1808, and later served on Moore's staff, but died either of dysentery or "an inflammation of the lungs" at Corunna, 14 January 1809.

Commissions: ensign 3rd Footguards 21 September 1785; lieutenant and captain 16 May 1792; major (brevet) 30 March 1797; major 66th Foot 17 August 1797; lieutenant colonel 68th Foot 31 August 1797; captain and lieutenant colonel 3rd Footguards 16 August 1799.
> WO25/3998

Richard Armstrong (1782-1854)

Born in Lincoln 24 January 1782; married Elizabeth Champion, Edgebaston November 1803/issue Served in Canada, Halifax and Gibraltar then throughout Peninsular War in Portuguese service and afterwards until 1821. Commanded brigade in Burma 1825-1826, commander of Canada West 1842-1848; commander in chief Madras 1851 but resigned due to ill-health early 1854 and died while sailing home 3 March 1854.

1. Hoppner, John, *Duke of Wellington: the original picture painted by Order of the Civil & Military Servants The Honble. East Indian Company Prints, Drawings and Watercolors from the Anne S.K. Brown Military Collection.* Brown Digital Repository. Brown University Library

2. Major General of Infantry by Charles Hamilton Smith. This is
the regulation uniform for general officers with rank displayed by the
arrangement of the buttons and embroidered loops, in this case paired for
a major general and in Wellington's case threes for a lieutenant general.
Wellington rarely wore dress uniform on active service, usually preferring
a plain blue or grey coat. This was no doubt in part a matter of practicality
but also a diplomatic acknowledgement that a substantial number of his
troops were Portuguese and Spanish.

3. Quartermaster General and Assistant Quartermaster General by Charles
Hamilton Smith. Once again these are formal uniforms (distinguished from
those worn by general officers by silver epaulettes and embroidery) which
normally gave way to slouch greatcoats on active service. Regimental officers
attached to staff departments retained their ordinary uniforms but once
again normally appeared in greatcoats or other manifestations of undress.

4. Major of Brigade, after William Loftie. This officer performed the functions of an adjutant General at brigade level. The dress uniform as depicted here was distinguished by silver embroidery. Normally the false buttonholes were plain and the customary slouch greatcoat was common.

5. Aide de Camp and Brigade Major of cavalry by Charles Hamilton Smith. Aide de Camps wore the same uniforms as brigade majors but were distinguished by gold rather than silver embroidery. Cavalry officers, as depicted here, wore aiguillettes rather than epaulettes. Extra ADCs retained their regimental uniforms.

6. Field Officer 1st (Royal) Regiment after William Loftie. As befitting their senior status, officers belonging to the Royals were permitted to have embroidered rather than laced button loops if they chose, but otherwise this officer's uniform is typical of those worn in the Peninsula. Note the low bicorne hat – a fashion which would grow quite extreme.

7. In December 1811 an entirely new uniform, (depicted here by Richard Knotel) was prescribed for officers with a short-tailed jacket instead of the old coat and a cap in place of the bicorne. How soon this uniform came into general use is unclear. Many officers no doubt had their old coats altered at least for active service in the Peninsula.

8. Private and Corporal of the 68th (Durham) Regiment. In March 1812 a new style of cap was prescribed for the Footguards and regiments of the Line but these light infantrymen continue to wear the earlier and plainer style, albeit evidence suggests it was reinforced with a leather crown.

9. Also continuing to wear the older style of cap were these Riflemen of the 5/60th and 95th Regiments as drawn by Charles Hamilton Smith. While Wellington's preference for fighting in line formation can suggest a conservative approach to tactics he was in fact very keen on employing trained riflemen and constantly requested more.

Hannover.

1. leichtes Bataillon.
Offizier und Mannschaften.

2. leichtes Bataillon.
Offizier und Mannschaften.

Englisch-Deutsche Legion.
1812.

10. Some of those additional riflemen came from the King's German Legion seen here after Knotel. The light infantry, who served in the 7th Division wore green jackets and were armed with both muskets and rifles. Conversely the red-jacketed line infantry with 1st Division also included detachments of rifle armed sharpshooters.

11. Officer and colour sergeant of the 9th (Norfolk) Regiment in the 1812 uniforms, by Charles Hamilton Smith. This regiment served under Wellington's command throughout the Peninsular War from Rolica and Vimeiro, and latterly in 5th Division.

IXᵀ or E.NORFOLK REGIMENT of INFANTRY.

12. Grenadiers of the 42nd and 92nd Highlanders. Together with the 79th these were the only kilted regiments in the Peninsula although over time many of their personnel migrated to wearing trousers and their bonnets became denuded of feathers. In addition to their facing colours (blue for the 42nd, green for the 79th and yellow for the 92nd) all three were distinguished by their tartans; the 4nd and 92nd had the regulation sett with a red over-stripe and yellow over-stripe respectively, while the 79th wore the unique Cameron of Erracht set. In addition, the 42nd flaunted their seniority as the "Old Highland Regiment" by wearing a red hackle.

13. Royal Artillerymen by Charles Hamilton Smith. In style the uniform worn was very similar to that of the infantry with the obvious difference that jackets were blue rather than red. On active service the usual trousers were worn over or instead of breeches and calf-length gaiters.

14. In contrast, the Royal Horse Artillery wore a quite different uniform; a short, braided dolman jacket and the distinctive fur-crested Tarleton helmet. With the addition of a carbine and belt this figure by Charles Hamilton Smith would serve equally well as an illustration of a light dragoon prior to the adoption of the 1812 uniform – the Royal Horse Artillery retained this uniform until after Waterloo.

15. Lieutenant Colonel 14th (or the Duchess of York's own) Regiment of (Light) Dragoons wearing the 1812 pattern uniform which replaced the earlier braided dolman and crested helmet. While more modern in style this uniform was initially unpopular as looking too similar to the French.

AN OFFICER (LIEUT COLL) of the 14TH LIGHT DRAGOONS.

The New COSTUME of the BRITISH LIGHT DRAGOONS

Pub. by Thos. Goddard & Son, 31 Pall Mall, 1st June 1812.

16. Trooper of the 12th (or Prince of Wales) Regiment of (Light) Dragoons wearing the 1812 pattern uniform. Note particularly the overalls worn instead of buckskin breeches, and the plain pelisse-like jacket or surtout. Dighton, Denis, *The new costume of the British Light Dragoons* (1812). *Prints, Drawings and Watercolors from the Anne S.K. Brown Military Collection.* Brown Digital Repository. Brown University Library.

Hannover.

Dragoner, feldmarschmässig.

17. King's German Legion Heavy Dragoons in marching order by Richard Knotel; these are the men who broke the French squares at Garcia Hernandez during the pursuit after Salamanca in 1812. The uniform and equipment are typical of other British heavy cavalry for much of the Peninsular War.

The NEW COSTUME of the BRITISH HEAVY DRAGOONS.

18. In 1812 the heavy dragoon uniform was also modernised largely as depicted here by Denis Dighton, although the crested helmet was quickly replaced by a maned version and may never have been worn in the Peninsula. The KGL Heavy Dragoons probably never adopted this uniform as they were converted to Light Dragoons in 1813. Dighton, Denis, *The new costume of the British Heavy Dragoons* (1812). Prints, Drawings and Watercolors from the Anne S.K. Brown Military Collection. Brown Digital Repository. Brown University Library.

Spanien.

Grenadier und Sappeur
vom Infanterie-Regimente Princesa.

Offizier und Mannschaften
vom leichten Regiment Catalonien.

Die Spanische Division de la Romana in Hamburg.
1807—1808.

19. Spanish troops belonging to La Romana's division by Richard Knotel. These were the best in the Spanish Army at the outset of the war and had been sent by the French to serve in the Baltic, before escaping with the aid of the Royal Navy. The indestructible Princesa Regiment in particular was an elite unit and from 1809 onwards, like most of the Spanish infantry, wore dark blue rather than the traditional white.

20. Unlike the Spaniards, the blue-coated Portuguese infantry
were fully integrated within Wellington's divisions. Arthur, Ribeiro,
*Soldado do Regimento d'Infanteria no. 19: (Guerra Peninsular 1810-
1814)*, (1900). *Prints, Drawings and Watercolors from the Anne S.K. Brown
Military Collection.* Brown Digital Repository. Brown University Library.

21. Dighton, Denis, *French infantry in the Peninsula, c. 1812. Prints, Drawings and Watercolors from the Anne S.K. Brown Military Collection.* Brown Digital Repository. Brown University Library.

Commissions: ensign West Meath Militia February 1794; ensign 24th Foot 23 June 1796; lieutenant 5th Foot 5 November 1799, half pay 1802; lieutenant 11th Foot May 1803; captain 9th Battalion of Reserve 9 July 1803; captain 89th Foot 2 August 1804; captain 9th Royal Veteran Battalion 10 April 1805; captain 97th Foot 7 July 1808; major (brevet) to serve with Portuguese Army in command of 16th Regiment 30 May 1811; lieutenant colonel "without purchase for conduct in action" 26 August 1813; lieutenant colonel 1st (Royal) Regiment 18 October 1821; lieutenant colonel 26th Foot 24 January 1829; colonel (India) 5 June 1829; colonel (brevet) 22 July 1830, then half pay as lieutenant colonel 13 February 1835; major general 12 August 1841; lieutenant general 11 November 1851.

WO25/790 f6; WO25/3998; Hall; Hart (1840)

Charles Ashworth (d.1832)

Served West Indies, where he survived a near fatal bout of Yellow Fever. In Portuguese service August 1808–February 1814. Commanded independent brigade at Fuentes d'Onoro, but assigned to 2nd Division after Albuera. Badly wounded at Nive while serving as Brigadier General on Portuguese Staff. Died in London 13 August 1832.

Commissions: ensign 68th Foot 13 October 1798; lieutenant 12 January 1799; captain 55th Foot 12 March 1801; major 6th West India Regiment 5 August 1805; major 62nd Foot 6 July 1808; lieutenant colonel (Staff Portugal) 18 January 1810; colonel (brevet) 1819; major general 22 July 1830.

Annual Biography and Obituary 1832; Hall; *ODNB*

Matthew, Lord Aylmer (1775-1850)

Eldest son of Henry, 4th Baron Aylmer, born 24 May 1775. First commissioned at the age of 12 but did not join his regiment until three years later. Served on San Domingo with a flank battalion 1794; took part in landing at Tiburon, assault on L'Acul, the "affair of Bombard near Cape Nicola Mole" and the capture of Port au Prince. After returning home was captured in the raid on Antwerp 1798, held prisoner for six months and exchanged in time for the Helder expedition. Served Hanover 1805, Copenhagen 1807 and then the Peninsula; as DAG to Sherbrooke. Appointed AAG 1 April 1809 and attached to 1st Division 18 June 1809. Served Oporto, Talavera, Busaco, Fuentes d'Onoro, Vittoria and Nivelle. DAG 1 January 1812 to 2 July 1813, then given brigade attached to 1st Division. Adjutant General in Ireland 22 December 1814 – July 1815. Governor General and C-in-C British North

America 30 July 1830 but dismissed 1835. Married Louisa Call 1801; no children but changed his name to Whitworth-Aylmer 1825 and died of heart attack 25 February 1850.

Commissions: ensign 49th Foot 19 October 1787; lieutenant 26 October 1791; captain 8 August 1794; major 2/85th 9 October 1800; lieutenant colonel 25 March 1802 but placed on half pay 1 October 1802 when battalion reduced, exchanged in Coldstream 9 June 1803, colonel (brevet) 25 July 1810; major general 4 June 1813; lieutenant general 27 May 1825.

> WO25/3998; WO25/744; Hart (1840); McGuigan & Burnham; *Royal Military Calendar*; Ward

Robert Barclay (1774–1811)

Served in both East Indies and West Indies, then Peninsula. Wounded at Busaco but never recovered and was reported to have died of his wounds in May 1811 after returning home.

Commissions: ensign 60th Foot 24 June 1783, but half pay same year; ensign 38th Foot 28 October 1789; lieutenant 31 March 1793; captain 8 April 1795; major 52nd Foot 17 September 1803; lieutenant colonel 29 May 1806.

> WO25/3998; Hall; *ODNB*

Andrew Francis Barnard (1773–1855)

Son of Rev Henry Barnard DD, born Fahan, Co. Donegal. Inspecting field officer of Militia in Canada and Nova Scotia 28 January 1808. Subs. Served in Peninsula where badly wounded at Barossa 5 March 1811; Cuidad Rodrigo and Badajoz, briefly commanding the Light Division afterwards. Badly wounded at the Nivelle and served at Waterloo. Appointed lieutenant governor of Chelsea Hospital 26 November 1849 and died there 17 January 1855.

Commissions: ensign 90th Foot 26 August 1794; lieutenant 81st Foot 23 September 1794; captain-lieutenant 13 November 1794; captain 29 September 1795, exch. 55th Foot 2 December 1795; captain and lieutenant colonel 1st Footguards 19 December 1799; major 7/West India Regiment 2 January 1808; lieutenant colonel (staff) 28 January 1808; lieutenant colonel 1st (Royal) Regiment 15 December 1808, exch. to 43rd Foot 29 March 1810, then 1/95th Rifles; colonel (brevet) 4 June 1813; major general 12 August 1819; lieutenant general 10 January 1837.

> Dalton; Hall; Hart (1840); *ODNB*

James Bathurst (1782-1850)
Second son of Henry Bathurst, Bishop of Norwich. Served Surinam, Egypt 1801 and Hanover 1805. Appointed Military Commissary to King's German Legion 10 October 1805. Served in Poland with Russian and Prussian armies and afterwards at Stralsund and Copenhagen. Served in Peninsula 1808-1810. AQMG 1 April 1809 but acted as military secretary to Wellington until returning home in December 1810, having become "deranged". Subsequently governor of Berwick.

Commissions: ensign 70th Foot 10 May 1794; lieutenant 16 November 1794; captain 7th West India Regiment 25 December 1799, half pay 25 June 1802; captain 2/1st (Royal) Regiment 25 May 1503; major 60th Foot 1 October 1803; lieutenant colonel (brevet) 10 October 1805; major QMG Staff 31 May 1810; major 5th Foot 7 February 1811, half pay Argyll Fencibles 13 June 1811; colonel (brevet) 4 June 1813; major general 12 August 1819; lieutenant general 10 January 1837.
WO25/3998; Hart (1840); Ward

Richard Beckett (1772-1809)
Son of John Beckett of Meanwood, an alderman of Leeds, born 18 June 1772. A noted cricketer associated with the MCC. Served Egypt, Germany, Denmark and Peninsula. Killed in action at Talavera 28 July 1809.

Commission: lieutenant and captain Coldstream Guards 16 July 1801.
Hall

Sir Thomas Sidney Beckwith (1772-1831)
Son of Major General John Beckwith; served in India and Ceylon. Joined Experimental Rifle Corps 1800; served Copenhagen and Peninsula; QMG Canada 1813. Died of fever at Mahabelshwar, India 15 January 1831.

Commissions: ensign 65th Foot 23 June 1790; lieutenant 71st Highlanders 2 February 1791; captain-lieutenant 4 October 1797; captain Experimental Rifle Corps 29 August 1800; major 15th Foot 11 March 1802; major Rifle Corps 28 April 1802; lieutenant colonel 95th Rifles 20 January 1803; colonel (brevet) 4 June 1811; major general 4 June 1814; lieutenant general 22 July 1830.
WO25/3998; Hall; *ODNB*

William Carr Beresford (1768-1854)
Illegitimate son of the Earl of Tyrone (later Marquess of Waterford) born 2 October 1768. Served at Toulon in 1794, took 88th Foot to India in 1799 and

served under Baird in Egypt 1801. Commanded a brigade at the capture of the Cape of Good Hope in 1806 and at Buenos Aires in the same year, where he was captured but escaped in time to be sent to occupy Madeira in 1807. Served throughout the Peninsular War; assigned to re-organise and lead the Portuguese Army, with the local British rank of lieutenant general and the Portuguese rank of *Marechal do Exercito*. An outstanding administrator, his limitations as a field commander were exposed at Albuera. Remained in Portuguese service until revolution in1819, becoming Master General of the Ordnance in 1828. Created viscount 1823, married cousin Louisa Beresford and died at Bedgebury Park, Kent 8 January 1854, leaving no legitimate issue.

Commissions: ensign 16th Foot 27 August 1785; lieutenant 25 June 1789; captain Independent Company 24 January 1791, exchanged to 69th Foot 31 May 1791; major 1 March 1794; lieutenant colonel 124th Foot 11 August 1794; lieutenant colonel 88th Foot 1 September 1795; colonel (brevet) 1 January 1800; brigadier general 11 February 1804; major general 25 April 1808; lieutenant general 1 January 1812; general 27 May 1825.

McGuigan & Burnham; *ODNB; Royal Military Calendar;*

George Henry Frederick Berkeley (1785-1857)

Eldest son of Admiral Sir George Cranfield Berkeley, born 9 July 1785. Educated at Harrow 1798-1800. Served Egypt 1807. AAG to army in Portugal 1 April 1809. Initially attached to 5th Division but transferred to 7th Division 5 March 1811, then back to 5th Division 7 December 1811. Served at Talavera, Bussaco, Fuentes d'Onoro, Badajoz, Salamanca, Vittoria, Nive and St. Sebastian. DAG Holland 11 August 1814, AAG and liaison officer at Prince of Orange's headquarters at Waterloo, where he was wounded. Served Kaffir War 1847, then C-in-C Madras Army 1848. Surveyor General of the Ordnance 1852. Died 25 September 1857.

Commissions: cornet Royal Horse Guards 21 January 1802; lieutenant 27 August 1803; captain 35th Foot 1 May 1805; major 9/Garrison Battalion 28 January 1808, exchanged to 35th Foot 25 March 1808; lieutenant colonel 13 June 1811; colonel (brevet) 27 May 1825; major general 10 January 1837; lieutenant general 9 November 1846; general 20 June 1857.

WO25/3998; Dalton; Hart (1840); Ward

Charles Bevan (1777-1811)

Served in Egypt, at Copenhagen, Walcheren and latterly in the Peninsula. Unfairly scapegoated for Brenier's escape from Almeida but denied a court-martial to clear his name and shot himself at Portalegre 8 July 1811.

Commissions: ensign 37th Foot 19 September 1793; lieutenant 4 September 1795; captain 5th Foot 14 March 1800 but exchanged to 28th Foot 2 May 1800; major 28th Foot 1 December 1804; lieutenant colonel 4th Foot 18 January 1810.

WO25/3998; Hall

Sir George Ridout Bingham (1777-1833)
Fourth son of Richard Bingham, born 21 July 1777. Served Corsica, then Cape 1796-1801, then Minorca 1801. Badly wounded at Salamanca 1812.

Commissions: ensign 69th Foot 3 June 1793; lieutenant 17 March 1794; captain 81st Foot 20 January 1796; major 82nd Foot 22 January 1801; lieutenant colonel 53rd Foot 14 March 1805; colonel (brevet) 4 June 1813.

WO25/3998; Hall; *ODNB*

William Williams Blake.

Commissions: cornet 20th Light Dragoons 26 April 1797; lieutenant 31 October 1799; captain 18 February 1802; major 21 March 1805; lieutenant colonel (brevet) 1 January 1812.

WO25/3998

Sir Edward Blakeney (1778-1868)
Fourth son of Colonel William Blakeney of Newcastle upon Tyne. Served Martinique, Helder; the Baltic and then the Peninsula where he was badly wounded at Albuera and at the storming of Badajoz but subsequently served at Vittoria and in the Pyrenees. Returning to serve in Portugal in 1826. Deputy Governor of Chelsea Hospital 1855 and then Governor in the following year. Died there 2 August 1868.

Commissions: cornet 8th Dragoons 28 February 1794; lieutenant 128th Foot 24 September 1794; captain 99th Foot 24 September 1794; major 17th Foot 17 September 1801, half pay 25 September 1802; major 47th Foot 9 July 1803, exchanged to 7th Royal Fusiliers 24 March 1804; lieutenant colonel (brevet) 25 April 1808; lieutenant colonel 7th Royal Fusiliers 20 June 1811; colonel (brevet) 4 June 1814; major general 25 May 1825; lieutenant general

(Ireland) 26 August 1836; lieutenant general 28 June 1838; general 20 June 1854; field marshal 9 November 1862.

> WO25/3998; Hall; Hart (1840); *ODNB*

Lord Blantyre – SEE Robert Alexander Stuart, Lord Blantyre

Daniel Macnamara Bourchier (d.1852)
Entered Royal Artillery as cadet 11 November 1801. Mentioned in dispatches at Badajoz. Retired 28 August 1826. Married/issue. Died in Dublin 22 October 1852.

Commissions: second lieutenant Royal Artillery 8 September 1803; lieutenant 24 October 1803; second captain 30 May 1812; major (brevet) 21 January 1819; major Royal Artillery (half pay) 26 June 1829.

Challis: Edinburgh Gazette;

Henry Frederick Bouverie (1783-1852)
Third son of Hon. Edward Bouverie, of Delapre Abbey, Northants. born 11 July 1783 and educated at Eton. Served in Egypt 1801 and then at Copenhagen 1807 as ADC to Lord Rosslyn. Afterwards served in Peninsula; slightly wounded at Talavera 28 July 1809 while serving as ADC and Assistant Military Secretary to Wellington. Appointed AAG 18 April 1812. Attached to 1st Division July 1812. AAG to Hill's corps October 1813. Commanded Brigade of Guards in Portugal 1826-28, then commanded Northern District 1828-36. Governor and CinC Malta 1 October 1836 to June 1843. Married 1826; died suddenly at Woolbeding House, Midhurst 14 November 1852, on the point of leaving to attend Wellington's funeral!

Commissions: cornet 2nd Dragoon Guards 2 February 1799, exch. ensign Coldstream 23 October 1799; lieutenant ad captain 19 November 1800; captain and lieutenant colonel 28 June 1810; colonel (brevet) 4 June 1814; major general 27 May 1812; lieutenant general 28 June 1838

> WO25/3998; Hall; Hart (1840); *ODNB; Royal Military Calendar; Times* obituary Notice, 17 Nov. 1852; Ward

Barnard Foord Bowes (1769-1812)
Born Barnard Bowes Foord 10 July 1769 but took his mother's rather than his father's name sometime after 1791. Served as 2IC Gibraltar before coming up to fight at Rolica and Vimeiro. Afterwards returned to Gibraltar but

again volunteered for service in Spain. Wounded at Badajoz – where he was shot through thigh and bayoneted, and then wounded again at attempted storm of San Cayetano fort outside Salamanca 23 June 1812. Having had the wound dressed he returned to assault only to be shot dead.

Commissions: ensign 26th Foot October 1781; lieutenant August 1783; captain Independent Company 24 January 1791, half pay; captain 26th Foot 2 February 1791; major 85th Foot 15 June 1796; lieutenant colonel 6th Foot 1 December 1796; colonel (brevet) 1 January 1805; major general 25 July 1810.

   WO25/3998; Hall; McGuigan & Burnham

Thomas Bradford (1777-1853)

Eldest son of Thomas Bradford of Woodlands, Doncaster,and Ashdown Park Sussex, born 1 December 1777. Served in Ireland 1798, commanding Nottingham Fencibles, then AAG Scotland 1801. Served Montevideo and Buenos Aires first as AAG then as DAG under Auchmuty. Served in Peninsula as AAG, commanded Portuguese brigade at Salamanca and after, slightly wounded at Bayonne. On return home appointed to staff Northern District 1814. C-in-C Bombay 1825-1829. Married twice/issue; died in Eaton Square, London 28 November 1853.

Commissions: ensign Independent company 20 October 1793; lieutenant 4th Foot 9 December 1793; captain 15 April 1794; major Nottinghamshire Fencible Infantry 9 September 1795; lieutenant colonel (brevet) 1 January 1801; major (late) 3/Garrison Battalion 28 September 1804; major 3/ Garrison Battalion 25 February 1805; major 87th Foot 30 May 1805; lieutenant colonel 34th Foot 1805, exchanged to 82nd Foot 21 December 1809; colonel (brevet) 25 July 1810; major general 4 June 1813; lieutenant general 27 May 1825; general 23 November 1841.

   WO25/2998; Hall; Hart (1840); *ODNB*

Thomas Brisbane (1773-1860)

Eldest son of Thomas Brisbane and Eleanor Bruce, born Brisbane House, Largs 23 July 1773. Served Flanders and Holland 1793-95 – wounded at Famars. Afterwards served in West Indies and in Peninsula; AAG at Vittoria, then commanded brigade under Picton in Pyrenees, Nivelle, Orthes and Toulouse – wounded there 10 April 1814. Went to North America, commanding brigade at Plattsburg September 1814. Narrowly missed Waterloo but commanded brigade and then a division in the Army of

Occupation. On Wellington's recommendation served as governor of New South Wales 1821–25 (founding Brisbane). Married/issue. Died 27 January 1860 at Brisbane house supposedly in the same room in which he had been born!

Commissions: ensign 71st Highlanders 10 January 1782, half pay 5 April 1783; ensign 38th Foot 2 April 1789; lieutenant 30 July 1791; captain Independent Company 12 April 1793; captain 53rd Foot 1 January 1794; major 5 August 1795; lieutenant colonel 69th Foot 4 April 1800; half pay York Rangers 24 February 1805; colonel (brevet) 25 July 1810; major general 4 June 1813; lieutenant general 27 May 1825; general 23 November 1841.

    Hall; Hart (1840); *ODNB; Royal Military Calendar*

John Bromhead (1776–1837)

Son of John Bromhead 24th Foot. Served QMG Department in Canada, Nova Scotia, Egypt 1801 and Hanover 1805 and throughout Peninsular War, including El Bodon, Badajoz and Bayonne. Married Maria Barclay/issue. Died in Lincoln 14 February 1837, aged 60.

Commissions: ensign 24th Foot 13 November 1793; lieutenant 16 June 1795; captain 31 October 1799; major 34th Foot 16 May 1803; lieutenant colonel (brevet) 26 June 1809; lieutenant colonel 77th Foot 3 August 1809; colonel (brevet) 1819; retired 3 January 1823.

    WO25/3998; *Gentlemen's Magazine, Royal Military Calendar*

Francis Brooke (1770–1826)

Second son of Francis Brooke of Colebrooke, County Fermanagh. Married Jane, daughter of George Burdett MP. Served in North America; Helder 1799; Copenhagen; Peninsula – Corunna, Badajoz, Salamanca, Vittoria and St. Sebastian. Wounded at New Orleans 1815. Commanded 1/4th Foot at Waterloo along with rest of Lambert's Brigade as latter was de facto commander of 6th Division. Retired 1819.

Commissions: ensign 4th Foot 20 April 1791; lieutenant 3 June 1794; captain 16 August 1797; major 14 August 1804; lieutenant colonel 14 February 1811

    WO25/3998; Dalton; *Royal Military Calendar*

Thomas William Brotherton (1785–1868)

Son of William Brotherton, born 1785. Served Egypt 1801 and Denmark 1805, then throughout Peninsular War as a cavalryman. Wounded at

Salamanca then wounded again and captured at Hasparren 13 December 1813 but exchanged shortly afterwards. Appointed commandant of Cavalry Depot, Maidstone 8 February 1832; Inspector General of Cavalry 1 January 1847. Married/issue. Died at Esher, Surrey, 21 January 1868.

Commissions: ensign Coldstream Guards 24 January 1800; lieutenant and captain 17 July 1801, half pay 1802; captain 53rd Foot and immediately exchanged to lieutenant and captain 3rd Footguards 3 December 1803; captain 6th Foot January 1807, but exchanged to 14th Light Dragoons 4 June 1807; major 3rd Dragoon Guards 28 November 1811, exchanged to 14th Light Dragoons 26 March 1812; lieutenant colonel (brevet) 19 May 1814; lieutenant colonel 12th Light Dragoons (Lancers) 12 October 1820, half pay 24 May1827; lieutenant colonel 95th Foot 15 June 1830; colonel (brevet) 20 July 1830; half pay 1831; lieutenant colonel 16th Light Dragoons 10 February 1832; major general 23 November 1841; lieutenant general 11 November 1851; general 1 April 1860.

WO25/3998; Hall; Hart; *ODNB*; *Reminiscences* (ed. B. Perrett)

William Henry Bunbury

Served in Peninsula September 1808 to February 1810; and again from June 1812 to December 1813; served at Douro, Talavera, Vittoria, Pyrenees, Nive, Nivelle; commanded 1st Battalion of Detachments February to September 1809; commanded 1/3rd Foot in 1813, but resigned rather than face court-martial after being accused of cowardice at St. Pierre 1813.

Commissions: ensign 60th Foot 24 October 1787; lieutenant 29 March 1791; captain-lieutenant 128th Foot 24 December 1794, exchanged to 35th Foot 1 September 1795; captain 35th Foot 5 August 1799; major (brevet) 1 January 1805; major 35th Foot 30 April 1805; lieutenant colonel 3rd Foot 31 December 1806.

WO25/3998; Oman 7:271, 280

John Fox Burgoyne (1782–1871)

Eldest of four illegitimate children of Lieutenant General John Burgoyne and Susan Caulfield, born 24 July 1782. Served on Malta at the blockade of Valetta, and afterwards in Egypt; Alexandria and Rosetta. Served in Peninsula; Corunna, Oporto; blew up Fort Concepcion; Busaco; siege of Badajoz; Salamanca; Burgos (slightly wounded); Vittoria; St. Sebastian (slightly wounded); Nive; Nivelle; Bayonne. Served at New Orleans and capture of Fort Bowyer. C-in-C Crimea after Lord Raglan's death 1855;

Constable of the Tower 1865. Married Charlotte Ross 31 January 1821/ issue. Died in London 7 October 1871.

Commissions: second lieutenant Royal Engineers 29 August 1798; lieutenant 1 July 1800; second captain 1 March 1805; captain 24 June 1809; major (brevet) 6 February 1812; lieutenant colonel (brevet) 27 April 1812; lieutenant colonel Royal Engineers 20 December 1814; colonel (brevet) 22 July 1830; major general 28 June 1838; lieutenant general 11 November 1851; general 5 September 1855.

WO25/3998; Hall; Hart (1840); *ODNB*

Robert Burne (1753?-1825)
Parentage unknown. Served in India 1783-1798; Bangalore, Sringapatman and the capture of Pondicherry 1793; once returned to Europe he went to Minorca, Hanover and South America, served in Portugal and Spain 1808-1809, including Vimeiro and Corunna. Afterwards at Walcheren before returning to Peninsula in 1811 to command a brigade in 6th Division from 5 March 1811-24 April 1812, including a stint commanding the division between 5 November 1811 and 9 February 1812. A probable combination of old age and ill-health saw him return later that year to serve on the home staff. He was also appointed governor of Carlisle in 1808, a position he held until his death at Berkeley Cottage Stanmore, Herts. 9 June 1825.

Commissions: ensign 36th Foot 28 September 1773; lieutenant 13 January 1777; captain and captain-lieutenant 7 May 1784; captain 28 October 1784; major (brevet) 1 March 1794; major 36th Foot 15 April 1796; lieutenant colonel (brevet) 1 January 1798; lieutenant colonel 36th Foot 13 November 1799; colonel (brevet) 25 April 1808; brigadier general 21 January 1811; major general 4 June 1811; lieutenant general 19 July 1821.

WO25/3998; McGuigan and Burnham; *Royal Military Calendar*

Hon. Henry Cadogan (1780-1813)
Seventh son of Charles, 1st Earl of Cadogan, born 26 February 1780. Wounded at Buenos Aires; served Peninsula, initially as ADC to Wellington at Talavera and then in command of 71st Highlanders. Killed in action while commanding brigade at Vittoria 21 June 1813.

Commissions: ensign 18th Foot 9 August 1797; lieutenant 18 July 1799; captain 60th Foot 21 November 1799; lieutenant and captain Coldstream Guards 9 December 1799; major 53rd Foot 8 December 1804; lieutenant colonel 18th Foot 22 August 1805; half pay Brunswick Fencibles 5 March 1807; lieutenant colonel 71st Highlanders 7 January 1808; colonel (brevet) 4 June 1813.

Hall; *ODNB*

Allan Cameron of Erracht (1750-1828)

Son of Ewen Cameron of Erracht and Marsali Maclean of Drimnin. Fled to America after killing a man in a duel and was arrested by Patriots in 1775 after taking a commission as a lieutenant in a putative loyalist unit. Released in 1778 he saw no service due to having broken both ankles in an escape attempt, but in 1793 was granted letters of service to raise 79th Highlanders. Served in Flanders and Holland 1794-95; Martinique 1795-97; Helder 1799; Ferrol 1800; Egypt 1801; Copenhagen 1807, then commanded brigade in Peninsula 1808-10, before returning home worn out and suffering from old wounds. He died at Fulham 9 March 1828. His eldest son, Phillips Cameron, was fatally wounded commanding the 79th Highlanders at Fuentes d'Onoro – see below)

Commissions: lieutenant Queen's Royal Regiment of Rangers (provincials) 6 November 1775; major commandant (temporary) 79th Highlanders 17 August 1793*; lieutenant colonel (temporary) 79th Highlanders 30 January 1794; colonel (brevet) 26 January 1797; colonel (permanent) 79th Highlanders 1 January 1805; brigadier general 1808; major general 25 July 1810; lieutenant general 12 August 1819.

*although this was his first real commission – and an irregularly obtained temporary one at that - he had been fraudulently styling himself Major Cameron since 1784!

WO25/3998; McGuigan and Burnham; Maclaine, L, *Indomitable Colonel* (London 1986); *ODNB*; Reid, S. *Wellington's Highland Warriors* (Barnsley 2010)

Phillips Cameron (1782-1811)

Eldest son of Allan Cameron of Erracht – see above – born 29 October 1782. Served Martinique 1796 and in Peninsula; fatally wounded at Fuentes d'Onoro and died 11 May 1813.

Commissions: ensign 82nd Foot February 1794; lieutenant 91st Foot 26 March 1794; captain-lieutenant 79th Highlanders 6 June 1794; captain 8 October 1794; major 3 September 1801; lieutenant colonel 19 April 1804.

WO25/3998; Hall

Sir Alexander Campbell (1760-1824)

Fourth son of Alexander Campbell of Balneed, Perthshire, and a "near relation" of Campbell of Melfort, born 20 August 1760. First served as a marine with the Channel Fleet 1780-81, then Gibraltar 1782-83. Served India, commanding 74th Highlanders at storming of Sringapatnam 1799. Appointed Adjutant General Ireland 25 January 1809 but served in Peninsula, (wounded at Talavera) in command of 4th Division 1809-10, then 6th Division 1811. Only resigned as AG Ireland September 1812 on being ordered to India. Knighted when standing proxy for Wellington at his installation as KB 1812. Served as C-in-C Mauritius and Bourbon 1813-16 and died as C-in-C Madras 11 December 1824. Married/issue.

Commissions: ensign 1/1st (Royal) 1 November 1776; lieutenant 25 December 1778; captain 97th Foot 13 April 1780, half pay 23 September 1783; captain 74th Highlanders 25 December 1787; major (brevet) 1 March 1794; major 74th Highlanders 1 September 1795; lieutenant colonel 74th Highlanders 4 December 1795; colonel (brevet) 25 December 1803; major general 25 July 1810; lieutenant general (East Indies) 9 March 1812; lieutenant general 4 June 1814.

WO25/3998; Hall; *ODNB; Royal Military Calendar*

Sir Colin Campbell (1776-1847)

Fifth son of John Campbell of Melfort. Served in West Indies and then East Indies; distinguished himself at storming of Ahmednuggur 1803 and had two horses shot from under him at Assaye. Served on staff throughout Peninsular War, as AAG and commandant at headquarters; and the same at Waterloo; governor of Nova Scotia then governor of Ceylon 1840-47. Married/issue. Died in London 13 June 1847, just days after returning from East Indies.

Commissions: lieutenant 3/Breadalbane Fencibles 1795; ensign West India Regiment 3 October 1799; lieutenant 35th Foot 21 August 1801 but immediately exchanged to 78th Highlanders; captain 9 January 1805; major 70th Foot 2 September 1808; lieutenant colonel 3 May 1810; colonel (brevet) 4 June 1814; captain and lieutenant colonel Coldstream Guards 15 July 1814; major general 27 May 1825; lieutenant general 28 June 1838.

Dalton; Hart (1840); Ward

Henry Frederick Campbell (1769-1856)

Son of Lieutenant Colonel Alexander Campbell of Cawdor and Frances Meadows, born 10 July 1769. Served Flanders 1793 and again in 1794 with staff. Served in Peninsula with second brigade of Guards, briefly commanded 1st Division. Badly wounded in face at Salamanca. Married Emma Williams 10 April 1808/issue. Died 2 September 1856.

Commissions: ensign 1st Footguards 20 September 1786; lieutenant and captain 25 April 1793; captain and lieutenant colonel 6 April 1796; colonel (brevet) 25 September 1803; major general 25 July 1810; 3rd Major 1st Footguards 2 October 1813; lieutenant general 4 June 1814; general 10 January 1837.

WO25/3998; Hart (1840)

James Campbell (1773-1835)
Served in India and in the Peninsula; notably at Badajoz in temporary command of Colville's brigade. Commanded brigade at Salamanca and Vittoria, being badly wounded on both occasions. Married Lady Dorothea Cuffe 18 March 1819; died in Paris 6 May 1835.

Commissions: ensign 1st Foot 30 March 1791; lieutenant 20 March 1794; captain Independent Company 6 September 1794, half pay; captain 42nd Highlanders 7 December 1797; major Argyle Fencibles 3 January 1799; major 94th Foot 7 April 1802; lieutenant colonel 94th Foot 27 September 1804; colonel (brevet) 4 June 1813; major general 12 August 1819.

WO25/3998; Hall; *ODNB; Royal Military Calendar*

Charles Fox Canning (1783-1815)
Third son of Stratford Canning, born 4 January 1783. Served Copenhagen 1807; ADC to Wellington in Peninsula and at Waterloo, where he was killed in action.

Commissions: ensign 3rd Footguards 29 December 1803; lieutenant and captain 25 December 1807; major (brevet) 27 April 1812; lieutenant colonel (brevet) 19 August 1813; captain and lieutenant colonel 3rd Footguards 31 March 1814.

Dalton; Hall

Hon. George Carleton (1781-1814)
Fourth son of General Sir Guy Carleton, Lord Dorchester, born 25 September 1781. Served Canada 1808 as inspecting field officer of militia, then in Peninsula, being badly wounded at Badajoz and subsequently killed in action at Bergen op Zoom 8 March 1814.

Commissions: ensign 9th Foot 14 July 1798; lieutenant 27 November 1798; captain 22 July 1800; captain 60th Foot 19 March 1803; captain 9th Foot 19 July 1803; major 40th Foot 22 October 1805; major 27th Foot 29 October 1805; lieutenant colonel (brevet) 28 January 1808; lieutenant colonel 44th Foot 22 August 1811.

    Hall

William Henry Carr (1777-1821)
Second son of Rev. Colston Carr, born Twickenham 6 October 1777. Served West Indies; Maroon War on Jamaica, then St. Domingo. Served throughout Peninsular war, but badly wounded at Orthez; "ball entered the chin and lodged in the roots of his tongue." Never fully recovered and died 10 August 1821.

Commissions: Ensign 68th Foot 12 March 1794; lieutenant 2 September 1795; captain 83rd Foot 4 May 1796; major 17 September 1807; lieutenant colonel (brevet) 27 April 1812; lieutenant colonel 83rd Foot 22 September 1814.

    Hall

Thomas Chamberlain (d.1828)
Served Canada, then Egypt, Cape and Peninsula.

Commissions: ensign 24th Foot 1793; lieutenant 3 September 1795; captain 25 April 1797; major 2 August 1804; lieutenant colonel (brevet) 4 June 1811; lieutenant colonel 24th Foot 11 June 1813, half pay on reduction of 2nd Battalion 1814; lieutenant colonel 8/Royal Veteran Battalion 25 November 1819.

Christopher Chowne: SEE Christopher Tilson

Lord Clinton: SEE Robert Cotton St. John Trefusis, Baron Clinton

Sir William Henry Clinton (1769-1846)
Eldest son of General Sir Henry Clinton, born in Lyons 23 December 1769. Served in Flanders 1793-94; Famars, Valenciennes, Dunkirk, Lannoi, Fremon, Cateau Cambresis, Fleurus etc. Inspector General of Foreign Corps 25 December 1800, Military Secretary to the Duke of York March 1803, QMG Ireland July 1804-1812, then served in Peninsula. Lieutenant General of the Ordnance 1825, served in Portugal 1826-1828, but declined command of the Portuguese Army. Died 16 February 1846.

Commissions: cornet 7th Light Dragoons 22 December 1784; lieutenant 7 March 1787; captain 45th Foot 9 January 1790; lieutenant and captain 1st Footguards 14 July 1790; captain and lieutenant colonel 29 December 1794; colonel (brevet) 1 January 1801; major general 25 April 1808; third major 1st Footguards 30 July 1812; second major 21 January 1813; first major 21 October 1813; lieutenant general 4 June 1813; general 22 July 1830.

WO 25/3998; Hart (1840); *ODNB*

Edward Charles Cocks (1786-1812)
Born in London 27 July 1786, the eldest son of John Cocks, Earl Somers. Served in Peninsula 1809-1812, becoming a noted exploring officer, but was killed at Burgos 8 October 1812 while serving as an infantry officer.

Commissions: cornet 16th Light Dragoons 29 April 1803; captain 48th Foot 25 December 1806, exchanged back to 16th Light Dragoons 12 April 1807; major 79th Highlanders 20 February 1812.

Hall; Page, J., *Intelligence Officer in the Peninsula*

James Robert Coghlan (k,1814)
Served in Peninsula; badly wounded at Talavera and captured on first day but subsequently escaped. Killed in action at Toulouse 10 April 1814.

Commissions: lieutenant 61st Foot 4 January 1797; captain 1 July 1803; major 9 January 1806; lieutenant colonel (brevet) 30 May 1811; lieutenant colonel 61st Foot 13 June 1811.

Hall

John Colborne (1778-1863)
Born 16 February 1778 the only son of Samuel Colborne of Lyndhurst, Hants. Educated at Christ's Hospital and Winchester College. Served Egypt 1801 and Maida 1806; military secretary to Sir John Moore; served throughout Peninsular War ant at Waterloo. C-in-C and governor General of Canada 1837-8; High Commissioner Ionian Islands 1843-1843; C-in-C Ireland January 1855-March 1860. Married/issue. Died at Valetta House, Torquay 17 April 1863.

Commissions: ensign 20th Foot 10 July 1794; lieutenant 4 September 1795; captain 12 January 1800; major 21 January 1808; lieutenant colonel (brevet) 2 February 1809; lieutenant colonel 52nd Foot 18 July 1811; colonel (brevet) 4 June 1814; major general 27 May 1825; lieutenant general 28 June 1838; general June 1854; field marshal April 1860.

Dalton; Hart (1840) *ODNB*

Galbraith Lowry Cole (1772-1842)
Born Dublin 1 May 1772, the second son of Willoughby Cole, Earl of Enniskillen. Served in West Indies under Sir Charles Grey in 1794 and in Egypt as military secretary to Sir John Hely Hutchinson. Commanded a brigade in Italy 1806 and served as ADC to Sir John Stuart at Maida. Commanded 4th Division in Peninsula; wounded at Albuera and again severely at Salamanca. Not at Waterloo but served in Army of Occupation 1815-1818. Governor of Cape Colony 1828-1833. Died 4 October 1842.

Commissions: cornet 12th Light Dragoons 31 March 1787; lieutenant 31 May 1791; captain 70th Foot 30 November 1792; major 31 October 1793; lieutenant colonel Ward's Regiment 26 November 1794; colonel (brevet) 1 January 1801; captain and lieutenant colonel 3rd Footguards 25 May 1803; major general 25 April 1808; lieutenant general 4 June 1813; general 22 July 1830.

Hall; Hart; *ODNB*

Francis John Colman
Died in Portugal 12 December 1811 "of fever and debility, brought on by exertions in his profession too great for his constitution". Was Serjeant at Arms in the House of Commons, in succession to his father Edward Colman. It was as the *Gentleman's Magazine* noted, a "valuable office" and his untimely death caused the old man some considerable financial embarrassment, requiring him to put up his coach and retire to Brighton!

Commissions: cornet 1st (Royal) Dragoons 13 September 1786; captain 15 July 1791; lieutenant and captain 1st Footguards 28 April 1793; lieutenant colonel 30 October 1799; lieutenant colonel 38th Foot 17 September 1802;

Gentleman's Magazine; Hall

Sir Charles Colville (1770-1843)
Second son of John, 9th Baron Colville, born 7 August 1770. Served St. Domingo 1793-1795; wounded during landing at Tiburon. Commanded 13th Foot in Ireland 1798 and Egypt 1801. Afterwards served in Martinique and then Peninsula; wounded while leading assault at Badajoz 6 April 1812 – shot through left thigh and lost finger of right hand. Wounded again at Vittoria. Commanded reserve at Hal on day of Waterloo and afterwards stormed Cambrai. Governor of Mauritius 1828. Married Jane Mure of Caldwell, Ayrshire 16 February 1818/issue. Died in Hampstead 27 May 1843.

Commissions: ensign 28th Foot 26 December 1781; lieutenant 30 September 1787; captain Independent Company 24 January 1791, half pay immediately and captain 13th Foot 26 May 1791; major 13th Foot 2 September 2 September 1795; lieutenant colonel 26 August 1796; colonel (brevet) 1 January 1805; colonel 5/Garrison Battalion 10 October 1812, half pay 25 December 1814; major general 25 July 1810; lieutenant general 12 August 1819; general 10 January 1837.

WO25/3998; Dalton; Hall: Hart; *ODNB*

Sir Stapleton Cotton (1773-1865)
Second son of Sir Robert Cotton Bt., born 14 November 1773. Served in Flanders and Holland 1793-94; the Cape and India 1799. Commanded a cavalry brigade in the Peninsula 1808-09. Went home on his father's death 1810 but soon returned to command all British cavalry withy the local rank of lieutenant general. Wounded after Salamanca but again returned after Vittoria to command cavalry for the rest of the war. C-in-C Leeward Islands 24 December 1816; C-in-C India 1825-30. Became first Baron Combermere in 1814 and Viscount Combermere in 1827. Died 21 February 1865.

Commissions: second lieutenant 23rd Fusiliers 26 February 1790; lieutenant 16 March 1791; captain 6th Dragoons 28 February 1793; major 59th Foot 28 April 1794 but promotion to lieutenant colonel 25th Light Dragoons backdated to 9 March 1794; colonel(brevet) 1 January 1800; lieutenant colonel 16th Light Dragoons 14 February 1800; major general 2 November 1805; lieutenant general 1 January 1812; general 27 May 1825; field marshal 2 October 1855.

WO25/3998; Hall; Hart (1840); *ODNB*

Sir John Francis Cradock (1762-1839)
Only son of John Cradock, bishop of Dublin, born 11 August 1762. An officer with wide though not particularly distinguished experience. Served in West Indies under Grey 1794. QMG Ireland 1797. Served on staff in Mediterranean and in Egypt 1801, then successively Corsica and Madras. Commanded in Portugal over winter of 1808-1809 until Wellesley's appointment Married/issue; died in London 26 July 1839.

Commissions: cornet 4th Dragoons1777; ensign Coldstream 1779; lieutenant and captain 12 December 1781; major 12th Dragoons 1785; major 13th Foot 16 June 1786; lieutenant colonel 16 June 1789; colonel 127th Foot 16

April 1795, half pay 1798; colonel 2/54th Foot 8 May 1801; major general 1 January 1798; lieutenant general 1 January 1804; general 4 June 1814

> WO25/3998; *ODNB; Royal Military Calendar*
>
> (NB: his entry in *Oxford Dictionary of National Biography* is eccentrically listed under Caradoc, a spelling of his name he only assumed in 1820!)

James Catlin Craufurd (1776-1810)

Illegitimate son of Captain James Craufurd, 3rd Footguards, born 23 January 1776 and generally known as Catlin Craufurd by way of distinguishing between father and son. Joined army 1791 but saw no service until going to South Africa 1797. Occupied a variety of staff posts until going to Portugal in 1808. Commanded brigade at Rolica and Vimerio, but supernumerary afterwards until given a brigade under Moore. Again commanded a brigade in 2nd Division 1809-10 but died of fever at Abrantes 25 December 1810. Married/issue.

Commissions: ensign 24th Foot 28 December 1791; lieutenant Independent Company 7 March 1793; captain Independent Company 10 September 1793; captain 30th Foot 22 October 1793; major Independent Companies 15 April 1795; major 98th Foot 18 May 1796; lieutenant colonel 98th Foot* 27 April 1797; colonel (brevet) 30 October 1805; brigadier general 14 June 1808 and 26 July 1809.
*subsequent re-numbered as 91st Highlanders

> WO25/3998; Hall; McGuigan & Burnham

Robert Craufurd (1764-1812)

Third son of Sir Alexander Craufurd, born Newark Ayrshire 5 May 1764. Served India 1790-92; resigned from Army to undertake intelligence work on the Continent, including liaison positions with Austrian staff 1793-97. DQMG Ireland 16 February 1798. Liaison officer with Austro-Russian forces in Switzerland 1799 and at Den Helder same year. AG East Indies 17 September 1801; commanded brigade at Buenos Aires, then commanded Light Brigade in Peninsula 1808 and again in 1809, expanding it to a division. Fatally wounded at storming of Cuidad Rodrigo 19 January 1812 and died five days later.

Commissions: ensign 25th Foot 1779; ensign 65th Foot 20 April 1780; ensign 26th Foot 28 April 1780; lieutenant 98th Foot 2 June 1780; lieutenant 26th Foot 7 March 1781; captain-lieutenant 45th Foot 19 March 1783; captain 92nd Foot 11 December 1782; captain 101st Foot 23 December 1783, then on half pay but exchanged to 75th Foot 1 November 1787, resigned 13 October

1793. Lieutenant Colonel (brevet) 26 January 1797; lieutenant colonel Hompesch Light Infantry, then 60th Foot 30 December 1797; lieutenant colonel 86th Foot 11 February 1802; half pay 60th Foot 24 February 1803; colonel (brevet) 30 October 1805; brigadier general 16 September 1806; major general 4 June 1811.

WO25/3998; Hall; *ODNB*

John Crowder (d.1838)
Served Copenhagen 1807 and then Peninsula; slightly wounded at Albuera, mentioned in despatches for Salamanca and badly wounded at Sorauren 1813. Died at Cheltenham 27 August 1838.

Commissions: lieutenant 7th Royal Fusiliers 16 June 1803; captain 5 November 1806; major (brevet) 17 August 1812; major 7th Fusiliers 9 September 1813; half-pay 23rd Fusiliers 25 May 1815; lieutenant colonel (brevet) 27 May 1825. Colonel (brevet) 28 June 1838.

Gentleman's Magazine; Hall; *Royal Military Calendar*

Henry John Cumming (1771-1856)
Son of Colonel Sir John Cumming, East India Company service. Served in Flanders and Holland 1793-1795 and at Helder 1799. Commanded 11th Light Dragoons in the Peninsula from May 1811 to May 1813; slightly wounded at El Bodon 25 September 1811 – a sabre cut in the arm. Died in London 28 November 1856, aged 85.

Commissions: cornet 11th Light Dragoons 12 May 1790; lieutenant 9 February 1793; captain 21 February 1794; major 25 October 1798; lieutenant colonel 17 February 1803; colonel (brevet) 1 January 1812; major general 4 June 1814; lieutenant general 22 July 1830; lieutenant general 1846.

WO25/3998; Hart; *Royal Military Calendar*

Edward Currie (1780-1815)
Born at Dalebank in Annandale he received his first commission as ensign 47th Foot at the age of 13 in consequence of his father's meritorious service. Served in Egypt 1801, then Peninsula as ADC to General Hill, before being killed at Waterloo as AAG.

Commissions: ensign 47th Foot 31 July 1793; lieutenant 58th Foot 5 September 1795; captain 5 April 1801; captain 90th Foot 25 December 1802; major 90th Foot 13 October 1814; lieutenant colonel (brevet) 19 June 1812.

Dalton

Dalhousie, Earl of SEE George Ramsay

William Gabriel Davy (1779-1856)
Elder son of Major Davy, East India Company service. Commanded 5/60th
at Rolica, Vimeiro and Talavera. Knighted by King William IV in 1836.
Married twice. Died at Tracy Park, Gloucestershire 25 January 1856, aged
77, and buried in family vault in Gloucester Cathedral.

Commissions: ensign March 1797; lieutenant 61st Foot 22 May 1797; captain
60th Foot 1 January 1802; major 5 February 1807; lieutenant colonel 7/
Garrison Battalion 28 December 1809, half pay by reduction 1814; colonel
(brevet) 12 August 1819; major general 22 July 1830; lieutenant general 23
November 1841; general 20 June 1854.
    Gentleman's Magazine; Hart; *Royal Military Calendar*

Hon. George de Grey (1776-1831)
Son of Thomas de Grey, Lord Walsingham and Augusta-Georgiana-Elizabeth
Irby, born 11 June 1776. Served Cape of Good Hope 1796 and then India;
Malvelly and Sringapatnam. Served Peninsula; commanded brigade at Albuera
but returned home due to ill-health 1812. Succeeded to Walsingham title 1818
but died with his wife, Matilda Methuen, in house fire 27 April 1831.

Commissions: cornet then lieutenant 1st Dragoons 1794; captain 25th Light
Dragoons 1795; major 25th Light Dragoons 25 May 1795; lieutenant colonel
26 Light Dragoons (?) 3 May 1799; lieutenant colonel 1st Dragoons 6 June
1799; colonel (brevet) 25 April 1808; major general 4 June 1811; lieutenant
general 19 July 1821.
    McGuigan & Burnham; *Royal Military Calendar; United Services Magazine*

Sir William Howe De Lancey (1781-1815).
Only son of Stephen de Lancey, American loyalist and governor of Tobago.
Served in West Indies 1795. Served on staff in Peninsula 1809-1814
as DQMG. Married Magdalen Hall 4 April 1815 but fatally wounded at
Waterloo while serving as QMG.

Commissions: cornet 16th Light Dragoons 7 July 1792; lieutenant 26
February 1793; captain Independent Company 25 March 1794, transferring
to 80th Foot; captain 17th Light Dragoons 20 October 1796; major 45th
Foot 17 October 1799; AQMG 1802; lieutenant colonel (permanent staff) 1
April 1809; colonel (brevet) 4 June 1813.
    Dalton; Ward

Robert Henry Dick (1787-1846)
Son of Dr. William Dick of Tullimet, Perthshire and EIC service, born in Calcutta 29 July 1787. Served Sicily, Maida, Egypt, then Peninsula; Busaco, Fuentes d'Onoro, Salamanca. Briefly succeeded to command of 1/42nd at Quatre Bras before himself being badly wounded. Following death of wife, Eliza MacNab in 1838 applied for further service; commanded centre division of Madras Army 1838 and temporarily C-in-C 1841-42, transferred to Bombay Army and killed in action at Sobraon 10 February 1846.

Commissions: ensign 75th Highlanders 22 November 1800; lieutenant 67th Foot 27 June 1802; captain 78th Highlanders 17 April 1804; major 24 April 1808; major 2/42nd Highlanders 14 July 1808; lieutenant colonel (brevet) 8 October 1812; lieutenant colonel 1/42nd Highlanders 18 June 1815, half pay colonel (unattached) 25 May 1825; major general 10 January 1837.
    Dalton; Hart; *ODNB*

Alexander Dickson (1777-1840)
Third son of Admiral William Dickson, born Roxburgh 3 June 1777. Entered Royal Artillry 1794, served Minorca 1798, the blockade of Malta and surrender of Valetta 1800, Buenos Aires 1807, then throughout Peninsular War and afterwards at New Orleans 1815; commanded battering train on Waterloo campaign. Afterwards Director General Field Train Department and DAG Royal Artillery. Married a Miss Briones/issue. Died 22 April 1840.

Commissions: second lieutenant Royal Artillery 6 November 1794; lieutenant 6 March 1795; captain 14 October 1801; major 6 February 1812; lieutenant colonel (brevet) 27 April 1812; colonel (brevet) 27 May 1825; major general 10 January 1837.
    Dalton; Hart (1840); *ODNB*

Sir Rufane Shaw Donkin (1773-1841)
Son of General Robert Donkin and Mary Collins. Served in West Indies 1793-1804 with a brief break to get himself wounded and captured at Ostend 1798; Served Copenhagen 1807 then Peninsula first as DQMG July 1808-April 1809; commanded brigade at Oporto and Talavera, then QMG Mediterranean. Married twice/issue. Hanged himself after a prolonged period of ill health 1 May 1841.

Commissions: ensign 44th Foot 21 March 1778; lieutenant 9 September 1779; captain 31 May 1793; major 1 September 1795; lieutenant colonel 11th Foot

24 May 1798; colonel (brevet) 24 April 1808; major general 4 June 1811; lieutenant general 19 July 1821; general 28 June 1838.

Hart; *ODNB; Royal Military Calendar*

Charles Donnellan (k.1809)

Fatally wounded at Talavera while commanding the 48th Foot; renowned as "the last of the powderers", due to his insistence on tying back and powdering his hair, notwithstanding the discontinuance of powder in 1795 and the abolition of queues in 1808. Another eccentricity was the wearing of his cocked hat athwart rather than fore and aft, as had been the fashion since the Helder in 1799!

Commissions: ensign 15th Foot 31 July 1789; captain 17 April 1793; captain 13th Foot 18 September 1793; major 62nd Foot 26 November 1799; lieutenant colonel (brevet) 28 September 1804; lieutenant colonel 48th Foot 14 November 1804.

Hall

James Dawes Douglas (1785–1862)

Eldest son of Major James Sholto Douglas of Grange, Jamaica and Sarah Dawes. Attended Royal Military college at Great Marlow; DQMG South America 1806; served Peninsula with Portuguese army, losing a leg at Toulouse 1814, then successively DQMG Scotland 1815–1822 and DQMG Ireland 1825–1830.

Commissions: ensign 42nd Highlanders 10 July 1799; lieutenant 19 June 1800; captain 16 September 1802; major (Spain and Portugal) 16 February 1809; lieutenant colonel (brevet) 30 May 1811; colonel (brevet) 19 July 1821; major general 22 July 1830;

Hart; *ODNB*

Charles William Doyle (1770–1842)

Eldest son of William Doyle of Bramblestown Co. Kilkenny, and Cecilia Salvini. British liaison officer with Spanish Army and raised the *Tiradores de Doyle*. Not to be confused with his half-brother, Sir John Milley Doyle, who served with the Portuguese Army. An officer of extensive previous experience in Flanders and Holland 1793-94; Texel 1796; West Indies 1796-98 and Egypt 1802. Married twice/issue. Died in Paris 25 October 1842.

Commissions: ensign 14th Foot 28 April 1783; lieutenant 12 February 1793, exchanged to Campbell's Regiment 30 October 1793; captain

21 June 1794; captain-lieutenant 97th Foot 3 September 1795; major general 9 July 1803; lieutenant colonel 22 August 1805; colonel (brevet) 4 June 1813; major general 12 August 1819; lieutenant general 10 January 1837.

Hall; *ODNB*

Sir John Milley Doyle (1784–1856).
Second son of Rev. Nicholas Milley Doyle of Bramblestown, Co. Kilkenny. A "gallant but eccentric" officer of very wide experience. Served Ireland and in the Mediterranean including Egypt, then Portuguese service 1809–1814 and again 1832-1834 before acrimoniously parting over arrears of pay. Married Miss Bryan 1 September 1817 but parted after trial for crim. con. No issue from marriage but illegitimate daughter by a Mrs McDonald. Died a Military Knight of Windsor 9 August 1856.

Commissions: ensign 107th Foot 31 May 1794; lieutenant 108th Foot 21 June 1794; lieutenant 92nd Highlanders 1800; captain 81st Foot 9 July 1803; captain 5th Foot 3 September 1803; captain 87th Foot 7 December 1804; major (Staff Portugal) 16 February 1809; lieutenant colonel (brevet) 26 September 1811. Colonel (brevet) 27 May 1825.

Gentleman's Magazine; *Royal Military Calendar*

Archibald Drummond (c.1810)
Archibald Drummond entered the Army as an ensign on 6 July 1784 and departed from it on 22 July 1810 by dying while on passage home from Lisbon.

Commissions: ensign 6 July 1784; ensign 16th Foot 30 April 1787; lieutenant 31 May 1790; captain 27 January 1794; major 2 May 1800; major 3rd Foot 9 July 1803; lieutenant colonel 3rd Foot 17 August 1809.

Hall

Saumaurez Dubourdieu (k.1814)
Son of Rev. John Dubordieu, rector of Annahilt County Down. Served Martinique 1808 and in Peninsula, mentioned in despatches for Vittoria and fatally wounded at St. Sebastian.

Commissions: Lieutenant Royal Artillery 18 April 1801; Second Captain 7 July 1805; Captain 8 February 1813.

Gentleman's Magazine; Hall

George Henry Duckworth, (1782–1811)
Son of Admiral Duckworth, married Penelope Fanshawe/issue, killed in action at Albuera 16 May 1811.

Commissions: captain 60th Foot 17 August 1803; Major 67th Foot 2 October 1806; Lieutenant-Colonel 1/West India Regiment 14 January 1808; lieutenant colonel 48th Foot 16 June 1808.

John Duffy (d.1855)
Served West Indies 1796; Helder 1799; Egypt 1807; Copenhagen; Peninsula; Cuidad Rodrigo, commanded 43rd at Badajoz, slightly wounded at Vittoria. Died in Jermyn Street 17 March 1855.

Commissions: ensign 10th Foot 21 October 1795; lieutenant 6 January 1796; captain 43rd Foot 12 August 19804; major (brevet) 6 February 1812; major 43rd Foot 17 June 1813; lieutenant colonel 95th Rifles 21 September 1815; lieutenant colonel 8th Foot 9 September 1819 – in November 1819 seniority as lieutenant colonel was antedated to 22 November 1813; half pay unattached 29 March 1828; colonel (brevet) 22 July 1830; major general 23 November 1841; lieutenant general 11 November 1851.
    Gentleman's Magazine; Hall; *Military Annual 1844*; *Royal Military Calendar*

Robert Lawrence Dundas (1780–1844)
Seventh and youngest son of Thomas Dundas, 1st Baron Dundas and Lady Charlotte Fitzwilliam born 7 July 1780. Served Helder 1799, Egypt 1800, transferred to Royal Staff Corps 1802 and served in North Germany 1805, then throughout Peninsular War. Died (unmarried) at Loftus, nr. Guisborough 23 November 1844.

Commissions: second lieutenant Royal Engineers 1 December 1797; lieutenant 2 May 1800; captain Royal Staff Corps 6 August 1802, major 14 July 1804; lieutenant colonel (brevet) 11 April 1811; half pay AQMG 1817; colonel (brevet) 19 July 1821; major general 22 July 1830; lieutenant general 23 November 1841.
    Gentleman's Magazine

William Bolden Dundas (1787–1858)
Son of Rear Admiral George Dundas, born Braddan, Isle of Man 3 July 1787. Mentioned in despatches at Cuidad Rodrigo but lost an arm at Badajoz. Married/issue. Died at Inveresk 8 August 1858.

Commissions: second lieutenant Royal Artillery 8 September 1803; lieutenant 12 September 1803; second captain 11 July 11; major (brevet) 21 January 1819; lieutenant colonel (brevet) 10 January 1837; major general 28 November 1854.

Hall; Hart (1840)

Benjamin D'Urban (1777-1849)

Son of Doctor Benjamin D'Urban, born at Halesworth 16 February 1777. Served Westphalia 1795; West Indies under Abercrombie. ADC to Earl of Pembroke, then General St. John. Superintendant Junior Department Royal Military College. Served Hanover 1805, then attached to QMG department 1806. Served throughout Peninsular War; AQMG 1 April 1809 then QMG Portuguese Army 20 April 1809- April 1816. Colonel Royal Staff Corps and DQMG 1817; Successively governor of Antigua and British Guiana 1819-1833. Governor and C-in-C Cape 1834-1838, continuing as C-in-C until 1846. CinC North America 1847 until his death at Montreal 25 May 1849.

Commissions: cornet 2nd Dragoon Guards April 1794; lieutenant 1 July 1794; captain 2 July 1794; captain 20th (Jamaica) Light Dragoons 25 December 1796; major Warwickshire Fencible Cavalry 21 November 1799; major 89th Foot 17 December 1802; lieutenant colonel 2/West India Regiment 1 January 1805; colonel (brevet) 4 June 1813; major general 12 August 1819; lieutenant general 10 January 1837.

Hart (1840); *ODNB*; *Royal Military Calendar*; Ward

Thomas Dyneley (1782-1860)

Entered Royal Artillery 1801; served with Royal Horse Artillery Maida, Peninsula and Waterloo. Married/issue. Died 21 June 1860.

Commissions: second lieutenant Royal Artillery 1 December 1801; lieutenant 1 July 1803; second captain 28 May 1808; major (brevet) 18 June 1815; lieutenant colonel brevet 10 January 1837; major general 1854; lieutenant general 16 November 1856.

Dalton; Hall; Hart (1840)

George Elder (d. 1837)

Born in Kilcoy. Ross & Cromarty "of humble but respectable parents". Served at Buenos Aires (wounded) and then in the Portuguese service June 1809 to April 1814. Mention in dispatches at Badajoz. Half Pay 27 December 1815. Staff at Madras June 1836 but died there in riding accident 4 December 1837.

Commissions: ensign 46th Foot 27 November 1799; second lieutenant 95th Rifles 5 November 1800; lieutenant 24 March 1803; captain 23 May 1805; major (brevet) 13 April 1809; lieutenant colonel EOPS "attached" to Portuguese Army 30 May 1811; colonel 19 July 1821; major general 22 July 1830.

> *Gentleman's Magazine*; Hall

Henry Walton Ellis (1782-1815)

Son of Lieutenant Colonel John Joyner Ellis, 89th Foot, born in Cambray, Cheltenham 29 November 1782. Served Ostend 1798, Helder 1799, Ferrol 1800, Alexandria 1801, Hanover 1805 and Copenhagen 1707. Served North America and West Indies, then Peninsula from 1810; wounded at Albuera, Badajoz, Salamanca and Pyrenees. Terminated a bullet-riddled career by being badly wounded at Waterloo. Riding to the rear he was thrown in a ditch sustaining further injuries, rescued and carried to an outhouse which caught fire on 19 June and although again rescued, received severe burns and died the next day.

Commissions: ensign 89th Foot 26 March 1783, (aged 4 months!) but half pay when disbanded in same year; ensign 41st Foot 21 September 1789; lieutenant 31 March 1792; captain 23rd Fusiliers 20 January 1796; major 23 October 1804; lieutenant colonel 23 April 1807.

> Dalton; Hall; *Medal Rolls 23rd Royal Welsh Fusiliers*

James Erskine (1765-1825)

Served in West Indies 1791-1797 including period on San Domingo, then Ireland 1798 and afterwards Peninsula; slightly wounded at Oporto and badly wounded at Badajoz. In New South Wales 1817-1823. To Madras 1825 but died on 7 June four days after his arrival.

Commissions: ensign 26th Foot 26 February 1788; lieutenant 22nd Foot 31 December 1791; captain 16 December 1794; major (brevet) 15 December 1803; major 48th Foot 14 February 1805; lieutenant colonel (brevet) 25 July 1810; lieutenant colonel 48th Foot 20 June 1811; colonel (brevet) August 1819.

> *1818 Pension Return*; Hall; *Royal Military Calendar*

Sir William Erskine bt. (1770-1813)

Eldest son of General William Erskine of Torrie, and Francis Moray, born 30 March 1770. Served in Peninsula but generally considered mad as well as incompetent. Committed suicide in Lisbon 13 February 1813.

Commissions: second lieutenant 23rd Fusiliers 23 September 1785; lieutenant 13th Light Dragoons 14 November 1787; captain 15th Light Dragoons 23 February 1791; major 1 March 1794; lieutenant colonel 14 December 1794, half pay February 1796; colonel (brevet half pay) 1 January 1801; colonel 14/Reserve Battalion 9 July 1803, half pay February 1805; major general 25 April 1808.

WO25/3998; Hall

William Cornwallis Eustace (1783-1855)
Son of Captain Charles Eustace 33rd Foot (later Lieutenant General Charles Eustace) and Alicia McCausland; originally named William Harnage Eustace but changed name sometime between 1798 and 1804. served in Ireland 1798 and later in the Peninsula; slightly wounded on Heights of Villares June 1812 and badly wounded 31 August 1813. Married twice/issue, died 1855.

Commissions: lieutenant (half pay 32nd Foot 27 September 1783; lieutenant 6th Foot 1 January 1797; captain 81st Foot 24 December 1802, half pay at Peace of Amiens but full pay again 25 May 1803; major 96th Foot 17 March 1808; lieutenant colonel *Chasseurs Britanniques* 23 August 1810; half pay by reduction 1814; lieutenant colonel 1st Footguards 25 March 1818; colonel (brevet) 12 August 1819, half pay (unattached) 18 May 1826.

WO25/757 f134; Hall.

Henry Samuel Eyre (1770-1851)
Son of Walpole Eyre, owner of St. Johns Wood, born in London 26 August 1770. Served at Gibraltar, then the Low Countries and Germany 1793-1795, Copenhagen 1807 then Portugal as major commanding 82nd Foot. As a reward for good service at Roliea and Vimeiro promoted into 19th Foot and subsequently served on Ceylon before exchanging into the Footguards. No longer in Army List 1814, later embarking on a second career in the church Died Marylebone 6 March 1851.

Commissions: ensign 11th Foot 23 July 1788; lieutenant 2 February 1792; captain 57th Foot 23 October 1793, half pay 94th Foot 1795; captain 12/Reserve Battalion 9 July 1803; major (brevet) 29 April 1804; major 82nd Foot 1 August 1804; lieutenant colonel 19th Foot 8 September 1808; captain and lieutenant colonel 1st Footguards 24 September 1812.

WO25/745

Sir Henry Fane (1779-1840)
Son of Hon. Henry Fane of Fullbeck, Lincolnshire, born 26 November 1779. ADC to his cousin the Earl of Westmorland (then Lord Lieutenant of Ireland) 1793-1794. Still serving in Ireland 1798. Afterwards served throughout Peninsular War. C in C India 1835 but resigned due to ill-heath and died while returning home at sea off the Azores 24 March 1840.

Commissions: cornet 7th Dragoon Guards 31 May 1792; lieutenant 55th Foot 29 September 1792; captain Independent Company 3 April 1793; captain-lieutenant and captain 4th Dragoon Guards 31 August 1793; captain 30 September 1793; major 24 August 1795; lieutenant colonel1 June 1797; colonel (brevet) 1 January 1805; major general 25 July 1810; lieutenant general 12 August 1819; general 10 January 1837.

    Hart (1840); McGuigan & Burnham

Ronald Craufurd Ferguson (1773-1841)
Son of William Ferguson of Raith, Kirkcaldy and Jane Crawford, born Edinburgh 8 February 1773. Served in Flanders 1793; and at the Cape of Good Hope in 1796 and 1806, was appointed major general 25 April 1808 and served at Rolica and Vimeiro, but not afterwards. Married daughter of Sir Hector Monro 1798/issue. Died 10 April 1841.

Commissions: ensign 53rd Foot 3 April 1790; lieutenant 24 January 1791; captain Independent Company 19 February 1793; captain 53rd Foot 23 October 1793; major 84th Foot 31 May 1794; lieutenant colonel 2/84th Foot 18 September 1794; colonel (brevet) 1 January 1800; major general 25 April 1808; lieutenant general 4 June 1813; general 22 July 1830.

    Gentleman's Magazine; Hart (1840*)*

John Forster Fitzgerald (1784-1877)
Son of Colonel Edward Fitzgerald of Carrigoran and Anne Catherine Burton. Served in Peninsula and slightly wounded at Badajoz and returned as missing during the fighting in the Pyrenees in July 1813. Served in Madras 1838 and afterwards in Bombay. Married Charlotte Hazen /issue. Died at Tours 24 March 1877 and buried there by the garrison with all the honours accorded to a Marshal of France.

Commissions: ensign Independent Company 29 October 1793; lieutenant 31 January 1794; captain Half Pay 79th Foot 9 May 1794; captain 46th Foot 1 October 1800; captain New Brunswick Fencibles 9 July 1803; major 25

September 1803; major 5/60th Foot 9 November 1809; lieutenant colonel (brevet) 25 July 1810; colonel (brevet) 12 August 1819; major general 22 July 1830; lieutenant general 23 November 1841; general 20 June 1841; field marshal 29 May 1875.

Hall; Hart (1840); *ODNB*; *Royal Military Calendar*

Richard Fletcher (1768-1813)
Son of Rev. Richard Fletcher, born Ipswich 1768. Married Elizabeth Mudge/ issue. Served West Indies 1791-1796, adjutant Royal Military Artificers 1796-1798; served Syria 1799 but then PoW Egypt 1800-1801. Served Copenhagen, then Peninsula as CRE to Wellington; substantially responsible for designing Lines of Torres Vedras. Slightly wounded during siege of Badajoz 1812 then killed in action at storming of St. Sebastian 31 August 1813.

Commissions: second lieutenant Royal Artillery 9 July 1788; transferred to Royal Engineers 29 June 1790; lieutenant Royal Engineers 16 January 1793; captain-lieutenant 18 August 1797; lieutenant colonel 24 June 1809.

Hall

Thomas Forbes (1774-1814)
Born 7 August 1774, third son of George Forbes, minister of Leochel Aberdeenshire and himself styled of Aberdeen. Mentioned in dispatches at Badajoz, slightly wounded at Salamanca, again at Orthes and killed in action at Toulouse 10 April 1814, leaving a widow and three children.

Commissions: captain 37th Foot 20 October 1796; major 45th Foot 20 October 1808; lieutenant colonel (brevet) 25 April 1812; lieutenant colonel 45th Foot 7 October 1813.

PROB 11/1570/255; Hall

Alexander Fordyce (k.1809)
Brigade major to Hill at Oporto, but when the latter took command of 2nd Division, Fordyce followed him as DAAG. Killed in action at Talavera.

Commissions: ensign 3 May 1796; ensign 81st Foot 24 August 1797; captain 3 September 1798.

Hall; Ward

Sir Haylett Framingham (1763-1820)
Son of Cozens Framingham and Frances Haylett, West Acrew, Norfolk. Served West Indies 1795, Minorca 1798. Served Peninsular War with RHA

until August 1812; slightly wounded at Talavera. Acted as CRA in absence of Major General Borthwick August 1811 to August 1812. Died at Cheltenham 10 May 1820.

Commissions: second lieutenant 29 April 1780; lieutenant Royal Artillery 8 March 1784; captain–lieutenant 14 August 1794; captain 28 September 1797; major (brevet) 20 July 1804; lieutenant colonel 29 December 1805; colonel (brevet) 4 June 1813; major general 12 August 1819.

Hall

John Fremantle (1790–1845)

Only son of General Stephen Francis Fremantle, born 17 January 1790. Attended junior department of Royal Military College, Great Marlow and afterwards served in Germany under Lord Cathcart 1806 and South America under Whitelocke 1807. Served throughout Peninsular War; was ADC to Wellington at Vittoria and sent home with the dispatch. ADC to Wellington again at Waterloo, Married/issue. Died at Tilney Street, London 6 April 1845.

Commissions: ensign Coldstream 17 October 1805; captain and lieutenant colonel 2 August 1810; major (brevet) 21 June 1813; lieutenant colonel (brevet) 21 March 1814; colonel (brevet) 22 July 1830; half-pay unattached 31 December 1839; major general 23 November 1841.

Dalton; *Gentleman's Magazine*; Hart (1840)

Daniel Gardner

Killed in action at Talavera while serving as brigade major to Richard Stewart.

Commissions: lieutenant 25 February 1802; lieutenant 43rd Foot 4 March 1802; captain 43rd Foot 27 August 1804.

Robert Gardiner (1781–1864)

Born 2 May 1781, the youngest son of Captain John Gardiner of the 3rd Foot. Entered Royal Artillery as cadet 1795 and went to Gibraltar in October 1797, then Minorca 1798, Hanover 1805, Peninsula 1808, Walcheren 1809 and back to Peninsula; mentioned in dispatches at Badajoz, commanded battery at Salamanca and afterwards commanded E troop RHA to end of war. Later at Quatre Bras and Waterloo. Subsequently Governor and Colonel in Chief Gibraltar 1848. Married/issue. Died at Melborne Lodge, Claremont 26 June 1864.

Commissions: second lieutenant Royal Artillery 7 April 1797; lieutenant 16 July 1799; captain 12 October 1804; major (brevet) 12 March 1812; lieutenant colonel (brevet) 3 March 1814; lieutenant colonel Royal Artillery 30 December 1828; colonel (brevet) 22 July 1830; colonel Royal Artillery 24 November 1839. Major general 23 November 1841; lieutenant general 11 October 1851; general 28 November 1854;
> Dalton; Hart (1840); *ODNB*

Edward Gibbs (1778?-1847)
Son of Samuel Gibbs of Horseley Park, Sussex. Served Ferrol, Sicily and Peninsula; Cuidad Rodrigo, Badajoz (lost an eye), and Vittoria. Latterly governor of Jersey. Died there 24 January 1847 "in his 70th year".

Commissions: ensign 59th Foot 14 November 1798, exch. immediately to 52nd Foot; lieutenant 52nd Foot 28 November 1799; captain 24 February 1803; major 4 February 1808; lieutenant colonel (brevet) 6 February 1812; colonel (brevet) 27 May 1825; major general 10 January 1837; lieutenant general 9 November 1846.
> *Gentleman's Magazine*; Hart (1840)

William Maynard Gomm (1784-1875)
Eldest son of Lieutenant Colonel William Gomm and Mary Allen Maynard, born Barbados 1784. Commissioned aged 10 just before his father was killed in action at the storming of Pointe a Pitre, Guadaloupe 1 July 1794. He himself served at Den Helder 1799 and afterwards at Ferrol, Copenhagen and the Peninsula, then Walcheren and back to the Peninsula. Appointed DAQMG 1 September 1810 and AQMG 6 December 1811. Attached to 5th Division for the duration of the war and AQMG at Waterloo. Subsequently C-in-C Jamaica 1839-41; Mauritius 1842-49 and India 1850-55. Married Elizabeth Kerr 1830 and died at Brighton 15 March 1875.

Commissions: ensign 9th Foot 24 May 1794; lieutenant 16 November 1794; captain 25 June 1803; major 10 October 1811; lieutenant colonel 17 August 1812; captain and lieutenant colonel Coldstream 25 July 1814; colonel (brevet) 12 February 1830; major general 10 January 1837; lieutenant general 9 November 1846; general 20 June 1854; field marshal 1 January 1868.
> Dalton; Hart (1840); *ODNB*; Ward

Hon. Alexander William Gordon (1786-1815)
Third son of John Gordon, Lord Haddo and Charlotte Baird. Served as ADC to his uncle, Sir David Baird, at the Cape 1806 and at Buenos Aires

and Corunna. Subsequently ADC to Wellington in the Peninsula and at Waterloo, where he was fatally wounded.

Commissions: ensign 3rd Footguards 26 May 1803; lieutenant and captain 3 April 1806; major (brevet) 26 May 1810; lieutenant colonel (brevet) 6 February 1812; captain and lieutenant colonel 3rd Footguards 15 January 1815.
    Dalton; *Gordons under Arms* (196); Hall

Sir Thomas Graham (1748-1843)

Third son of Thomas Graham of Balnagowan and Lady Christian Hope, born 19 October 1748. Had no military experience prior to July 1793 when he served as ADC to Lord Mulgrave at Toulon. According to a well-known story this arose from his outrage at the desecration of his late wife's body by French officials who searched her coffin for hidden valuables. Subsequently raised 90th Foot and was at Quiberon then British military commissioner to Austrian Army in Italy 1796-98. Served in Mediterranean 1798-1802; Minorca 1798; appointed to command land forces for Malta expedition and blockaded Valetta until capitulation in September 1800. Went on the abortive Swedish expedition of 1808 and then to Spain and Corunna. Commanded brigade at Walcheren 1809 but invalided home then to command garrison of Cadiz where he won the battle of Barossa February 1811. Appointed to command 1st Division under Wellington in June 1811 and also had additional responsibility for the 6th and 7th Divisions. Went home shortly before Salamanca due to an eye infection but returned to Peninsula 1813 in time for Vittoria. Again entrusted with a wing of the army and took San Sebastian before again going home sick. Thereafter served in Holland from November 1813 to the end of the war. Created Baron Lyndoch of Balnagowan May 1814 and died in London 18 December 1843.

Commissions: lieutenant colonel commandant 90th Foot (temporary) 10 February 1794*; colonel (brevet) 22 July 1795; brigadier general (Mediterranean) November 1799; major general 25 September 1803; lieutenant general 25 July 1810; general 19 July 1821.
*commissions remained temporary until made substantive after Corunna in 1809
    Hart; *ODNB*

William Grant

Served in North America and in West Indies during Revolution, then India; Sringapatnam 1792. Cochin and Columbo 1795 and 1796. Returned to Britain 1802, served Walcheren 1809 then Peninsula. Badly wounded at Vittoria 21 June 1813 while commanding brigade in 7th Division. Slightly wounded at Maya 25 July 1813 and wounded again five days later outside Pamplona. Purchased Tanachie, near Findhorn 1816 and died c.1824.

Commissions: ensign 42nd Highlanders 24 October 1773; ensign 55th Foot 24 October 1778; adjutant 27 December 1778; lieutenant 7 February 1781; captain Independent Company 24 January 1791; captain 77th Foot 16 March 1791; major (brevet) 1 January 1798; lieutenant colonel 14/Reserve Battalion 9 July 1803; lieutenant colonel 1/82nd Foot 15 August 1805; colonel (brevet) 1 January 1812; major general 4 June 1813.

   1818 Pension Return; Hall; Royal Military Calendar

George Gray (k.1812)

Served in Peninsula April to May 1809, and again from June 1810. Fatally wounded at Badajoz 6 April 1812 and died the following day.

Commissions: lieutenant 6th Dragoon Guards 22 April 1794; captain 12 January 1799; captain 30th Foot 12 March 1799; major 30th Foot 1 December 1804; lieutenant colonel (brevet) 4 June 1811.

Charles John Greville (1780-1837)

Second son of George Greville, 2nd Earl of Warwick and Henrietta Vernon, born 5 April 1780. Served in India and then with Baird in Egypt. Served in Peninsula at Corunna, then Walcheren before returning to the Peninsula and serving throughout the war. Died in Hill Street Berkeley Square 2 December 1837.

Commissions: ensign 10th Foot 1796; lieutenant 12 July 1796; captain 26 December 1799; major 38th Foot 13 April 1803; lieutenant colonel 21 March 1805; colonel (brevet) 4 June 1813; major general 12 August 1819 (retaining regimental commission).

   Gentleman's Magazine

John Grey (1772-1856)

Younger son of Charles Grey of Morwick Hall and Catherine Maria Skelly, baptised at Embleton, Northumberland 18 March 1772. Served in India; Malavelley and Sringapatnam. Afterwards in Peninsula; slightly wounded during the siege of Cuidad Rodrigo and badly wounded during the storm on 19 January 1812. After a long period on half pay from 1816 he again served in India 1840-1852 culminating in the appointment as C-in-C Bombay December 1850. Died 19 February 1856.

Commissions: ensign 75th Highlanders 18 July 1798; lieutenant 8 May 1799; major 27 November 1806; captain 15/Reserve Battalion 31 October 1803; captain 82nd Foot 23 August 1804; major 9/Garrison Battalion 27 November 1806; major 99th Foot 13 June 1811; lieutenant colonel (brevet) 6 February 1812; half-pay 1816; colonel (brevet) 22 July 1830; major general 28 June 1838; lieutenant general (East Indies) 30 December 1850; lieutenant general 11 November 1851.

Hall; *ODNB*

John Wright Guise (1777-1865)

Second son of Sir John Guise and Elizabeth Wright, born Highnam Court, Gloucestershire 20 July 1777. Served in Egypt 1801 and Hanover 1805, then Peninsula; Fuentes d'Onoro, Salamanca, Vittoria and the Nive. Married Charlotte Diana Vernon 12 August 1815/issue. Died at Elmore, Gloucestershire 1 April 1865.

Commissions: ensign 70th Foot 4 November 1794; ensign 3rd Footguards 4 March 1795; lieutenant and captain 25 October 1798; captain and lieutenant colonel 25 July 1805; colonel (brevet) 4 June 1813; major general 12 August 1819; lieutenant general 10 January 1837; general 11 November 1851.

Hall; Hart; *ODNB*

John Gurwood (1790-1845)

Son of "poor but honest parents in the East Riding of Yorkshire". Served in Peninsula, initially with 52nd, badly commanding one of the forlorn hopes at Cuidad Rodrigo He was promoted to a company in the Royal African corps and served for a while as ADC to Lord Edward Somerset. He exchanged to the 9th Light Dragoons and was appointed brigade-major of the household cavalry on the arrival of the service squadrons of the Life Guards and Blues in the Peninsula before transferred as brigade-major to Lambert's brigade of the 6th Division. He was one of the officers brought into the 10th Hussars after Colonel Quentin's acquittal in 1814. Gurwood then served as ADC to Sir Henry Clinton when second in command under the Prince of Orange in the Netherlands and was briefly DAQMG at the prince's headquarters, He had received three wounds in the Peninsula, and was again wounded (in the knee) at Waterloo. Deputy Lieutenant of the Tower of London 15 November 1839. Gurwood was for many years private secretary to the Duke of Wellington and was entrusted with the difficult task of editing of the Duke's general orders and selections from his despatches, but eventually succumbed to depression and committed suicide 25 January 1845.

Commissions: ensign 52nd Foot 30 March 1808; lieutenant 3 August 1809; captain 9th Light Dragoons 6 February 1812; major (brevet) 6 March 1817; lieutenant colonel (unattached) 15 March 1827; half-pay 1/West India 20 July 1830; colonel 23 November 1841.

Dalton; Hart (1840); *Royal Military Calendar*

Colin Halkett (1774-1856)
Eldest son of Major General Frederick Godar Halkett and Georgina Robina Seton, born at Venlo, Holland, 7 September 1774. Served in Dutch and Hanoverian armies before finally entering British service as lieutenant colonel King's German Regiment (afterwards King's German Legion). Served Hanover 1805 and Copenhagen 1807, then Peninsula; Albuera, Salamanca, Vittoria and passage of the Nive. Badly wounded at Waterloo. Lieutenant Governor of Jersey July 1821-August 1830, commander-in-chief Bombay July 1831-January 1832. Married Letitia Crickett/issue. Died 24 September 1856 while serving as Governor of Chelsea Hospital.

Commissions: ensign 3rd Foot 3 January 1799 (never joined); captain 2/ Dutch Light Infantry 1800; lieutenant colonel King's German Regiment 17 November 1803; colonel (brevet) 1 January 1812; major general 4 June 1814; lieutenant general 22 July 1830; general 9 November 1846.

Dalton; Hart (1840); *ODNB*

John Hamilton (1755-1835)
Son of James Hamilton of Woodbrooke and Strabane, Co. Tyrone, and Elinor Stewart, born 4 August 1755. Originally entered East India Company service 1771, transferred to British Army 1788 and served at Sringapatnam1792, then on San Domingo 1797-1797; appointed Inspector General of Portuguese infantry October 1809 then appointed to command a Portuguese division 16 December 1809 until November 1813 when he retired and became Governor of Duncannon 10 May 1814. Married Emily Sophia Mock 1794/issue. Died at Tunbridge Wells 24 December 1835.

Commissions: ensign Bengal Native Infantry 22 March 1773; lieutenant 22 March 1778; captain 15 October 1781; captain 76th Foot 1 November 1788; major (brevet) 1 March 1794; lieutenant colonel 61st Foot 20 February 1795;

lieutenant colonel 81st Foot 23 December 1795; colonel (brevet) 29 April 1802; major general 25 October 1809; lieutenant general 4 June 1814.
ODNB; *Royal Military Calendar*

Charles Amédée Harcourt (1771-1831)

Amédée Louis André Marie Charles François d'Harcourt was born France in 1771. Entered British Army as volunteer in Flanders 1793 as ADC to Lieutenant General Lord Harcourt then commanded troop of Salm Hussars. Resigned to accept British commission December 1794. ADC to General Don 1798, served on staff in Helder 1799; on mission to Russia 1800; ADC to General Fox Malta 1801 then AQMG in Ireland 1803-1809; DQMG at Cape of Good Hope 1809; commanded 1/40th Foot in Peninsula May 1810 to May 1811; again in Peninsula October 1811 to April 1812; commanded a brigade in 4th Division and wounded at Badajoz. Died when thrown from a horse at Windsor 14 September 1831.

Commissions: ensign 127th Foot 11 December; lieutenant 99th Foot 20 December 1794; lieutenant 16th Light Dragoons 7 April 1795; captain 20th Foot 22 October 1799; major half-pay 40th Foot 25 September 1802; lieutenant colonel 1 November 1804; lieutenant colonel 40th Foot 25 January 1810; colonel (brevet) 4 June 1813; half pay 1814; major general 12 August 1819.
1818 Pension Return; Hall; *Royal Military Calendar*

William Maundy Harvey (1774-1813)

Only son of Samuel Harvey Esq. of Ramsgate, Kent. Served Copenhagen and afterwards in Peninsula in Portuguese service August 1809 until death. Badly wounded at Badajoz while serving as brigadier in 4th Division. Died at sea 10 June 1813 while returning home to recover his strength. Married/issue.

Commissions: captain 1/West India Regiment 22 July 1797; lieutenant colonel (brevet) 17 December 1803; major 1/West India Regiment 4 June 1805; major 79th Highlanders 27 February 1806; colonel (brevet) 30 December 1811.
Hall

James Hay (d.1854)

Son of John Hay, born in Braco, Perthshire. Served in Peninsula; wounded at Salamanca and later badly wounded at Waterloo. Died at Kilburn, Co. Longford 25 February 1854.

Commissions: cornet 16th (Queens) Light Dragoons 10 June 1795; lieutenant 26 April 1798; captain 28 February 1805; major 2 January 1812; lieutenant colonel 18 February 1813; colonel (brevet) 22 July 1830; half-pay as lieutenant colonel 27 October 1837; major general 23 November 1841; lieutenant general 11 November 1851.

> Dalton; *Gentleman's Magazine*; Hart; *Royal Military Calendar*

Felton Elwell Hervey (1782-1819)
Eldest son of Fenton Lionel Hervey, born 24 June 1782. Lost an arm at Oporto but continued in the service and was an AQMG at Waterloo and ADC to Wellington in the Army of Occupation. Married Louisa Catherine Caton of Maryland 24 April 1817. Created baronet in 1818 but died 24 September 1819.

Commissions: cornet 3rd Dragoon Guards 6 May 1800; captain 9 July 1803; captain 14th Light Dragoons 28 July 1803; major 14th Light Dragoons 8 May 1806; lieutenant colonel 12 July 1810; colonel (brevet) 4 June 1814.

> Dalton; *Waterloo Roll Call*; Hall

Clement Hill (1781-1845).
Younger brother of Sir Rowland Hill, born 6 December 1781. Served as ADC to his brother being slightly wounded at Oporto and badly wounded at Waterloo. C-in-C Madras 1837. Died at Falls of Gairsoppa, Canara, Madras 20 January 1845.

Commissions: cornet 22 August 1805; lieutenant 6 March 1806; captain Royal Regiment of Horse Guards 4 April 1811; major (brevet) 19 December 1811; lieutenant colonel (brevet) 30 December 1813; colonel (brevet) 21 June 1827; major general 10 January 1837.

> Dalton; Hart; *Gentleman's Magazine*

Dudley St. Leger Hill (1787-1851)
Eldest son of Dudley Hill of Co. Carlow; married twice/issue. Served South America 1807, then throughout Peninsula War seconded to Portuguese service until 1821, first with the Loyal Lusitanian Legion, then the 8th Line. Appears to have made a career of getting wounded; wounded in thigh and captured Buenos Aires; slightly wounded at Rolica, Vimeiro and Benavente; wounded and captured at river Carrion 25 October 1811, but subsequently escaped; badly wounded at Salamanca; slightly wounded at Burgos; badly

wounded at St. Sebastian and wounded again at Bayonne. Later lieutenant governor of St. Lucia 1834–1838. Commanded a division in Bengal 1848 and died of apoplexy at Ambala 21 February 1851.

Commissions: ensign 82nd Foot 6 September 1804; lieutenant 95th Rifles 10 October 1805; captain Royal West India Rangers 16 August 1810; major (brevet) 27 April 1812; lieutenant colonel (brevet) 21 June 1813; major 95th (Derbyshire) Regiment December 1823; half pay January 1826; major general 23 November 1841.

WO25/762 f48; Hall; *ODNB; Royal Military Calendar*

George Hill (d.1830)

Served in Holland and Germany 1794–95; Helder 1799; then Peninsula – wounded and captured at Fuentes d'Onoro while commanding forward picquets of Guards Brigade and remained a prisoner until the war's end. Died in Bury Street, St. James's 31 October 1830.

Commissions: ensign 3rd Footguards 4 April 1794; lieutenant and captain 9 February 1797; captain and lieutenant colonel 8 November 1804; colonel (brevet) 4 June 1813; lieutenant colonel 3rd Footguards 25 July 1814; major general 12 August 1819.

Gentleman's Magazine; Royal Military Calendar

Sir Rowland Hill (1772–1842)

Second son of Sir John Hill and Mary Chambre, born at Prees, Shropshire 11 August 1772 and studied at Strasbourg military academy. Entered army 1790 and served as ADC to General O'Hara at Toulon, then served in Egypt 1801 and commanded brigade on Hanover expedition. Served throughout Peninsular War, becoming Wellington's most trusted subordinate. Created Baron Hill of Almaraz and Hardwick 1814. Commanded I Corps at Waterloo and afterwards second in command of Army of Occupation 1815–1818. In retirement for next ten years but C-in-C from 1828 until death at Hardwick Grange 10 December 1842.

Commissions: ensign 38th Foot 31 July 1790; lieutenant 53rd Foot 24 January 1791; captain (brevet) 23 March 1793*; captain 86th Foot 30 October 1793; major 90th Foot 10 February 1794; lieutenant colonel 90th Foot 13 May 1794; colonel (brevet) 1 January 1800; major general 30 October 1805; lieutenant general 1 January 1812; general 27 May 1825; colonel Royal Horse Guards 19 November 1830.

*An unusual promotion; ordinarily the lowest rank conferred by brevet was that of major. This brevet captaincy was presumably connected with his appointment as ADC to General O'Hara.

ODNB; Dalton; Hart

Samuel Venables Hinde (d.1837)

Eldest son and heir of Robert Hinde of Hunsdon House, Hitchin. Served as a marine with the Mediterranean Fleet 1793-1797, including ashore at Toulon and on Corsica. Received brevet majority for helping quell an incipient mutiny on board HMS *St.George* 1797. Served Helder 1799, Copenhagen 1807; Peninsula 1808, Walcheren 1809 and back to Peninsula 1811, commanding a brigade 1812-1813 but badly wounded during a demonstration covering the crossing of the Bidassoa and invalided home. Died at Hitchin 25 September 1837.

Commissions: ensign 25th Foot 24 January 1788; lieutenant 28 March 1792; captain 3 April 1795; major (brevet) 6 July 1797; major 32nd Foot 5 November 1800; lieutenant colonel (brevet) 29 April 1802; colonel (brevet) 4 June 1811; major general 4 June 1814; lieutenant general 22 July 1830

Royal Military Calendar

Harcourt Fort Holcombe (1778-1847)

Born 6 January 1778, son of Canon William Holcombe of St. Davids Pembrokeshire and Mary Aldridge. Entered Royal Artillery 1795 but saw no active service until going to the Peninsula in 1808. In 1811 he volunteered to either join an embassy to Persia or go to the Peninsula and so ended up at Lisbon. Mentioned in despatches at Cuidad Rodrigo. After Badajoz went to Sicily and served on east coast of Spain. Latterly appointed Commander Royal Artillery at Lisbon and responsible for recovering all the magazines and other Royal Artillery materiel dumped throughout the Peninsula over the course of the war. Married/ issue. Died in Edinburgh 6 March 1847 and buried Dunkeld Cathedral.

Commissions: second lieutenant Royal Artillery 6 March 1795; lieutenant 1 July 1796; captain-lieutenant and captain 12 September 1803; captain 3 December 1806; major (brevet) 6 February 1812; lieutenant colonel (brevet) 27 April 1812; lieutenant colonel Royal Artillery 25 August 1825.

Hart (1840); *Royal Military Calendar*

James Archibald Hope (1786-1871)

Son of Lieutenant Colonel Erskine Hope 26th Foot, born 14 April 1786. Served Hanover 1805 and DAG under Cathcart at Copenhagen 1807. Served Peninsula

1808-9, then Walcheren and again in Peninsula 1810 to the end of the war; Barossa, Cuidad Rodrigo; Badajoz; Salamanca forts; Vittoria; St, Sebastian, Bidassoa; Nivelle, Nive, Orthes and Toulouse. Appointed AAG 25 February 1813, acting with Graham's column, but transferred to Beresford's autumn 1813. Afterwards served as major general on the staff in Lower Canada 1841-1847. Married/issue. Died at Balgowan House, Pittville, Cheltenham 30 December 1871.

Commissions: ensign 26th Foot 12 January 1800; lieutenant 3 June 1801; captain 18 February 1806; major 90th Foot 6 March 1811; lieutenant colonel (brevet) 21 June 1813; captain and lieutenant colonel 3rd Footguards 25 July 1814; colonel (brevet) 22 July 1830; Retired on half pay as lieutenant colonel 1 November 1839; major general 23 November 1841; lieutenant general 11 November 1851; general 12 June 1859.

    Hart (1840); *ODNB*; Ward

John Hope (1765-1836)

Not to be confused with Sir John Hope, later Earl of Hopetoun, he was the son of the writer and politician John Hope and was born 15 July 1765. From 1778-1782 he served in the Dutch Army's Scotch Brigade, then on British half-pay until commissioned in the 60th Foot 1787. Served Flanders and Germany 1793-95 as ADC to Sir William Erskine, then Cape with 28th Light Dragoons and West Indies with 37th Foot. Briefly AAG Scotland then DAG under Cathcart in Hanover 1805 and Denmark 1807. Served in Peninsula, commanding 7th Division at Salamanca but invalided home in September, afterwards serving on staff in Ireland and in Scotland. Married twice/issue. Died August 1836.

Commissions: captain 60th Foot 29 September 1787; captain 13th Light Dragoons 30 June 1788; major 25 March 1795; lieutenant colonel 28th Light Dragoons 20 February 1796; lieutenant colonel 37th Foot 19 April 1799; lieutenant colonel 60th Foot November 1804; colonel (brevet) 1 January 1805; major general 25 July 1810; lieutenant general 12 August 1819.

    ODNB

Sir William Houston (1766-1842)

Born 10 August 1766, Served West Indies and Flanders, then at taking of Minorca, Egypt 1801, then Mediterranean and Ireland, Walcheren 1809 and the Peninsula as commander of 7th Division from formation in March 1811 until invalided home due to Walcheren Fever sometime before 1 August. Married Lady Jane Maitland 1808/issue. Died at Bromley Hill, Kent 8 April 1842.

Commissions: ensign 31st Foot 18 July 1781; lieutenant Independent Company 2 April 1782; captain 77th Foot 13 March 1783, half pay; captain 19th Foot 20 July 1785; major 19th Foot 1 March 1794; lieutenant colonel 84th Foot 18 March 1795; lieutenant colonel 58th Foot 10 June 1795; colonel (brevet) 29 April 1802; major general 25 October 1809; lieutenant general 4 June 1814; general 10 January 1837.

> Hart; *ODNB*; *Royal Military Calendar*

Sir Edward Howorth

Commanded Royal Artillery at Talavera, Busaco and Fuentes d'Onoro. Died March 1827.

Commissions: first lieutenant Royal Artillery 7 July 1779; captain 1 December 1782; major (brevet) 1 March 1794; lieutenant colonel (brevet) 1 January 1798; lieutenant colonel Royal Artillery 18 April 1801; colonel 29 December 1805; major general 4 June 1811; lieutenant general 12 August 1819.

> *Royal Military Calendar*

Edward Hull (1771-1810)

Son of Major Trevor Hull 36th Foot and a mulatto named Ann Gibbons, born Jamaica c.1771. Served Peninsula and killed in action at the Coa 24 July 1810.

Commissions: lieutenant Independent company 24 January 1791; lieutenant 43rd Foot 31 December 1791; captain 1 September 1795; major 10 August 1804; lieutenant colonel 8 September 1808.

> Hall

Richard Hulse (c1775-1812)

Third son of Sir Edward Hulse, third baronet. Served in Flanders 1793, Hanover 1805, Copenhagen 1807, and Peninsula from 1809, successively commanding 1/Coldstream, a brigade in 6th Division and finally 5th Division only to die of typhus at Arevalo on 7 September 1812.

Commissions: ensign Coldstream 24 March 1790; lieutenant and captain 25 April 1793; captain-lieutenant and lieutenant colonel 23 September 1799; captain and lieutenant colonel 9 May 1800; colonel (brevet) 25 October 1809; brigadier 23 July 1811; major general (Spain and Portugal) 26 October 1811; major general 1 January 1812.

> McGuigan & Burnham; Hall

William Inglis (1764–1835)
Third son of William Inglis MD, born in Edinburgh 1764. Served in North America during the Revolution, then Canada. Served Flanders in 1793 and again 1794–95. Afterwards in West Indies 1796–1802, present at taking of St Lucia. Served Channel Islands and Gibraltar to 1809 then Peninsula. Wounded at Albuera and carried off the field exhorting his men to "Die Hard". Subsequently commanded a brigade in 7th Division May 1813 to end of war. Lieutenant Governor of Kinsale 1827 then Governor of Cork 1829. Married/issue. Died at Ramsgate, Kent 29 November 1835.

Commissions: ensign 57th Foot 11 October 1779; lieutenant 3 May 1782; captain-lieutenant and captain 11 July 1785; captain 30 June 1787; major (brevet) 6 May 1795; major 57th Foot 1 September 1795; lieutenant colonel (brevet) 1 January 1800; lieutenant colonel 57th Foot 16 August 1804; colonel (brevet) 25 July 1810; brigadier general 21 January 1813; major general 4 June 1813; lieutenant general 27 May 1825.
     Hall; *ODNB*; McGuigan & Burnham

William Iremonger (1776–1852)
Son of Joshua Iremonger, born Donnington, Berkshire 31 September 1776. Served Toulon, Egypt, Buenos Aires, and Peninsula. Seemingly a very inefficient officer and reckoned culpable for Brenier's escape from Almeida, but perhaps fortunately for himself had already arranged to sell out with effect from 2 May 1811. Died at Andover, Hants. 21 January 1852.

Commissions: ensign 18th Foot 29 February 1792; lieutenant 1794; captain 44th Foot 10 February 1796; major 11/Reserve Battalion 1804; major 88th Foot September 1804; lieutenant colonel 2nd Foot 17 March 1808.

John Thomas Jones (1783–1843)
Eldest of five sons of John Jones, general superintendent of Landguard Fort, where he was born 25 March 1783. Entered Royal Engineers 1798 and served Gibraltar 1798–1803 and on return to England employed on Chelmsford Lines. Served Mediterranean 1805–06. Appointed adjutant at Woolwich 1 January 1807, Served Peninsula 1808 then Walcheren. Returning to Peninsula was appointed brigade major of Engineers at Cuidad Rodrigo and Badajoz. Wounded at Burgos, spending time while convalescing writing a *Journal of Sieges carried on by the Allies in Spain in 1810, 1811 and 1812*. Afterwards served in Army of Occupation. Married Catherine Maria Lawrence 1816/issue. Died at Cheltenham 25 February 1843.

Commissions: second lieutenant Royal Engineers 30 August 1798; lieutenant 14 September 1800; second captain 1 March 1805; captain 24 June 1809; major (brevet) 6 February 1812; lieutenant colonel (brevet) 27 April 1812; lieutenant colonel Royal Engineers 16 November 1816; colonel (brevet) 27 May 1825; major general 10 January 1837.

Hall; *ODNB*; *Royal Military Calendar*

William Kelly (d.1818)
Served in Canada (Quebec garrison); Egypt 1801; Cape 1806 and the Peninsula; badly wounded in Pyrenees 2 August 1813. Afterwards served Nepal 1816.

Commissions: ensign 28th Foot 14 December 1785; ensign 24th Foot 31 August 1787; lieutenant 27 June 1792; captain-lieutenant and captain 3 September 1795; captain 28 October 1795; major 5 April 1799; lieutenant colonel (brevet) 1 January 1805; lieutenant colonel 24th Foot 22 February 1810; colonel (brevet) 4 June 1813.

WO25/3998; Hall

James Kemmis (1751-1820)
Second son of Thomas Kemmis of Shaen Castle, Queens County, Ireland, born 1 January 1751. Taken prisoner at Saratoga 1777. Subsequently served Flanders and Holland 1794-1795, then West Indies to 1798. Served Helder 1799 and Egypt 1801, then Irish Staff 1807-1808 before going to Portugal; Rolica and Vimeiro. Afterwards in garrison at Elvas and then Seville before commanding brigade in 4th Division until 1812 when removed to Irish Staff. Died at Cheltenham 2 April 1820.

Commissions: ensign 9th Foot 7 July 1775; lieutenant 3 June 1777; captain 21 January 1784, then half-pay; captain 40th Foot 31 March 1790; major (brevet) 1 March 1794; lieutenant colonel (brevet) 1 January 1798; major 40th Foot 5 August 1799; lieutenant colonel 40th Foot 1 August 1804; colonel (brevet) 25 April 1808; brigadier general 23 January 1811; major general 4 June 1811.

WO25/3998; McGuigan and Burnham; *Royal Military Calendar*

William Howe Knight (Erskine) (1782-1843)
Son of Colonel Henry Knight and Mary Erskine of Pittodrie, Aberdeenshire; subsequently adopted name Erskine on inheriting his mother's estate in 1813. Aged 12 on receiving his first commission; "In consequence of my Father's services, His late Royal Highness the Duke of York was pleased to grant me an

Ensigncy at a very early age." Served in Peninsula where he was badly wounded at Badajoz and in consequence retired as a major on the half pay of Bradshaw's Recruiting Corps in 1813. Married in London 12 August 1812/issue.

Commissions: ensign 27th Foot 1794; lieutenant 3 September 1795; captain 19 December 1799; major 12 December 1805; lieutenant colonel (brevet) 1 January 1812.
    WO25/757 f107; Hall

George Augustus Frederick Lake (1781–1808)
Son of Lieutenant General Gerard Lake. Had previously served in India, being wounded at Laswaree while helping his father to remount. Killed on action at Rolica 1808 – seemingly ambushed in a defile while leading his grenadier company.

Commissions: lieutenant 20th Foot 24 May 1797; captain 17 January 1799; captain 4th Foot 5 September 1799; lieutenant colonel 29th Foot 12 November 1803.
    Hall

Robert Lawson (d.1826)
Son of Lieutenant General Robert Lawson RA. Served throughout Peninsular War and mentioned in despatches for Vittoria.

Commissions: first lieutenant Royal Artillery 17 January 1793; captain-lieutenant and captain 4 March 1797; captain (brevet) 1 March 1804; captain Royal Artillery 29 June 1808; major (brevet) 17 August 1812.
    Hall

John Thomas Leaky (b. 1783)
Born in Cork 1783. Served Helder 1799, Copenhagen 1807, Martinique 1809, the Peninsula; Badajoz and Albuera 1811, commanded brigade light companies at Aldea de Ponte after Thomas Pearson was wounded and himself wounded while commanding 23rd Fusiliers at Badajoz 1812.

Commissions: ensign 69th Foot 18 June 1799; lieutenant 4th Foot August 1799; lieutenant 69th Foot 14 July 1802; captain 2/23rd Fusiliers 12 January 1805; major (brevet) 27 February 1812; major 23rd Fusiliers 17 June 1813, exchanged to half pay 7th Royal Fusiliers early 1815 but returned to full pay as major 21st Royal Scots Fusiliers 22 April 1819; lieutenant colonel 24 Augusts 1821; retired 16 October 1834.
    WO25/789 f1; *1818 Pension Return*; Hall; *Medal Rolls 23rd RWF*

Sir James Leith (1763-1816)
Third son of John Leith of Leith Hall, Aberdeenshire, and Harriet Steuart, born 8 August 1763. Served at Gibraltar from 1784, then Toulon 1793 as ADC to David Dundas. Raised and commanded Aberdeen (Princess of Wales) Fencibles. Served on Irish staff, then Walcheren and the Peninsula, latterly in command of 5th Division. Wounded badly, but not dangerously at Salamanca and again badly wounded at storming of San Sebastian 1813. Afterwards governor of Barbados but died there of yellow fever 16 October 1816.

Commissions: second lieutenant 7th Royal Fusiliers 1780; captain 81st Highlanders 23 November 1782; captain 50th Foot 25 June 1784; lieutenant colonel Aberdeen (Princess of Wales) Fencibles 25 October 1794; colonel (brevet) 1 January 1801; colonel 13/Reserve Battalion 9 July 1803; major general 25 April 1808; lieutenant general (Spain and Portugal) 6 September 1811; lieutenant general 4 June 1813.

> *ODNB*; Westminster Abbey

John Gaspard Le Marchant (1766-1812)
Eldest son of John Le Marchant and Marie Hirzel, born near Amiens 9 February 1766. Served Gibraltar 1783-1787, then Flanders 1793. Subsequently responsible for Sword Exercise and 1796 pattern light cavalry sword. Founder and superintendent of Royal Military College at High Wycombe 1807. Served in Peninsula 1812 but killed in action at Salamanca 22 July 1812. Married/issue.

Commissions: ensign Wiltshire Militia 25 September 1781; ensign 2/1st (Royal) Regiment 18 February 1783; cornet 6th Dragoons 30 May 1787; lieutenant 2nd Dragoon Guards 18 November 1789; captain 31 December 1791; major 16th Light Dragoons 11 March 1794; lieutenant colonel (brevet) 6 April 1797; lieutenant colonel Hompesch Hussars 16 April 1797; lieutenant colonel 29th Light Dragoons 29 May 1797; lieutenant colonel 2nd Dragoon Guards 19 July 1799; half pay 1803; colonel (brevet) 2 November 1805; lieutenant colonel 6th Dragoon Guards 25 July 1811; major general 4 June 1811.

> Hall; *ODNB*

Henry Blois Lynch (d.1823)
Of Partry House, Ballinrobe, co. Mayo. Normally styled Blois Lynch. Served Copenhagen 1807; Major 16th Portuguese Line 18 September 1811.

Mentioned in dispatches Cuidad Rodrigo. Salamanca, Burgos, Vittoria, Biddasoa. Retired 13 October 1814. Married/issue – 11 sons.

Commissions: ensign 20th Foot 28 March 1795; lieutenant 29th Foot 6 May 1795, transf. to Experimental corps of Riflemen 25 August 1800; captain 95th Rifles 25 June 1803; half pay Royal York Rangers 1805; Major (brevet) 1 January 1814; captain 73rd Foot 28 June 1815; half pay 27th Foot.
>   Challis; *Royal Military Calendar*

Sir James Frederick Lyon (1775-1844)
Son of Captain James Lyon 35th Foot, killed at Bunker Hill; commanded detachment on board HMS Marlborough in "Glorious First of June" 1794; Grenada 1796; Mediterranean 1799 and Egypt 1801. Commanded 97th Foot during the Peninsular War; sent to Germany in 1813, commanding Hanoverian troops at Gohrde, Hamburg and Waterloo. Married Anne Cox; died at Brighton 14 October 1844.

Commissions: ensign 25th Foot 4 August 1791; lieutenant 26 April 1793; captain 5 April 1795; major 97th Foot 21 February 1799; lieutenant colonel 13 May 1802; colonel (brevet) 4 June 1811; major general 4 June 1814; lieutenant general 22 July 1830.
>   Dalton; Hart; *ODNB*

Archibald MacDonnell (d.1814)
With 92nd Highlanders from first raising. Served Peninsula 1808-9, then Walcheren before returning to Peninsula. Died in Lochaber 1814.

Commissions: ensign 79th Highlanders; lieutenant 100th/92nd Highlanders 11 February 1794; captain 17 January 1799; major 29 August 1805; lieutenant colonel (brevet) 30 May 1811; lieutenant colonel 9/Royal Veterans 9 September 1813.
>   Bulloch, J.M. *Territorial Soldiering in the North East of Scotland* (Aberdeen 1914)

Aeneas MacIntosh (d.1814)
Served in West Indies, then Helder, Walcheren and afterwards the Peninsula; Fuentes d'Onoro and failed attempt to take the San Christobal fort at Badajoz 6 June 1811. As a result of destructive dissention within the 85th Foot he was court-martialled in 1812. Although he was acquitted it was thought best to disperse the officers amongst other regiments; MacIntosh was to have gone to the 79th Highlanders but died suddenly in January 1814.

Commissions: captain 85th Foot 23 March 1797; major 7 April 1808; lieutenant colonel (brevet) 30 May 1811; major 79th Highlanders 25 January 1813.

    Hall

John Randoll Mackenzie of Suddie (1763 – 1809)

Son of William Mackenzie of Suddie and Margaret Mackenzie of Coull. Commanded 2/78th Highlanders at Maida. Served in the Peninsula first in command of a brigade and then 3rd Division on formation but killed in action at Talavera 28 July 1809.

Commissions: adjutant of Marines 28 May 1780; lieutenant 3 November 1780; captain 78th Highlanders 13 March 1793; lieutenant colonel (brevet) 15 November 1794; lieutenant colonel 78th Highlanders 27 February 1796; colonel (brevet) 1 January 1801; major general 25 April 1808.

    Hall

Henry McKinnon (1773-1812).

Youngest son of William McKinnon and Louisa Vernon, born Longwood 15 July 1773. Married Miss Colt 1804/issue. Served with Coldstream in Holland 1793. Served as Brigade Major to Sir George Nugent in Ireland 1798. Served Egypt 1801; Hanover 1805 and Copenhagen 1807. Commanded a brigade in 3rd Division and died a major general at Cuidad Rodrigo.

Commissions: ensign 43rd Foot 31 May 1790; lieutenant 30 November 1792; captain Independent Company 11 April 1793; lieutenant and Captain 2nd Coldstream 9 October 1793; captain and lieutenant colonel 18 October 1799; colonel (brevet) 25 October 1809; major general Spain & Portugal 26 October 1811; major general 1 January 1812.

    Hall; McGuigan & Burnham; *ODNB*

Charles MacLeod (1784-1812)

Son of Lieutenant General John MacLeod and Wilhelmina-Frances Kerr. Served Copenhagen 1807, *Peninsula*; Coa, Cuidad Rodrigo, killed in action at Badajoz 6 April 1812.

Commissions: ensign 71st Highlanders 199; lieutenant 62nd Foot 21 March 1800; captain 3/West India Regiment 22 April 1802; major 43rd Foot 26 November 1806; lieutenant colonel 16 August 1810.

George MacLeod
Served in Peninsula; mentioned in dispatches at Cuidad Rodrigo and badly wounded at Badajoz while serving as a brigade major.

Commissions: lieutenant Royal Engineers 1 July 1801; second captain 1 July 1806; captain 1 May 1811; major (brevet) 6 February 1812; lieutenant colonel Royal Engineers 21 June 1817.
> Hall; *Royal Military Calendar*

Thomas McMahon (1779-1860)
Son of John McMahon and Mary Stackpoole born 27 September 1779. Married Emily Ann Westropp 27 August 1809 / issue. Served with Portuguese Army during Peninsular War and afterwards in India and Nepal, latterly as Adjutant General there. Died 10 April 1860.

Commissions: ensign 22nd Foot 2 February 1797; lieutenant 40th Foot 24 October 1799; captain 3 October 1803; major Royal West India Rangers 6 November 1806; major 2/West India Regiment April 1809; lieutenant colonel 17th Foot 20 June 1811; colonel (brevet) 4 June 1814; major general 27 May 1825; lieutenant general 28 June 1838.

Russell Manners (1771-1840)
Son of Colonel Russell Manners 2nd Dragoon Guards and Mary Rayner, born London 1771; served in India 1791 to 1793; served in Peninsula February 1810 to February 1813 and again January to April 1814; retired 18 April 1822. Married Catherine Pollock / issue, but divorced 1813 for adultery and desertion. Died Southampton 16 January 1840.

Commissions: ensign 75th Highlanders 1 September 1791; ensign 74th Highlanders 23 May 1792; lieutenant 9 June 1794; captain 3 May 1801; major 11 March 1808; lieutenant-Colonel (brevet) 6 February 1812.
> *Gentlemen's Magazine; Royal Military Calendar*

John May (1778-1847)
Son of Sir John May, Storekeeper of the Ordnance, Fort George, Guernsey. Entered Royal Artillery 1795 and served afloat with Bomb Service 1 December 1797-16 April 1801, then Copenhagen and Peninsula. Wounded by two musket balls in left thigh when riding in pursuit of French army after Salamanca and received a contusion at Vittoria. AAG Royal Artillery at Waterloo. Married a Miss Broff 1819 and died in London 8 May 1847.

Commissions: second lieutenant Royal Artillery 6 March 1795; lieutenant 7 October 1795; captain 18 April 1803; major (brevet) 6 Februart 1812; lieutenant colonel (brevet) 27 April 1812; major Royal Artillery 2 May 1825; lieutenant colonel Royal Artillery 29 July 1825; colonel (brevet) 22 July 1830; colonel Royal Artillery 10 January 1837; major general 28 June 1838.

Dalton; Hall; Hart (1840)

Hon. John Meade (1775-1849)

Third son of John Meade, 1st Earl Clanwilliam and Theodosia Magill, born 1775. Served Flanders and Holland 1794-1795; Ferrol 1800 and Peninsula, commanding 45th Foot at Busaco. Married Urania-Caroline Ward 2 October 1816. Died 6 August 1849.

Commissions: ensign 30 October 1794; lieutenant 12 November 1794; lieutenant 12th Foot 8 September 1795, captain 29 August 1799; major 30th Foot 4 June 1801; lieutenant colonel 45th Foot 1 December 1804; colonel (brevet) 4 June 1813; half pay 1814; major general 12 August 1819; lieutenant general 10 January 1837.

Hart

Henry Francis Mellish (1782-1817)

Second son of Charles Mellish MP of Blyth, near Bawtry, and Judith Stapleton.

Commissions: lieutenant 11th Light Dragoons 28 August 1801; captain 87th Foot and DAAG, lieutenant colonel (brevet) 20 February 1812; Major Sicilian Regiment 7 March 1811 and AAG 11 May 1811.

Ward

George Middlemore (d.1850)

Served Cape, Madras and Egypt. ADC to Baird on return from Egypt. Served Peninsula, succeeding to command of 48th Foot at Talavera. After going home due to ill-health was appointeg AQMG Severn District 1814 then Inspecting Field Officer Nottingham; lieutenant governor of Grenada 1833-1835, then governor of St. Helena 1836-1842. Married/issue. Died at Tunbridge Wells 18 November 1850.

Commissions: ensign 48th Foot 6 February; lieutenant Independent Company 5 April 1793; lieutenant 86th Foot 30 October 1793; captain-lieutenant and captain 15 October 1794; captain 1 September 1795; major 48th Foot 14

September 1804; lieutenant colonel (brevet) 2 November 1809; half pay 12/
Garrison Battalion due to ill-health 1811; colonel (brevet)12 August 1819;
major general 22 July 1830; lieutenant general 23 November 1841.

> Hart; *Royal Military Calendar*

James Miller

In Portuguese service, first as a "general" of Militia, then major Portuguese
23rd Regiment, 7 May 1810 lieutenant colonel and (temporarily) brigade
commander.

Commissions: ensign 74th Highlanders 21 September 1800; lieutenant 8 July
1802; captain 26 September 1806; major Portuguese 23rd Regiment, 7 May
1810 then lieutenant colonel; major (brevet) 21 June 1813; but notwithstanding
was still only a substantive captain in the 74th Highlanders in 1815.

Sir George Murray (1772-1846)

Second son of Sir William Murray of Ochtertyre and Lady Augusta
Mackenzie, born at Ochteryre, Perthshire 6 February 1772. Served Flanders
and Holland 1793-95; ADC to Major General Alexander Campbell for
Quiberon expedition; AQMG Helder expedition 1799 – wounded; AQMG
Egypt 1801; Adjutant General West Indies, then AQMG Hanover and
Denmark 1807; QMG for abortive Swedish expedition 1808, then QMG
under Sir John Moore 1809; Appointed QMG Peninsula 1 April 1809;
struck off strength on promotion to major general 7 May 1812 but resumed
appointment 26 December 1812. QMG Army of Occupation 18145-1818;
Governor RMC Sandhurst 1819-1824; C-in-C Ireland 1825-1828; Colonial
Secy. 1828-1830; Master General of the Ordnance 1834-35, and again 1841
to his death in 1846. Married Lady Louisa Erskine 28 April 1825/issue.
Died in Belgrave Square, London, 28 July 1846.

Commissions: ensign 71st Highlanders 12 March 1789; ensign 3rd Footguards
1790; lieutenant and captain 16 January 1794; captain and lieutenant colonel
5 August 1799; colonel 9 March 1809; brigadier 4 June 1811; major general
1 January 1812; lieutenant general (North America) 1814; lieutenant general
27 May 1825; general 23 November 1841.

> Hart; *ODNB*

James Patrick Murray (1782-1834)

Son of General Jon. James Murray, born 21 January 1782. Served as ADC
at Helder 1799, then Peninsula, losing right arm (gun-shot wound) at

Oporto 12 May 1809. AAG Athlone February 1811. 31 January 1803, with 12 children – all living in 1829!

Commissions: ensign 44th Foot 10 November 1797; lieutenant 16 March 1798; captain-lieutenant 9th Foot 25 December 1799; half pay 25 February 1802 "by reduction"; captain 66th Foot 9 July 1803; major 9 February 1804; lieutenant colonel 25 May 1809; lieutenant colonel 5/Garrison Battalion 2 November 1809; half pay 6 February 1815 "by reduction"; colonel (brevet) 12 August 1819.

    WO25/768 f254; WO164/113; *1818 Pension Return*; Hall

Sir John Murray (1768-1827)
Eldest son of Sir Robert Murray and Susan Renton. Married Elizabeth Cholmondley Phipps 27 August 1807. A guardsman, he was ADC to the Duke of York 1795; served at the Cape 1796 and in India; commanded a force sent to the Red Sea in 1799 and was QMG under Baird in Egypt the following year. Returned from India in 1805 and served unsatisfactorily in Peninsula 1808-09; later served in Malta and Italy and made a complete cock of an expedition to the east coast of Spain in 1813, for which he was subsequently court-martialled and although nominally acquitted thanks to influence at Court, he never served again and was denied the KB. Died at Frankfurt am Main 15 October 1827.

Commissions: ensign 3rd Footguards 24 October 1788; lieutenant and captain 3rd Footguards 25 April 1793; lieutenant colonel 2/84th Foot 31 May 1794; colonel (brevet) 1 January 1800; major general 30 October 1805; lieutenant general 1 January 1812; general 27 May 1825.

    ODNB; Ward

Sir William James Myers (1783-1811)
Son of Sir William Myers, born 27 November 1783 and usually referred to as Sir James Myers by way of distinguishing him from his father. Fatally wounded at Albuera.

Commissions: lieutenant 15th Foot 1 October 1794; captain 18 December 1794, unattached full pay 11 March 1795; lieutenant and captain Coldstream Guards 11 January 1800; lieutenant colonel (brevet) 24 May 1802; lieutenant colonel 62nd Foot 10 July 1802; lieutenant colonel 7th Fusiliers 15 August 1804.

    WO25/2965; Hall

George Napier (1784-1855)

Second son of Colonel the Hon. George Thomas Napier and Lady Sarah Lennox, born in Whitehall 30 June 1784. Served Martinique 1809 then afterwards in Peninsula, initially as ADC to Sir John Moore. Wounded at Casal Nova 14 March 1811 and again at Cuidad Rodrigo, losing his right arm. Appointed AAG 29 January 1814 and attached to 6th Division, but appointment cancelled. Married twice/issue. C-in-C Cape 1839-43. Died at Geneva 16 September 1855.

Commissions: cornet 24th Light Dragoons 25 January 1800; lieutenant 46th Foot 18 June 1800; exch. 52nd Foot 25 December 1802; captain 5 January 1804; major (brevet) 30 May 1811; major 52nd Foot 27 June 1811; lieutenant colonel (brevet) 6 February 1812; lieutenant colonel 71st Highlanders 24 March 1814; captain and lieutenant colonel 3rd Footguards 25 July 1814; lieutenant colonel 44th Foot 22 February 1821 but retired on half pay Sicilian Regiment 19 April 1821; colonel (brevet) 27 May 1825; major general 10 January 1837; lieutenant general 9 November 1846; general 20 June 1854.

    Hall; Hart (1840); *ODNB*; Ward

William Nicholas (1785-1812)

Third son of Robert Nicholas, esq., of Ashton Keynes, near Cricklade, Wiltshire, and Charlotte, sixth daughter of Admiral Sir Thomas Frankland, bart., born 12 Dec. 1785. Served Sicily 1806; QMG at Maida; Egypt 1807; Spain 1809 on mission to Spanish Army; and in 1810 to Cadiz where he acted as engineer. Served at Barossa and then transferred to Wellington's army in time to take part in the siege of Badajoz. Badly wounded in storm and died 14 April.

Commissions: second lieutenant Royal Engineers 1801; lieutenant 1 July 1802; second captain 25 August 1806;

    Hall; *ODNB*

Sir Miles Nightingall (1768-1829)

Illegitimate son of Charles, Earl Cornwallis and Ann Nightingall, born 25 December 1768. Entered army 1787 and served in India and West Indies, latterly as DAG St. Domingo. Served Ireland 1798 as ADC to his father and afterwards at Helder. Served again in India before returning to England in 1805. Commanded brigade at Rolica and Vimiero. Afterwards declined governorship of New South Wales and instead returned to Peninsula, 1809 commanding brigade in 1st Division. Slightly wounded at Fuentes d'Onoro but then appointed to Bengal staff and remained in India until 1819, latterly as C-in-C Bombay. Married Flora Darrell 1800. MP for Eye 1820 until his death 17 September 1829.

Commissions: ensign 52nd Foot 1787; lieutenant 52nd Foot 12 November 1788; successively captain 125th Foot 1794; major 121st Foot and lieutenant colonel 115th Foot 1795; lieutenant colonel 38th Foot 28 October 1795; colonel (brevet) 25 December 1803; lieutenant colonel 69th Foot 8 May 1806; major general 25 July 1810; lieutenant general 4 June 1814.

> Hall; McGuigan & Burnham

Robert Nixon (b.1761)

Seventh son of Alexander Nixon of Mullynesker, Co. Fermanagh. Served Egypt 1801 with 28th Foot, then Peninsula, being appointed to command 2nd Cacadores May 1810–July 1811, then back to 28th Foot; subsequently wounded while commanding 28th Foot at Waterloo and retired 1816. Receiving his first commission aged 32 indicates he began his military career in the ranks.

Commissions: ensign 28th Foot 31 January 1793; lieutenant 17 May 1794; captain 5 April 1801; major 15 December 1804; lieutenant colonel (brevet) 30 May 1811.

> Dalton

John Nugent (d.1836)

Served Flanders 1793-1794, then West Indies; St. Lucia 1796 and Trinidad 1797; afterwards ADC to General Trench in Ireland. Served Cape and South America, then Peninsula. Mentioned in dispatches commanding 2/38th at Badajoz.

Commissions: ensign 13th Foot 31 July 1789; lieutenant 1791; captain 38th Foot 31 July 1793; major (brevet) 29 April 1802; major 38th Foot 1 August 1804; lieutenant colonel 38th Foot 8 February 1807; colonel (brevet) 4 June 1814, half pay by reduction 1814.

> Hall; *Royal Military Calendar*

Hon. Robert William O'Callaghan (1777-1849)

Younger son of Cornelius O'Callaghan, 1st Baron Lismore of Shanbally, and Frances Ponsonby, born October 1777. Served Maida and Peninsula, temporarily commanding brigade in 2nd Division 1813 – mentioned in despatches for

Vittoria. He served with the Army of Occupation in France and then became Commander in Chief Scotland in 1825 and Commander-in-Chief of the Madras Army in 1831 before retiring in 1836 Died unmarried 9 June 1849.

Commissions: ensign 128th Foot 29 November 1794; lieutenant 30th Light Dragoons 6 December 1794; captain 31 January 1795; captain 22nd Light Dragoons 19 April 1796, half pay 23 June 1802; captain 18th Light Dragoons 3 December 1802; major 40th Foot 17 February 1803; lieutenant colonel 39th Foot 16 July 1803; colonel (brevet) 25 July 1810; major general 4 June 1814; lieutenant general 22 July 1830.

WO25/3998; Hall; Hart (1840)

Peter O'Hare (k.1812)

Commissioned from the ranks. Served in Peninsula until killed in action at Badajoz 6 April 1812.

Commissions: ensign 69th Foot 20 August 1796; lieutenant 20 January 1797; lieutenant 95th Rifles 28 August 1800; captain 6 August 1803; major 11 April 1811.

WO25/2964; WO25/3998; Hall

Bryan O'Toole

In Portuguese service November 1811 to April 1814 as lieutenant colonel 7th Cacadores. Badly wounded at Sorauren.

Commissions: lieutenant 6/Irish Brigade 1 October 1794; captain-lieutenant and captain 31 December 1795; captain Hompesch Corps 30 December 1797; half pay 1802; captain 39th Foot 9 July 1803; major (brevet) 25 April 1808; lieutenant colonel (brevet) 21 June 1813; half pay same day but still listed as Captain 39th Foot 1815.

WO25/3998; *1818 Pension Return; Hall.*

John Oswald (1771-1840)

Son of James Townshend Oswald of Dunnikier, Fife, born 2 October 1771. Served Martinique, St. Lucia and Guadaloupe. Badly wounded at the Helder 1799, then served in Mediterranean; Malta, Maida and the capture of Scylla, where was described as a handsome 6-footer who was very formidable in hand to hand combat. Served in Peninsula, commanding 5th Division in absence of Sir James Leith and slightly wounded at St. Sebastian. Married (twice), died at Dunnikier 8 June 1840.

Commissions: second lieutenant 7th Fusiliers 1 February 1788; lieutenant 29 June 1789; captain Independent Company 24 January 1791; captain 35th Foot 23 March 1791; major 1 September 1795; lieutenant colonel 30 March 1797; colonel (brevet) 30 October 1805; major general 4 June 1811; lieutenant general 12 August 1819; general 10 January 1837.

WO25/3998; Hall; Hart (1840)

Denis Pack (1773-1823)

Only son of Very Reverend Thomas Pack, Dean of Ossory, born in Kilkenny 7 October 1777. Served in Flanders, Quiberon and Ireland. Commanded 71st Highlanders at the Cape and then Buenos Aires; badly wounded and taken prisoner but escaped and commanded provisional battalion of light companies until evacuation. Served in Peninsula; Rolica, Vimeiro and Corunna, then Walcheren. As 1/71st was then in no immediate condition to return to the Peninsula Pack received permission to command a brigade in Portuguese service July 1810-April 1813. Subsequently commanded a British brigade in 6th Division; slightly wounded while commanding 6th Division at Sorauren 28 July 1813 and badly wounded at Toulouse. Commanded brigade at Waterloo where he was again wounded. Married Lady Elizabeth Beresford 10 July 1816/ issue. Died of heart problems at Lord Beresford's house in Wimpole Street 24 July 1823.

Commissions: cornet 14th Light Dragoons 30 November 1791; lieutenant 12 March 1795; captain 5th Dragoon Guards 27 February 1796; major 4th Dragoon Guards 25 August 1798; lieutenant colonel 71st Highlanders 6 December 1800; colonel (brevet) 25 July 1810; major general 4 June 1813.

Dalton, Hall; McGuigan & Burnham; *ODNB*

Hon. Edward Paget (1775-1849)

A gallant but unfortunate officer, the second son of Henry Batly (later Paget) and Jane Champagne, born 3 November 1775. Served in Flanders and Holland 1794-95 and as a marine at the battle of Cape St. Vincent 1797. Served Egypt 1801 but wounded at Alexandria. Served in the Mediterranean 1806 and assigned to the abortive Swedish expedition and afterwards with Moore at Corunna. Led the attack over the Douro at Oporto but badly wounded and lost his left arm. Returned to the Peninsula late 1812 as commander of 1st Division and 2IC to Wellington, only to be taken prisoner on 17 November during the retreat from Burgos. Was not at Waterloo but briefly served as

C-in-C India 1822–1825 and later as governor of Chelsea Hospital. Married twice, with issue, and died at Cowes Castle 13 May 1849.

Commissions: cornet and sub-lieutenant Lifeguards 23 March 1792; captain 54th Foot 7 December 1792; major 14 November 1793; lieutenant colonel 28th Foot 30 April 1794; colonel (brevet) 1 January 1798; brigadier general October 1803; major general 1 January 1805; lieutenant general (Portugal and Spain) 1809; lieutenant general 4 June 1811; general 27 May 1825.

> Hall; Hart (1840); *ODNB*

Hon. Edward Michael Pakenham (1778–1815)

Second son of Edward Michael Pakenham 2nd Baron Longford and Catherine Rowley, born at Longford Castle 2 April 1778. Served Ireland 1798, then West Indies 1801–1803; wounded St. Lucia 1803. Served Copenhagen 1807 and Martinique 1809, where wounded in the assault 1 February. Served in Peninsula 1809–1814, initially on staff; AAG 15 November 1809 and DAG 3 March 1810; commanded brigade in 1st Division August 1810, then took command of 3rd Division after Picton was wounded at Badajoz before taking command of 6th Division early 1813; appointed Adjutant General 10 May 1813 but temporarily resumed command of 6th Division 30 July at Sorauren. Otherwise remained Adjutant General until war's end. Appointed to command North America 24 October 1814 and killed in action at New Orleans 8 January 1815.

Commissions: ensign (late) 92nd Foot 28 May 1794; captain June 1794; major 33rd Light Dragoons 6 December 1794, exchanged to 23rd Light Dragoons 1 June 1798; lieutenant colonel 64th Foot 17 October 1799, exchanged to 7th Fusiliers 1805; colonel (brevet) 1 January 1805; major general (Portugal and Spain) 26 October 1811; major general 1 January 1812.

> *ODNB*; Ward

Hon. Hercules Robert Pakenham (1781–1850)

Third son of Edward Michael Pakenham, 2nd Baron Longford and Catherine Rowley, born 29 September 1781. Served Peninsula; appointed DAAG 1 September 1809 and attached to 3rd Division. Appointed AAG 1 October 1810, badly wounded at Badajoz 7 April 1812. Retired on half-pay Portuguese Service 1816 on account of wounds – especially an open one on his hip-bone. Married Emily Stapylton 10 November 1817/issue. Died at Langford Lodge, Co. Antrim 7 March 1850.

Commissions: ensign 40th Foot 23 August 1803; lieutenant 2/West India Regiment 3 February 1804; lieutenant 95th Rifles 24 April 1804; captain 95th Rifles 2 August 1805; major 7/West India Regiment 30 August 1810; lieutenant colonel (brevet) 27 April 1812; lieutenant colonel 26th Foot 3 September 1812; captain and lieutenant colonel Coldstream 25 July 1814; colonel (brevet) 27 May 1825; major general 10 January 1837; lieutenant general 9 November 1846.

WO25/770; Hall; Hart (1840); *ODNB*; Ward

Sir William Payne (1759-1831)
Youngest son of Sir Ralph Payne and Margaret Gallwey of St. Kitts, becoming Payne-Gallwey by royal licence in consequence of a legacy 1814. Served in Flanders 1794 and on Irish staff 1798-1805, subsequently served in Peninsula in command of the cavalry 1809-1810. Married Lady Harriet Quinn 19 November 1804/issue. Died 16 April 1831.

Commissions: lieutenant 1st Dragoons 14 July 1777; captain 15 April 1782; major 1794; lieutenant colonel 1 March 1794; lieutenant colonel 3rd Dragoon Guards 5 October 1796; colonel (brevet) 1 January 1798; brigadier general (Ireland) 1802-1805; major general 1 January 1805; lieutenant colonel 10th Light Dragoons 12 September 1805; lieutenant general 4 June 1811; General 27 May 1825.

Gentleman's Magazine; *Royal Military Calendar*

Sir Thomas Picton (1758-1815)
Seventh of 12 children of Thomas Picton of Poyston, Pembrokeshire and Cecil Powell, born Haverfordwest 24 August 1758. Entered army 1771; ADC to Sir Charles Grey in West Indies 1794. Governor of Trinidad 1801-1803; dismissed following conviction for cruelty, but reinstated 1808. Served Walcheren and appointed governor of Flushing but invalided home. Served in Peninsula 1810-1814 as commander of 3rd Division except for a year after being wounded at Badajoz 1812. Commanded 5th Division 1815, Badly wounded at Quatre Bras and killed in action at Waterloo. Unmarried but fathered four children by his mistress, Rosetta Smith, on Trinidad.

Commissions: ensign 12th Foot 14 November 1771; captain 75th Foot 1778; captain 12th Foot but half pay 12th Foot 24 December 1787; lieutenant colonel (brevet) 19 November 1794; lieutenant colonel 56th Foot 1 May 1796; colonel (brevet) 1 January 1801; major general 25 April 1808; lieutenant general (Spain and Portugal) September 1811; lieutenant general 4 June 1813.

Dalton; *ODNB*

Frederick Cavendish Ponsonby (1783-1837)
Second son of Frederick Ponsonby 3rd Earl of Bessborugh, and Lady Henrietta Spencer, born 6 July 1783. Served in Peninsula at Talavera and then afterwards as AAG 2 January 1810 attached to Fane's cavalry brigade. Served at Barossa and Busaco, commanded 12th Light Dragoons at Salamanca and Vittoria. badly wounded at Waterloo but survived various attempts to finish him off. Afterwards Inspecting Field Officer Ionian Islands 20 January 1824 and C-in-C May 1825. Governor of Malta 22 December 1826-May 1835. Married/issue, died suddenly in an inn near Basingstoke 11 January 1837.

Commissions: cornet 10th Light Dragoons January 1800; lieutenant 20 June 1800; captain 20 August 1803; captain 60th Foot 1806; major 25 June 1807; major 23rd Light Dragoons 6 August 1809; lieutenant colonel (brevet) 15 March 1810; lieutenant colonel 12th Light Dragoons 11 June 1811; colonel (brevet) 4 June 1814; half pay 26 August 1820; major general 27 May 1825.
    Dalton; Hall; Ward

Hon. William Ponsonby (1772-1815)
Second son of William Brabazon Ponsonby, 1st Baron Ponsonby, of Imokilly, Co. Cork, born 13 October 1772. Served in Peninsula; assumed command of Le Marchant's brigade at Salamanca and led it at Vittoria. Killed in action at Waterloo while commanding "Union Brigade".

Commissions: ensign Independent Company 1793; captain 83rd Foot September 1794; major (permanent) Loyal Irish Fencible Infantry 15 December 1794; major 5th Dragoon Guards 1 March 1798; lieutenant colonel 24 February 1803; colonel (brevet) 25 July 1810; major general 4 June 1813.
    Dalton; *ODNB*

Manley Power(1772-1826)
Son of Captain-lieutenant Bolton Power 20th Foot. Served Helder 1799; Minorca 1800 and Egypt. AAG and Inspecting Field Officer of Militia October 1803-1805; served Peninsula, commanding a Portuguese brigade, then North America 1814-1815. Lieutenant governor of Malta 1820-1826, but died suddenly in Berne, Switzerland while returning home 7 July 1826.

Commissions: ensign 20th Foot 27 August 1785; lieutenant 4 May 1789; captain Independent Company 28 June 1793; captain 20th Foot 16 January 1794; major 7 October 1799; lieutenant colonel 20 June 1801, half pay by reduction 1802; lieutenant colonel 32nd Foot 8 June 1805; colonel(brevet) 25 July 1810; major general 8 August 1814; lieutenant general 27 May 1825.

McGuigan & Burham; *Royal Military Calendar*

William Greenshields Power (1781–1863)

Served throughout Peninsular War and afterwards in Ceylon 1829–1834. Died at Shanklin, Isle of Wight 23 January 1863.

Commissions: second lieutenant Royal Artillery 31 May 1800; lieutenant 11 February 1802; second captain 13 June 1807; major (brevet) 21 September 1813; captain Royal Artillery 1 August 1815, half pay 1 April 1817; lieutenant colonel (brevet) 21 June 1817. Lieutenant colonel Royal Artillery 12 June 1835; Colonel (brevet) 10 January 1837; colonel Royal Artillery 4 May 1846; major general 9 November 1846; lieutenant general 20 June 1854; general 4 February 1857.

Hart (1840); *Royal Military Calendar*

William Henry Pringle (1772–1840)

Son of Major General Henry Pringle of Caledon, born in Dublin 21 August 1772. Served at Helder 1799, Peninsula; Salamanca, Maya, Nive, Nivelle, badly wounded at St. Palais 15 February 1814. Married/issue. Died in London 23 December 1840.

Commissions: cornet 16th Light Dragoons 6 July 1792; lieutenant 24 February 1793; captain 15 October 1794; major 111th Foot 19 September 1794, half pay 1 March 1798; major 4th Foot 6 August 1799; captain and lieutenant colonel Coldstream 17 September 1802; colonel (brevet) 25 October 1809; major general 1 January 1812; lieutenant general 27 May 1825.

Hall; Hart (1840)

Henry Pynn

Served Peninsula with 82nd at Rolica and Vimeiro. With Portuguese Army April 1809 to August 1813; major 3rd Portuguese Line then lieutenant colonel 18th Portuguese Line. Commanded light companies of Ashworth's Brigade at Fuentes d'Onoro. Badly wounded in Pyrenees 30 July 1813.

Commissions: lieutenant Royal Newfoundland Fencibles 1795; ensign 83nd Foot October 1799; lieutenant 28 November 1799; adjutant 7 September 1804; captain 30 May 1805; major (brevet) 15 November 1809; lieutenant colonel (brevet 4 June 1814.

Hall; *Royal Military Calendar*

Ramsay, George, Earl of Dalhousie (1770-1838)

Son of George Ramsay 8th Earl of Dalhousie and Elizabeth Glen, born Dalhousie Castle, Midlothian, 23 October 1770. Served on Gibraltar then commanded 2nd Foot on Martinique; badly wounded there 1795. Served Ireland 1798, Helder 1799 and Egypt 1801, then Walcheren and Peninsula. Appointed to command 7th Division 25 October 1812. Captain General and C-in-C North America 1819. Lieutenant Governor of Nova Scotia 1816-1820, then Governor of Canada 1820-1828. C-in-C India 18128 but resigned to ill-health 1832. Married/issue. Died at Dalhousie Castle 21 March 1838.

Commissions: cornet 3rd Dragoon Guards 2 July 1787; captain Independent Company 1790; captain 2/1st (Royal) Regiment 4 January 1791; major 2nd Foot 27 June 1792; lieutenant colonel 2nd Foot 22 August 1794; colonel (brevet) 1 January 1800; major general 25 April 1805; lieutenant general 4 June 1813; general 22 July 1830.

> *Dictionary of Canadian Biography*; *Royal Military Calendar*

Ramsay, William Norman (1782-1815)

Born in Edinburgh 1782, eldest son of Captain David Ramsay RN. Entered the Royal Military Academy as a cadet on 17 Jan. 1797. Served in the Egypt 1800-1. Served in Peninsula with Major Bull's Troop RHA and attracted some fame for mounted action at Fuentes d'Onoro. Subsequently served at New Orleans 1815 and then killed in action at Waterloo while commanding H Troop.

Commissions: second lieutenant Royal Artillery 27 October 1798; lieutenant 1 August 1800; second captain 24 April 1806; major (brevet) 22 November 1813; captain Royal Artillery 17 December 1813.

> Dalton

Henry Ridge (1778-1812)

Born in Hampshire 1778. Served Canada, then Helder 1799 and as ADC to General Richard England. Served Hanover 1805-06, Buenos Aires 1806 and Peninsula. Killed in action at Badajoz 6 April 1812.

Commissions: ensign 5th Foot 1796; lieutenant 12 January 1797; captain 9 October 1803; major 25 March 1808; lieutenant colonel [brevet] 19 January 1812.

> Hall

William Robe (1765-1820)

Son of Lieutenant William Robe RA and Mary Broome, born Woolwich 1765. Served Jamaica and the Canadas, marrying Sarah Watt in Quebec

1788/issue; served Flanders and Holland 1793-1794 and Helder 1799. Served Canada again and then Copenhagen. Afterwards served throughout the Peninsular War and died at Shooter's Hill near Woolwich 5 November 1820.

Commissions: second lieutenant Royal Artillery 24 May 1781; lieutenant 22 November 1787; captain-lieutenant and captain 9 September 1790; quartermaster 25 November 1794; captain 2 October 1799; major (brevet) 1 January 1805; major Royal Artillery 1 June 1806; lieutenant colonel 13 January 1807; colonel (brevet) 4 June 1814.

ODNB; Hall

Frederick Philipse Robinson (1763-1852)

Fourth son of noted American Loyalist Colonel Beverley Robinson and Susanna Philipse, born Highlands, New York September 1763. Served in Revolutionary War including 18 months as POW. In 1790s served West Indies with a grenadier battalion under Grey; at Martinique, St.Lucia and Guadaloupe, but returned to England totally debilitated. Accepted appointment as Inspecting Field Officer of Recruiting Service at Bedford in 1796. Eventually went to Peninsula 1812, distinguishing himself in command of a brigade at Vittoria. Badly wounded at Storming of St. Sebastian and again at Nive. Served North America 1814-15; Plattsburg. Married (twice)/issue. Died at Brighton 1 January 1852.

Commissions: ensign Loyal American Regiment February 1777; ensign 17th Foot 11 September 1778; lieutenant 4/60th Foot 1 September 1779; lieutenant 38th Foot 4 November 1780; captain-lieutenant 24 March 1794; captain 3 July 1794; major 127th Foot 1 September 1794; major 32nd Foot 1795; major 134th Foot 29 July 1796, half pay 1 March 1798; lieutenant colonel (brevet) 1 January 1800; major 86th Foot 19 February 1807; major 28th Foot 26 March 1807; major 18th Foot 16 April 1807; half pay 91st Foot 30 April 1807; colonel (brevet) 25 July 1810; major general 4 June 1813; lieutenant general 27 May 1825; general 23 November 1841.

WO25/748 R14; *Gentleman's Magazine*; Hall; Hart (1840); McGuigan & Burnham

John Charles Rooke (d.1813)

Eldest son of Colonel Charles Rooke. Served Ireland 1798, Egypt 1801 (wounded 21 March). Major of Brigade, Jersey May 1804-November 1805. Served Hanover December 1805-February 1806; Copenhagen 1807 then

Peninsula – appointed AAG 14 November 1810 and attached to 2nd Division until fatally wounded at Nivelle 10 November and died 19 December 1813.

Commissions: cornet Windsor Foresters Fencible Cavalry; ensign 3rd Footguards 12 August 1795; lieutenant and Captain 26 December 1798; captain and lieutenant colonel 26 January 1809.

> WO25/748 R17; Hall; Ward

John Ross (d.1843)

One of six officers of this name holding field rank during the Revolutionary and Napoleonic wars. This one served in the East Indies until August 1798, then Ferrol, Sicily, Portugal, Spain and Walcheren, then back to Spain until 1811 when appointed Adjutant General Ceylon, then DAG Ireland 1815-1818; Commandant Isle of Wight Depot 1819 but retired on half pay 1820; lieutenant governor of Guernsey 1828-1837. Died in Southampton 17 May 1843.

Commissions: ensign 36th Foot 2 January 1793; lieutenant 52nd Foot 8 May 1796; captain 11 January 1800; major 14 August 1804; lieutenant colonel 91st Highlanders 27 January 1808, immediately exchanging back to 52nd Foot; lieutenant colonel 66th Foot 18 July 1811; colonel (brevet) 4 June 1814; major general 27 May 1825; lieutenant general 28 June 1838.

> WO25/748 R27; Hart; *London Gazette*; *Royal Military Calendar*

Lord George William Russell (1790-1846)

Second son of John, 6th Duke of Bedford, born 8 May 1790. Served Copenhagen 1807, then Peninsula; wounded at Talavera and ADC to Wellington at Toulouse; brought home despatches. Married Elizabeth Anne Rawdon 1817/issue. Died 16 July 1846.

Commissions: lieutenant 1st Dragoons 11 September 1806; captain 25 March 1808; captain 23rd Light Dragoons 18 May 1808; major 102nd Foot 4 February 1813; lieutenant colonel (brevet) 12 April 1814; half-pay 42nd Highlanders; lieutenant colonel 90th Foot May 1829; colonel (brevet) 22 July 1830; half-pat unattached as lieutenant colonel 17 May 1831; major general 23 November 1841.

> Hall; Hart (1840); *Royal Military Calendar*

George Scovell (1774-1861)

Son of George Scovell of Cirencester, born in London 21 March 1774. Attended RM College 1808 and served throughout Peninsular War;

appointed DAQMG 1 April 1809; initially attached to Cotton's cavalry brigade but then placed in charge of Corps of Staff Guides 23 May 1809; AQMG 30 May 1811 and placed in charge of "all military communications" 14 August 1811, specialising in intelligence work and cyphers. AQMG at Waterloo. Lieutenant Governor of the Royal Military College, Sandhurst 25 April 1829–2 February 1837 and Governor to 31 March 1856.

Commissions: adjutant 4th Dragoons 5 April 1798; cornet 20 June 1798; lieutenant 4 May 1800; captain 10 March 1804; captain 57th Foot 12 March 1807; major (brevet) 30 May 1811; lieutenant colonel (brevet) 17 August 1812; major commandant Royal Staff Corps 15 April 1813, half pay 25 October 1814, returning to full pay 10 August 1815; lieutenant colonel commandant Royal Staff Corps Cavalry 22 February 1816, half pay 25 December 1818; colonel (brevet) 17 May 1825; major general 10 January 1837; lieutenant general 9 November 9 November 1846; general 20 June 1854.

     WO25/3998; Dalton; Hart (1840); *ODNB*; Ward

Sir John Coape Sherbrooke (1764–1830)
Son of William Sherbrooke and Sarah Coape; baptised in Arnold, Notts. 29 April 1764. Served in the 33rd Foot as second in command to Wellesley in Flanders 1793–94, then to India, taking part in the storming of Sringapatnam 1799. Again served under Wellesley in Peninsula 1809 as commander of 1st Division but returned home in April 1810, due to ill-health. Lieutenant Governor of Nova Scotia August 1811, then Governor General of British North America April 1816 until forced to resign due to a paralytic stroke February 1818. Married Katherina Pyndar 24 August 1811. Died in Calverton, Notts. 14 February 1830.

Commissions: ensign 4th Foot 7 December 1780; lieutenant 22 December 1781; captain 85th Foot 6 March 1783, then half-pay; captain 33rd Foot 23 June 1784; major 30 September 1793; lieutenant colonel 1 March 1794; colonel (brevet) 1 January 1798; half pay 5th Foot 29 October 1802; major general 1 January 1805; lieutenant general 4 June 1811.

     WO25/3998; *Royal Military Calendar*

John Byne Skerrett (1778–1814)
Only son of Lieutenant General John Nicholas Skerrett and Anne Byne, born 1777 or 1778. Served West Indies; St. Lucia 1794 and afterwards Jamaica. Served Peninsula; Cadiz, Tariffa and Seville, then under Wellington commanding a brigade in the Light Division. Served in Holland 1814 and

injured in a riding accident; consequently, led his then brigade into the assault on Bergen-op-Zoom supported by a crutch. Twice wounded but refused to retire and eventually shot through the head, dying on 10 March 1814 "in the 36th year of his age".

Commissions: ensign 86th Foot 26 April 1783; lieutenant 79th Foot 25 October 1783, half pay 5 February 1784; lieutenant 10th Foot 27 July 1791, exchanged to 48th Foot 6 January 1792; captain 123rd Foot 27 August 1794; captain 69th Foot 23 March 1795; major 83rd Foot 29 March 1798; lieutenant colonel 23 October 1800; lieutenant colonel 10/Reserve Battalion 17 September 1803; lieutenant colonel 47th Foot 16 January 1804; colonel (brevet) 25 July 1810; major general 4 June 1813.

WO25/3998; McGuigan & Burnham; St. Nicholas Cathedral, Newcastle upon Tyne

John "Black Jack" Slade (1762-1859)
Son of John Slade of Maunsel Grange, Bridgewater, Somerset and Charlotte Portal, born 31 December 1762. Married twice, fathering 11 sons and 4 daughters! Saw no active service before going to the Peninsula in command of the Hussar Brigade 1808-09. Again in command of a brigade August 1809 to June 1813 and for a time commander of 2nd Cavalry Division. Generally regarded as brave but incompetent. Died at Monty's Court, Norton Fitzwarren 13 August 1859.

Commissions: Cornet 10th Dragoons 11 May 1780; lieutenant 28 April 1783; captain 10th Light Dragoons 24 October 1787; major 1 March 1794; lieutenant colonel 29 April 1795; exchange to 1st Dragoons 18 October 1798; colonel (brevet) 29 April 1802; brigadier general (Ireland) 28 May 1807. ; major general 25 October 1809; lieutenant general 4 June 1814; general 10 January 1837.

WO30/3998; Hart; McGuigan & Ross; *ODNB*

William Smith
Served with the 45th Foot throughout his career; ensign 45th Foot 26 February 1793; lieutenant 15 October 1794; captain 25 June 1803; major 13 July 1810 – killed in action at Busaco.

WO 25/3998; Hall

Fitzroy Somerset (1788-1855)
Youngest son of 5th Duke of Beaufort and Elizabeth Boscawen, born at Badminton 30 September 1788. Served in Peninsula as ADC to Wellington

and was wounded at Busaco. Served as military secretary to Wellington 1815 and although lost right arm at Waterloo continued in that role until Wellington's resignation as CinC in 1828, but eventually because C-in-C himself in succession to Rowland Hill. Best known as Lord Raglan (since 1852) for commanding British Army in the Crimea and died there 28 June 1855. Married/issue

Commissions: cornet 4th Dragoons 9 June 1804; lieutenant 30 May 1805; captain 6/Garrison Battalion 5 May 1808; captain 43rd Foot 18 August 1808; major (brevet) 9 June 1811; lieutenant colonel (brevet) 27 April 1812; captain and lieutenant colonel 1st Footguards 25 July 1814; colonel (brevet) 28 August 1815; major general 27 May 1825; lieutenant general 28 June 1838; general (temporary) 28 February 1854; general (substantive) 20 June 1854; field marshal 5 November 1854.

WO25/3998; Dalton; Hall; Hart (1840); *ODNB*

John Sontag (1747-1816)
Dutch (?) officer, born at Den Haag 28 October 1747, his full name was revealed in his will to be Sebastian Balthasar John Sontag. Appears to have been largely employed on various special services on behalf of the Foreign Office and Treasury – his first known commission came as late as 1780; sold out as captain-lieutenant 1792, but served on staff in Flanders 1793-94, appointed military commandant of hospitals in Flanders 1 March 1795; DQMG West Indies 1795, ADC to Sir Ralph Abercromby at Helder 1799 – wounded 2 October - and military commissary to Dutch troops 19 October 1799 and subsequently appointed Inspector General of Reduced Foreign Officers 1808-1814. Served with allied army at Eylau then Sweden, Portugal and Spain first as a liaison officer, before commanding a brigade in 4th Division at Talavera, serving at Walcheren, next to Cadiz 1810. Commanded a brigade in 7th Division March - August 1811 and temporarily commanded 7th Division August-October 1811. Invalided home due to ill health October 1811 – no doubt age-related.

"To the memory of General John Sontag born at Hague the 28th of October 1747. He served with the British Armies in Flanders, in the West Indies and at the Helder, with the Russian and Prussian Armies in Poland, was a civil and military Governor of Walcheren and shared the glories of the British Army in the Peninsula, in Spain and Portugal under the Duke of Wellington. He died at Earls Court, Old Brompton 4 May 1816 aged 69.

"In testimony of the highest and tenderest regard. This monument erected by his affectionate widow."

Commissions: cornet 12th Light Dragoons 8 September 1780; Lieutenant 12th Light Dragoons 19 November 1781; captain-lieutenant 8th Light Dragoons 16 September 1786, sold out 1792; captain of Guides 1793; major (brevet) 1 March 1795; lieutenant colonel (brevet) 5 October 1795; colonel (brevet) 25 September 1803, brigadier general on the Staff 1808-1810; Major General 25 July 1810;Lieutenant General 4 June 1814.

> McGuigan & Burnham; *Royal Military Calendar*; Memorial inscription St. Mary Abbott's church, Kensington; PROB 11/1585/36 (will).

Sir Brent Spencer (1760-1828)

Son of Conway Spencer of Trummery Co. Antrim. Served in West Indies during the American Revolution and again on Jamaica 1790-1794 as major 13th Foot. Took flank battalion to St. Domingo (Haiti) early in 1794. Badly beaten in fight at Bombarde on 1 May 1794 but did well at capture of Port au Prince. Served briefly on St. Vincent and against the Maroons on Jamaica but returned to St. Domingo in 1795 and remained there until the final evacuation in 1798. Served in Europe for the first time on Helder expedition 1799 and Egypt 1801; Eastern District staff 1803-1807. Major General 1 January 1805. Commanded a brigade at Copenhagen 1807 and assigned to abortive Swedish expedition 1808 but diverted instead to southern Spain. On his own initiative joined British forces in Portugal and fought at Rolica and Vimeiro. Afterwards supported Wellesley in inquiry into Convention of Cintra and served again in Peninsula May 1810 to July 1811, commanding 1st Division and acting as second in command of the army. Effectively retired after his supersession by Thomas Graham. Napier's assessment that he was "more noted for intrepidity than for military quickness" out of his depth at higher command. Rumoured to have secretly married Princess Augusta, he died at Lee, Great Missenden, Bucks. 29 December 1828.

Commissions: ensign 15th Foot 18 January 1778; lieutenant 15th Foot 12 November 1779; captain 90th Foot 29 July 1783, exchanged back to 15th Foot 4 September 1783; major 13th Foot 6 March 1791; lieutenant colonel (local) Dillon's Foot then lieutenant colonel (late) 115th Foot 2 May 1794; lieutenant colonel 40th Foot 22 July 1795; brigadier (St. Domingo) 9 July 1797; colonel (brevet) 28 May 1798; major general 1 January 1805; colonel 9/Garrison Battalion 25 November 1806; colonel 2/West India

Regiment 25 June 1808; colonel commandant 2/95th Rifles 31 August 1809; lieutenant general 4 June 1811; colonel 40th Foot 2 July 1818; general 27 May 1828.

WO 25/3998; *ODNB*

William Frederick Spry (1770-1814)
Son of Lieutenant General William Spry RE. Served in India, including the storming of Sringapatnam. Subsequently in Peninsula, latterly commanding a Portuguese brigade. Mentioned in despatches for Salamanca. Also served Vittoria and St. Sebastian. Died of wounds in Southampton 21 January 1814.

Commissions: ensign 70th Foot 6 March 1782; lieutenant 73rd Highlanders 4 October 1783, half pay; lieutenant 64th Foot 2 June 1786; captain 77th Foot 25 December 1787; major (brevet) 6 May 1785; major 77th Foot 1 September 1795; lieutenant colonel (brevet) 1 January 1782; colonel (brevet) 25 July 1810; major general 4 June 1813

WO25/3998

John Squire (1780-1812)
Eldest son of Samuel Squire DD of Ely Place, London. Served Helder 1799 and Egypt 1801, then South America as CRE. Afterwards on abortive expedition to Sweden then to Peninsula with Moore. Served Walcheren and back to Peninsula. Mentioned in despatches at Badajoz but died of died suddenly of a paralytic stroke at Truxillo 19 May 1812.

Commissions: second lieutenant Royal Artillery 27 April 1796; second lieutenant Royal Engineers 1 January 1797; lieutenant 29 August 1798; second captain 2 December 1802; captain 1 July 1806; major (brevet) 5 December 1811; lieutenant colonel (brevet) 27 April 1812.

WO25/3998; Hall

Hon. Leicester Fitzgerald Charles Stanhope (1784-1862)
Fourth son of 3rd Earl of Harrington and Jane Fleming, born in Dublin 2 September 1784. Married Elizabeth Green/issue. Succeeded elder brother as 5th Earl of Harrington in 1859 but died 7 September 1862.

Commissions: cornet 1st Lifeguards 25 September 1799; lieutenant 20 October 1802; lieutenant 9th Foot 10 March 1803; captain 31 March 1803; captain 6th Dragoon Guards 5 November 1803; captain 17th Light Dragoons

21 January 1813; major (brevet) 4 June 1814; lieutenant colonel (brevet) 29 June 1815; major 47th Foot 4 July 1816; lieutenant colonel (unattached) 26 June 1823.

WO25/3998

Hon. Lincoln Edwin Robert Stanhope (1781-1840)

Second son of 3rd Earl of Harrington and Jane Fleming, born 26 November 1781. Served Peninsula; slightly wounded 10 May 1809 but commanded 16th Light Dragoons at Talavera. Died 29 February 1840.

Commissions: cornet 16th Light Dragoons 26 April 1798; lieutenant 7 February 1800; captain 25 October 1802; major 11 June 1807; lieutenant colonel 17th Light Dragoons 2 January 1812; colonel (brevet) 22 July 1830; major general 28 June 1838.

WO25/3998; Hall

Hon. Charles William Stewart (1778-1854)

Second son of Robert Stewart, 1st Marquess of Londonderry and Frances Pratt, born in Dublin 18 May 1778. Served in Flanders on Lord Moira's staff and afterwards on Craufurd's mission to the Austrian army, where he was wounded in the head at Donauworth. Afterwards at Helder 1799, where he was again wounded, Served in Peninsula 1808-1812, then Germany and northern France 1813-14, taking part in the battle of Leipzig. Married twice/issue. Changed name to Vane in consequence of marriage to his second wife in 1819 and succeeded his elder brother Lord Castlereagh as 3rd Marquess of Londonderry 1822. Died of influenza at Holdernesse House, Park Lane, London 6 March 1854.

Commissions: ensign 108th Foot 3 April 1794; lieutenant 30 October 1794; captain 12 November 1794; major 106th Foot 31 July 1795; lieutenant colonel 5th (Royal Irish) Dragoons 1 January 1797; lieutenant colonel 18th Light Dragoons 12 April 1799; colonel 25 September 1803; major general 25 July 1810; lieutenant general 4 June 1814; general 10 January 1837.

WO25/3998; Hart (1840); *ODNB*; Ward

Richard Stewart/Stuart (1756-1810)

Born in Kingarth, Bute in 1756 and probably related to the Stuarts of Bute. DAG Portugal 1796 and AG 1798. Returned to Peninsula 1809 and commanded a brigade at Talavera but died in Lisbon 19 October 1810 "in consequence of a fall from a balcony, whose banister had been removed."

Commissions: ensign 51st Foot 6 December 1775; lieutenant 23 December 1778; adjutant 31 August 1790; captain-lieutenant and captain 29 October 1793; major (brevet) 12 September 1794; lieutenant colonel (brevet) 30 November 1796; major 72nd Highlanders 11 October 1798; major 32nd Foot 30 October 1800; lieutenant colonel 43rd Foot 5 November 1800; colonel (brevet) 25 September 1803; brigadier general 1807; major general 25 July 1810.

   WO 25/3998; Hall; McGuigan & Burnham

Robert Walter Stuart, Lord Blantyre (1775-1830)

Son of Alexander Stuart, Lord Blantyre, born 26 December 1775. Served on staff in Portugal under Sir Charles Stewart, then the Helder 1799; Egypt 1801; Denmark and then Peninsula in command of 2/42nd. At various times acted up to command brigade in 1st Division 1810-1812. Married Frances Rodney/issue. Killed in Brussels 22 September 1830, shot by a stray musket ball while observing a riot from his hotel window!

Commissions: ensign 3rd Footguards 13 March 1795; captain 31st Foot 8 March 1798, exchanged to 12th Light Dragoons 24 March 1798 and then 7th Light Dragoons 5 September 1799; major 17th Light Dragoons 7 April 1804; lieutenant colonel 42nd Highlanders 19 September 1804; half pay 8/ Garrison Battalion 6 May 1813; colonel (brevet) 4 June 1813; major general 12 August 1819.

   WO25/3998; *Gentleman's Magazine*

Hon. William Stewart (1774-1827)

Fourth son of John Stewart, Earl of Galloway, and Anne Dashwood, born 10 January 1774. Served in West Indies 1793-1794; Martinique and Guadaloupe. Served Quiberon 1795 then back to San Domingo; commandant at Mole St. Nicholas until August 1798. Afterwards served with Austrian and Russian armies 1799, taking part in the battle of Zurich. Instrumental in creation of Experimental Rifle Corps/95th Rifles; commanding it at Ferrol and Copenhagen. Served in Peninsula, latterly as commander of 2. Division; slightly wounded at Albuera and badly wounded at Maya 25 July 1813 but fought on, strapped to the saddle. Popularly known as "Auld Grog Wullie". Married Frances Douglas 21 April 1804/issue. Died at Cumloden, Newton Stewart 7 January 1827.

Commissions: ensign 42nd Highlanders March 1786; lieutenant 67th Foot 14 October 1787; captain Independent Company 24 June 1791; captain 22nd Foot 31 October 1792; major 31st Foot December 1794; lieutenant colonel (unattached) 14 January 1795; lieutenant colonel 67th Foot 1 September 1795; licutenant colonel Experimental Rifle Corps 25 August 1800; colonel (brevet) 2 April 1801; major general 25 April 1808; lieutenant general 4 June 1813.

WO25/3998; Hall; *ODNB*

Thomas William Stubbs (1776–1844)

Not, strictly speaking, a British officer. Born in Basingstoke 7 June 1776 the son of Captain Thomas Stubbs. Served in Portugal 1797–1799, married there, converted to Catholicism, and was a captain in Portuguese service by 1800. Fled to Britain when Portuguese Army was disbanded by French in 1807, but soon returned and served for a time with the Loyal Lusitanian Legion before taking command of the 23rd Regiment in 1810 and being promoted to colonel 20 February 1811; brigadier 4 June 1813, subsequently major general and lieutenant general. Died at Lisbon 27 April 1844.

British Commissions: ensign 50th Foot 20 July 1793, lieutenant 50th Foot 3 April 1795.

Gentleman's Magazine; *Naval and Military Magazine 1828*

Henry Sturgeon (1781–1814)

Born c1781, son of Lady Henrietta Alicia Watson-Wentworth, sister of the Marquess of Rockingham, and her former footman William Sturgeon. Appears in Army List simply as Henry Sturgeon but actually appears to have been named either Richard Henry Sturgeon or Robert Henry Sturgeon. Entered Royal Artillery 1796 but after transferring to Royal Staff Corps was attached to QMG department 1 June 1809. Mentioned in despatches at Cuidad Rodrigo. Appointed AQMG 25 April 1813 and appointed to command Corps of Staff Guides vice Scovell. Noted talent for building bridges but was killed in action at Vic-en-Bigorre 19 March 1814. There is no evidence to support a popular story that he deliberately exposed himself to fire following criticism of his running of the Army's post office.

Commissions: second lieutenant Royal Artillery 1 January 1796; lieutenant 21 August 1797; captain Royal Staff Corps 1 June 1809; lieutenant colonel (brevet) 6 February 1812.

WO25/3998; *Burke's Peerage*; Dalton; Ward

Charles Sutton (1775–1828)

Eldest son of Admiral Evelyn Sutton of Screveton, Nottingham. Served Helder 1799 and Hanover 1805, then throughout Peninsular War; largely attached to Portuguese Army. Died of a sudden attack of apoplexy at Bottesford nr. Belvoir 26 March 1828.

Commissions: cornet 11th Light Dragoons 6 August 1799; ensign 3rd Footguards 10 July 1800; lieutenant and captain 17 December 1802, half pay 25 December 1802; captain 23rd Fusiliers 25 May 1803; major 23rd Fusiliers 23 April 1807; lieutenant colonel (brevet) 30 May 1811; lieutenant colonel 23rd Fusiliers 17 June 1813, half pay 1814; colonel (brevet) 19 July 1821.

    WO25/3998; *Gentleman's Magazine*; *Medal Rolls 23rd RWF*

Charles Taylor (1772-1808)
Only son of Dr Taylor of Reading. educated at Westminster and Christchurch, Oxford. He gained a BA in 1794 and an MA in 1797. Killed in action at Vimeiro 21 August 1808.

Commissions: cornet 7th Light Dragoons 1793; captain 16 September 1795; major 16 May 1801; lieutenant colonel 20th Light Dragoons 24 February 1803.

    Hall

Alexander Thompson
Mentioned in despatches at Cuidad Rodrigo 1812, slightly wounded at Badajoz and again while serving as an engineer at the Salamanca forts. Badly wounded at Salamanca 22 July 1812. Afterwards at St. Sebastian.

Commissions: ensign 74th Highlanders 23 September 1803; lieutenant 29 February 1804; captain 14 May 1807; major (brevet) 9 April 1812; lieutenant colonel (brevet) 21 September 1813; half pay 89th Foot 1 April 1819.

    WO25/776 f99; Hall

Christopher Tilson (1771-1834)
Son of John Tilson of Watlington Park, Oxford. Served Egypt 1801, Sicily 1805 and West Indies 1806, then Peninsula; commanded brigade at various points between 1808 and 1810, returned to command 2nd Division, as Hill's deputy, for a short time late in 1812. Confusingly he had by then become Christopher Chowne in consequence of a legacy. Married Jane Craufurd 12 October 1823. Died 15 July 1834.

Commissions: second lieutenant 23rd Fusiliers 13 February 1788; lieutenant 1790; captain Independent Company 25 April 1793; major 99th Foot 1794;

lieutenant colonel 99th Foot 15 November 1794, half pay March 1798; lieutenant colonel 44th Foot 24 January 1799; Colonel (brevet) 1 January 1800; brigadier general (Mediterranean 25 March 1805; major general 25 April 1808; lieutenant general 4 June 1813.

Royal Military Calendar

Henry Torrens (1779-1828)

Fourth son of Very Reverend Thomas Torrens and Elizabeth Curry, born in Londonderry 1779. Served West Indies; wounded at the capture of St. Lucia and afterwards fought in the Carib War on St. Vincent. ADC first to Whitelocke (1798) then Cuyler (1799) in Portugal. Served Helder 1799 and badly wounded at Egmont op See. Took Surrey Rangers (Fencibles) to Nova Scotia in 1801 before transferring to 86th Foot to serve Egypt and India under Baird until 1803. AAG Kent District then served as military secretary to Whitelock in Argentina. Assistant Military Secretary to Commander in Chief 1807, then to Portugal 1808 on staff as Military Secretary. Afterwards returned to post as Assistant Military Secretary and then Military Secretary to Commander in Chief for the remainder of the war, and then Adjutant General 25 March 1820. Married Sarah Patton on St. Helena in May 1803/ issue. Died suddenly of an apoplexy while riding at Welwyn, Herts, 23 August 1828.

Commissions: ensign 52nd Foot 2 November 1793; lieutenant (late) 92nd Foot 14 June 1794; lieutenant 63rd Foot 11 November 1795; captain 6/West India Regiment 28 March 1797; captain 20th Foot 8 August 1799; major Surrey Rangers 3 November 1799; major 86th Foot 4 February 1802; lieutenant colonel (brevet) 1 January 1805; major 89th Foot 19 February 1807; captain and lieutenant colonel 3rd Footguards 13 June 1811; colonel (brevet) 20 February 1812; major general 4 June 1814.

Gentleman's Magazine; ODNB; Royal Military Calendar

Nicholas Trant (1769-1839)

Son of Thomas Trant, born in Dingle 1769. Married Sarah Georgina Horsington 1799/issue. Served at Flushing and Cape of Good Hope with 89th Foot, then Portugal and Minorca with the Irish Brigade. Helped form the Queen's German Regiment and served with it in Egypt, but left army at Peace of Amiens in 1802. Joined Royal Staff Corps in December 1803, serving as a confidential agent and returning to Portugal in 1808; helped raise Loyal Lusitanian Legion, officially a foreign corps in British pay and afterwards commanded large bodies of Portuguese troops engaged in partisan operations. He was highly regarded by Wellington but ultimately ill-rewarded.

British Commissions: lieutenant 89th Foot 31 May 1794; captain 1 October 1794, captain 1/Irish Brigade 1 October 1796; major Queen's German Regiment 13 January 1799, lieutenant colonel Queen's German Regiment (97th Foot) 5 April 1801, retired 1802; ensign Royal Staff Corps 25 December 1803; lieutenant Royal Staff Corps 28 November 1805; lieutenant colonel (Portugal) 1808; captain Royal Staff Corps 1 June 1809; major (brevet) 6 June 1815; half pay 25 December 1816.

   ODNB; *Royal Military Calendar*

Robert Travers (1770-1834)

Son of John Travers and Mehetabel Colthurst, born 13 October 1770. Served Ireland 1798 as a volunteer under Moore, then Helder 1799 and Ferrol 1800, Hanover, Buenos Aires and Peninsula 1808. Commanded 2/10th Foot on Malta from 1810, then Peninsula 1812-1813, and Genoa 1814. Resident High Commissioner at Cephalonia 1817-1823. Married/issue. Died as a result of a fall from his horse in Patrick Street, Cork 24 December 1834.

Commissions: ensign 85th Foot 1793; lieutenant 112th Foot 21 July 1794; captain 1 September 1795, half pay 1 March 1798; captain 79th Highlanders 3 July 1799; captain Experimental Rifle Corps 25 August 1800; major 95th Rifles 6 May 1805; lieutenant colonel 8/Garrison Battalion 22 December 1808; lieutenant colonel 10th Foot 15 February 1810; colonel (brevet) 4 June 1814; major general 27 May 1825.

   Burke's Irish Family Records; *Royal Military Calendar*; *United Services Magazine*

Robert Cotton St. John Trefusis, Lord Clinton (1787-1832)

Eldest son of Robert Trefusis, 17th Baron Clinton, born 28 April 1787, Served as extra ADC to Wellington in Peninsula. Married 1814/issue. Died near Florence while en route to Naples, October 1832.

Commissions: lieutenant 16th Dragoons 1805; captain 18 June 1807; captain 16th Light Dragoons 17 September 1807; exch, 60th Foot 13 June 1812; major 41st Foot 13 August 1812; exchanged to half pay 8/Garrison Battalion 1814; lieutenant colonel (brevet) 20 August 1812; colonel (brevet) 16 July 1825.

   Challis; *Gentleman's Magazine*

Hon Richard le Poer Trench (1767-1837)
Son of William Trench, 1st Earl of Clancarty, and Anne Gardiner, born 19 May 1767; succeeded to title as 2nd Earl of Clancarty 1805 but continued to serve as Hon. R. Le Poer Trench. Initially served in Canada and appointed Inspecting Field Officer of Militia 1808, but afterwards served throughout Peninsular War. Mentioned in dispatches at Badajoz. Married Henrietta Margaret Staples 6 February 1796/issue. Died 24 November 1837.

Commissions: ensign 27th Foot 30 October 1799; lieutenant 67th Foot 9 December 1800; captain 93rd Highlanders 25 May 1803; major 96th Foot 25 October 1806; lieutenant colonel (brevet) 28 January 1808; lieutenant colonel 74th Highlanders 21 September 1809; colonel (brevet) 4 June 1814.
    ODNB; *Royal Military Calendar*

John Goulston Price Tucker. (1777-1841)
Fourth son of Henry Tucker and Frances Bruere, born on Bermuda 27 July 1777. Served in India, Cape of Good Hope, and Argentina on the staff latterly as AQMG under Sir Samuel Auchmuty before coming out to Portugal. Appointed AAG 24 November 1808 but does not appear to have served again in the Peninsula. Appears to have retired on half pay 1810 before going to 41st Foot at Niagara 1814 and serving in American War. Married Ann Mulcaster/issue. Died in Paris 1841.

Commissions: ensign 2/78th Highlanders 29 April 1795; lieutenant 25 May 1796; then lieutenant 72nd Highlanders; captain 72nd Highlanders 31 August 1801; major 13 January 1805; lieutenant colonel (brevet) 16 April 1807; major 8/Garrison Battalion 2 October 1808; major 41st Foot 27 January 1814; colonel (brevet) 4 June 1814; major 5/West India Regiment 30 November 1815.
    Royal Military Calendar

Alexander Tulloh (d. 1826)
Served Royal Horse Artillery. Interned while on leave in France during the Peace of Amiens but escaped 1810 and served with Portuguese army from 1811. Wounded at Badajoz and badly wounded at Nive. Married/issue. Died 28 May 1826.

Commissions: second lieutenant Royal Artillery 2 May 1794; lieutenant 11 August 1794; second captain 19 July 1804; captain 8 May 1811; major (brevet) 1 January 1812; lieutenant colonel (brevet) 27 April 1812; half pay 1 August 1820.

Hall; Kane; *Royal Military Calendar*

Hon, Arthur Percy Upton (1777-1855)

Third son of Clotworthy Upton, 1st Baron Templeton, born 13 June 1777. Served Peninsula and appointed AQMG 28 October 1812. Attached to 1st Division until returned home 30 April 1814. A noted cricketer and MP for Bury St. Edmunds 1818-1826. Died in Brighton 22 January 1855.

Commissions: ensign Coldstream 28 April 1793; lieutenant and captain 1st Footguards 2 December 1795; major 13th Foot 7 May 1807; lieutenant colonel (brevet) 14 May 1807; captain and lieutenant colonel 1st Footguards 21 May 1807; colonel (brevet) 4 June 1814; major 1st Footguards 25 July 1814; major general 19 July 1821; lieutenant general 10 January 1837.

WO25/3998; Hart (1840); *Royal Military Calendar*; Ward

John Ormsby Vandeleur (1763-1849)

Only son of Captain Richard Vandeleur of Rutland, Queen's County. Served in Flanders 1794 and at the Cape 1799-1802. Served under Lord Lake in India and took over 8th Light Dragoons after his cousin Thomas Pakenham was killed in action at Laswaree. Served in Peninsula; Cuidad Rodrigo (wounded) Salamanca, Vittoria and Nive. Fought at Waterloo. Married Catherine Glasse 1829/issue. Died 1 November 1849.

Commissions: ensign 5th Foot 29 December 1781; lieutenant 67th Foot 21 July 1783, half pay; lieutenant 9th Foot 16 July 1788; captain 7 March 1792; captain-lieutenant 8th Light Dragoons 1 March 1794; major 1 March 1794; lieutenant colonel (brevet) 1 January 1798; lieutenant colonel 8th Light Dragoons 16 April 1807; colonel (brevet) 25 April 1808; major general 4 June 1811; lieutenant general 19 July 1821; general 10 January 1838.

WO25/3998; Dalton; Hall; Hart (1840)

Richard Hussey Vivian (1775-1842)

Eldest son of John Vivian of Truro and Betsey Cranch, born 28 July 1775. Served in Holland 1794-95. Subsequently at Helder 1799. In Peninsula led 7th Light Dragoons at Benevente and Corunna. Returned to Peninsula 1813 commanding Hussar Brigade. Served Nive and Orthes then badly wounded at bridge of Croix d'Orade in the advance to Toulouse. Subsequently served at Waterloo and was Inspector General of Cavalry 1825-31, C-in-C Ireland

1831–35, Master General of the Ordnance 1835–41. Created baronet 1828. Married twice/issue. Died of heart attack at Baden–Baden 20 August 1842.

Commissions: ensign 20th Foot 31 July 1793; lieutenant Independent Company 20 October 1793; lieutenant 54th Foot 30 October 1793; captain 28th Foot 7 May 1794; captain 7th Light Dragoons 8 August 1798; major 9 March 1803; lieutenant colonel 25th Light Dragoons 28 September 1804; lieutenant colonel 7th Light Dragoons 1 December 1804; colonel (brevet) 20 February 1812; major general 4 June 1814; lieutenant general 22 July 1830.

WO25/3998; Dalton; Hart (1840); McGuigan and Burnham; *ODNB*; *Royal Military Calendar*

George Townshend Walker (1764–1842)
Eldest son of Major Nathaniel Walker and Henrietta Bagster, born 25 May 1764. Served briefly in India and then Flanders on QMG staff. Inspector of Foreign Corps 1795 and involved in raising of Roll's Regiment. Served briefly in Portugal, as ADC first to General Fraser and then to the Prince of Waldeck. Served Helder 1799 as British Commissioner with Russian contingent, then took command of 50th Foot at Malta. Served Copenhagen 1807 and Peninsula 1808. Commanded 50th Foot at Vimeiro. Served at Walcheren, before returning to Peninsula as liaison officer with Spanish Army 1810. On promotion to major general was given a brigade in 5th Division. Badly wounded at Badajoz 6 April 1812 and according to legend would have been murdered had he not made a masonic sign of distress. Invalided home he returned to the Peninsula in 1813 and was again wounded, less seriously at Orthez 27 February 1814, while commanding 7th Division. Governor of Grenada 1815–1816; C-in-C Madras 1826–1831; lieutenant governor of Chelsea Hospital 24 May 1837, dying there 14 November 1842.

Commissions: ensign 95th Foot 4 March 1782; lieutenant 13 March 1783; lieutenant 71st Highlanders 22 June 1783; lieutenant 36th Foot 15 March 1784; lieutenant 35th Foot 25 July 1787; captain-lieutenant and captain 14th Foot 13 March 1789; captain 60th Foot 4 May 1791; major 28 August 1794; lieutenant colonel 50th Foot 6 September 1798; colonel (brevet) 25 April 1808; major general 4 June 1811; lieutenant general 19 July 1821; general 28 June 1838.

Hall; Hart; McGuigan and Burnham; *ODNB*

John Alexander Dunlop Agnew Wallace (1775–1857)
Only son of Sir Thomas Wallace of Craigie, Ayrshire and Eglantine

Maxwell. Served India; Sringapatnam 1791-9, then Minorca 1798; and Egypt 1801 before commanding 88th Foot with great distinction throughout the Peninsular War. Married Janette Rodger 23 June 1829/issue. Died at Lochryan House, Stranraer 11 November 1857.

Commissions; ensign 75th Highlanders 28 December 1789; lieutenant 6 April 1790; captain 58th Foot 8 June 1796; major 9 July 1803; lieutenant colonel 28 August 1804; lieutenant colonel 88th Foot 6 February 1805; colonel (brevet) 4 June 1813; major general 12 August 1819; lieutenant general 10 August 1837; general 11 November 1851.

Hall; Hart; *ODNB*

John Waters (1773-1842)
Born at Margam, Glamorgan, grandson of Edward Waters (High Sheriff of Glamorgan 1754) Served Helder 1799 and Egypt then the West Indies. Served Peninsula first as ADC to Stewart and then with 1st Portuguese Line. Appointed AAG 15 April 1811 and employed as an exploring officer, captured at Sabugal 3 May 1811 but escaped next day. Acting AG during autumn 1811, served Badajoz and Salamanca, slightly wounded in Pyrenees 28 July 1813; AAG Waterloo – slightly wounded. Died at Park Place, St. James's 21 November 1842.

Commissions: ensign 2/1st (Royal) Regiment 2 August 1797; lieutenant 15 February 1799, captain (brevet) 24 September 1803; captain 2/1st (Royal) Regiment 28 February 1805; major (Spain and Portugal) 16 February 1809 "not holding regimental commission"; lieutenant colonel (brevet) 30 May 1811; captain and lieutenant colonel Coldstream 15 May 1817; colonel (brevet) 19 July 1821, half pay 15 February 1827; major general 22 July 1830; lieutenant general 23 November 23 November 1841.

Dalton; Hart (1840); *ODNB*; Ward

Gregory Holman Bromley Way (1776-1844)
Fifth son of Benjamin Way FRS and Elizabeth Anne Cooke, born in London 28 December 1776. Served in Malta at the siege of Valetta 1799–1800, South America and the Peninsula; wounded at Rolica and at Albuera. Half-pay as lieutenant colonel 24 October 1814 in consequence of wounds, but appointed DAG Scotland in the following year. Married Marianne Weyland 19 May 1815. Died at Brighton 19 February 1844.

Commissions: ensign 26th Foot 24 August 1797; lieutenant 35th Foot 3 November 1799; captain 13 August 1802, but half pay by reduction; captain

5th Foot 20 January 1803; major 29th Foot 25 February 1808; lieutenant colonel (brevet) 30 May 1811; lieutenant colonel 29th Foot 4 July 1811; lieutenant colonel 22nd Foot 29 September 1814, but half pay 24 October 1814 in consequence of wounds; colonel (brevet) 19 July 1821; colonel 3/ Royal Veteran Battalion 24 November 1822, but half pay by reduction 24 April 1825; major general 22 July 1830; lieutenant general 23 November 1841.

> WO25/777 f41; *1818 Pension Return*; Hart 1840; *ODNB*

Daniel White (k.1809)

Served in marine detachments 1793 and in West Indies 1793 to 1796; served at Helder 1799, wounded at Bergen; served in Peninsula July 1808 to June 1811; succeeded to command of 29th Foot after Rolica; fatally wounded at Albuera and died at Elvas 3 June 1811.

Commissions: lieutenant 29th Foot 25 August 1787; captain 1 March 1794; major 5 December 1799; lieutenant colonel (brevet) 1 January 1805; lieutenant colonel 29th Foot 2 September 1808.

> Hall

Samuel Ford Whittingham (1772-1841)

Eldest son of William Whittingham of Bristol, born 29 January 1772; worked as a commercial traveller in Spain in 1790s before entering army in 1803; attended Royal Military College 1806 and afterwards sent on confidential mission to Spain. Served Buenos Aires as extra ADC to General Whitelocke and afterwards appointed DAQMG Sicily, but on arrival at Gibraltar was attached to General Castanos' forces and present at Baylen. Appointed DAQMG 25 April 1809 but remained with Spanish Army and was wounded at Talavera; appointed major general in Spanish service12 August 1809 and lieutenant general June 1814. Organised Spanish division in Minorca 1812 and led it at Castalla. Subsequently played a prominent role in military coup in 1814, destroying Spain's liberal government and returning Fernando to the throne. Returning to British service he was governor of Dominica 1818-1821; QMG India 1821-1833. C-in-C Windward and Leeward Islands 1836, then commander Madras Army until dying suddenly at Madras 19 January 1841. Married Magdalena de Creus y Jimenez in Gibraltar January 1810/issue.

British Commissions: ensign 20 January 1803; lieutenant 25 February 1803; lieutenant 1st Lifeguards 10 March 1803; captain 20th Foot 14 February

1805; captain 13th Light Dragoons 13 June 1805; major 12 March 1810; lieutenant colonel 30 May 1811; colonel (brevet) 4 June 1814; major general 27 May 1825; lieutenant general 28 June 1838. It seems extremely unlikely that he ever did a day's regimental soldiering during his career.

Hall; Hart (1840); *ODNB;* Ward

John Archer Williams
Served in Peninsula from August 1808; present at Torres Vedras, Cuidad Rodrigo and Badajoz, where badly wounded guiding Light Division into breach. Killed in action at Burgos 24 September 1812.

Commissions: second lieutenant Royal Engineers 1 January 1804; lieutenant 1 March 1805; second captain 24 June 1809.

Hall

William Williams (1776-1832)
Slightly wounded at Busaco 27 September 1810 and badly wounded at Fuentes d'Onoro 3 May 1811, while commanding light infantry battalions belonging to 3rd Division. Again wounded at Badajoz and Salamanca 1812. Afterwards served in North America and responsible for retraining 13th Foot as light infantry; served Plattsburg and Lacolle Mill. Died 17 June 1832.

Commissions: ensign 40th Foot 23 June 1794; lieutenant 7 April 1795; captain 23 September 1799; major (brevet) 24 June 1802; major 16/Reserve Battalion 9 July 1803; major 81st Foot 26 October 1804; lieutenant colonel 5/60th Foot 15 November 1809; lieutenant colonel 13th Foot 25 June 1812; colonel (brevet) 12 August 1819; retired 8 November 1819; major general 22 July 1830.

Gentleman's Magazine; Hall; *Royal Military Calendar*

James Wilson (1780-1847)
A gallant but unfortunate officer. Served at the Helder 1799; Ferrol 1800 and Egypt 1801; slightly wounded at Albuera 16 May 1811, again at Badajoz 6 April 1812 and then badly wounded in the Pyrenees 26 July. Served at Toulouse 1814 but unfit for further service as a result of "continuall sufferings from severe wounds recd. In Peninsula." Married in Winchester 24 March 1805, he died at Bath in February 1847.

Commissions: ensign 27th Foot 12 December 1798; lieutenant 27 August 1799; captain 27 May 1801, but half pay "by reduction"; captain 48th Foot 9 July 1803; major 20 June 1811; lieutenant colonel (brevet) 19 April 1812, half pay 25 September 1814 "by reduction"; colonel (brevet) 22 July 1830; major general 28 June 1838.

WO25/778 f 35; *1818 Pension Return*; Hall

Sir Robert Thomas Wilson (1777-1849)

Third son of Benjamin Wilson FRS and Jane Hetherington, born in Bloomsbury 17 August 1777. Served in Flanders and Holland 1793-95; Ireland 1798; Egypt 1801 and Cape 1806. Attached to Russian Army in Poland 1807 and present at Eylau and Friedland. Served in Peninsula; raised and commanded Loyal Lusitanian Legion 1808-09, but far too independent-minded to work with Wellington. Again served with Russian and then Austrian armies throughout 1812-14 campaigns, including Dresden and Leipzig, but latterly with Austrian Army in Italy. Married Jemima Belford 1797/issue. Died suddenly at Marshall Thompson's Hotel, Oxford Street 9 May 1849.

Commissions: cornet 15th Light Dragoons 2 April 1794; lieutenant 31 October 1794; captain 21 September 1796; major Hompesch' Mounted Rifles 28 June 1800; lieutenant colonel 27 February 1802, then half pay; lieutenant colonel 19th Light Dragoons 30 August 1804; lieutenant colonel 20th Light Dragoons 7 March 1805; colonel (brevet) 25 July 1810; lieutenant colonel 22nd Light Dragoons 10 December 1812; major general 4 June 1813; lieutenant general 27 May 1825; general 23 November 1841.

Hart (1840); *ODNB*

Alexander George Woodford(1782-1870)

Eldest son of Lieutenant Colonel John Woodford and Lady Susan Gordon, born in London 14 June 1782. Served at the Helder 1799 and wounded at Bergen. Served at Copenhagen, Sicily, and the Peninsula; Cadiz, Cuidad Rodrigo, Badajoz, Salamanca (commanded light battalion of Guards Brigade), Vittoria, Nive. Commanded 2/Coldstream at Waterloo. Afterwards commanded a brigade on Malta 1825-1827, then Corfu 1827-1832, Ionian Islands 1832-1835 then lieutenant governor of Gibraltar February 1835. Successively lieutenant governor and governor of Chelsea Hospital 1856-1868. Married/issue. Died at Chelsea Hospital 26 August 1870.

Commissions: ensign 9th Foot 6 December 1794; lieutenant Independent Company 15 July 1795, company taken into 22nd Foot, but he himself placed on half pay as under age; captain-lieutenant and captain 9th Foot 11 December 1799; lieutenant and captain Coldstream 20 December 1799; captain and lieutenant colonel 8 March 1810; colonel (brevet) 4 June 1814;

second major Coldstream 25 July 1814; first major 18 January 1820; lieutenant colonel Coldstream 25 July 1821; major general 27 May 1925; lieutenant general 28 June 1838; general 20 June 1854; field marshal 1 January 1868.

Dalton; Hall; Hart (1840); *ODNB*

William Woodgate (1780–1861)
Served Canada and the West Indies, then in Peninsula August 1808 to March 1812, commanding 3rd Division light battalions at Fuentes d'Onoro and afterwards at Badajoz and Salamanca. Retired from active service on reduction of battalion in 1817. Died in Paris 12 January 1861.

Commissions: lieutenant 6th Foot 19 November 1800; captain 5/60th Foot 6 April 1803; major 5/60th Foot 13 August 1807; lieutenant colonel (brevet) 30 May 1811; lieutenant colonel 5/60th Foot 16 June 1814; colonel (brevet) 19 July 1821.

Hall; Hart; *Royal Military Calendar*

Wellington's Armies 1808–1814

T he organisation of British infantry brigades set out below can be deceptive in that their administrative and tactical matrices differed. On paper, a brigade normally comprised three battalions of line infantry and a single company of green-jacketed riflemen. Each of those battalions included a light company which flung skirmishers ahead of the main battle line. However, this company was not entirely independent for it was joined out there with the other light companies of the brigade and with the rifle company formed into a small light battalion under the command of the senior captain.[1] This was a permanent arrangement and it is common to find captains recording in their post-war returns of service that they had commanded the light companies of their brigade.

Moreover, whilst notionally comprised of only four companies, these light battalions were comparatively strong for not only was it customary to try and maintain the regimental light companies at something approaching their proper establishment, but in action they were also thickened out first by skirmishers, "marksmen" or "flankers" sent forward from the ordinary battalion companies, then by whole companies and finally by complete battalions.

This practice of consolidating the light companies did not end at brigade level, for by the end of the war, at division level these provisional light battalions were in turn being consolidated with a Portuguese cacadore battalion[2] to form a divisional light brigade, usually commanded by a major or a lieutenant colonel, with the assistance of an adjutant.

Consequently, in action, a typical brigade would actually deploy four battalions; that is three nine-company strong line battalions and a four-company

---

1 This was under the authority of the 1792 *Rules and regulations for the Formations, Field Exercises and Movements of his Majesty's Forces*, which clearly stated (p.332) that "When two or more companies are together they are to consider themselves a battalion, the senior officer is to take command, leaving the immediate command of his own company to the next officer belonging to it."

2 Or the KGL Light Battalion of 1st Division.

light battalion, while a division might eventually field two British brigades, a Portuguese brigade and a consolidated light brigade as well.

1808

The army which Lieutenant General Sir Arthur Wellesley, as he then was, commanded at Rolica and Vimeiro was rather haphazardly organised, since the troops which constituted it were drawn from a variety of different sources and indeed some of them were quite literally still arriving in theatre as the battles were being fought.

1st Brigade (Hill):
5th Foot
9th Foot
38th Foot

2nd Brigade (Ferguson):
36th Foot
40th Foot
71st Highlanders

3rd Brigade (Nightingall):
28th Foot
82nd Foot

4th Brigade (Bowes):
6th Foot
32nd Foot

5th Brigade (Catlin Craufurd):
50th Foot
91st Highlanders

6th Brigade (Fane):
45th Foot
5/60th Foot
2/95th Rifles

NB: before Vimeiro the 45th and 50th Foot changed places.

1809 Oporto

The Memorandum of Operations for 1809 opens with the statement that "The British army, intended for the service in Portugal and Spain, was complete in the end of April, with the exception of one brigade of infantry not arrived, and some troops expected from Gibraltar, when relieved by others to be sent from Portugal."

Morning State of the British Forces in Portugal, under Sir Arthur Wellesley, K.B.

Headquarters, Coimbra, May 6, 1809

		Sergeants, Drummers, Rank and File &c				
	Officers	Present	Sick	On Command	Total	Total Efficients Present, Officers and Men
CAVALRY						
1st Brigade (Stapleton Cotton)						
14th Light Dragoons	27	628	21	73	749	655
16th Light Dragoons	37	673	20	35	765	710
20th Light Dragoons (two sqdns)	6	237	6	63	312	243
3rd Light Dragoons K.G.L. (one sqdn)	3	57	2	77	139	60
						1,668
2nd Brigade (Fane)						
3rd Dragoon Guards	25	698	10		733	723
4th Dragoons	27	716	13		756	743
						1,466
Total Cavalry	125	3,009	72	248	3,454	3,134
INFANTRY						
Brigade of Guards (H. Campbell)						
Coldstream Guards, 1st Batt.	33	1,194	75	3	1,305	1,227

(*continued*)

	Officers	Sergeants, Drummers, Rank and File &c				Total Efficients Present, Officers and Men
		Present	Sick	On Command	Total	
3rd Footguards, 1st Batt.	34	1,228	79	8	1,349	1,262
1 company 5/60th Foot	2	61	4	–	67	63
						2,552
1st Brigade (Hill)						
3rd Foot, 1st Batt.	28	719	104	50	901	747
48th Foot, 2nd Batt.	32	721	52	–	805	753
66th Foot, 2nd Batt.	34	667	38	10	749	701
1 company 5/60th Foot	2	61	4	–	67	63
						2,264
2nd Brigade (Mackenzie)						
27th Foot, 3rd Batt.	28	726	134	2	890	754
31st Foot, 2nd Batt.	27	765	99	6	897	792
45th Foot, 1st Batt.	22	671	125	27	845	693
						2,239
3rd Brigade (Tilson)						
5/60th Foot (5 companies)	14	306	32	2	354	320
87th Foot, 2nd Batt.	32	669	88	1	790	701
88th Foot, 1st Batt.	30	608	143	28	809	638
1st Portuguese, 1st Batt.	–	–	–	–	–	–
						1,659
4th Brigade (Sontag)						
97th Foot	22	572	74	20	688	594
2nd Batt. of Detachments	35	787	221	16	1,059	822
1 company 5/60th Foot	2	61	6	–	69	63
16th Portuguese, 2nd Batt.	–	–	–	–	–	–
						1,479

(*continued*)

	Officers	Sergeants, Drummers, Rank and File &c				Total Efficients Present, Officers and Men
		Present	Sick	On Command	Total	
5th Brigade (A. Campbell)						
7th Foot, 2nd Batt.	26	559	50	3	638	585
53rd Foot	23	691	59	3	776	714
1 company 5/60th Foot	4	64	11	1	80	68
10th Portuguese, 1st Batt.	-	-	-	-	-	-
						1,367
6th Brigade (R. Stewart)						
29th Foot	26	596	85	7	714	622
1st Batt, of Detachments	27	803	169	24	1,023	830
16th Portuguese, 1st Batt.	-	-	-	-	-	-
						1,452
7th Brigade (Cameron)						
9th Foot, 2nd Batt.	27	545	227	22	821	572
83rd Foot, 2nd Batt.	39	833	73	23	968	872
1 company 5/60th Foot	2	60	3	1	66	62
10th Portuguese, 2nd Batt.	-	-	-	-	-	-
K.G.L. Brigade (Murray)						
1st Line Batt. K.G.L.	34	767	125	9	935	801
2nd Line Batt. K.G.L.	32	804	52	9	897	836
5th Line Batt. K.G.L.	28	720	101	12	861	748
7th Line Batt. K.G.L.	22	688	83	10	803	710
						3,095

(*continued*)

| | Officers | Sergeants, Drummers, Rank and File &c | | | | Total Efficients Present, Officers and Men |
		Present	Sick	On Command	Total	
Unattached troops (Lisbon)						
24th Foot, 2nd Batt.	18	750	26	3	797	768
30th Foot, 2nd Batt.	15	447	49	197	708	462
Independent Light Co. K.G.L.	3	35	14	4	56	38
						1,268
Total Infantry	703	18,178	2,405	501	21,787	18,881
Artillery						
British	31	550	83	499	1,163	581
King's German Legion	18	331	34	134	517	349
Wagon Train attached	3	61	18	83	165	64
Total Artillery	52	942	135	716	1,845	949
Engineers	12	27	1	–	40	39
Wagon Train	2	65	21	17	105	67
General Total	894	22,221	2,634	1,482	27,231	23,115

The ensuing campaign was strikingly successful in driving the French out of Portugal, but the army was found too big to control effectively through its brigade commanders alone and with effect from 18 June 1809, its infantry units were reorganised into four divisions and an independent Light Brigade. This proved successful and over the next two years three more divisions were added and the Light Brigade was expanded into a full division.

The powerful 1st Division usually had four brigades (including one and then two of Footguards), each comprising two large battalions, while the other divisions initially had only two brigades, each of two or three battalions. In addition to the infantry, each division had its own organic artillery support, staff and commissariat officers.

The divisions did not, however as a rule, have an organic cavalry element, although the Light Division enjoyed the almost permanent attachment of the 1st Hussars King's German Legion (KGL), reflecting their frequent employment on detached operations.

Within a short time most divisions (1st Division being the exception) were also reinforced by the addition of a strong Portuguese brigade, normally comprising two ordinary infantry regiments (each of two battalions) and a cacadore or light infantry battalion. This practice was resented by the Portuguese government, which would undoubtedly have preferred their army to operate as a distinct national corps, but it effectively increased the size of the British Army by perhaps as much as 50 per cent while avoiding most of the operational difficulties traditionally associated with co-ordinating independent allied forces.

1st Division "The Gentlemen's Sons"

The 1st Division was formed on 18 June 1809 and derived its nickname from the inclusion of first one and then two brigades of Footguards. It also included a brigade drawn from the highly regarded King's German Legion (KGL) but otherwise its composition seemed at times transient and perhaps variable in quality.

1st Division 18 June 1809 Sir John Coape Sherbrooke
Brigadier General Henry Frederick Campbell's Brigade
Coldstream Guards (1 battalion)
Scots Guards (1 battalion)

Brigadier General Allan Cameron of Erracht's Brigade
2/9th Foot
2/83rd Foot

Brigadier General Ernst von Langwerth's Brigade
1/King's German Legion
2/King's German Legion

Brigadier General Sigismund von Löw's Brigade
5/King's German Legion
7/King's German Legion

Subsequent alterations 1809:

Campbell was wounded at Talavera and replaced by Hon. Edward Stopford, except for a brief period between 8 November and 15 December when Richard Hulse had the brigade.

Cameron's brigade saw some confusing changes; 1/40th Foot came up from Cadiz to temporarily replace 2/9th Foot sometime before 21 June. 2/9th Foot then relieved 1/61st Foot at Gibraltar, who joined the brigade shortly before Talavera and in turn replaced 1/40th which transferred to 4th Division. After Talavera 2/24th Foot and 2/42nd Highlanders joined and 2/83rd Foot were then sent down to Lisbon.

Langwerth was killed at Talavera and succeeded by Beck of 1/KGL, but all four King's German Legion battalions were subsequently amalgamated into a single brigade under Löw on 1 November.

1st Division: 1 January 1810 Sir John Coape Sherbrooke
Brigadier General Hon. Edward Stopford's Brigade
Coldstream Guards (1 battalion)
Scots Guards (1 battalion)

Brigadier General Allan Cameron of Erracht's Brigade
2/24th Foot
2/42nd Highlanders
1/61st Foot

Brigadier General Sigismund von Löw's Brigade
1/ King's German Legion
2/ King's German Legion
5/ King's German Legion
7/ King's German Legion
Det. King's German Legion Light Battalion

Subsequent alterations 1810:

Sir Stapleton Cotton briefly took command of the division on 26 April after Sherbrooke went home sick, but then he in turn was given command of the newly formed cavalry division on 3 June and replaced by Major General Sir Brent Spencer.

Cameron appears to have been on the sick list from March onwards, although he was not officially replaced by Lieutenant Colonel Lord Blantyre of 2/42nd until 4 August. Cameron resumed command again on 1 October before being finally invalided home on 26 November. His own 1/79th Highlanders came up from Cadiz on 12 September to replace 1/61st Foot, which was in turn intended to form the nucleus of a 4th

Brigade. The exchange, however, was delayed until after Busaco and the meantime 1/79th and 1/7th Fusiliers formed a temporary brigade under Edward Pakenham. After Busaco the delayed exchange between 1/61st and 1/79th finally took place and Pakenham's Brigade (1/7th Fusiliers and 1/61st) transferred to 4 Division on 6 October. They in turn were then replaced in 1 Division by a new brigade under Sir William Erskine – see below.

1st Division: 1 January 1811 Sir Brent Spencer
Brigadier General Hon. Edward Stopford's Brigade
Coldstream Guards (1 battalion)
Scots Guards (1 battalion)
Coy. 5/60th (rifles)

Lieutenant Colonel Lord Blantyre's Brigade
2/24th Foot
2/42nd Highlanders
1/79th Highlanders
Coy. 5/60th (rifles)

Brigadier General Sigismund von Löw's Brigade
1/ King's German Legion
2/ King's German Legion
5/ King's German Legion
7/ King's German Legion
Det. KGL Light

Major General Sir William Erskine's Brigade
1/50th Foot
1/71st Highlanders
1/92nd Highlanders
Coy. 3/95th Rifles

Subsequent alterations 1811:

Spencer was promoted to lieutenant general on 4 June but was manoeuvred into going home on leave 25 July and was replaced by Lieutenant General Sir Thomas Graham.

Campbell returned to the Guards brigade on 8 June while Stopford went off to command a brigade in 4 Division.

Blantyre's temporary command of 2 Brigade came to an end with the appointment of Major General Sir Miles Nightingall on 23 January, however Nightingall then left for Bengal on 25 June and Stopford returned from 4 Division to take over the brigade on 21 July. On the same day 1/26th also joined the brigade. Stopford, however, developed a history of going sick and Blantyre retained effective command.

Erskine was promoted to the command of 5 Division on 6 February and replaced by Major General Sir Kenneth Howard, however the whole brigade was then transferred to 2 Division in the re-organisation which followed Albuera

In Löw's Brigade the detachments from the King's German Legion Light battalions were ordered to rejoin their parent units on 6 June, while 7/KGL was ordered to be drafted on 26 June and the cadre returned to England.

1st Division: 1 January 1812   Sir Thomas Graham
Major General Henry Frederick Campbell's Brigade
Coldstream Guards (1 battalion)
Scots Guards (1 battalion)
Coy. 5/60th (rifles)

Lieutenant Colonel Lord Blantyre's Brigade
2/24th Foot
1/26th Foot
2/42nd Highlanders
1/79th Highlanders
Coy. 5/60th (rifles)

Brigadier General Sigismund von Löw's Brigade
1/ King's German Legion
2/ King's German Legion
5/ King's German Legion

Subsequent alterations 1812:

Graham went home sick on 6 July and Henry Campbell temporarily took over the division until 11 October when Lieutenant General the Hon. Edward Paget was appointed, only to be taken prisoner on 17 November during the retreat from Burgos and consequently the division ended the year under Lieutenant General Sir William Stewart.

While Campbell was commanding the division, his brigade was looked after by the Hon. T.W. Fermor of the Scots Guards.

Stopford resumed command of his brigade from Blantyre sometime before 1 February but was absent again by 8 April. Major General William Wheatley took over on 7 May but died of typhus on 1 September and was himself replaced by Colonel James Stirling of 1/42nd.

The brigade itself went through an equally confusing succession of changes. 1/26th proved to be too sickly for field service and by 8 March had been sent down to Gibraltar to relieve 1/82nd. They were replaced by 1/58th Foot, who arrived on 2 April only to ordered to join 5th Division on 1 June, although it actually remained with the brigade until the post Burgos re-organisation. This was probably because although 1/42nd Highlanders also joined the brigade on 23 April, 2/42nd then went home on 19 May. The whole brigade then went to 6th Division on 10 November and was replaced by another brigade of Footguards (1/1st and 3/1st) under Kenneth Howard and then on 6 December another King's German Legion brigade (1/ King's German Legion Light Battalion and 2/ King's German Legion Light Battalion) joined under Colin Halkett.

1st Division:1 January 1813   Sir William Stewart
Major General Sir Kenneth Howard's Brigade
1/1st Footguards
3/1st Footguards
Coy. 5/60th (rifles)

Major General Hon. T. W. Fermor's Brigade
Coldstream Guards (1 battalion)
Scots Guards (1 battalion)
Coy. 5/60th (rifles)

Brigadier General Sigismund von Löw's Brigade
1/ King's German Legion
2/ King's German Legion
5/ King's German Legion

Brigadier General Colin Halkett's Brigade
1/ King's German Legion Light Battalion
2/ King's German Legion Light Battalion

Subsequent alterations 1813:

Command of the division passed to Howard on 25 March. Although Sir Thomas Graham was officially re-appointed to it on 19 May, he was also serving as commander of the Left Wing of the army and so Howard remained in day to day charge of the division until Graham again went sick on 8 October and was replaced by Sir John Hope, but Howard still continued to exercise de facto command of the division as Hope also followed Graham in leading the army's left wing.

While Howard was acting up his brigade was looked after by Colonel Sir John Lambert of 1st Footguards. However, Lambert was promoted major general on 4 June and transferred to 6. Division so the brigade then passed to Colonel Peregrine Maitland, again of 1st Footguards.

Löw went home to Germany on 6 May and at that point all of the KGL battalions were consolidated into a single brigade under Halkett, who was himself succeeded by Major General Heinrich von Hinhuber on 20 October.

A new 4th Brigade came out in July under Lord Aylmer and joined the division sometime in August. Initially it comprised:

76th Foot
2/84th Foot
85th Foot

However, on 17 October 2/84th Foot was transferred to 5. Division and replaced by 2/62nd and on 24 November 77th Foot came up from Lisbon and was also added to the brigade.

1st Division:1 January 1814   Sir John Hope (Sir Kenneth Howard)
Colonel Peregrine Maitland's Brigade
1/1st Footguards
3/1st Footguards
Coy. 5/60th (rifles)

Major General Hon. Edward Stopford's Brigade*
Coldstream Guards (1 battalion)
Scots Guards (1 battalion)
Coy. 5/60th (rifles)

---

*It is not clear exactly when Stopford returned to take command of the brigade

Major General Heinrich von Hinhuber's Brigade
1/ King's German Legion
2/ King's German Legion
5/ King's German Legion
1/ King's German Legion Light Battalion
2/ King's German Legion Light Battalion

Major General Lord Aylmer's Brigade
2/62nd Foot
76th Foot
77th Foot
85th Foot

Subsequent alterations 1814:

Stopford was wounded at Bayonne on 14 April and command of his brigade passed to Colonel John Guise of the Scots Guards. Otherwise, with the war drawing to a close, the only other alteration was the addition of 1/37th Foot to Aylmer's Brigade sometime before 25 March.

2nd Division "The Observing Division"

The 2nd Division was formed on 18 June 1809 and latterly nicknamed "The Observing Division", since most of its early service was spent as part of a corps of observation marking the French forces in Extramadura and Andalusia.

2nd Division 18 June 1809   Sir Rowland Hill
Major General Christopher Tilson's Brigade
1/3rd Foot
2/48th Foot
2/66th Foot

Brigadier General Richard Stewart's Brigade
29th Foot
1/Battalion Detachments (Lt. Col. William Bunbury, 3rd Foot)[3]

---

3 This was a provisional unit formed by Sir John Cradock and comprised of detachments and stragglers left behind in Portugal when Moore marched into Spain. Its composition on 6 February 1809 is set out per the return below and further units were represented by the time it reached Talavera.

Subsequent Alterations 1809:

In September 2/31st which had been serving with 3rd Division was added to Tilson's Brigade. Tilson himself was replaced by Lieutenant Colonel George Duckworth of 2/48th on 15 September. Also, in September, a third brigade was added under Catlin Craufurd comprising 2/28th Foot; 2/34th Foot and 2/39th Foot. In Stewart's brigade 1/48th had come up from Gibraltar in time for Talavera and by 1 November 1/ Detachments had been broken up and replaced by 1/57th Foot – also from Gibraltar.

2nd Division 1 January 1810   Sir Rowland Hill
Lieutenant Colonel George Duckworth's Brigade
1/3rd Foot
2/31st Foot
2/48th Foot
2/66th Foot

Unit	Field Officers	Captains	Subalterns	Staff	NCOs & Men
3rd Foot	1	0	0	0	0
20th Foot	0	1	1	0	47
28th Foot	0	1	6	1	120
32nd Foot	0	0	0	1	0
38th Foot	1	3	2	0	59
42nd Highlanders	0	0	2	1	23
2/43rd Foot	0	1	2	1	119
50th Foot	0	0	0	1	0
52nd Foot	0	1	3	2	123
79th Highlanders	0	0	4	1	64
91st Highlanders	0	1	2	1	164
92nd Highlanders	0	1	2	2	74
95th Rifles	0	0	0	0	35
Totals	2	9	24	11	58 NCOs 770 Men

Brigadier General Richard Stewart's Brigade
29th Foot
1/48th Foot
1/57th Foot

Brigadier General Catlin Craufurd's Brigade
2/28th Foot
2/34th Foot
2/39th Foot

Subsequent Alterations 1810:

On 20 June 1810 Major General Sir James Leith was nominated to command both the division "under Hill" and Duckworth's Brigade, but then on 8 July Leith was given command of a newly arrived brigade which became the nucleus of 5th Division. Instead, Sir William Stewart became Hill's deputy from 8 August and took over the division when Hill went home sick in November.

Duckworth's brigade was taken over by Leith on 20 June and then by Stewart on 27 July. In practice when Stewart was commanding the division the brigade was looked after by Lieutenant Colonel Sir John Colborne of 2/66th Foot.

Richard Stewart went home on sick leave before 1 September, leaving Colonel William Inglis of 1/57th Foot to command his brigade, although he was in turn superseded by Major General Daniel Hoghton on 8 October.

Catlin Craufurd died of fever at Abrantes on 25 September and his brigade was temporarily commanded at Busaco by Lieutenant Colonel George Wilson of 2/39th Foot, before Sir William Lumley took over on 30 September.

2nd Division 1 January 1811   Sir William Stewart
Lieutenant Colonel Sir John Colborne's Brigade
1/3rd Foot
2/31st Foot
2/48th Foot
2/66th Foot
Company 5/60th Foot

Major General Daniel Hoghton's Brigade
29th Foot
1/48th Foot
1/57th Foot
Company 5/60th Foot

Major General Sir William Lumley's Brigade
2/28th Foot
2/34th Foot
2/39th Foot
Company 5/60th Foot

Subsequent Alterations June 1811:

Hill returned from sick leave before the end of May and resumed command of the division, which had suffered very heavy losses at Albuera on 16 May, necessitating a radical re-organisation with effect from 6 June.

With the exception of 1/48th and 2/48th the survivors of Colborne's and Hoghton's brigades were consolidated into a single provisional battalion! This was then posted to Lumley's Brigade (which had been commanded at Albuera by Lieutenant Colonel Alexander Abercromby of 2/28th Foot), while the survivors of 2/48th Foot were drafted into 1/48th and posted to 4th Division. Two new brigades were then posted in to replace the two destroyed ones; Howard's Brigade from 1st Division and Charles Ashworth's Portuguese Brigade.

2nd Division 6 June 1811   Sir Rowland Hill
Major General Sir Kenneth Howard's Brigade
1/50th Foot
1/71st Foot
1/92nd Highlanders
Company 3/95th Rifles

Major General Sir William Lumley's Brigade
2/28th Foot
2/34th Foot
2/39th Foot
Provisional Battalion

Lieutenant Colonel Charles Ashworth's (Portuguese) Brigade
6th Line   (2 Bns)
18th Line   (2 Bns)
6th Cacadores   (1 Bn)

Subsequent Alterations August 1811:

On 22 July, 1/28th Foot came up from Gibraltar and was attached to Lumley's Brigade in place of the provisional battalion. Sufficient reinforcement drafts had arrived to bring both 1/3rd and 1/57th Foot back up to strength and together with the remainder of the provisional battalion formed into a new brigade under Colonel William Inglis of the 57th, with effect from 7 August.

2nd Division 7 August 1811   Sir Rowland Hill
Major General Sir Kenneth Howard's Brigade
1/50th Foot
1/71st Foot
1/92nd Highlanders
Company 3/95th Rifles

Colonel William Inglis' Brigade
1/3rd Foot
1/57th Foot
Provisional Battalion[4]

Major General Sir William Lumley's Brigade
1/28th Foot
2/28th Foot
2/34th Foot
2/39th Foot

Lieutenant Colonel Charles Ashworth's (Portuguese) Brigade
6th Line   (2 Bns)
18th Line   (2 Bns)
6th Cacadores   (1 Bn)

---

4 By this point it comprised:
   3 Coys 29th Foot
   4 Coys 2/31st Foot
   3 Coys 2/66th Foot

Subsequent Alterations 1811:

On 21 August the 3/95th Rifles company attached to Howard's Brigade was posted to the Light Division and a company of 5/60th received in exchange. Inglis' Brigade was taken over by Colonel John Byng on 21 September and on 3 October the remnants of 29th Foot were ordered home.

Lumley's Brigade underwent a number of changes. He himself went home sick in early August but was not officially replaced until Lieutenant Colonel George Wilson of 1/39th took over on 9 October. In the meantime, 2/28th were drafted into 1/28th and the cadre sent home to recruit. However, they were not replaced until 1/39th arrived from Sicily in October, but then on 17 December the effectives of 2/39th were drafted in 1/39th and the remainder sent home.

2nd Division 1 January 1812   Sir Rowland Hill
Major General Sir Kenneth Howard's Brigade
1/50th Foot
1/71st Foot
1/92nd Highlanders
Company 5/60th Foot

Colonel John Byng's Brigade
1/3rd Foot
1/57th Foot
Provisional Battalion (4 Coys 2/31st Foot and 3 coys 2/66th Foot)
Company 5/60th Foot

Lieutenant Colonel George Wilson's Brigade
1/28th Foot
2/34th Foot
1/39th Foot
Company 5/60th Foot

Lieutenant Colonel Charles Ashworth's (Portuguese) Brigade
6th Line   (2 Bns)
18th Line   (2 Bns)
6th Cacadores (1 Bn)

Subsequent Alterations 1812:

On 14 April Major General Christopher Tilson (who had changed his name to Chowne thanks to a fortunate legacy) returned to the army and was named commander of the division "under Hill". On 10 November Howard was transferred to 1st Division and his brigade temporarily taken over by Lieutenant Colonel Henry Cadogan of 1/71st Foot

2nd Division 1 January 1813   Sir Rowland Hill
    (Christopher Chowne/Tilson)
Lieutenant Colonel Henry Cadogan's Brigade
1/50th Foot
1/71st Foot
1/92nd Highlanders
Company 5/60th Foot

Colonel John Byng's Brigade
1/3rd Foot
1/57th Foot
Provisional Battalion (4 Coys 2/31st Foot and 3 coys 2/66th Foot)
Company 5/60th Foot

Lieutenant Colonel George Wilson's Brigade
1/28th Foot
2/34th Foot
1/39th Foot
Company 5/60th Foot

Lieutenant Colonel Charles Ashworth's (Portuguese) Brigade
6th Line   (2 Bns)
18th Line   (2 Bns)
6th Cacadores   (1 Bn)

Subsequent Alterations 1813:

On 25 March Lieutenant General Sir William Stewart was appointed to command the division "under Hill's direction."

On the same day Howard was appointed to command 1. Division and so his old brigade was officially given to Major General George Townshend Walker.

However Cadogan was still commanding it when he was killed in action at Vittoria on 21 June. Lieutenant Colonel John Cameron of Fassfern (1/92nd Highlanders) took over but was wounded at Maya on 25 July; Lieutenant Colonel John Foster Fitzgerald of 5/60th next took over until Walker finally arrived in August. However, on 18 November Walker was promoted to command 7. Division and so the brigade went to Major General Sir Edward Barnes on 20 November.

George Wilson died of fever at Moralejo on 5 January 1813 and Colonel Hon. Robert William O'Callaghan of 1/39th took over until 23 July when he was succeeded by Major General William Pringle.

Ashworth was badly wounded (as a Portuguese Brigadier) at the Nive on 13 December and was succeeded by Lieutenant Colonel Henry Hardinge.

2nd Division 1 January 1814   Sir Rowland Hill (Sir William Stewart)
Major General Sir Edward Barnes' Brigade
1/50th Foot
1/71st Foot
1/92nd Highlanders
Company 5/60th Foot

Colonel John Byng's Brigade
1/3rd Foot
1/57th Foot
Provisional Battalion (4 Coys 2/31st Foot and 3 coys 2/66th Foot)
Company 5/60th Foot

Major General Sir William Pringle's Brigade
1/28th Foot
2/34th Foot
1/39th Foot
Company 5/60th Foot

Lieutenant Colonel Henry Hardinge's (Portuguese) Brigade
6th Line   (2 Bns)
18th Line   (2 Bns)
6th Cacadores   (1 Bn)

Subsequent Alterations 1814:

Sir William Pringle was badly wounded at St. Palais on 15 February 1814 and Colonel Robert Callaghan once again took over his brigade.

3rd Division "The Fighting Division"

The 3rd Division was formed on 18 June 1809 under Mackenzie and the nickname speaks for itself.

18 June 1809   Major General John Randoll Mackenzie of Suddie
Major General Mackenzie's Brigade
3/27th Foot
2/31st Foot
1/45th Foot

Brigadier General Christopher Tilson's Brigade
2/87th Foot
1/88th Foot
5 Coys. 5/60th Foot

Subsequent Alterations 1809:

Tilson was assigned to 2. Division on 21 June 1809 and replaced by Colonel Sir Rufane Shaw Donkin, while 3/27th Foot were sent down to Lisbon just before Talavera and replaced by 2/24th.

Mackenzie was killed in action at Talavera resulting in a considerable re-organisation. Brigadier General Robert Craufurd was appointed to command the division in his place, while the two existing brigades were amalgamated under Donkin and Craufurd's Light Brigade was added to the division.

On 15 September 2/87th Foot were ordered down the Lisbon and at about the same time 2/24th Foot and 2/31st Foot were transferred to 2nd Division. In October Donkin gave up command of his brigade and was replaced by Colonel Henry Mackinnon, while on 8 January the decision to attach a company of riflemen to each brigade saw two of the five companies of 5/60th withdrawn and dispersed around the army.

It was therefore a very different division which saw the start of 1810, with more alterations to come.

3rd Division 8 January 1810 Major General Robert Craufurd
Major General Craufurd's Brigade
1/43rd Foot
1/52nd Foot
1/95th Rifles

Colonel Henry Mackinnon's Brigade
1/45th Foot
1/88th Foot
3 Coys 5/60th Foot

On 22 February the division was completely re-organised under Sir Thomas Picton, with Craufurd and his brigade departing to form the nucleus of the Light Division. In its place Major General Stafford Lightburne's brigade was brought across from 4th Division and Jose Champelimuad's Portuguese brigade added, while Mackinnon's brigade lost its three remaining companies of 5/60th but was reinforced by 1/74th Highlanders. The 5/60th companies going to Lightburne's brigade.

3rd Division 22 February 1810 Major General Sir Thomas Picton
Colonel Henry Mackinnon's Brigade
1/45th Foot
1/74th Highlanders
1/88th Foot

Major General Stafford Lightburne's Brigade
2/5th Foot
2/58th Foot
3 Coys 5/60th Foot

Champelimaud's Brigade
9th Line   (2 Bns)
21st Line   (2 Bns)

Subsequent alterations 1810:

Lightburne's Brigade underwent a number of changes. 2/83rd Foot was posted to the brigade on 12 September but did not actually join until after Busaco, at which point 2/58th Foot was assigned to garrison duty in Lisbon and replaced by 94th Foot on 6 October. Lightburne himself went home in October and Sir Charles Colville was given command of the brigade in his place on 6 October. Finally, Champelimaud was wounded at Busaco, on 27 September, but not replaced by Charles Sutton until 29 October.

3rd Division 1 January 1811 Major General Sir Thomas Picton
Colonel Henry Mackinnon's Brigade
1/45th Foot
1/74th Highlanders
1/88th Foot

Major General Sir Charles Colville's Brigade
2/5th Foot
2/2/83rd Foot
94th Foot (Scotch Brigade)
3 Coys 5/60th Foot

Charles Sutton's Brigade
9th Line   (2 Bns)
21st Line   (2 Bns)

Subsequent alterations 1811:

On 5 March the three 5/60th companies were transferred to Mackinnon's Brigade and replaced by 2/88th Foot. However, on 10 July 2/88th were drafted into 1/88th in Mackinnon's Brigade and replaced by 77th Foot.

Mackinnon was absent sick between 1 July and 31 October with his brigade being commanded in the meantime by Lieutenant Colonel John Wallace of 1/88th Foot. Sutton's brigade was led by Manly Power at Fuentes d'Onoro, but Luis Pelmerim took command shortly afterwards.

Finally, Colville was temporarily transferred to the command of 4th Division on 22 December

3rd Division 1 January 1812 Major General Sir Thomas Picton
Colonel Henry Mackinnon's Brigade
1/45th Foot

1/74th Highlanders
1/88th Foot
3 Coys 5/60th Foot

Lieutenant Colonel James Campbell's Brigade
2/5th Foot
77th Foot
2/83rd Foot
94th Foot (Scotch Brigade)

Luis Palmeirim's Brigade
9th Line   (2 Bns)
21st Line   (2 Bns)

Subsequent alterations 1812:

A brisk series of command changes took place in the first half of the year, beginning with the death of Colonel Henry Mackinnon at Cuidad Rodrigo on 19 January. His brigade was taken over by Major General Sir James Kempt on 8 February, but when Sir Thomas Picton was wounded at Badajoz on 6 April Kempt briefly took charge of the division only to be quickly wounded in his turn. This meant that on 7 April the senior surviving officer was Lieutenant Colonel John Wallace of 1/88th Foot. With Wallace temporarily in command of the division, Kempt's brigade passed to Major Thomas Forbes of 1/45th. When Picton returned to duty shortly afterwards, Wallace took over the brigade until himself being invalided home after the retreat from Burgos.

Although Picton was only slightly wounded and returned to duty shortly afterwards an infection developed, and he eventually went home on sick leave shortly before Salamanca, so the division then went to Major General Edward Pakenham, who commanded it for the rest of the year. Pakenham had originally been appointed to command Colville's Brigade on 28 June, but as he was almost immediately elevated to command the division, Campbell of the 94th remained in command of the brigade.

Champelimaud had returned to command the Portuguese brigade before 17 March but was wounded at Badajoz and replaced by Manly Power on 8 April.

As to the constituent regiments; 77th Foot was sent down to Lisbon after Badajoz, due to being very low in numbers. Instead 1/5th Foot was posted to the brigade on 1 June and both battalions of the regiment served together at Salamanca on 22 July. Five days later 2/5th was drafted into 1/5th and on 17 October 2/87th Foot was posted into the brigade.

On 8 April 12th Cacadores were added to the Portuguese brigade.

3rd Division 1 January 1813 Major General Hon. Edward Pakenham
Major Thomas Forbes' Brigade
1/45th Foot
1/74th Highlanders
1/88th Foot
3 Coys 5/60th Foot

Lieutenant Colonel James Campbell's Brigade
1/5th Foot
2/83rd Foot
2/87th Foot
94th Foot (Scotch Brigade)

Manley Power's Brigade
9th Line   (2 Bns)
21st Line   (2 Bns)
12th Cacadores (1 Bn)

Subsequent alterations:

Colville returned to the division in January, taking temporary command in place of Pakenham who was transferred to 6th Division on 26 January. Picton also returned in May and Colville thereupon reverted to commanding Campbell's Brigade until 8 August, when Picton again went sick until December, at which point Colville was transferred to 5. Division.

In the meantime, Kempt's Brigade continued under temporary command until Colonel Thomas Brisbane was appointed on 25 March, while Colville's Brigade was taken over by Sir John Keane on 8 August at first temporarily and then officially from 8 September. Power was succeeded by Charles Sutton in command of the Portuguese Brigade in July.

12th Cacadores had left the brigade before 26 April and were replaced by 11th Cacadores. Otherwise there were no alterations in the division's command structure or composition until the war's end in April 1814.

4th Division "The Supporting Division/The Enthusiastics"

The 4th Division was formed on 18 June 1809 under Campbell. The reason for its early nickname is unclear but it supposedly earned the later one at Albuera.

18 June 1809   Major General Alexander Campbell
Major General Alexander Campbell's (Lieutenant Colonel William Myers)
    Brigade
2/7th Fusiliers
2/53rd Foot

Brigadier General John Sontag's Brigade
97th Foot
2/Battalion of Detachments (Lieutenant Colonel Edward Copeson 5th
    Foot)[5]

Subsequent Alterations 1809:

Campbell was wounded at Talavera, but not replaced as commander of the division until Major General Galbraith Lowry Cole arrived in October. In the meantime, Sontag's Brigade had been taken over by Colonel James

---

5 This was another provisional unit formed by Sir John Cradock and comprised of
   detachments and stragglers left behind in Portugal when Moore marched into Spain.
   Its composition on 6 February 1809 is set out per the return below and further units
   were represented by the time it reached Talavera

Unit	Field Officers	Captains	Subalterns	Staff	NCOs & Men
2nd Foot	0	1	3	0	96
4th Foot	0	0	3	2	78
5th Foot	1	0	2	1	93
6th Foot	1	0	0	0	38
32nd Foot	0	1	8	1	74
36th Foot	0	0	5	1	75
42nd Highlanders	0	0	0	1	0
50th Foot	0	1	1	1	75
71st Highlanders	0	0	3	0	107
82nd Foot	0	1	7	1	96
Totals	2	4	32	8	734

Kemmis before Talavera, so as the senior officer Kemmis must have looked after the division until Cole took over.

Kemmis had brought his own 1/40th Foot and in September 1/11th Foot joined Myers' Brigade. In October 2/Battalion of Detachments was sent home and replaced by 3/27th Foot.

4th Division 1 January 1810 Major General Galbraith Lowry Cole
Lieutenant Colonel William Myers' Brigade
2/7th Fusiliers
1/11th Foot
2/53rd Foot

Colonel James Kemmis' Brigade
3/27th Foot
1/40th Foot
97th Foot

Major General Stafford Lightburne's Brigade
2/5th Foot
2/58th Foot

Lightburne's Brigade joined the division on 2 January but was then transferred to 3rd Division on 22 February. This was part of a much larger re-organisation on that date, when Major General Alexander Campbell returned to resume command of his brigade (Myers') but not the division. At that point Kemmis' men were re-designated the senior brigade in the division and McMahan's Portuguese brigade joined to replace Lightburne's Brigade.

4th Division 22 February 1810 Major General Galbraith Lowry Cole
Colonel James Kemmis' Brigade
3/27th Foot
1/40th Foot
97th Foot

Major General Alexander Campbell's Brigade
2/7th Fusiliers
1/11th Foot
2/53rd Foot

Thomas McMahon's Brigade
3rd Line   (2 Bns.)
15th Line   (2 Bns.)

Subsequent alterations 1810:

On 17 May McMahon's Brigade was transferred to 5th Division and replaced by Richard Collins' Brigade comprising the Portuguese 11th and 23rd Line.

On 6 October Campbell left with his brigade to form the nucleus of 6th Division, being replaced by Pakenham's Brigade. This initially comprised 1/7th Fusiliers; 1/61st Foot and the Brunswick Oels Jager. On 12 November all but one company of the Jagers were transferred to the Light Division and replaced by 1/23rd Fusiliers and on 17 November 1/61st Foot exchanged with 2/7th Fusiliers, who came back from 6th Division to form the Fusilier Brigade.

4th Division 1 January 1811   Major General Galbraith Lowry Cole
Colonel James Kemmis' Brigade
3/27th Foot
1/40th Foot
97th Foot
Coy. 5/60th Foot

Major General Hon. Pakenham's (Fusilier) Brigade
1/7th Fusiliers
2/7th Fusiliers
1/23rd Fusilers
Coy. Brunswick Oels Jager

Richard Collins' Brigade
11th Line   (2 Bns.)
23rd Line   (2 Bns.)

Subsequent alterations 1811:

The Fusilier Brigade was taken over by Major General William Houston on 23 January, and then once again by Myers on 5 March when Houston was promoted to command the new 7th Division. Myers was then killed at

Albuera and replaced by Edward Stopford on 18 June, but he in turn was transferred to 1th Division on 28 July, whereupon Pakenham returned to command it again. In the meantime, 2/7th Fusiliers were drafted into 1/7th Fusiliers and replaced by 1/48th Foot on 26 June.

Collins' Portuguese brigade was temporarily commanded by William Harvey at Albuera, while Collins commanded a provisional brigade drawn out of the Elvas garrison (comprising the 5th Line and 5th Cacadores). Previously, it had been joined by 1/Loyal Lusitanian Legion on 14 March, and the battalion was absorbed into the Portuguese Army proper by September and redesignated the 7th Cacadores.

The only other change in personnel during the year concerned Kemmis' Brigade. The Brunswick Oels Jager briefly joined the brigade after being thrown out of the Light Division sometime before 1 February but were quickly shuffled off to the newly formed 7. Division.

At the end of the year 97th Foot were ordered home to recruit on 3 October and Major General Cole went home sick on 22 December, being replaced as divisional commander by Sir Charles Colville.

4th Division 1 January 1812   Major General Sir Charles Colville
Colonel James Kemmis' Brigade
3/27th Foot
1/40th Foot
Coy. 5/60th Foot

Major General Hon. Pakenham's (Fusilier) Brigade
1/7th Fusiliers
1/23rd Fusilers
1/48th Foot
Coy. Brunswick Oels Jager

Richard Collins' Brigade
11th Line   (2 Bns.)
23rd Line   (2 Bns.)
7th Cacadores (1 Bn.)

Subsequent alterations 1812:

Again, a complicated year. Colville was wounded at Badajoz on 6 April, but command of the division was kept open until Cole returned in June.

However, he in turn was wounded at Salamana on 22 July and the division then appears to have been commanded by Sir William Anson until Cole returned again in 15 October.

Kemmis had gone before 1 April and his brigade was commanded at Badajoz by Lieutenant Colonel Charles Harcourt of 1/40th before passing to Major General Sir William Anson on 9 April.

Pakenham's Brigade was taken over by Major General Barnard Bowes on 9 February, but he in turn was posted to 6. Division on 2 May and the brigade commanded by Lieutenant Colonel Henry Ellis of 1/23rd Fusiliers until Colonel John Skerrett took over at the end of the year. Confusingly, although Skerrett was appointed to command the brigade on 17 October, he actually appears to have remained in command of a quite different one which he brought up with him from Cadiz; comprising 3/1st Footguards, 2/47th Foot. 2/87th Foot and two companies of 2/95th Rifles. This brigade also served with 4. Division from 26 October until the division went into winter quarters at the end of the year. At this point it was broken up and only then did Skerrett take over what had been the Fusilier Brigade.

In the meantime, a number of other changes in personnel had taken place. On 17 October 1/82nd Foot joined the Fusilier Brigade, displacing 1/48th Foot which transferred to Anson's Brigade. However, 1/82nd Foot was then transferred to 7. Division on 28 November and replaced by 20th Foot, while Anson's Brigade was further reinforced by 2/Provisional Battalion (2nd Foot and 1/53rd Foot) on 6 December.[6]

There were no alterations to the composition of the Portuguese brigade, which was taken over by William Harvey sometime before 17 March, and then after he was badly wounded at Badajoz was commanded by Thomas Stubbs.

---

6   This unit is not to be confused with the Provisional Battalion which served with 2nd Division for a time. The usual practice was for understrength units to be rotated home to recruit and refit, but Wellington resisted this so far as he was able, preferring instead to form such units into provisional battalions and so retain veteran officers and men in theatre for as long as possible.

4th Division 1 January 1813 Major General Sir Galbraith Lowry Cole
Major General Sir William Anson's Brigade
3/27th Foot
1/40th Foot
1/48th Foot
2/Provisional Battalion
Coy. 5/60th Foot

Colonel John Skerrett's (Fusilier) Brigade
1/7th Fusiliers
20th Foot
1/23rd Fusiliers
Coy. Brunswick Oels Jager

Thomas Stubbs' Brigade
11th Line   (2 Bns.)
23rd Line   (2 Bns.)
7th Cacadores (1 Bn.)

Subsequent Alterations:

Skerrett transferred to the Light Division on 2 July 1813 and replaced by
Major General Robert Ross, while James Miller took over Stubbs' Brigade
before 1 September 1813, although it was commanded at the Nivelle by Jose
da Vasconcelos. Otherwise the command structure and composition of the
division was unchanged until the war's end. Ross was wounded at Orthez on
27 February, but no replacement was ever appointed.

5th Division – "The Pioneers"

This division had a rather slow gestation and the nickname probably
indicates that at least some of its units were employed on labouring
duties until it was fully assembled and ready for service. The nucleus of
the division was a brigade commanded by Sir James Leith, comprising
three regiments which had served at Walcheren: 3/1st (Royals), 1/9th
Foot and 2/38th Foot. Although arriving in Lisbon in April 1810 they
were very sickly with "Walcheren Fever" and do not appear in army
returns until 8 July. On 4 August the brigade was temporarily placed
under the command of Lieutenant Colonel James Stevenson Barnes of

3/1st (Royals) while Leith began preparations for forming the division. On 30 September Barnes was superseded by Brigadier General Andrew Hay (also of 3/1st) and on 6 October Leith was formally appointed to command the division. At the same time two more brigades were added; a Portuguese one under Colonel William Frederick Spry and a second British one under Major General James Dunlop, although the latter was only appointed on 5 November and one of his battalions, 1/4th Foot does not appear in returns until 15 November. In the meantime, both British brigades had received a company of Brunswick Oels Jager on 12 November.

5th Division 1 January 1811 Major General Sir James Leith
Brigadier General Andrew Hay's Brigade[7]
3/1st (Royals)
1/9th Foot
2/38th Foot
Coy. Brunswick Oels Jager

Major General James Dunlop's Brigade
1/4th Foot
2/30th Foot
2/44th Foot
Coy. Brunswick Oels Jager

Colonel William Spry's Brigade
3rd Line   (2 Bns.)
15th Line   (2 Bns.)

Subsequent alterations 1811:

Leith was absent from 1 February, being replaced by Sir William Erskine on 6 February. Erskine was in turn absent between 7 March and 22 April and then left the division for good on 11 May. During the interregnums Major General Dunlop acted up until Major General George Townshend Walker took over on 2 October. Leith then returned to command the division on

---

7 Hay was promoted to major general 4 June 1811.

1 December, having been appointed a lieutenant general 'in Spain and Portugal. On 6 September.

On 14 March 2/Loyal Lusitanian Legion was added as the light infantry element of Spry's Brigade and re-designated 8th Cacadores by September.

5th Division 1 January 1812 Lieutenant General Sir James Leith
Major General Andrew Hay's Brigade
3/1st (Royals)
1/9th Foot
2/38th Foot
Coy. Brunswick Oels Jager

Major General George Townshead Walker's Brigade
1/4th Foot
2/30th Foot
2/44th Foot
Coy. Brunswick Oels Jager

Colonel William Spry's Brigade
3rd Line   (2 Bns.)
15th Line   (2 Bns.)
8th Cacadores (1 Bn.)

Subsequent alterations 1812:

Leith was wounded at Salamanca on 22 July and invalided home. He was succeeded by Major General Richard Hulse, but Hulse died of typhus on 7 September and the division was looked after by Major General William Pringle until Major General John Oswald was appointed on 25 October.

Hay went absent on 8 June and his brigade was temporarily commanded by Lieutenant Colonel the Hon. Charles Greville of 1/38th Foot until Richard Hulse was appointed on 31 July. However, since Hulse was actually commanding the division in Leith's absence, Greville probably continued to look after the brigade until Sir Edward Barnes was given the brigade on 28 October, although this turned out to be a temporary appointment as he was transferred to 7th. Division to make way for Hay's return by the end of the year.

Walker was wounded at Badajoz and his brigade then had no designated commander until William Pringle was appointed on 28 June, but as he was commanding the division, the brigade was looked after by Lieutenant Colonel Francis Brooke of 1/4th Foot, who had commanded it after Badajoz.

In terms of personnel, 1/38th came out to the Peninsula in June and fought at Salamanca along with 2/38th, which was subsequently drafted into 1/38th on 6 December.

Similarly, 2/4th Foot were posted to the second brigade on 10 May and was also drafted into 1/4th Foot on 6 December. On the same date 2/30th Foot and 2/44th Foot were temporarily amalgamated as 4/Provisional Battalion. In the meantime, 2/47th Foot was posted to the brigade on 17 October.

5th Division 1 January 1813 Lieutenant General Sir James Leith
Major General Andrew Hay's Brigade
3/1st (Royals)
1/9th Foot
1/38th Foot
Coy. Brunswick Oels Jager

Major General George Townshead Walker's Brigade
1/4th Foot
2/47th Foot
4/Provisional Battalion
Coy. Brunswick Oels Jager

Colonel William Spry's Brigade
3rd Line   (2 Bns.)
15th Line   (2 Bns.)
8th Cacadores (1 Bn.)

Subsequent alterations 1813:

Oswald was absent at the beginning of the year and Hay appears to have commanded the division until he returned sometime in April. Sir James Leith then returned to reclaim the command on 30 August but was wounded two days later at San Sebastian on 1 September. Oswald was still on hand and briefly took over the division again, but by 9 October command had temporarily reverted to Hay, pending Sir Charles Colville's appointment sometime in December. As usual, while Hay was acting up, Greville of 1/38th Foot looked after his brigade.

Colonel Frederick Phillipse Robinson was appointed to command Pringle's Brigade on 9 March. On Robinson's being wounded outside Bayonne on 10 December command passed to Lieutenant Colonel John Piper of 1/4th Foot, but he in turn was wounded the following day and succeeded by Lieutenant Colonel Jacob Tonson of 2/84th Foot. Luiz da Rego Barreto was in command of the Portuguese brigade at the Bidassoa on 9 October and thereafter to the end of the war.

2/59th Foot was posted to Robinson's Brigade on 12 April and 4/ Provisional Battalion ordered home on 10 May. On 17 October 2/84th Foot was posted in from 1st Division and 2/47th transferred to Hay's Brigade.

5th Division 1 January 1814 Major General Sir Charles Colville
Major General Andrew Hay's Brigade
3/1st (Royals)
1/9th Foot
1/38th Foot
2/47th Foot
Coy. Brunswick Oels Jager

Major General Frederick Robinson's Brigade
1/4th Foot
2/59th Foot
2/84th Foot
Coy. Brunswick Oels Jager

da Rego Barreto's Brigade
3rd Line   (2 Bns.)
15th Line   (2 Bns.)
8th Cacadores   (1 Bn.)

Subsequent Alterations:

Hay was killed outside Bayonne on 14 April and presumably Greville of 1/38th Foot took over his brigade again. Robinson had initially returned to duty shortly after being wounded but was compelled to go home on 1 February and Tonson took over again.

6th Division – "The Marching Division"

The division was ordered to be formed on 6 October 1810 by taking Alexander Campbell's Brigade from 4th Division and adding Baron Eben's Independent Portuguese Brigade. Since Campbell was to have the division, Colonel Richard Hulse was appointed to command his brigade on 14 November and on 17 November 1/61st Foot replaced 2/7th Fusiliers, who went back to 4th Division on the formation of the Fusilier Brigade.

6th Division 1 January 1811   Major General Alexander Campbell

Colonel Richard Hulse's Brigade
1/11th Foot
2/53rd Foot
1/61st Foot
Coy. 5/60th Foot

Baron Eben's Brigade[8]
8th Line   (2 Bns.)
Loyal Lusitanian Legion   (2 Bns.)

Subsequent alterations 1811:

Campbell was ordered out to India in November and temporarily replaced by Major General Robert Burne until Major General Sir Henry Clinton took over on 9 February 1812.

A new brigade was formed under Burne on 5 March 1811; initially comprising 2nd Foot and 1/36th Foot, it was joined by 1/32nd Foot on 21

---

8 Friedrich Christian Baron von Eben was a German adventurer, born at Creutzburg in Silesia in 1773 the son of a Prussian general. He initially served in the Prussian Army between 1787 and 1799 when he entered British service as a Captain in the York Hussars before joining the 10th Light Dragoons. He left the 10th Light Dragoons in 1806 and went home for a time before appearing in Portugal, where he married Elisabetha Contessa d`Astigarraga, the daughter of a Portuguese Admiral, in Porto 1808. He subsequently helped raise and command the Loyal Lusitanian Legion – a Portuguese corps in British pay. In 1817 Eben was implicated in a conspiracy against the King of Portugal, and but for his association with the Prince of Wales would probably have been executed. Instead he was exiled and ended his colourful military career in the service of Simon Bolivar before dying in Bogota in Columbia in 1835.

July. Eben and the Loyal Lusitanian Legion were separated (probably for the good of the service) on 14 May when the two battalions were posted as cacadores to 4th Division and 5th Division respectively and were replaced by the 12th Line. Baron Eben himself was temporarily replaced at the same time by George Madden.

6th Division 1 January 1812 Major General Robert Burne
Colonel Richard Hulse's Brigade
1/11th Foot
2/53rd Foot
1/61st Foot
Coy. 5/60th Foot

Major General Robert Burne's Brigade
2nd Foot
1/32nd Foot
1/36th Foot

George Madden's Brigade
8th Line   (2 Bns.)
12th Line   (2 Bns.)

Subsequent alterations 1812:

Lieutenant General Sir Henry Clinton assumed command of the division on 9 February.

Burne had left by 1 April and was replaced by Major General Barnard Bowes on 2 May. However, Bowes was then killed at the storming of the San Cayetano fort at Salamanca on 24 June and Colonel Samuel Venables Hinde of 1/32nd Foot took over.

Hulse was transferred to command a brigade in 5. Division on 31 July and Lieutenant Colonel George Bingham of 2/53rd Foot took over from him.

At the end of the year it became necessary to amalgamate 2nd Foot and 2/53rd Foot to form 2/Provisional Battalion. This was then transferred to 4th Division and what was left of both Bingham's and Hinde's brigades were amalgamated into a single brigade under Hinde on 11 November.

On the same day Colonel James Stirling's (Highland) Brigade was drafted in from 1st Division. Initially it only consisted of 1/42nd

Highlanders and 1/79th Highlanders but was joined by 1/91st Highlanders[9] on 14 December.

The Portuguese brigade remained nominally under Eben's command until the Conde da Rezende took command on 30 April but was himself invalided on 4 October whereupon George Madden resumed command. In the meantime 9th Cacadores had joined the brigade on 10 April.

6th Division 1 January 1813 Lieutenant General Sir Henry Clinton
Colonel James Stirling's (Highland) Brigade
1/42nd Highlanders
1/79th Highlanders
1/91st Highlanders
Coy. 5/60th Foot

Colonel Samuel Hinde's Brigade
1/11th Foot
1/32nd Foot[10]
1/36th Foot
1/61st Foot
Coy. 5/60th Foot

George Madden's Brigade
8th Line   (2 Bns.)
12th Line   (2 Bns.)
9th Cacadores   (1 Bn.)

Subsequent alterations:

Clinton was replaced by Pakenham on 26 January but on the latter being appointed Adjutant General on 25 June Clinton returned briefly until Denis Pack took over on 22 July, only to be badly wounded at Sorauren on 28 July. Both Pakenham and Colville successively took over for brief periods until his return to duty, before Clinton returned shortly before 9 October Clinton and commanded the division to the end of the war.

---

9 While retaining their Argyleshire title, the 91st Highlanders had lost their kilts by this time
10 1/32nd missed the battle of Toulouse due to it having been sent back to St. Jean de Luz for reclothing.

Pack and Sir John Lambert had both been given brigades in the Division on 2 July[11]. Lambert took over Hinde's Brigade and Pack took over the Highland Brigade, although Stirling again commanded the latter when Pack moved up to command the division. On Clinton's return, Pack reverted to command of the Highland Brigade and Stirling went home.

James Douglas of the 8th Line took over Madden's Brigade in August, but otherwise there were no other alterations in the command structure or composition of the division until the war's end.

7th Division   "The Mongrels"

The division was ordered to be formed under Major General William Houston on 5 March 1811 although not completed until after the siege of Badajoz in that year. At that point its cosmopolitan nature was readily apparent since its first brigade, Alten's, had two battalions in green and one in black; its second had all three battalions in red[12]; while the third brigade was in a mixture of blue and brown. Six of the eleven battalions in the division were designated as light infantry and its officers tried hard to convince anyone who would listen that they were a second Light Division. Unfortunately, the rest of the army unkindly, but accurately, simply referred to them as "The Mongrels"

7th Division 5 March 1811 Major General William Houston
Major General Karl von Alten's Brigade
1/KGL Light Battalion
2/KGL Light Battalion
Brunswick Oels Light Infantry[13]

Colonel Robert Long's Brigade
51st Foot
85th Foot
Chasseurs Britanniques

---

11 This was in consequence of both being gazetted major generals on 4 June.
12 One of these, the *Chasseurs Britanniques* was originally a French émigré unit but was now comprised of mercenaries and deserters.
13 Not to be confused with the green-jacketed Brunswick Oels Jager, this corps was dressed all in black and armed with muskets rather than rifles.

Francis Colman's Brigade
7th Line   (2 Bns)
19th Line   (2 Bns)
2nd Cacadores (1 Bn)

Subsequent alterations 1811

A certain lack of cohesion was evident, no doubt due to the cosmopolitan nature of the division. On 19 March Long was transferred to command Beresford's cavalry and replaced on 31 March by Major General John Sontag. However, Houston was invalided home sometime before 1 August, whereupon Sontag was promoted to command the division in his place, and Colonel de Bernewitz of the Brunswickers took over his brigade.[14] Sontag, however, was also invalided on 15 October and replaced in command of the division by Karl von Alten, whose brigade then passed to Colin Halkett. Colman's Brigade meanwhile was taken over first by Carlos Frederico Le Cor shortly after joining the division, then by Luis Palmeirim between May and August, with Colman resuming command on 12 August. Unfortunately, Colman died on 12 December 1811 "from fever and debility, brought on by exertions in Portugal" but would not be replaced until 27 February 1812.

Otherwise the only alterations were the arrival of the 68th Foot on 19 July and the departure of the 85th on 3 October to return home and recruit.

7th Division 1 January 1812 Major General Karl von Alten
Colonel Colin Halkett's Brigade
1/KGL Light Battalion
2/KGL Light Battalion
Brunswick Oels Light Infantry

Major General John de Bernewitz' Brigade
51st Foot
68th Foot
Chasseurs Britanniques

---

14 More properly Johann Heinrich Karl von Bernewitz (1760–1821) he was promoted major general in the British service as of 23 November.

Francis Colman's Brigade
7th Line   (2 Bns)
19th Line   (2 Bns)
2nd Cacadores (1 Bn)

Subsequent alterations 1812

Colman's brigade, vacant since his death on 12 December 1811, was taken over by Richard Collins on 27 February. On 2 May Alten was transferred to take command of the Light Division and replaced in command of 7th Division by Major General John Hope[15]. Unfortunately Hope went sick on 23 September and was not replaced by Major General George, Earl of Dalhousie until 25 October. In the meantime, de Bernewitz acted up but by December Wellington was actively engaged in trying to get rid of him.

Otherwise a number of changes in personnel took place towards the end of the year. On 28 November two battalions arrived; 1/6th going to Halkett's Brigade and 1/82nd to de Bernewitz'. Then Halkett's brigade was taken over by Colonel Edward Barnes on 3 December and three days later both KGL battalions were transferred to 2nd Division and replaced by 3/ Provisional Battalion (2/24th and 2/58th Foot).

7th Division 1 January 1813   Major General George, Earl of Dalhousie
Colonel Edward Barnes' Brigade
1/6th Foot
3/Provisional Battalion
Brunswick Oels Light Infantry

Major General John de Bernewitz' Brigade
51st Foot
68th Foot
1/82nd Foot
Chasseurs Britanniques

Richard Collins' Brigade
7th Line   (2 Bns)
19th Line   (2 Bns)
2nd Cacadores (1 Bn)

---

15 Not to be confused with Lieutenant General Sir John Hope, later Earl of Hopetoun.

Subsequent alterations 1813 and 1814

Dalhousie went home after the crossing of the Bidassoa on 9 October and was temporarily replaced in command of the division by the Portuguese general Carlos Le Cor. However, Le Cor was almost immediately transferred to take command of Hamilton's Portuguese Division on 18 November and Major General George Townshend Walker was appointed to command 7th Division "in Dalhousie's absence". Walker was then wounded at Orthez on 27 February, but Dalhousie returned to resume command of the division almost at once.

At brigade level Collins was killed on 17 February and between March and October the Portuguese brigade was commanded by Frederico Le Cor, and thereafter by John Doyle. On 27 February de Bernewitz was relieved of his command and ordered home, ostensibly at the request of the Duke of Brunswick. However, Brigadier General William Inglis was not named to command the brigade on 21 May (and promoted major general on 4 June) but did not actually take over until the campaign in the Pyrenees. In the meantime, Lieutenant Colonel William Grant of 1/82nd was badly wounded while commanding the brigade at Vittoria. Finally, on 20 November Barnes went to 2. Division on 20 November and his brigade was taken over by Lieutenant Colonel John Gardiner of 1/6th Foot.

The Light Division "The Division"

Formed on 22 February 1810 under Brigadier General Robert Craufurd, it was initially no more than a reinforced brigade comprising 1/43rd Foot, 1/52nd, and 1/95th from 3rd Division, and two Portuguese battalions; 1st and 3rd Cacadores. On 4 August they were re-organised into two brigades which were unique in their integration of British and Portuguese units. In addition, 1st Hussars KGL were attached for most of the war and after them the Cavalry Staff Corps.

Light Division 4 August 1810   Brigadier General Robert Craufurd
Colonel Thomas Beckwith's Brigade
1/43rd Foot
1st Cacadores
4 Coys. 1/95th Rifles

Lieutenant Colonel Robert Barclay's Brigade
1/52nd Foot
3rd Cacadores
4 Coys. 1/95th Rifles

Subsequent alterations 1810

Barclay of 1/52nd was wounded at Busaco and replaced by Lieutenant Colonel James Wynch of 1/4th Foot, who in turn died of typhus on 6 January 1811.

One company of 2/95th Rifles joined Beckwith's Brigade at some time before 1 October, and the Brunswick Oels Light Infantry were posted to Wynch's Brigade on 12 November.

Light Division 1 January 1811 Brigadier General Robert Craufurd
Colonel Thomas Beckwith's Brigade
1/43rd Foot
1st Cacadores
4 Coys. 1/95th Rifles
1 Coy 2/95th Rifles

Lieutenant Colonel James Wynch's Brigade
1/52nd Foot
3rd Cacadores
Brunswick Oels Light Infantry
4 Coys. 1/95th Rifles

Subsequent alterations 1811

Craufurd went on leave shortly before 8 February and the division was temporarily commanded by Major General Sir William Erskine between 7 March and Craufurd's return on 22 April. Wynch died of typhus on 6 January but was not replaced by Colonel George Drummond of 1/52nd until 7 February. Drummond himself died of a "malignant fever" on 8 September and was succeeded by Major General John Ormsby Vandeleur on 30 September. Meanwhile Beckwith was invalided home on 1 August and replaced by Lieutenant Colonel Andrew Barnard of 1/43rd Foot.

The Brunswick Oels Light Infantry seemingly did not fit and were posted to the newly formed 7th Division on 5 March and were replaced on the same day by the newly arrived 2/52nd Foot. In Barnard's Brigade, the regimental headquarters and five companies of 3/95th were posted in on 21 August and by 1 October a second company of 2/95th had also joined the brigade.

Light Division 1 January 1812 Major General Robert Craufurd
Lieutenant Colonel Andrew Barnard's Brigade
1/43rd Foot
1st Cacadores
4 Coys. 1/95th Rifles
2 Coys. 2/95th Rifles
5 Coys. 3/95th Rifles

Major General John Ormsby Vandeleur's Brigade
1/52nd Foot
2/52nd Foot
3rd Cacadores
4 Coys. 1/95th Rifles

Subsequent alterations 1812

Craufurd was killed at Cuidad Rodrigo on 19 January and as Vandeleur was wounded, Lieutenant Colonel Barnard took temporary command. Vandeleur was fit for duty by 15 April but Karl von Alten was appointed to command the division on 2 May. In the meantime, Lieutenant Colonel Edward Gibbs of 1/52nd had been looking after Vandeleur's brigade but he in turn was wounded at Badajoz, losing an eye.

2/52nd Foot were drafted into 1/52nd on 23 February and the cadre sent home to rebuild. When Alten took over the division all the 1/95th companies were consolidated in Vandeleur's brigade, but on 24 August they were split up, with half returning to what was still being referred to as Beckwith's Brigade, before being followed by the rest of the battalion by the end of the year. Also in May 1812 the two companies of 2/95th were transferred to Vandeleur's Brigade and joined by four others from 2/95th.

Light Division 1 January 1813 Lieutenant General Karl von Alten
Lieutenant Colonel Andrew Barnard's Brigade
1/43rd Foot
1/95th Rifles
1st Cacadores
5 Coys. 3/95th Rifles

Major General John Ormsby Vandeleur's Brigade
1/52nd Foot
3rd Cacadores
6 Coys. 2/95th Rifles

Subsequent alterations 1813-1814

Barnard remained in acting command of what was still being referred to as
Beckwith's Brigade until 23 March when Major General Sir James Kempt
formally took over. On 2 July Vandeleur was given a cavalry brigade and was
at first replaced by Major General John Byne Skerrett, but he went home
in September and so was succeeded by Lieutenant Colonel John Colborne
of 1/52nd Foot. Because this brigade was weaker than the other the two-
battalion strong 20th (Portuguese) Line was assigned to it in October 1812,
but never actually joined and eventually the 17th Line was posted to the
brigade instead on 26 April 1813.

Otherwise there were no further alterations to the war's end although
1/43rd Foot and 1/95th Rifles missed Orthez on 27 February 1814 due to
their being absent re-fitting.

Wellington's Cavalry

The Duke was bred as an infantryman and while there is no doubting that
he could ride a horse well he never understood cavalry and consequently
never fully trusted cavalry officers to behave themselves when not under
his immediate eye. This in turn meant that although he created two cavalry
divisions they were never actually employed as such. Unlike the infantry
divisions they were merely administrative units and both were eventually
abolished. Sir Stapleton Cotton, who commanded the 1st Cavalry Division
for most of the war, effectively acted throughout as Wellington's chief of
cavalry, a staff appointment comparable to the CRA (Commander Royal
Artillery) rather than a tactical role.

The highest level of tactical control exercised on and off the battlefield was therefore the brigade, initially comprising two and later three regiments.

At the outset of the war cavalry regiments normally consisted of 10 troops, each with a notional strength of 63 troopers plus the usual allowance of commissioned and non-commissioned officers. Junior subalterns were styled cornets rather than ensigns but otherwise ranks corresponded to their infantry colleagues.

On service troops were paired off to form squadrons. However, because cavalry units did not have the equivalent of a second battalion, two of the troops were designated as a depot and did not serve overseas. Heavy cavalry regiments, variously designated as Dragoon Guards[16] or Dragoons therefore had four service squadrons until 1811 when they were reduced to three. Light cavalry, variously known as Light Dragoons or Light Dragoons (Hussars)[17] not only retained their four squadrons but had a fifth authorised in September 1813.

Otherwise the only differences were traditional and sartorial – with the sole exception of the Royal Horse Guards (Blues) heavy cavalry wore red jackets and light cavalry blue ones. Both heavy and light cavalry followed the same 1796 *Instructions and Regulations for the Formations and movements of the Cavalry*, and while Continental armies allocated large horses to their heavy cavalry and ponies to their hussars, all British cavalrymen preferred the same large horses. Furthermore, British light cavalry were notoriously negligent of training in scouting and outpost duties, preferring to concentrate on the charge. They were, in short, trained as battle cavalry and as will be seen below it was not at all uncommon for heavy and light cavalry units to be promiscuously brigaded together.

---

16 Confusingly Dragoon Guards were not Household troops. Originally, they were the premier heavy cavalry designated simply as Horse, and sometimes armoured in cuirassier style. However, as an economy measure in the 1740s they were re-designated as dragoons and placed on the lower pay scale with the hollow consolation of the title Guards appended as a reminder of their original higher status.

17 A number of dragoon regiments were trained as light cavalry after the Seven Years War but were not regarded as a different branch of the service and so retained their existing seniority with the word Light added to their title in parenthesis by way of distinction; thus, for example the 14th Dragoons became the 14th Regiment of (Light) Dragoons. Similarly, when some of those regiments subsequently dressed and styled themselves as hussars, the title was also grudgingly added in parenthesis which produced the 7th (or the Queen's Own) Regiment of (Light) Dragoons (HUSSARS)!

Unsurprisingly, in addition to his other complaints, Wellington soon found his own cavalry to be inferior to foreign ones when it came to scouting and outpost duties, and preferred to place his trust in the Light Dragoons and Hussars of the King's German Legion (KGL).

The Duke's ambivalent attitude towards his cavalry, and to its officers, was reflected in the uncertainty of their organisation and constant changes, although in fairness to Wellington the frequency of the transfers also appears to reflect considerable inter-regimental rivalries.

In June 1809 a cavalry Division was formed under Major General Sir William Payne.

Initially there were two brigades each of two regiments:

Colonel Henry Fane's Brigade
3rd Dragoon Guards
4th Dragoons

Major General Stapleton Cotton's Brigade
14th Light Dragoons
16th Light Dragoons

In addition to these units, but not brigaded were:

20th Light Dragoons (2 squadrons)
23rd Light Dragoons
1st Light Dragoons KGL
Det. 3rd Light Dragoons KGL

Sometime before 21 June the 23rd Light Dragoons and 1st Light Dragoons KGL were brigaded under Colonel William Anson, while the two squadrons of the 20th Light Dragoons and the detachment of the 3rd Light Dragoons KGL were sent home in July. Then in November there were some wholesale changes. Lieutenant Colonel Granby Calcraft of 3rd Dragoon Guards temporarily took over Fane's brigade at the end of October, while Black Jack Slade took over Cotton's Brigade since the latter was fully occupied in acting as 2IC of the division. Slade had brought his own 1st Dragoons so at about the same time the 16th Light Dragoons were transferred to Anson's Brigade, replacing the 23rd Light Dragoons, who had suffered badly at Talavera and needed to be sent home.

Cavalry Division 1 January 1810   Major Genenal Sir William Payne
Fane's Brigade
3rd Dragoon Guards
4th Dragoons

Slade's Brigade
1st (Royal) Dragoons
14th Light Dragoons

Anson's Brigade
16th Light Dragoons
1st Hussars KGL[18]

Subsequent alterations 1810:

Payne went home before 1 June and Stapleton Cotton officially took command of the division on 3 June. Fane was assigned to Hill's corps of observation in Extramadura and his brigade was taken over by Colonel the Hon. George de Grey on 13 May.

Cavalry Division 1 January 1811   Major General Stapleton Cotton
De Grey's Brigade
3rd Dragoon Guards
4th Dragoons

Slade's Brigade
1st Dragoons
14th Light Dragoons

Anson's Brigade
16th Light Dragoons
1st Hussars KGL

---

18 Formerly 1st Light Dragoons KGL.

Alterations

Cotton went home between 15 January and 22 April and in his absence the division was commanded first by Slade until 7 March and then by Sir William Erskine. While Slade had the division, his brigade was looked after by Colonel Samuel Hawker of 14th Light Dragoons. Similarly, Anson was absent between 1 March and 15 May, leaving his brigade to Arentschilt of 1st Hussars KGL

An additional brigade was formed under Robert Ballard Long on 13 June, comprising the 13th Light Dragoons and 2nd Hussars KGL, but on 18 June the 13th Light Dragoons were transferred to Slade's brigade and replaced by the 11th Dragoons. This was only a pre-positioning move for on the following day, 19 June the whole cavalry was reorganised into two divisions as set out below.

Wellington's Cavalry 19 June 1811

1st Cavalry Division Major General Stapleton Cotton
Slade's Brigade
1st Dragoons
13th Light Dragoons
14th Light Dragoons

Anson's Brigade
16th Light Dragoons
1st Hussars KGL

George Madden's Portuguese Brigade[19]
1st Cavalry
7th Cavalry
5th Cavalry
8th Cavalry

---

19 Madden's Portuguese contingent was actually comprised of two brigades; his own 1st and 7th Cavalry, and Loftus Otway's 5th and 8th Cavalry.

2nd Cavalry Division Major General Sir William Erskine
De Grey's Brigade
3rd Dragoon Guards
4th Dragoons

Long's Brigade
11th Light Dragoons
2nd Hussars KGL

This arrangement proved unsatisfactory and a further reorganisation took place just a month later on 19 July.

1st Cavalry Division Major General Stapleton Cotton
Slade's Brigade
1st Dragoons
12th Light Dragoons

Anson's Brigade
13th Light Dragoons
16th Light Dragoons

Victor Alten's Brigade
11th Light Dragoons
1st Hussars KGL

George Madden's Portuguese Brigade
1st Cavalry
7th Cavalry
5th Cavalry
8th Cavalry

2nd Cavalry Division Major General Sir William Erskine
De Grey's Brigade
3rd Dragoon Guards
4th Dragoons

Long's Brigade
14th Light Dragoons
2nd Hussars KGL

Notwithstanding, the organisation of the two divisions remained in a state of flux. The 9th Light Dragoons joined Long's Brigade in 2nd Cavalry Division on 1 August, and at the same time the 14th Light Dragoons exchanged with the 13th Light Dragoons. Then on 30 August a new brigade arrived under Major General John Gaspard Le Marchant comprising the 4th Dragoon Guards and 3rd Dragoons. Initially it was posted to 2nd Cavalry Division and joined by 5th Dragoon Guards on 1 October before the whole lot were transferred to 1st Cavalry Division on 8 November – replacing Madden's Brigade which was struck off strength. As De Grey's Brigade had also been transferred to 1st Cavalry Division on 5 October, this meant that 2nd Cavalry Division was reduced to a single brigade. Perhaps not surprisingly Erskine, finding himself superfluous, was then absent between 8 December 1811 and 8 April 1812.

At the outset of 1812 the cavalry divisions were therefore looking decidedly lopsided, but it is worth re-emphasising that unlike the infantry divisions they were not discrete tactical units.

Wellington's Cavalry 1 January 1812

1st Cavalry Division Lieutenant General Stapleton Cotton
Slade's Brigade
1st Dragoons
12th Light Dragoons

De Grey's Brigade
3rd Dragoon Guards
4th Dragoons

Anson's Brigade
14th Light Dragoons
16th Light Dragoons

Le Marchant's Brigade
4th Dragoon Guards
3rd Dragoons

Victor Alten's Brigade
11th Light Dragoons
1st Hussars KGL

2nd Cavalry Division

Long's Brigade
9th Light Dragoons
13th Light Dragoons
2nd Hussars KGL

Subsequent alterations:

Cotton was wounded at Salamanca and temporarily replaced by a King's German Legion officer, Major General Eberhardt Otto Georg von Bock. Cotton returned before 15 October but was again invalided in December. For his part Erskine returned to command 2nd Cavalry Division on 6 April. Otherwise the numerous alterations are best dealt with brigade by brigade.

Victor Alten's Brigade
Alten was absent from 1 August until mid-September. On 1 July the 11th Light Dragoons had been ordered to exchange with the 14th Light Dragoons in Anson's Brigade, and on 17 October the 2nd Hussars KGL were transferred from Long's Brigade.

Anson's Brigade
Anson was absent during the first half of the year and the brigade looked after until 1 July by Colonel Henry Cumming of 11th Light Dragoons. On 29 January the 12th Light Dragoons were transferred in, and then on 1 July the 14th Light Dragoons were ordered to exchange with 11th Light Dragoons in Alten's Brigade.

Bock's Brigade
A new formation comprising 1st and 2nd Dragoons KGL commanded by Major General von Bock. Initially assigned to 2nd Cavalry Division on 23 March but then transferred to 1st Cavalry Division on 14 April.

De Grey's Brigade
This was broken up on 29 January with 3rd Dragoons passing to Slade's Brigade and 4th Dragoons to Le Marchant's.

Le Marchant's Brigade
On 29 January the 4th Dragoon Guards were transferred to Slade's Brigade and replaced by the 4th Dragoons. Le Marchant himself was killed at

Salamanca and replaced on 23 July by Sir William Ponsonby of 5th Dragoon Guards.

Long's Brigade
As noted above 2nd Hussars KGL were transferred to Alten's Brigade on 17 October.

Slade's Brigade
On 29 January the 3rd and 4th Dragoon Guards were transferred to the brigade and in exchange the 12th Light Dragoons were posted to Anson's Brigade. Slade and his brigade were transferred to 2nd Cavalry Division.

Wellington's Cavalry 1 January 1813

Bock appears to have acted as chief of cavalry until Cotton's return on 25 June, but in the meantime neither division had a designated commanding officer present and they were abolished on 21 April.

1st Cavalry Division

Ponsonby's Brigade
5th Dragoon Guards
3rd Dragoons
4th Dragoons

Anson's Brigade
11th Light Dragoons
12th Light Dragoons
16th Light Dragoons

Alten's Brigade
14th Light Dragoons
1st Hussars KGL
2nd Hussars KGL

Bock's Brigade
1st Dragoons KGL
2nd Dragoons KGL

2nd Cavalry Division

Slade's Brigade
3rd Dragoon Guards
4th Dragoon Guards
1st Dragoons

Long's Brigade
9th Light Dragoons
13th Light Dragoons

Subsequent alterations

Alten's Brigade
2nd Hussars KGL were ordered home on 13 March. 14th Light Dragoons were transferred to Long's Brigade on 2 July and replaced by 18th Light Dragoons (Hussars) from Grant's Brigade.

Anson's Brigade
11th Light Dragoons were ordered home on 13 March and Anson assigned to Home staff on 2 July, being replaced by Major General John Ormsby Vandeleur.

Grant's Brigade
A new brigade under Colonel Sir Colquhon Grant joining the army on 15 April, comprising 10th Light Dragoons (Hussars). 15th Light Dragoons (Hussars) and 18th Light Dragoons (Hussars). Grant was replaced by Lord Edward Somerset on 2 July and on the same date 18th Light Dragoons (Hussars) were transferred to Alten's Brigade. Subsequently the 7th Light Dragoons (Hussars) were assigned to the brigade in October but do not appear in orders until 24 November.

Long's Brigade
9th Light Dragoons were ordered home on 13 March, but only replaced by the 14th Light Dragoons on 2 July. Long was replaced by Colquhon Grant on 6 September, but he was in turn replaced by Sir Hussey Vivian on 24 November.

Rebow's Brigade
A new brigade led by Major General Francis Slater Rebow and comprising just two squadrons apiece of 1st Lifeguards, 2nd Lifeguards and Royal Horse

Guards (Blues). Initially posted to 2nd Cavalry Division on 25 January before transferring to 1st Cavalry Division on 5 February. Rebow returned home shortly afterwards and by March the brigade was commanded by Lieutenant Colonel Sir Robert Hill of the Blues. In October the brigade was taken over by Major General Terence O'Brien O'Loghlin.

Slade's Brigade

4th Dragoon Guards were ordered home on 13 March and Slade himself followed on 23 April, being replaced on 20 May by Major General Henry Fane

Wellington's Cavalry 1 January 1814

Alten's Brigade

18th Light Dragoons (Hussars)
1st Hussars KGL
Alten returned to Germany and was replaced by Vivian on 16 January. Vivian was then wounded on 8 April and replaced by Arentschildt

Bock's Brigade

1st Dragoons KGL
2nd Dragoons KGL
Bülow took over the brigade on 16 January[20]. Arentschild was then given command on 25 March only to be transferred to take over Alten's old brigade when Vivian was wounded on 8 April – whereupon Bülow resumed command.

Fane's Brigade

While Fane was running his ad hoc division from 16 January, his brigade was looked after by Lieutenant Colonel Arthur Clifton of 1st (Royal) Dragoons.

O'Loghlin's Brigade

1st Lifeguards (2 squadrons)
2nd Lifeguards (2 squadrons)
Blues (2 squadrons)

---

20 Bock was ordered to Germany but was drowned in a shipwreck off the coast of Brittany on 21 January.

Ponsonby's Brigade
5th Dragoon Guards
3rd Dragoons
4th Dragoons
Ponsonby was recorded as absent on 25 January and Lord Charles Manners
of 3rd Dragoons had the brigade.

Vandeleur's Brigade
12th Light Dragoons
16th Light Dragoons

Vivian's Brigade
13th Light Dragoons
14th Light Dragoons
Vivian was transferred to the command of Alten's Brigade on 16 January and
officially replaced by Fane. However, Fane also retained his own brigade and
in effect commanded a small division. Consequently, day to day command of
what had been Vivian's Brigade was exercised by Lieutenant Colonel Patrick
Doherty of 13th Light Dragoons.

Endnotes

Chapter 1: 1808

1   The best of the Portuguese troops were sent off to Germany, while the rest were simply disbanded.

2   It was intended to have landed at Cadiz but the Spanish authorities were suspicious of British motives and politely declined to receive them.

3   The relative seniorities of the officers concerned were: (1) Sir Hew Whitefoord Dalrymple, lieutenant general 1 January 1801; (2) Sir Harry Burrard, lieutenant general 1 January 1805; (3) Sir John Moore, lieutenant general 2 November 1805; (4) Sir Arthur Wellesley, lieutenant general 25 April 1808.

4   Only Dalrymple was actually recalled. Wellesley had already returned and appeared at the inquiry more in the character of a witness than a defendant.

5   *Dispatches* 4: 168-179

At a Meeting of the Board of General Officers appointed to inquire into the Convention, &c. in Portugal, by His Majesty's Warrant bearing date the 1st day of November, 1808, at the Great Hall in Chelsea College, on Monday the 14th day of the same month…

"Having received the directions of the Judge Advocate General to attend you here this day, with as much detailed information in writing as I may think proper to offer, of my proceedings from the time I sailed with the troops from Ireland to the time I gave up the command to Lieut. General Sir Harry Burrard, I have now the honor to submit to the Court of Inquiry copies of my dispatches to the Secretary of State, detailing my proceedings.

"As these proceedings are fully detailed in the dispatches which contain an account of my motives for my actions at the moment I carried them into execution, I should be satisfied if the Court were to form an opinion upon a consideration of their contents; but as the Court have expressed a desire, at the same time, to have a narrative of my proceedings, I have drawn one out principally from the dispatches."

6   *Dispatches* 4: 180. These paragraphs were actually some of the answers given by Wellesley to the Court by way of clarification after the memoranda had been read.

7   HMS *Donegal*, a 74-gun ship of the line, commanded by Captain Sir Pulteney Malcolm.

8   HMS *Crocodile*, a 22-gun frigate commanded by Captain Hon. George Cadogan.

9   This was the battle of Medina de Rio Seco fought on 14 July 1808 between the combined armies of Don Gregorio de la Cuesta, then Captain-General of Old Castile and Joaquin Blake, commander of the Galician army, on the one hand and a French army under Marshal Bessieres on the other.
Joaquin Blake y Joyes [1759-1827], the son of an Irish father and a Galician mother was one of the best of the Spanish commanders, and his Galicians were the larger and better trained of the two armies, but Cuesta (1741-1811), outranked Blake by seniority and therefore insisted on assuming the chief command and led the combined force to its destruction by a French army half its size.

10 The 5,000 men in question were newly levied, inadequately clothed and armed and as yet quite unfit for service, nor was their commander, General Bernardino Freire, much inclined to co-operate with Wellesley.

11 Brief notes on all British officers mentioned in the memoranda and dispatches are to be found in Appendix I.

12 This was the remarkable battle of Bailen fought on 19 July 1808 when a Spanish army under General Castanos not only defeated a French army commanded by General Dupont but forced it to capitulate on the battlefield. The convention provided for the repatriation of the surrendered French forces and whilst this particular stipulation was eventually repudiated by the Supreme Junta in Cadiz, it provided the precedent for the same provision in the Convention of Cintra.

13 Sir Harry Burrard (1755-1813) was seeming well-liked and competent, but his reputation has suffered for restraining Wellesley's pursuit of Junot after Vimeiro because he was acutely conscious that he in turn was about to hand the army over to Dalrymple.

14 Charles Stuart (1779-1845) son of General Charles Stuart, a career diplomat appointed as an envoy to Spain in 1808 and later ambassador to Portugal and at the end of the war became ambassador to France in 1814.

15 Insurrecto/"insurrection" – *levee en masse*.

16 Wellington wrote this as the Battle of Roleia, *Dispatches* 4: 96-100. Wellesley to Lord Castlereagh, Secretary of State. Villa Verde, 17 August, 1808.
Robert Stewart, Viscount Castlereagh and from 1820, Marquess of Londonderry [1769-1822] was Secretary of State for War and the Colonies at the time and together with his colleague George Canning ensured Wellesley's

Surrey Artists'
Open Studios
ONLINE SHOP
An opportunity to buy original
art and craft from Surrey based artists
www.surreyopenstudios.org.uk/shop

SURREY ARTS

SaOS
surrey artists' open studios

www.surreyopenstudios.org.uk/shop

Surrey Artists'
Open Studios
ONLINE SHOP

re-appointment. Forced from the cabinet in September 1809, he returned to government in 1812 as Foreign Secretary for the remainder of the war.

17   See Appendix 2 for the composition of the six infantry brigades which fought under Wellesley at Rolica and Vimeiro.

18   Anstruther's Brigade, from Ramsgate, comprised: 2/9th Foot; 43rd Foot; 52nd Foot and 97th Foot, mustering some 2,703 men. Acland's Brigade, from Harwich, was rather weaker since not all of them came ashore in time. Only the 2nd (Queen's); 20th Foot; and 1/95th Rifles were present, of which only the first was complete. Two and a half companies of the 20th did not land until late on 21 August after the battle was fought, and only two companies of 1/95th were ashore to give a total of 1,332 men.

19   Lieutenant General the Hon. Charles Stuart, KB led an earlier British expedition to Portugal in 1796. He died in 1801 and is not to be confused with his son, Charles Stuart, the British ambassador to Portugal or with the Hon. Charles William *Stewart*, younger brother of Lord Castlereagh.

20   The memoranda ends abruptly since Wellesley, in agreeing to appear before the court of inquiry, had only engaged to cover the period between his appointment and his supersession by Sir Harry Burrard – and did just that. Subsequent testimony as to events afterwards took the form of responses to cross-examination rather than a continuous narrative.

21   *Dispatches* 4: 108-111. Wellesley to Sir Harry Burrard, Vimeiro 21 August, 1808; *ibid* 115 Wellesley to Viscount Castlereagh, Vimeiro, 22d August, 1808
"Sir Harry did not land till late in the day in the midst of the attack, and he desired me to continue my own operations; and as far as I am personally concerned in the action, I was amply rewarded for any disappointment I might have felt in not having had an opportunity of bringing the service to a close, by the satisfaction expressed by the army that the second and more important victory had been gained by their old General."

22   Otherwise known as Marshal Junot; the title of Duc de Abrantes was bestowed by Napoleon as a reward for conquering Portugal. Wellington was happy to acknowledge these titles including that of Napoleon's brother, King Joseph.

23   *Dispatches* 4: 119, Wellesley to Hon. Charles Stewart 25 August 1808.

24   *Dispatches* 4: 261 *Memorandum on the Defence of Portugal* 7 March 1809.

Chapter 2: Memorandum of Operations In 1809

1   *Dispatches* 5 347-364.

2   See Appendix 2.

3   Francisco Javier Venegas de Saavedra y Ramínez de Arenzana (1754-1838).

4   Lieutenant General Don Pedro Caro y Sureda, Marques de la Romana (1761-1811). He had been sent with a picked division of troops to the Baltic when Spain was still in alliance with France, but afterwards he and most of his men escaped on British ships and returned to Spain. There he assumed command of the Army of Galicia and in spite of severe difficulties kept it in being and co-operated wholeheartedly with Wellesley until his sudden death on 23 January 1811.

5   Wellesley to Viscount Castlereagh, Secretary of State; Oporto, 12 May, 1809, (*Dispatches* 4:322–326).

6   Ernest, Baron von Langwerth, a Hanoverian officer, was serving on the staff of the army at the time, so Murray's command of the brigade was temporary. Langwerth (1757-1809) resumed command of the brigade after Oporto but was killed in action at Talavera on 28 July 1809.

7   The first battalion of Detachments was one of two provisional units formed by Cradock from strays left behind in Portugal when Moore marched into Spain the previous year.

8   *Dispatches* 4: 326.

9   Wellesley to Viscount Castlereagh, Secretary of State; Talavera de la Reyna, 29th July, 1809.
    Vol.4: 532-540.

10 A reference to the Spaniards' failure to supply food and transport to their British allies.

11 Major General John Randoll Mackenzie of Suddie, commanding 3. Division – the infantry brigades had been grouped into divisions on 18 June 1809 – see Appendix II for their composition. Confusingly, Mackenzie had not yet relinquished command of his own brigade within the division.

12 Jose Maria de la Cueva, Ducque de Alburquerque (1775-1811) commanded the 2nd Cavalry Division of the Spanish army at Talavera, and was defeated at battle of Arzobispo 8 August 1809. On 4 February 1810 he took 11,000 men of Army of Estramadura into Cadiz, securing it ahead of the French army. He was appointed governor of the city but resigned in March and was sent to London as Spanish ambassador, where he died in 1811 and was buried in Westminster Abbey.

13 This was the result of a breakdown in control. A staff officer, Lieutenant Colonel John Elley, delivered the order for Anson to charge with his brigade, but as soon as the 23rd were formed Colonel Elley led them forward without waiting for the 1st KGL Dragoons. Anson made no attempt to restrain the 23rd and they tumbled into a wide ditch. To complete their discomfiture the French counter-attacked and consequently the 23rd suffered some 40 per cent casualties and had to be sent home.

14   *Dispatches* 4: 538.

15   Francisco Ramon Lopez de Letona Eguia (1750-1827); by all accounts an extremely unpopular officer. On October 21, 1809, a British liaison officer, Colonel Roche, wrote that General Areizaga "has been appointed commander of the army in place of General Eguía, who has been finally dismissed for almost everyone's satisfaction".

16   Diego Vicente Maria de Canas y Portocarrero, Duque del Parque (1755-1823).

17   Juan Carlos de Aréizaga (? – 1816).

Chapter 3: Memorandum of Operations in 1810

1   *Dispatches* 7:291-313 [23rd February, 1811].

2   A note comments that: "They were stated to be 20,000 men, but I doubt that they ever collected 15,000."

3   Blank in original. A note states that: "The Duque del Parque stated that he should march on the 24th January… but they did not march till later in the month and the beginning of February."

4   Nicolas de Mahy y Romo [1757-1822] – second in command to Romana.

5   The Walcheren regiments were seriously weakened for some time afterwards, not only by the casualties suffered there, but by the lingering effects of Walcheren Fever; now believed to be a compound of malaria, typhus, typhoid and paratyphoid fever, and perhaps dysentery as well. Not only were the survivors debilitated by it, but in the longer term it proved to be an intromittent, triggered especially by wet weather.

6   These were Portuguese troops commanded by Thomas McMahon.

7   Craufurd's despatch to Wellington describing the action was dated from Carvalhal, 25th July, 1810. (*Dispatches* 6:294):

"I have the honor to report to your Lordship, that yesterday morning the enemy advanced to attack the light division, with between 3000 and 4000 cavalry, a considerable number of guns, and a large body of infantry.

"On the first appearance of the heads of their columns, the cavalry and brigade of artillery attached to the division advanced to support the piquets and Captain Ross, with four guns, was for some time engaged with those attached to the enemy's cavalry, which were of much larger calibre. As the immense superiority of the enemy's force displayed itself, we fell back gradually towards the fortress, upon the right of which the infantry of the division was posted, having its left in some enclosures near the windmill, about eight hundred yards from the place, and its right to the Coa, in a very broken and extensive position, which it was absolutely necessary to occupy, in order to cover the passage of the cavalry and artillery through the long defile leading to the bridge; after this was effected, the infantry retired by degrees, and in as good order as it is possible in ground so extremely intricate; a position close in front of the bridge was maintained, as long as was necessary to give time for the troops which had passed to take up one behind the river, and the bridge was afterwards defended with the greatest gallantry, though, I am sorry to say, with considerable loss by the 43rd and part of the 95th regiments. Towards the evening the firing ceased, and after it was dark I withdrew the troops from the Coa and retired to this place. The troops behaved with the greatest gallantry.

"Those returned as prisoners and missing were taken in a charge with the enemy's cavalry, just after our cavalry and guns had begun to retire."

Return of the number of Killed, Wounded, and Missing, of a Division of the Army under the Command of His Excellency Lieut. General Wellington, K.B., in an action with the French Army, near Almeida, on the 24th July, 1810.

	Officers	Serjeants	Drummers	Rank and File	Troop Horses	Total loss of Officers, Non-commissioned Officers, and Rank and File
Killed	4	3	–	29	–	36
Wounded	23	10	2	164	–	199
Missing	1	1	1	80	..	83

8   *Dispatches* 6:472 Wellington to Liverpool 30 September 1810.
     Robert Banks Jenkinson, 2nd Earl of Liverpool (1770-1828) – a career politician formerly known as Lord Hawkesbury, he became secretary of state for war and the colonies in September 1809 and succeeded Spencer Perceval as prime minister after the latter's assassination in May 1812.

9   *Not* Major General the Hon. Robert Meade, but his younger brother, lieutenant Colonel the Hon. John Meade (1775-1849).

10   Probably Captain Walter Birmingham of the 29th Foot, then serving with the Portuguese Army – he was killed at Toulouse commanding the 21st Portuguese Regiment (WO25/3998; Hall).

11   An error, 3/1st Royals served in the Peninsula while 1/1st (Royals) were in the West Indies at the time.

12   Francis John Colman, died in Portugal 12 December 1811 "of fever and debility, brought on by exertions in his profession too great for his constitution".

13   *Dispatches* 6:476.

14   The battle on 11 August was that of Villagarcia, outside Llerena. The French
      commander on this occasion was Jean Baptiste Girard and Romana's defeat was
      largely down to faulty intelligence, which badly underestimated the strength
      of the French army. Afterwards, Romana replaced all his cavalry officers with
      General La Carrera, and appointed Carlos D'Espana to command the remains
      of his old infantry division.
15   The rearguard action at Fuente Canos, near Monastario, was in fact a French
      victory but a timely charge by Madden's Portuguese brigade very successfully
      covered Romana's retreat.

Chapter 4: Memorandum of Operations In 1811

1   *Dispatches* 8:474-499 Freneda, 28th December, 1811.
2   Roger-Bernard-Charles Espagnac de Ramefort (1775-1839), more familiarly
     known as Don Carlos de Espana, a French emigre officer whose brigade and latterly
     division was closely associated with Wellington's forces throughout most of the war.
3   This Portuguese division with only two brigades was formed on 16 December
     1809 under John Hamilton and attached to the 2nd Division.
4   A reference to the battle of Villanuevo de Castillejos, a successful rearguard
     action by Ballasteros.
5   To the Earl of Liverpool, Secretary of State, Villa Fermosa 8 May 1811.
     Dispatches 7:528-534.
6   Jean Baptiste Drouet, Comte D'Erlon's 9th Corps was a scratch formation
     formed of the newly raised 4th battalions of regiments already serving in the
     Peninsula. (see Oman 4:17-20).
7   See Appendix II; this is a mistake for the Light Infantry *brigade* belonging to
     Picton's division.
8   Don Julian Sanchez "El Charro" (1774-1832) to the British the best known of
     the Spanish guerrilla leaders. His lancers were taken into the regular army in
     1810 as the *Lanceros de Castilla*.
9   The black-coated Brunswick Light Infantry are not to be confused with the
     green-jacketed riflemen of the Brunswick Jager.
10   Captain William Wilde 87th Foot, later killed in action at Badajoz 26 March
     1812.
11   William Iremonger (1776-1852).
12   A *cause celebre*: while there was no doubting Iremonger's incompetent
     culpability, Lieutenant Colonel Charles Bevan (1778-1811) was unfairly
     blamed. Far from receiving his orders at 13.00 hours, it appears that Sir
     William Erskine failed to pass them on and so they did not arrive until about
     twelve hours later, when Bevan not unreasonably decided to wait until daylight

before moving. Afterwards he requested a court martial to clear himself but on Wellington's refusal to grant one he shot himself at Portalegre on 8 July 1811.

13   *Dispatches* 8:303-310: To the Earl of Liverpool, Secretary of State. Quadraseis, 29th Sept., 1811.

Chapter 5: 1812 to 1814

1   General Viscount Wellington, K.B., to the Earl of Liverpool, Secretary of State, Gallegos, 20th January, 1812, *Dispatches* 8:527-533.

2   A defensive wall outside the main trace of the fortifications.

3   An independent Portuguese brigade.

4   General Viscount Wellington, K.B., to the Earl of Liverpool, Secretary of State, Camp before Badajoz 7th April 1812.

5   Wellington to Earl Bathurst, Flores de Avila 14 July 1812, *Dispatches* 9:301-309. Henry Bathurst, 3rd Earl Bathurst (1762-1834) succeeded Liverpool as Secretary of State for War and the Colonies in May 1812.

6   Otto Eberhard von Bock, commanding the heavy cavalry of the King's German Legion, subsequently drowned in a shipwreck while returning to Germany in 1814.

7   Wellington to Earl Bathurst, Salvatierra, 22nd June, 1813, *Despatches* 10:446-453.

8   Pablo Morillo(1775-1837) an ex-ranker, commissioned after Bailen and for a time a guerrilla leader before bringing his men into the regular Spanish army.

9   Francisco Anchia y Urquiza (10 April 1783 – 1831) a former guerrilla better known as Francisco de Longa from his place of birth.

10 Pedro Agustín Girón, later 4th Marquis de las Amarilas, and Duque de Ahumada (1778–1842), a competent if not particularly distinguished Spanish officer, and himself the son of a general.

11 Francisco da Silveira Pinto da Fonseca Teixeira (1 September 1763 – 27 May 1821).

12 Return of the Ordnance, Carriages and Ammunition, captured from the enemy in the action at Vitoria, on the 21st June, 1813:

151	Brass Ordnance, on travelling carriages
415	Caissons
14,248	Rounds of ammunition
1,973,400	Musket Ball cartridges
40,668	lbs. of Gunpowder
56	Forage waggons
44	Forge waggons

DICKSON, Lieut. Col. Commanding the Artillery.

13 Or perhaps had gone astray amid the plundering of the French baggage train.
14 Wellington to Earl Bathurst, Toulouse 12 April 1814, *Dispatches* 11:632-637.
15 *Despatches* 11:648.
16 *Despatches* 11:660.

Index

Bolded references indicate biographical notes

Abadia, General [Sp.] 88, 94, 95
Abercromby, Hon. Alexander 123,
    138, 238
Abrantes 8, 27, 28, 44, 68, 71, 72
Abrantes, Duc de [Fr.] See Junot,
    Marshal
Acland, Wroth Palmer 5, 7, 13, 14, 15,
    16, **139**
Alameda 78
Alamedilla 89
Alava, Don Miguel [Sp.] 118, 124, 130
Alba de Tormes 112
Alba de Tormes [battle] 41
Albergueria 91, 92
Albuera 85, 86, 110
Albuera [battle] 83, 84
Alburquerque, Duque de [Sp.] 33, 41,
    43, 44, 45
Alcantara 26, 27, 52
Alcobaca 8, 9
Aldea da Ponte 92, 93
Aldea del Obispo 80
Aldea Tejada 113
Aldea Velha 91
Alentejo 5, 8, 64, 75, 86, 87
Algeo, John Henry 108, **139**
Alfayetes 91–92
Almaraz 27, 37, 69
Almeida 3, 4, 51, 52–53, 74, 75, 76–77,
    81, 82, 88

Almonacid 39
Alten, Karl von [KGL] 89, 90,
    91, 92, 93, 127, 261, 262, 263,
    266, 267
Alten, Victor [KGL] 272, 273, 274,
    275, 276, 277
Aly, Karl August [KGL] 77, 80
Amarante, Conde de [Port.] 122
Anson, George 32, 35, 89, 90, 115, 116,
    121, **140**, 252, 253, 269, 270, 271,
    273, 274, 275, 276
Anstruther, Robert 13, 14, 15, 18, **140**
Aranjuez 36, 38
Arentschilt, Col. [KGL] 57, 93, 126,
    271, 277
Areyzaga, General [Sp.] 40–41, 45
Armstrong, Richard 58
Arzobispo 27, 38, 39, 41, 48
Ashworth, Charles 79, **141**, 238, 239,
    240, 241, 242
Astorga 27, 28, 44, 47, 48, 49, 87
Augereau, Marshal [Fr.] 45
Ayamonte 45, 76, 86, 96
Aylmer, Matthew Lord 124, **141**,
    234, 235

Bacellar, Colonel [Port.] 45, 67, 93
Badajoz 39, 45, 47, 68, 69, 70–73,
    74–75, 76, 83, 84, 85, 86
Badajoz [storm] 104–111

Bailen [battle] 5

Ballasteros, General [Sp.] 40, 65, 68, 69, 73, 74, 75, 97, 110

Barba de Puerco 82

Barcenas, Don Pedro [Sp.] 129

Barclay, Robert 58, **142**, 265

Bargas 30

Barnard, Andrew Francis 102, 105, 107, **142**, 265, 266, 267

Barnes, Sir Edward 242, 255, 263, 264

Barnes, James Stevenson 253–254

Barreto, Luiz da Rego [Port.] 257

Barrie, General [Fr.] 104

Bassecourt, Lieut. General [Sp.] 33, 37

Bathurst, James 12, 18, 25, 35, 59, **143**

Baurot, General [Fr.] 129

Beckett, Richard 34, **143**

Beckwith, Sir Thomas Sidney 58, 107, **143**, 264, 265

Belchite 27

Beresford, William Carr 22, 23, 29, 36–37, 39, 64, 74–75, 76, 81, 83, 107, 114, 116, 123, 126, 127, 128, **143**

Berekeley, George Henry 123, **144**

Bernewitz Johann de [Brunswick] 262, 263, 264

Bessieres, Marshal [Fr.] 3, 7, 21, 76, 87

Bingham, George Ridout 35, 117, **145**, 259

Birmingham, [Walter?] 57

Bismula 92

Bisset, Commissary 103, 118

Blake, General Joaquin [Sp.] 2, 3, 7, 27, 76, 85, 86, 96, 97, 98

Blake, William Williams 23, 25, **145**

Blakeney, Sir Edward 108, **145**

Blantyre, Lord SEE Stewart, Robert Walter

Bligh, Captain RN 6, 9, 13

Bock, Otto Eberhardt [KGL] 115, 121, 274, 275, 277

Bonnet, General [Fr.] 54, 88

Bornos 97

Borthwick, William 109

Bouchier, Daniel Macnamara 109, **146**

Bouverie, Henry Frederick 123, **146**

Bowes, Barnard Foord 10, 15, 16, 107, **146**, 224, 252, 259

Bradford, Thomas 113, 114, 116, 121, 122, **147**

Brenier, General [Fr.] 17, 82

Brisbane, Thomas 129, **147**, 247

British Army
1st Division 22, 30, 32, 34, 77, 78, 79, 80, 101, 102, 114, 115, 121, 123, 228, 229–235

2nd Division 22, 32, 44, 47, 51, 54, 56, 62, 75, 235–243

3rd Division 56, 77, 78, 79, 80, 83, 89, 90, 91, 92, 100, 101, 102, 105, 108, 113, 114, 115, 117, 120, 123, 127, 129, 243–247

4th Division 72, 73, 89, 91, 92, 101, 102, 105, 106, 107, 113, 114, 115, 116, 117, 120, 123, 128, 248–253

5th Division 77, 89, 91, 105, 108, 113, 114, 115, 116, 117, 121, 122, 253–257

6th Division 77, 89, 113, 115, 116, 122, 128, 258–261

7th Division 77, 78, 79, 83, 89, 91, 92, 112–113, 114, 120, 123, 261–264

Light Division 77, 79, 89, 90, 100, 101, 102, 105, 106, 114, 115, 120, 123, 127, 228, 264–267

Royal Engineers 103

Royal Staff Corps 117

1st Lifeguards 276, 277

2nd Lifeguards 276, 277

Royal Horse Guards [Blues] 276, 277

3rd Dragoon Guards 225, 269, 270, 272, 273, 275, 276

4th Dragoon Guards 273, 275, 276, 277

5th Dragoon Guards 273, 275, 278

1st [Royal] Dragoons 269, 270, 271, 272, 273, 276

3rd Dragoons 273, 274, 275, 278

4th Dragoons 117, 269, 270, 272, 273, 274, 275, 278

7th Light Dragoons 276

9th Light Dragoons 273, 274, 276

10th Light Dragoons 276

11th Light Dragoons 93, 271, 272, 273, 274, 275, 276

12th Light Dragoons 117, 272, 273, 274, 275, 278

13th Light Dragoons 56, 74–75, 271, 272, 273, 274, 276, 278

14th Light Dragoons 24, 89–90, 113, 114, 117, 225, 269, 270, 271, 273, 274, 275, 276, 278

15th Light Dragoons 276

16th Light Dragoons 25, 89–90, 225, 269, 270, 271, 273, 275, 278

18th Light Dragoons 125, 276, 277

20th Light Dragoons 16, 17, 25, 225, 269

23rd Light Dragoons 26, 30, 33, 269

Cavalry Staff Corps 264

KGL 1st Hussars 33, 93, 228, 264, 270, 271, 273, 275, 277

KGL 2nd Hussars 271, 272, 274, 275, 276

KGL 3rd Light Dragoons 225, 269

KGL Heavy Dragoons 115, 274, 275, 277

Footguards 22, 24, 33, 34, 35, 80, 103, 117, 225, 226, 229, 230, 231, 232, 233, 252

1st [Royal] Regiment 51, 57, 253–4, 255, 256, 257

2nd [Queen's] Regiment 77, 252, 258, 259

3rd Foot [Buffs] 23, 25, 226, 235, 236, 237, 239, 240, 241, 242

4th Foot 82, 108, 254, 255, 256

5th Foot 11, 12, 90, 91, 92–93, 103, 108. 224, 244, 245, 246, 247, 249

6th Foot 224, 263

7th Fusiliers 34, 35, 117, 227, 231, 248, 249, 250, 251, 253, 258

9th Foot 11, 12, 51, 57, 224, 227, 229, 230, 254, 254, 256, 257

11th Foot 249, 258, 259, 260

20th Foot 252, 253

23rd Fusiliers 108, 117, 250, 251, 253

24th Foot 78, 80, 227, 230, 231, 243, 263

26th Foot 232, 233

27th Foot 226, 243, 249, 250, 251, 253

28th Foot 224, 236, 237, 238, 239, 241, 242

29th Foot 11, 12, 16, 23, 24, 33, 35, 227, 235, 237, 238, 240

30th Foot 35, 108, 227, 254, 255, 256

31st Foot 32, 226, 236, 237, 243

32nd Foot 224, 258, 259, 260

34th Foot 236, 237, 238, 239, 241, 242

36th Foot 16, 17, 82, 128, 224, 258, 259, 260

37th Foot 235,

38th Foot 51, 57, 106, 108, 117, 224, 254, 255, 256

39th Foot 236, 237, 238, 239, 240, 241, 242

40th Foot 16, 17, 102, 224, 230, 249, 250, 251, 253

42nd Highlanders 80, 128, 230, 231, 233, 259–260

43rd Foot 16, 23, 24, 57, 100, 108, 244, 264, 265, 266, 267

44th Foot 108, 254, 255, 256

45th Foot 11, 32, 35, 56, 102, 108, 129, 224, 226, 243, 244, 245, 247

47th Foot 252, 256, 257

48th Foot 23, 25, 26, 30, 33, 34, 35, 108, 226, 235, 236, 237, 238, 251, 252, 253

50th Foot 11, 15, 16, 17, 224, 231, 238, 239, 240, 241, 242

51st Foot 261, 262, 263

52nd Foot 16, 17, 23, 24, 57, 58, 100, 108, 244, 264, 265, 266, 267

53rd Foot 34, 35, 117, 227, 248, 249, 252, 258, 259

57th Foot 236, 237, 238, 239, 240, 241, 242

58th Foot 71, 233, 244, 245, 249, 263

59th Foot 257

60th Rifles 11, 12, 15, 16, 17, 24, 32, 35, 108, 116, 224, 226, 227, 230, 230, 232, 233, 237, 238, 240, 241, 242, 243, 244, 245, 246, 247, 250, 251, 258, 260

61st Foot 26, 90, 128, 230, 231, 250, 258, 259, 260

62nd Foot 234, 235

66th Foot 23, 25, 226, 235, 236, 237

68th Foot 262, 263

71st Highlanders 16, 17, 78, 80, 120, 224, 231, 238, 239, 240, 241, 242

74th Highlanders 57, 80, 91, 102, 108, 244, 245, 246, 247

76th Foot 234, 235

77th Foot 90, 91, 93, 234, 235, 246, 260

79th Highlanders 46, 78, 80, 128, 230, 231

82nd Foot 11, 16, 17, 123, 224, 233, 252, 263

83rd Foot 77, 78, 108, 227, 229, 230, 244, 245, 246, 247

84th Foot 234, 257, 257

85th Foot 78, 234, 235, 261, 262

87th Foot 32, 46, 124, 226, 243, 247, 252

88th Foot 56, 71, 80, 102, 117, 226, 243, 244, 245, 246, 247

91st Highlanders 11, 224, 260

92nd Highlanders 231, 238, 239, 240, 241, 242

94th Foot 46, 100, 108, 116–117, 245, 247

95th Rifles 11, 12, 15, 16, 17, 23, 57, 80, 100, 108, 224, 231, 238, 239, 240, 244, 252, 264, 265, 265, 266, 267

97th Foot 16, 17, 34, 35, 226, 248, 249, 250, 251

Chasseurs Britanniques 79, 261, 262, 263

Duke of Brunswick's Light Infantry 79, 261, 262, 263, 265, 266

Brunswick Oels Jager 250, 251, 253, 254, 255, 257

1st Bn. Detachments 35, 227, 235, 236

2nd Bn. Of Detachments 226, 248, 249

4th Royal Veteran Bn. 2

King's German Legion [KGL] 22, 23, 25, 33, 227, 229, 230, 231, 232, 233, 235

KGL Light Infantry 77, 228, 230, 231, 232, 233, 235, 261
Bromhead, John 93, **148**
Brooke, Francis 108, 256
Brotherton, Thomas 90, **148**
Bulow, Col. Von [KGL] 277
Bunbury, William Henry 35, **149**, 235
Burgoyne, John Fox 109, **149**
Burne, Robert 17, **150**, 258, 259
Burrard, Sir Harry 2, 7, 14
Busaco [battle] 54–60
Byng, John 240, 241, 242

Cabrerizos 112
Cadogan, Hon. Henry 78, 80, 81, 83, 120, **150**, 241, 242
Cadiz 45, 46, 67, 68, 69, 71, 74, 97
Calcraft, Granby 269
Caldas 10
Callaghan, Hon, Robert William 122–123, 243
Cameron, Allan, of Erracht 22, 35, **151**, 229, 230
Cameron, John, of Fassfern 242
Cameron, Phillips 78, 80, 81, **151**
Campbell, Sir Alexander 22, 32, 33–34, 35, 77, 82, 86, **152**, 248, 249, 250, 258
Campbell, Colin 24, 124, **152**
Campbell, Henry Frederick 35, 103, **152**, 229, 232
Campbell, James 100, 101, 108, 116–117, **153**, 246, 247
Campillo 89
Campo Mayor 68, 73, 74, 75, 84
Canning, Charles Fox 110, **153**
Carleton, Hon. George 108, **153**
Carr, William Henry 77, 108, **154**
Carrera, General [Sp.] 45, 48

Cartaxo 62, 68, 69
Castanos, General [Sp.] 4
Castello Branco 85
Castillejos 92
Cazalegas 30, 31, 36
Celerico 50, 54
Chamberlain, Thomas 78, **154**
Champilmaud, Gen. [Port.] 57, 80, 107, 244
Chapman, Captain 59
Chaves 21
Chowne, Christopher – SEE Tilson, Christopher
Cintra, Convention of 2, 18
Claparede, General [Fr.] 67, 71, 73
Clausel, General [Fr.] 112, 122
Clifton, Arthur 277
Clinton, Lord, SEE Robert Trefusis
Clinton, Sir William Henry 113–114, 115, 116, 128, **154**, 258, 259, 260
Cocks, Edward Charles 90, **155**
Coghlan, James Robert 128, **155**
Coimbra 22, 26, 61, 72, 73
Colborne, John 101, 102, **155**, 237, 238, 267
Cole, Sir Galbraith Lowry 75, 92, 93, 113, 114, 116, 123, 128, **156**, 248, 249, 250, 251, 252, 253
Collins, Richard 250, 251, 263, 264
Colman, Francis John 57, **156**, 262, 263
Colville, Hon. Charles 90, 93, 102, 105, 107, 123, **156**, 245, 247, 251, 256–257, 260
Condeixa 74
Cooke, Colonel 130, 131
Copeson, Edward 248
Copons, General [Sp.] 45, 97
Corunna 2, 7, 19
Cotton, Admiral Sir Charles RN 3–5

Cotton, Sir Stapleton 32, 34, 78, 79,
    89, 92, 113, 114, 115, 116, 126,
    157, 230, 267, 269, 270, 271, 272,
    273, 274
Cradock, Sir John 19, 21, **157**
Craufurd, James Catlin 10, 16, **158**,
    224, 236, 237, 265
Craufurd, Robert 28, 36, 52, 55, 57, 58,
    79, 91, 100, 101, 102, **158**, 243,
    244, 264, 265, 266
Croix d'Orade 126, 127
Crowder, John 117, **159**
Cuesta, Don Gregorio 2, 3, 7, 21, 27,
    28, 29, 30, 34–35, 36, 37–38, 39
Cuidad Real 21, 48
Cuidad Rodrigo 29, 39, 40, 41, 44, 47,
    50, 51, 52, 64, 74, 75, 76, 85,
    87–88, 89, 90, 91, 94, 95, 97,
    110, 112
Cuidad Rodrigo [storm] 99–104
Cumming, Henry John 93, **159**, 274
Currie, Edward 24, **159**

Dalhousie, Earl of SEE Ramsay, George
Dalrymple, Sir Hew 2, 5, 18
Dansey,Capt. 57
Daroca 97
D'Aramante, Conde [Port.] 110
Davy, William Gabriel 17, 35, **160**
De Grey, Hon. George 72–73, 89, 91,
    160, 270, 272, 274
De Lancey, William Howe 24, 117,
    123, **160**
Deleytosa 38, 39
Desbareaux, General [Fr.] 129
Dessolles, General [Fr.] 44
Dick, Robert Henry 77, 80, **161**
Dickson, Alexander 103, 109, 124,
    130, **161**

Do Rego, Luiz [Port.] 106, 108
Doherty, Patrick 278
Donkin, Rufane Shaw 32–33, **161**, 243
Donellan, Charles 35, **162**
Douglas, James Dawes 56, 57, 117,
    128, **162, 261**
Doyle, Charles William 7, **162**
Doyle, Sir John Milley 24, **163**, 264
Drouet, General [Fr.] 67, 70–71, 85,
    86, 109
Drummond, Archibald 25, **163**
Drummond, George 265
Dubordieu, Saumaurez 121, **163**
Duckworth, George Henry 25, **164**,
    236, 3=237
Duffy, John 102, **164**
Dundas, Robert Lawrence 117, **164**
Dundas, William Bolden 103, **164**
Dunlop, James 254
Dupont, General 5
D'Urban, Benjamin 112, 113, 114, 117,
    128, **165**
Dynely, Thomas 103, **165**

Eben, Baron Friedrich Christian **258**,
    259, 260
Eguia, Francisco [Sp.] 39, 40
El Bodon [battle] 88–95
Elder, George 102, 108, **165**
Ellis, Henry Walton 108, 117, **166**, 252
Elvas 4, 5, 8, 71, 72, 75, 76, 83, 86
Empecinado [Sp. Guerrilla] 97
Erskine, James 108, **166**
Erskine, Sir William 77, 81, **166**, 231,
    254, 265, 272, 273, 274
Escalona 30, 31, 36
Espana, Carlos de [Sp.] 68, 69, 89, 91,
    103, 113, 114, 118
Espeja 89

Eustace, William Cornwallis 79, 81, **167**
Ezpeleta, Don J. de [Sp.] 127, 129
Eyre, Henry Samuel 17, **167**

Fane, Sir Henry 10–11, 12, 15, 18, 33,
    56, 62, **168**, 224, 269, 270, 277
Ferguson, Ronald Craufurd 7, 10, 15,
    16, 17, 18, **168**, 224
Fermor, Hon. Thomas William 233
Ficalho, Conde de [Port.] 117
Fitzgerald, John Forster 108, **168**, 242
Fletcher, Sir Richard 35, 59, 103, 109,
    124, **169**
Forbes, Thomas 108, 129, **169**,
    246, 247
Forcalhos 92
Fordyce, Alexander 24, 33, **169**
Fort Concepcion 77
Foy, General 63, 71, 89, 122
Framingham, Sir Haylett 109, 117, **169**
Francheschi, General 28
Freire, Bernardino [Port.] 8–9
Fremantle, John 124, **170**
Freyre, Don Manuel [Sp.] 125, 126,
    127, 128
Fuente Guinaldo 89, 90, 91, 92
Fuentes d'Onoro [battle] 76–82

Gallegos 50
De Gand, Visconde [Sp.] 45
Gardanne, General [Fr.] 63, 64
Gardiner, John 264
Gardiner, Robert 109, **170**
Gardner, Daniel 33, **170**
Gazan, Comte [Fr.] 132
Gerona 27
Gibbs, Edward 102, 108, **171**, 266
Giron, Pedro Augustin [Sp.] 121, 124
Gomm, William Maynard 123, **171**

Gordon, Hon. Alexander William
    104, **171**
Graham, Sir Thomas 89, 90, 91, 101,
    102, 103, 110, 121, 122, 123, 124,
    172, 231, 232, 234
Grant, Sir Colquhon 276
Grant, William 123, **172**, 264
Gray, George 108, **173**
Greville, Charles John 117, **173**,
    255, 257
Grey, John 101, **173**
Guadalcanal 83, 85
Guard, William 35
Guarda 67, 71, 73
Gurwood, John 102, **174**
Guise, John Wright 80, **174**, 235

Halkett, Colin 121–122, **175**, 233, 262
Hamilton, Sir John 47, 72–73, 75, **175**
Harcourt, Charles Amedee 102, 108,
    176, 252
Hardinge, Henry 242
Harispe, General [Fr.] 129
Harvey, William Maundy 107, **176**,
    251, 252
Hawker, Samuel 271
Hay, Andrew 254, 255, 256, 257
Hay, James 90, 117, **176**
Hervey, Felton Elwell 24, 25, 90, 113,
    114, 117, **177**
Hesse-Darmstadt Regiment [Fr.]
    106, 111
Hill, Clement 24, 47, **177**
Hill, Dudley St. Leger 58, 106,
    108, **177**
Hill, George 80, **178**
Hill, Sir Robert 277
Hill, Rowland 7, 10, 11, 12, 14, 16, 22,
    23, 24, 32, 33, 35, 44, 48, 49, 51,

52, 53–4, 62, 64, 110, 119, 120, 123, 126, 129, **178**, 224, 235, 237, 238, 239, 240

Hinde, Samuel Venables 116, **179**, 259, 260, 261

Hinhuber, Heinrich von [KGL] 234, 235

HMS *Alfred* 6, 9

HMS *Crocodile* 2

HMS *Donegal* 2, 7

HMS *Lively* 26

Hoghton, Daniel 237, 238

Holcombe, Harcourt Fort 103, 109, **179**

Hope, James Archibald 123, **179**

Hope, Sir John 114, **180**, 234,

Hope, John 263

Houston, Sir William 78, 79, **180**, 250, 261

Howard, Kenneth 77, 232, 233, 238, 239, 240, 241

Howorth, Sir Edward 35, 59, **181**

Hull, Edward **181**

Hulse, Richard 116, **181**, 229, 255, 258, 259

Inglis, William 123, **182**, 237, 239, 264

Iremonger, William **182**

Jaen 45

Jaraicejo 39

Jones, John Thomas 103, 109, **182**

Joseph, King of Spain [Fr.] 1, 7, 28, 31, 36, 45, 119, 122

Jourdan, Marshal [Fr.] 31, 119

Junot, Marshal [Duc de Abrantes] 1, 7, 14, 17, 21, 45, 46, 47, 48, 50, 78

Keane, Sir John 247

Kellerman, General [Fr.] 18, 21, 26, 27, 28, 38, 39, 50, 54

Kelly, William 81, **183**

Kemmis, James 17, **183**, 250, 251, 252

Kempt, Sir James 105, 106, 246, 248–249, 267

Kennedy 59

Knight, William Howe 108, **183**

La Carolina 21, 29, 39, 41, 44

La Motte, Colonel [Fr.] 79

La Serna 115

Laborde, General [Fr.] 7, 8, 9, 10, 14

Lacy, General [Sp.] 96

Lake, George 11, **184**

Lambert, John 128, 234, 261

Lamego 67

Langwerth, Ernst von [KGL] 22, 25, 34, 229, 230

Las Torres 113

Lawson, Robert 121, **184**

Le Cor, Carlos Frederico [Port.] 53, 56, 262

Le Marchant, John Gaspard 114, **185**, 273, 274

Leaky, John Thomas 108, **184**

Leite, General [Port.] 72

Leith, Sir James 51, 57, 105, 106, 113, 114–115, 116, **185**, 237, 253, 254, 255, 256

Leon de Sicilia, Colonel [Sp.] 127

Lerida 95–96

Leyria 7, 8, 9, 67

Lhuillier, General [Fr.] 129

Lightburne, Stafford 244, 249

Llerena 83, 85, 110

Loison, General [Fr.] 5, 8, 9, 10, 13, 14, 47, 50, 58

Long, Robert 261, 262, 272, 273, 274, 276

Longa, Francisco de [Sp.] 121

Los Santos 76, 85
Lourinha 15, 16
Loverdo, General [Fr.] 131
Low, Sigismund von [KGL] 229, 230, 231, 232, 234
Lugo 26
Lumley, Sir William 237, 238, 239, 240
Lynch, Henry Blois 100, **185**
Lyon, James Frederick 17, 35, **186**

MacBean, Forbes 57–58
McDonald, Major 80
Macdonald, Marshal Etienne [Fr.] 45
McDonnell, Archibald 77, **186**
McGrigor, Dr. James 118
Macintosh, Aeneas 78, 81, **186**
Mackenzie, John Randoll 31, 32–33, 34, **187**
Mackinlay, Capt. RN 26
Mackinnon, Henry 57, 80–81, 100, 101, **187**, 243, 244, 245
Macleod, Charles 102, 108, **187**
Macleod, George 102, **188**
McMahon, Thomas 51, 92, **188**, 249, 250
Machado, Colonel [Port.] 24
Madden, George 70, 259, 260, 271, 272, 273
Mafra 14
Mahy, Nicolas de [Sp.] 44, 51, 96
Maitland, Peregrine 234
Malcolm, Capt. Pulteney RN 3, 7
Manners, Lord Charles 278
Manners, Russell 80, 101, 108, **188**
Marchand, General [Fr.] 40
Marcilla, Don A. Garces de [Sp.] 129
Marmont, Marshal [Fr.] 84, 85, 86, 87, 97, 110, 112, 116

Massena, Marshal [Fr.] 67, 70, 71–72, 73, 76, 97
Maucune, General [Fr.] 58
May, John 103, 109, **188**
Meade, Hon. R 56, 57, **189**
Medellin 21, 44, 68
Mellish, Henry Francis 24, **189**
Mendizabal, Don Gabriel [Sp.] 65, 68, 127
Merida 27, 68, 85
Merle, General [Fr.] 58
Middlemore, George 35, **189**
Miller, James 67, **190**
Mina, General [Sp.] 94, 95, 97
Monasterio 21, 27, 45
Mondego Bay 3, 4–5, 6
Montauban 131, 132
Montblanc 127, 128
Moore, Sir John 2, 7, 19
Morillo, Pablo [Sp.] 119, 120, 122
Mortier, Marshal [Fr.] 21, 27, 28, 39, 40, 44, 47, 64, 65
Mozinho, Brito [Port.] 128
Murray, Sir George 25, 35, 124, 132, **190**
Murray, James Patrick 25, **190**
Murray, Sir John 22, 23, 24, **191**
Myers, Sir William James 35, **191**, 248, 249, 250–251

Napier, George 101, 102, **192**
Navalmoral 38
Nave d'Aver 77, 78, 91
Nazareth 9
Ney, Marshal [Fr.] 26, 27, 28, 39, 40, 44, 46, 47, 50, 52, 55
Nicholas, William 109, **192**
Nightingall, Sir Miles 10, 11, 15, 16, 18, 77, 80, **192**, 224, 232

Nixon, Robert 78, 81, **193**
Nugent, John 106, 108, **193**

O'Callaghan, Hon. Robert 123, **193**, 242
O'Donoju, Don Thomas [Sp.] 124
O'Hare, Peter 80, 108, **194**
O'Lalor, Don Jose [Sp.] 35, 118, 124
O'Loghlin, Terence O'Brien 277
O'Toole, Bryan 100, 101, **194**
Obidos 9, 10
Olivenca 68, 69, 73, 75
Oporto 3, 21, 22–25
Orange, Prince of 94, 118, 124
Orense 27
Oropesa 37, 39, 40, 96
Oswald, John 121, 122, **194**, 255, 256
Otway, Loftus 271

Pack, Denis 17, 55, 57, 58, 77, 89, 91,
     92, 100, 112, 114, 117, 121, 128,
     195, 260, 261
Paget, Hon. Edward 22, 23, 24, **195**, 232
Pakenham, Edward 92, 93, 113, 114,
     116, 122, **196**, 231, 246, 247, 250,
     251, 260
Pakenham, Hon. Hercules 108, **196**
Payne, Sir William 22, 32, 33, 35, **197**,
     269, 270
Palmerin, Luis [Port.] 245, 246, 262
Parque, Duque del [Sp.] 39, 40, 41, 47
Pastores 90
Penaranda 115
Peniche 4, 5, 9, 13
Penne Villemur, Conde de [Port.] 110
Penrose, Admiral RN 129
Philippon, General [Fr.] 106
Picton, Sir Thomas 56–57, 77, 93, 100,
     105, 106, 113, 120, 123, 127, 129,
     197, 244, 245, 246, 247

Pinto, Major [Port.] 80, 101
Piper, John 257
Plascencia 27, 28, 29, 30, 37, 39, 40,
     85, 86
Pombal 72
Ponsonby, Hon, Frederick 117, **198**
Ponsonby, Hon. William 116, 127, **198**,
     275, 278
Pontedo Abade 67
Portalegre 47, 74
Portuguese Army 1, 3, 6, 7, 8, 9, 11,
     13, 16–17, 19, 20, 21, 36–37, 39,
     44, 45–46, 49, 51, 59, 60, 71
  1st Cavalry 271, 272
  4th Cavalry 47
  5th Cavalry 271, 272
  7th Cavalry 271, 272
  8th Cavalry 271 272,
  1st Line 58, 226
  3rd Line 250, 254, 256, 257
  5th Line 251
  6th Line 239, 240, 241, 242
  7th Line 262, 263
  8th Line 56, 82, 117, 258, 259, 260
  9th Line 57, 244, 245, 246, 247
  10th Line 227
  11th Line 250, 253
  12th Line 259, 260
  15th Line 106, 108, 250, 254, 256, 257
  16th Line 22, 24–24, 58, 226
  18th Line 239, 240, 241, 242
  19th Line 57, 262, 263
  20th Line 46, 267
  21st Line 57, 90, 91, 93, 244, 245,
     246, 247
  23rd Line 253
  24th Line 71
  1st Cacadores 264, 265, 266, 267
  2nd Cacadores 78, 81, 103, 262, 263

3rd Cacadores 57, 102, 264, 265, 266, 267

4th Cacadores 55, 58, 112, 121

5th Cacadores 251

6th Cacadores 80, 239, 240, 241, 242

7th Cacadores 251, 253

8th Cacadores 106, 108, 121, 128, 255, 256, 257

9th Cacadores 260

12th Cacadores 247

Loyal Lusitanian Legion 51, 81, 251, 255, 258

Power, Manley 105, 116, 123, **198**, 245, 247

Power, William Greenshields 103, **199**

Pozo Velho 79

Pringle, William Henry 116, **199**, 242, 243, 255, 256

Puerte de Banos 29, 36, 39, 40, 85

Puerte de Mirabete 28, 41

Puerte de Perales 28, 37, 89, 91

Pynn, Henry 80, **199**

Ramsay, George, Earl of Dalhousie 120, 123, 129, **200**, 263, 264

Ramsay, William Norman 121, **200**

Rebolosa 92

Rebow, Francis Slater 276–277

Regnier, General [Fr.] 47, 52, 53, 55, 64

Regoa, Lt. Col. Luis de [Port.] 58

Retberg, Captain de [KGL 109

Rezende, Conde de [Port.] 117, 260

Ricard, Colonel [Fr.] 132

Ridge, Henry 90, 93, 100, 101, 108, **200**

Robe, William 12, 17, 109, **200**

Robinson, Frederick Philipse 121, **201**, 257

Robleda 91

Rolica [battle] 10–13

Romana, Marquis de la 21, 26–27, 39–40, 45, 48, 49, 60, 64–65, 68, 69 [death]

Rooke, John Charles 123, **201**

Ross, John 17, **202**

Ross, Robert 253

Russell, Lord William 130, **202**

St. Cyr, Marshal [Fr.] 21, 27

St. Hilaire, General [Fr.] 129

St. Martin de Trebejo 44

St. Simon, Colonel [Fr.] 130, 131

Sabugal 63, 79

Salamanca 21, 39, 40, 46, 47, 49, 84, 88

Salamanca [battle] 111–118

Salvador, Don E.S. [Sp.] 129

San Antonio de Cantaro 55

San Christoval 70

Santa Olalla 30, 31

Sanchez, Don Julian [Sp.] 77, 79, 87, 89, 91, 103, 118

Santarem 62, 63, 64

Sardao 58, 59, 60

Scovell, George 117, **202**

Sebastiani, General [Fr.] 21, 27, 28, 29, 31, 36, 39, 44, 45

Serras, General [Fr.] 50, 54, 63

Setuval 8

Seville 45, 46, 67, 86, 96, 109, 110

Sherbrooke, Sir John Coape 22, 23–24, 31, 34, 35, **203**, 229, 230

Silviera, Francisco da [Port.] 63, 67, 71

Simon, General [Fr.] 58

Skerrett, John Byne 97, **203**, 252, 253, 267

Slade, Sir John ["Black Jack"] 46, 47, 89, 91, **204**, 269, 270, 271, 272, 273, 275, 276, 277

Smyth/Smith, William 55, 57, **204**

Sobral 64

Somerset, Lord Edward 117, 126, 276

Somerset, Lord Fitzroy 117, 124, 130, **204**

Sontag, John 22, **205**, 248, 262

Souham, General [Fr.] 94

Soult, Marshal [Fr.] 21, 23, 26, 28, 36, 37, 38, 39, 40, 44, 67–68, 83, 84, 85, 86, 96, 109–110, 130, 131, 132

Spanish Army
  4th Army 129
  El Rey [cavalry] 34
  Tiradores de Cantabria 127

Spencer, Sir Brent 1, 4, 5, 6, 12, 17–18, 59, 82, 85, **206**, 230, 231

Spry, William Frederick 114, 116, **207**, 254, 255, 256

Squire, John 106, 109, **207**

Stanhope, Hon. Leicester 25, **207**

Stanhope, Lincoln Edwin Robert 25, **208**

Starkenfels, Laroche [KGL] 102

Stewart, Hon. Charles 23, 24, 35, 93, **208**

Stewart/Stuart, Richard 22–23, 33, 35, **208**, 235, 237

Stewart, Robert, Lord Blantyre 80, 81, **209**, 230, 231. 232

Stewart, Hon. William 46, 122, **209**, 232, 237, 241, 242

Stirling, James 233, 259, 260, 261

Stopford, Hon. Edward 229, 230, 232, 233, 234, 251

Stubbs, Thomas William 115, 116, 123, **210**, 252, 253

Sturgeon, Henry 103, 117, **210**

Suchet, Marshal [Fr.] 27, 45, 96, 97, 98

Sutton, Charles 57, 80, **210**, 245, 247

Talavera de la Reyna 27, 29, 30, 36, 37–38, 39, 44, 86, 110

Talavera [battle] 31–36

Taupin, General [Fr.] 122

Taylor, Charles 16, 17, **211**

Thomar 8

Thomiere, General [Fr.] 4, 7

Thompson, Alexander 102, **211**

Tilson, Christopher 33, 35, **211**, 235, 236, 241, 243

Toledo 27, 28, 36, 39

Tonson, Jacob 257

Torrens, Henry 18, **212**

Torres Vedras 13, 14, 60, 71

Torrijos 30, 31

Tortosa 95

Toulouse [battle] 125–130

Trant, Nicholas 8, 9, 55, 58, 59, 60, 110, **212**

Tras os Montes 3

Travers, Robert 17, **213**

Trefusis, Robert, Lord Clinton 111, 118, **213**

Trench, Richard Le Poer 57, 80, 91, 108, **214**

Truxillo 85

Tucker, John Goulston Price 12, 18, **214**

Tulloh, Alexander 109, **214**

Upton, Arthur Percy 123, **215**

Valladolid 21, 27, 38, 39

Van der Maesen, General [Fr.] 122

Vandeleur, John Ormsby 101, 102, 107, 123, **215**, 265, 266, 267, 278

Venegas, Francisco [Sp.] 21, 27, 28, 29, 30, 31, 36, 38–39

Victor, Marshal [Fr.] 21, 26, 27, 28, 29, 30, 31, 36, 39, 40, 44

Victoria, General [Port.] 109
Vielande, General [Fr.] 106
Vigo 26, 27
Villa da Ponte 67
Villafranca 44, 69
Vimeiro [battle] 15–18
Viseu 43, 50
Vittoria [battle] 119–125
Vivian, Richard Hussey 125–126,
    215, 276, 277, 278

Walcheren fever 95
Walker, George Townshend 17, 105,
    107, 120, **216,** 241, 242, 254, 255,
    256, 264
Wallace, John 56, 57, 80, 117, **216,**
    245, 246
Waters, John 117, **217**
Watson, Major 35
Way, Gregory Holman 22, 24, **217**

Wheatley, William 233
White, Daniel 35, **218**
Whittingham, Samuel Ford 35, **218**
Williams, John Archer 109, **219**
Williams, William 77, 78, 81, 89, 91,
    108, 117, **219**
Wilson, George 237, 240, 241, 242
Wilson, James 105, 109, **219**
Wilson, Sir Robert 30, 31, 36, 39, 64,
    67, 110, **220**
Wimpffen, Don Luis [Sp.] 124,
    130, 132
Woodford, Alexander George
    117, **220**
Woodgate, William 80, **221**
Wynch, James 265

Zafra 85, 86
Zamora 27, 36
Zaragosa 21, 27